TRADIVOX

VOLUME XVIII

TRADIVOX

CATHOLIC CATECHISM INDEX

VOLUME XVIII

Peter Gasparri

Edited by
Aaron Seng

SOPHIA INSTITUTE PRESS
MANCHESTER, NEW HAMPSHIRE

South Bend, Indiana
www.Tradivox.com

This book is an original derivative work comprised of newly typeset and reformatted editions of the following Catholic catechisms, once issued with ecclesiastical approval and now found in the public domain:

Gasparri, Peter Cardinal. *The Catholic Catechism.*
Toronto: Longmans, Green and Co., 1932.

Scripture references follow the Douay-Rheims Bible,
per the imprint of John Murphy Company (Baltimore, 1899).

Cover and interior design by Perceptions Design Studio.
Unless otherwise noted, all illustrations are in the public domain.

Sophia Institute Press
Box 5284, Manchester, NH 03108
1-800-888-9344

www.SophiaInstitute.com

Sophia Institute Press® is a registered trademark of Sophia Institute.

ISBN 978-1-64413-384-2
LCCN 2023949202

Dedicated with love and deepest respect
to all the English Martyrs and Confessors.
Orate pro nobis.

CONTENTS

CONTENTS

ACKNOWLEDGMENTS

THE publication of this series is due primarily to the generosity of countless volunteers and donors from several countries. Special thanks are owed to Mr. and Mrs. Phil Seng, Mr. and Mrs. Michael Over, Mr. and Mrs. Jim McElwee, Mr. and Mrs. John Brouillette, Mr. and Mrs. Thomas Scheibelhut, Mr. and Mrs. Kyle Barriger, as well the visionary priests and faithful of St. Stanislaus Bishop and Martyr parish in South Bend, Indiana, and St. Patrick's Oratory in Green Bay, Wisconsin. May God richly reward their commitment to handing on the Catholic faith.

FOREWORD

The Catholic faith remains always the same throughout the centuries and millennia until the coming of our Lord at the end of the time, likewise "Jesus Christ is the same yesterday, today and forever" (Heb 13:8). The Catholic faith is "the faith, which was once delivered unto the saints" (Jude 1:3). The Magisterium of the Church teaches us solemnly the same truth in the following words of the First Vatican Council: "The doctrine of the faith which God has revealed, is put forward not as some philosophical discovery capable of being perfected by human intelligence, but as a divine deposit committed to the spouse of Christ to be faithfully protected and infallibly promulgated. Hence, too, that meaning of the sacred dogmas is ever to be maintained, which has once been declared by holy mother Church, and there must never be any abandonment of this sense under the pretext or in the name of a more profound understanding. May understanding, knowledge and wisdom increase as ages and centuries roll along, and greatly and vigorously flourish, in each and all, in the individual and the whole Church: but this only in its own proper kind, that is to say, in the same doctrine, the same sense, and the same understanding (cf. Vincentius Lerinensis, *Commonitorium*, 28)."[1]

An authentically Catholic catechism has the function of learning and teaching the unchanging Catholic faith throughout all generations. The Roman Pontiffs indeed, taught: "There is nothing more effective than catechetical instruction to spread the glory of God and to secure the salvation of souls."[2] Saint Pius X said, that "the great loss of souls is due to ignorance

[1] Vatican I, Dogmatic Constitution *Dei Filius de fide catholica*, Ch. 4

[2] Pope Benedict XIV, Apostolic Constitution *Etsi minime*, n. 13

of divine things."[3] Therefore, the traditional catechisms have enduring value in our own day and age, which is marked by an enormous doctrinal confusion, which reigns in the life of the Church in the past six decades, and which reaches its peak in our days.

I welcome and bless the great project of the "Tradivox" in cataloguing and preserving the hundreds of long-lost Catholic catechisms issued with episcopal approval over the last millennium. This project will convincingly show the essentially unchanging nature of the apostolic doctrine across time and space, and so I invite the faithful of the entire world to support this historic effort, as we seek to restore the perennial catechism of the Church. The project of a catechism restoration on behalf of "Tradivox" will surely be of great benefit not only to many confused and disoriented Catholic faithful, but also to all people who are sincerely seeking the ultimate and authentic truth about God and man, which one can find only in the Catholic and apostolic faith, and which is the only religion and faith willed by God and to which God calls all men.

+Athanasius Schneider, O.R.C.,
Titular Bishop of Celerina
Auxiliary Bishop of the Archdiocese of Saint Mary in Astana

[3] Cf. Pope St. Pius X, Encyclical *Acerbo nimis,* n. 27

SERIES EDITOR'S
PREFACE

SOME are surprised to find that when a given Catholic is asked to "look something up in the catechism," he may well respond: "Which one?" The history of the Catholic Church across the last millennium is in fact filled with the publication of numerous catechisms, issued in every major language on earth; and for centuries, these concise "guidebooks" to Catholic doctrine have served countless men and women seeking a clear and concise presentation of that faith forever entrusted by Jesus Christ to his one, holy, Catholic, and apostolic Church.

Taken together, the many catechisms issued with episcopal approval can offer a kind of "window" on to the universal ordinary magisterium — a glimpse of those truths which have been held and taught in the Church *everywhere, always, and by all.* For, as St. Paul reminds us, the tenets of this Faith do not change from age to age: "Jesus Christ yesterday and today and the same for ever. Be not led away with various and strange doctrines" (Heb 13:8-9).

The catechisms included in our *Tradivox Catholic Catechism Index* are selected for their orthodoxy and historical significance, in the interest of demonstrating to contemporary readers the remarkable continuity of Catholic doctrine across time and space. Long regarded as reliable summaries of Church teaching on matters of faith and morals, we are proud to reproduce these works of centuries past, composed and endorsed by countless priests, bishops, and popes devoted to "giving voice to tradition."

In This Volume

This volume features the universally acclaimed catechism of Cardinal Pietro Gasparri, simply entitled *The Catholic Catechism* and restored here from its first approved English translation of 1932.

Born in 1852 as the tenth child of humble Italian shepherds, little Pietro would go on to become one of the most influential clerics of the twentieth century. After teaching with distinction at the Catholic University of Paris, he was summoned to Rome by Pope St. Pius X in 1904 to preside over the creation of the first major compendium of Church law in Catholic history: the 1917 Code of Canon Law, which would prove to be the first major task of nearly twenty-five years spent in service at the Vatican. Throughout his work, Gasparri's personal gifts for theological study were matched by amiability, good sense, and fatherly concern for those under his direction, leading many to consider him as a candidate for the papacy in the conclave of 1922. The same decade witnessed the two other great achievements of his career: reconciliation with post-revolutionary France in 1920, and Italy in 1929.

Gasparri's catechism first appeared in Latin as the fruit of some six years of personal study and writing, and despite the author's claims to the contrary, it was rumored that the text would soon be adopted as a standard throughout the Church. While such universal promulgation was never officially ordered, the rumors proved to be nearly self-fulfilling: the merits of the cardinal's catechism were recognized immediately upon publication, and it was rapidly translated into nearly every major language. As an instructor's reference and theological sourcebook, the strength of the work is tremendous: the body text in fact comprises three different catechisms, each written for gradually higher levels of comprehension, and showing the author's penchant for both brevity and precision. However, the most unique aspect of the work is the compendious amount of primary source material included in the appendixes and footnotes: in this, readers are granted not only the cardinal's personal distillation of Catholic doctrine, but are also placed in direct contact with the many magisterial texts upon which it is founded.

Dying in 1934, the cardinal was regarded by all as a faithful son of the Church, and his catechism endures as a remarkable capitulation of the common and received doctrine of the Church in the interwar period. Beyond the usual correction of typographical errors present in the original, our only notable change in this edition has been to standardize the numerous references to the *Catechism of the Council of Trent*, so that they uniformly cite specific pages of that catechism as found in Volume VII of the current series.

Editorial Note

Our *Catholic Catechism Index* series generally retains only the doctrinal content of those catechisms it seeks to reproduce, as well as that front matter most essential to establishing the credibility of each work as an authentic expression of the Church's common doctrine, e.g., any episcopal endorsement, *nihil obstat*, or *imprimatur*. However, it should be noted that especially prior to the eighteenth century, a number of catechisms were so immediately and universally received as reliably orthodox texts (often simply by the reputation of the author or publisher), that they received no such "official" approval; or if they did, it was often years later and in subsequent editions. We therefore include both the original printing date in our Table of Contents, and further edition information in the Preface above.

Woodcut depicting an early method used in the production of Catholic catechisms, circa 1568.

Our primary goal has been to bring these historical texts back into publication in readable English copy. Due to the wide range of time periods, cultures, and unique author styles represented in this series, we have made a number of editorial adjustments to allow for a less fatiguing read, more rapid cross-reference throughout the series, and greater research potential for the future. While not affecting the original content, these adjustments have included adopting a cleaner typesetting and simpler standard for capitalization and annotation, as well as remedying certain anachronisms in spelling or grammar.

At the same time, in deepest respect for the venerable age and subject matter of these works, we have been at pains to adhere as closely as possible to the original text: retaining archaisms such as "doth" and "hallowed," and avoiding any alterations that might affect the doctrinal content or authorial voice. We have painstakingly restored original artwork wherever possible, and where the rare explanatory note has been deemed necessary, it is not made in the text itself, but only in a marginal note. In some cases, our editorial refusal to "modernize" the content of these classical works may require a higher degree of attention from today's reader, who we trust will be richly rewarded by the effort.

We pray that our work continues to yield highly readable, faithful reproductions of these time-honored monuments to Catholic religious instruction: catechisms once penned, promulgated, and praised by bishops across the globe. May these texts that once served to guide and shape the faith and lives of millions now do so again; and may the scholars and saints once involved in their first publication now intercede for all who take them up anew. *Tolle lege!*

Sincerely in Christ,
Aaron Seng

TRADIVOX

VOLUME XVIII

THE CATHOLIC CATECHISM

DRAWN UP BY
PETER CARDINAL GASPARRI

LONGMANS, GREEN AND CO.
128–132 UNIVERSITY AVENUE, TORONTO
1932

THE CATHOLIC CATECHISM

DRAWN UP BY

PETER CARDINAL GASPARRI

LONGMANS, GREEN AND CO.
128–132 UNIVERSITY AVENUE, TORONTO
1932

IMPRIMATUR
✠ FR. A. ZAMPINI, EP. PORPHYREONEN.
VIC. GEN. CIVITATIS VATICANAE.

CENSOR DEPUTATUS
HILARIUS CARPENTER, O.P., S.T.L., B.LITT.
PRINTED IN GREAT BRITAIN.

AUTHOR'S INTRODUCTION

All who are occupied in spreading Christian doctrine must echo the wish expressed both by the Council of Trent,[1] and by that of the Vatican,[2] that a catechism should be published for use in the universal Church with the view that "as there is one Lord and one faith, so too there should be some one general rule and method employed in teaching the faithful the duties of the Christian religion."[3] The need of some such uniform catechism has become all the greater since people now move from one place to another so freely. To meet this need, then, we have endeavored to the best of our ability to draw up such a catechism.

In order to foster knowledge of Christian doctrine throughout the Church, the Roman pontiffs, in accordance with the desires expressed by the fathers at Trent, were at pains to have a catechism drawn up, which they called *A Catechism for Parish Priests according to the Decree of the Council of Trent*, or more briefly, the *Roman Catechism*, or the *Catechism of the Council of Trent*; this was done with the object of providing the clergy with a reliable summary of Catholic doctrine. But though this catechism is, of course, of very great value in catechetical work,[4] yet, as its title shows, it is primarily meant for parish priests and catechists who have to instruct the faithful; it was not meant precisely for simple folk, nor, in point of fact, does it deal

[1] Cf. Council of Trent, Session 25, "On Reformation"; "Decree on the Index of books, on the catechism," etc.

[2] See Appendix I: "Scheme of the Constitution on the shorter catechism, remodeled in accordance with emendation accepted by the General Congregation (of the Vatican Council)."

[3] *Catechism of the Council of Trent*, Preface [Editor's note: See p. 38-39 of Volume VII of this series, which includes in full the *Catechism of the Council of Trent.* All subsequent references to that catechism have been updated to reflect the pagination of the appropriate volume in this series, e.g., see TCCI 7:38-39 here.]

[4] In his constitution *In Dominico Agro* of June 14, 1761, Pope Clement XIII says that this catechism was "compiled with much labor and toil, that is was universally approved of and received great praise"; further, that the Roman pontiffs set forth in it "doctrine commonly taught in the Church and wholly removed from error." Pius XI in his epistle *Unigenitus Dei Filius* of March 19, 1924, says: "In the Roman Catechism, one hardly knows which to admire the most—the abundance of sound doctrine or the elegant Latinity." This catechism deals with the Creed, the sacraments, the commandments, and with prayer. The English version is known simply as the *Catechism of Trent.*

with all the material. There was also published by the great theologian Cardinal St. Robert Bellarmine a catechism for children,[5] which has received high commendation from various popes. So too the late pope Pius X gave his approval to several catechisms drawn up to meet the needs of people of different ages, especially in dioceses of the Roman province; several bishops, too, both in Italy and elsewhere, have decided that the people of their dioceses should be taught out of their own particular catechism. In compiling the present catechism, we have taken account of all the abovementioned publications, and have in fact incorporated into it all that seemed useful in them.

Further, there are three classes of people who need catechetical instruction adapted to their age and capacity. Little children preparing for their first Communion; older children who, as in duty bound, are learning their catechism; grown-up folk who desire to have a fuller acquaintance with Catholic doctrine. Hence this threefold catechism.[6] The three catechisms are, for the convenience of teachers, printed together in this volume, but they may, and indeed should, be printed separately for the use of the different people concerned—though in printing the First Catechism separately, the notes should be omitted, since they are meant for teachers only.

Pope Pius X in his decree *Quam singulari* of August 8th, 1910, published by the Sacred Congregation of the Discipline of the Sacraments,[7] definitely fixed the time when children begin to be bound by the law of sacramental confession and Communion; he also made it clear how far they must be instructed in Christian doctrine before they can and ought to be admitted to their first Communion.[8] In harmony, then, with this decree we present

[5] Editor's note: St. Robert Bellarmine's catechism spoken of here, *A Shorte Catechisme*, is included in full in Volume II of this series.

[6] Older people who are entirely ignorant of Christian doctrine but wish to receive the sacraments should, so as not to delay their first Communion, learn the First Catechism (for little children) and then be admitted to their first Communion; then they should learn the Second Catechism (for children). For the method of dealing with people who are in danger of death, and, though not knowing their Christian doctrine, yet ask for the Church's sacraments, see Appendix III.

[7] See Appendix II.

[8] See the Third Catechism (for adults), q. 262, 264.

a brief scheme of catechetical instruction for children.[9] The bishop of the diocese at his discretion, and the teacher with the advice of his bishop or parish priest, can add a few other points, provided he does not burden their minds or keep them long from their first Communion, when it is a question of children. Nor is it necessary that a child should know the answers to the questions by heart; it is enough if he understands the meaning of the words.[10] The teacher should of course explain when necessary the doctrine contained in the questions, using simple and easy words and illustrations which will help a child to grasp what is said. Before a person is admitted to his first Communion, he should promise his parish priest that he will continue to study his catechism; and, if it is a question of children, his parents or those responsible should satisfy that promise.[11]

After his first Communion, a child should continue to receive Holy Communion as often as his confessor judges fit,[12] and meanwhile he should gradually learn the entire catechism according to his capacity;[13] the obligation of seeing that he does so lies on his parents or those otherwise

[9] We have taken this catechism, save for a few modifications, from the decree *Quam singulari, pubblicato di ordine del Sommo Pontefice Pio PP. X dalla S. Congregazione dei Sacramenti, il di 8 agosto 1910*, edited by the Rev. Domenico Iorio, secretary of the above congregation. In compiling it, the author had before him a commentary (*Sulla eta della prima Comunione dei fanciulli—Breve commento del Decreto* "*Quam singulari*") by Cardinal Gennari, who had a great deal to do with the framing of the decree and therefore had a clear grasp of its meaning.

[10] So Cardinal Gennari, *Breve commento del Decreto* "*Quam singulari*"

[11] The parish priest can, if we mistake not, after consultation with his bishop, defer the admission of a child to his first Communion for a short time, provided he is convinced of these two points: a) that after making his first Communion, the child will not attend the catechism classes; b) that if his first Communion is put off, he will attend the catechism classes till he is admitted to his first Communion. For a brief postponement such as this is a lesser evil than defective and imperfect knowledge of his catechism; and so long as the Church does not clearly state the opposite, we must presume that, for the child's sake, she prefers the lesser evil.

[12] The words of the decree *Quam singulari* are: "Once, if not several times in the year, parish priests should take care to arrange for a general Communion of the children and should admit to it not only the first communicants but also those who, with the consent of their parents and their confessor, as we have said above, have already made their first Communion. In either case, a few days of instruction and preparation should precede."

[13] Cf. Pius X, Decree *Quam singulari*, n. 2

responsible.[14] By "the entire catechism," we do not mean a catechism like the one given further on for grown-up or educated people, but a brief one so developed that a child may know sufficient Christian doctrine to enable him to lead an ordinary Christian life. In our Second Catechism, therefore, we have felt it better to follow an arrangement by which the questions and answers are given in the same words as in the Third Catechism (for adults); hence a child who later on wants to acquire a fuller knowledge of Christian doctrine can readily get it by turning to our Third Catechism. The bishop of the diocese can of course substitute for our plan any other he thinks more suitable; he can also amplify it or cut it down as he thinks fit. The teacher, too, in talking to the children can add explanations of doctrines, stories from the Bible, or devotional comments; of these he will find examples in our Third Catechism. In learning his catechism, a child will experience a good deal of difficulty; that is why, as the decree of the S. Congregation points out, it has to be learned by degrees, and according to a child's age and capacity. It will be for the bishop to provide a proper series of instructions for teaching catechism to different classes of children; it is much to be wished that these instructions should be the same for all parishes of the same nationality and language.[15]

Finally, our aim in the compilation of the Third Catechism has been to set down only those doctrines which the Church herself has defined, or which are generally received in the theological schools, or are in accord with general Catholic practices that the Church has never repudiated. We have tried to express these doctrines in as few words as possible, but always with a view to helping clergy and teachers alike, while affording grown-up and educated people an opportunity of getting to know their doctrine

[14] See below, Third Catechism, q. 263.

[15] In order to secure the attendance of the children at the catechism classes, there is in some districts a solemn renewal of the promises made at baptism; at least once in every two years, the children come to the school and, after an instruction and an examination, special instructions by way of preparation are given; then, on an appointed day, they receive Holy Communion, and in the presence of their parents or others responsible, make a solemn renewal of the promises made at their baptism, while the witnesses ratify the promises so made. In other places, they have a public distribution of prizes for those children who have proved most assiduous in attending catechism and have shown real progress.

thoroughly. Fuller explanations can of course be left to the theologians. Moreover, it will, unless we are mistaken, be found that in the apologetic classes given in the ordinary curriculum of our colleges, this catechism will prove very useful, as providing a standard in order, method, and statement, for teaching students how to acquire a deeper knowledge of their religion and also how to defend it.

With regard, too, to this fuller catechism, we would draw special attention to the following remarks, which can, in their degree, be applied also to the catechism to be taught after children have made their first Communion.

If it is found that, for the refutation of certain local errors or fuller illustration of Catholic teaching some doctrinal points call for fuller treatment, or that additional material or other biblical and historical illustrations than those already given are required; these can of course be added with the bishop's leave, though such additions should be kept distinct from the catechism as we have drawn it up.

As regards matters of discipline, only the general practice is given in this catechism. When in any district or diocese some change in this respect has been authorized, such modifications should be printed at the foot of the page and explained by the teacher. Mere local concessions can be sufficiently explained orally by the parish priest or the teacher.

If the catechism is used in the Churches of the East, then note:

a) When some disciplinary question arises, for example in the Third Catechism (for adults), Ch. 5, "On the Precepts of the Church," q. 242 *et seq.*, the usage in vogue in the Western Church is to be explained, and then, if the usage approved in some Eastern Church differs, it will be for the local bishops to substitute the requisite questions and answers pertinent to their particular Church.

b) In this catechism too are given some of the prayers in use in the Western Church; for these should be substituted similar prayers better known in the East.

c) The same applies to the Creed. In this catechism we have given and explained the Apostles' Creed. But many of the Eastern Churches make use in their catechisms as well as in their liturgy of the Nicene-Constantinopolitan

Creed, which we use (with the addition of the *Filioque*) in the Mass; but the Eastern Churches should keep their Creed in the catechism, provided they make due profession of the doctrine of the procession of the Holy Spirit from the Father and the Son, and, since there neither is nor can be any real difference, make use of the explanations we have given.

d) Finally, omitting other points of difference, the matter and form of some of the sacraments is not expressed in the Latin Church in the same terms as those used by some at least of the Eastern Churches. In the catechism, we have given the matter and form as received in the Latin Church, but at the foot of the page have added the matter and form in use in the East. The Eastern bishops can reverse the proceeding and put the matter and form usual with them in the text and ours in a footnote.

Inasmuch as we do not teach catechism solely for intellectual instruction, but primarily with a view to stirring up men's hearts and making them lead moral lives in harmony with that teaching, a teacher will be failing in his duty if he does not explain the doctrine so far as his pupils are capable of appreciating it, or if he does not make use of favorable opportunities for urging on them the necessity of leading a good life. At the foot of the page, then, the teacher will find specimens of such explanations and exhortations; these he can develop at will, nor will he find any difficulty in adding to them himself. He will also find—in addition to citations from the ecumenical councils, the Roman pontiffs, the fathers of the Church, the Roman Congregations, and the Code of Canon Law—passages from the Bible dealing with the doctrine given in the text. If the teacher thus gets accustomed to use holy scripture, which "is profitable to teach, to reprove, to correct, to instruct in justice,"[16] then his flock will day by day grow in knowledge and veneration for the word of God.[17]

[16] 2 Tm 3:16

[17] These citations from the councils, the Roman pontiffs, and Congregations, are given together in the Appendix. When taken together with the passages from the Bible given in the footnotes, it will be seen that they afford solid proof that the doctrine enshrined in the catechism is in no sense new, but founded on holy scripture and the perpetual teaching office of the Church.

Lastly we would draw attention to the fact that this catechism has been revised by a special body of the Consultors of the Congregation of the Council, under the presidency of the Cardinal Prefect; that it has been submitted to several professors of theology in Catholic universities and read by many of the cardinals and other learned men; while some of the principal consultors and theological professors in the Roman schools have generously given assistance in its compilation.[18] Needless to say that if perchance we have written anything contrary to, or not in precise accord with, the mind of the Apostolic See, we regard it as already withdrawn and expunged.

— PETER, CARD. GASPARRI.

[18] The Gregorian University under the Jesuit Fathers, the Dominican Collegio Angelico, the Roman Seminary, the Pontifical Institute for Oriental Studies, and the Urban College for the Propagation of the Faith have been particularly helpful in this respect.

INDULGENCES

Granted to those who devote themselves to teaching or learning the catechism

I. A plenary indulgence to all the faithful who shall for approximately half an hour or not less than twenty minutes devote themselves to learning or teaching the catechism at least twice in the month; this indulgence can be gained on any two days in the month that they may choose, provided always that, being truly penitent, they have been to confession and Holy Communion and have visited some Church or public oratory and there prayed for the intention of the Roman pontiff.

II. A partial indulgence of one hundred days to the same members of the faithful so often as for the abovementioned space of time they teach or learn the catechism—provided always that they are sorry for their sins.[19]

All should, according to their capacity, carefully learn their Christian catechism and should also take care that those under their charge do the same. For there is no teaching more important than this, since it points out to us the way of eternal salvation, which is our final goal. "For what doth it profit a man if he gain the whole world but suffer the loss of his own soul? Or what exchange shall a man give for his soul?"[20]

[19] See the full Decree of March 12, 1930, given in Appendix IV.

[20] Mt 16:26

THE PRINCIPAL THINGS THAT IT IS NECESSARY OR NOTABLY USEFUL FOR EVERYONE TO KNOW[21]

The Sign of the Cross

In the name of the Father and of the Son and of the Holy Ghost. Amen.

The Lord's Prayer

Our Father who art in heaven, hallowed be thy name, thy kingdom come, thy will be done on earth, as it is in heaven.

Give us this day our daily bread; and forgive us our trespasses, as we forgive them that trespass against us, and lead us not into temptation, but deliver us from evil. Amen.

The Hail Mary

Hail Mary, full of grace, the Lord is with thee; blessed art thou among women, and blessed is the fruit of thy womb, Jesus.

Holy Mary, Mother of God, pray for us sinners now and at the hour of our death. Amen.

The Apostles' Creed

1. I believe in God the Father Almighty, Creator of heaven and earth.
2. And in Jesus Christ, his only Son, our Lord.
3. Who was conceived by the Holy Ghost, born of the Virgin Mary.
4. Suffered under Pontius Pilate, was crucified, dead, and buried.
5. He descended into hell; the third day he rose again from the dead.
6. He ascended into heaven; sitteth at the right hand of God the Father Almighty.
7. From thence he shall come to judge the living and the dead.

[21] The teacher should see that the older children learn all these by heart; for those who are to be admitted to first Communion, see the First Catechism, p. 20, note 24.

8. I believe in the Holy Ghost.
9. The holy Catholic Church, the communion of saints.
10. The forgiveness of sins.
11. The resurrection of the body.
12. And life everlasting. Amen.

Hail Holy Queen

Hail, holy Queen, Mother of mercy; hail, our life, our sweetness, and our hope. To thee do we cry, poor banished children of Eve; to thee do we sigh, mourning and weeping in this vale of tears. Turn then, most gracious advocate, thine eyes of mercy toward us. And after this our exile, show unto us the blessed fruit of thy womb, Jesus. O clement, O loving, O sweet Virgin Mary.

Glory Be to the Father

Glory be to the Father, and to the Son, and to the Holy Ghost, as it was in the beginning, is now, and ever shall be, world without end. Amen.

Prayer to One's Guardian Angel

O angel of God, my guardian, enlighten, guard, rule, and govern me, who have been committed to thee by the Divine Majesty.

Prayer for the Holy Souls

Eternal rest give unto them, O Lord, and let perpetual light shine upon them. May they rest in peace. Amen.

The Principal Mysteries of Faith

1. The mystery of one God in three distinct Persons, the Father, the Son, and the Holy Ghost.
2. The mystery of man's redemption by the incarnation, passion, and death of Jesus Christ, the Son of God.

The Decalogue or Ten Commandments of God

I am the Lord thy God;

1. Thou shalt not have strange gods before me.
2. Thou shalt not take the name of the Lord thy God in vain.
3. Remember that thou keep holy the sabbath day.[22]
4. Honor thy father and thy mother.
5. Thou shalt not kill.
6. Thou shalt not commit adultery.
7. Thou shalt not steal.
8. Thou shalt not bear false witness against thy neighbor.
9. Thou shalt not covet thy neighbor's wife.
10. Thou shalt not covet thy neighbor's goods.

The Precepts of the Church

1. To hear Mass and to refrain from servile works on Sundays and other feasts of obligation.
2. To fast and abstain from flesh meat on days appointed by the Church.
3. To confess one's sins at least once a year.
4. To receive the sacrament of the Holy Eucharist at least at Easter.
5. To contribute to the support of the Church and her clergy.

[22] This answer should be explained in the manner suggested under q. 203ff, below.

The Sacraments

1. Baptism.
2. Confirmation.
3. Holy Eucharist.
4. Penance.
5. Extreme unction.[23]
6. Holy orders.
7. Holy matrimony.

An Act of Faith

O my God, I firmly believe that thou art one God in three distinct Persons, the Father, the Son, and the Holy Ghost; and that the Son, being made man for our salvation, suffered and died, rose from the dead, and renders to each man according to his merits either reward in paradise or punishment in hell. These and all other things that the Catholic Church believes and teaches, I believe, because thou hast revealed them who canst neither deceive nor be deceived.

A Short Act of Faith

O my God, because thou art the truth itself, I believe in thee; increase my faith.

An Act of Hope

O my God, as thou art almighty, infinitely merciful and faithful to thy promises, I hope that thou wilt give me, through the merits of Jesus Christ, life everlasting and the graces necessary to obtain it; for thou hast promised it to those who do good works, and these, with thy help, I am determined to do.

[23] In the Eastern Church, confirmation is known as "chrism," extreme unction as "the blessing of the sick," and among the Latins too as "holy oils."

A Short Act of Hope

O my God, because thou art powerful, merciful, and faithful to thy promises, I hope in thee; increase my hope.

An Act of Charity

O my God, I love thee with my whole heart above all things, because thou art infinitely good and infinitely to be loved; and for thy sake I love my neighbor as I love myself, and I forgive him if he has injured me in any way.

A Short Act of Charity

O my God, because thou art so good, I love thee; increase my love.

An Act of Contrition

O my God, I am sorry with my whole heart for all my sins, and I hate them, not only because by sinning I have deserved the punishments appointed them by thee, but especially because I have offended thee, the supreme good, who art worthy to be loved above all things. Therefore, I firmly resolve with the help of thy grace not to sin again, and carefully to avoid the immediate occasions of sin.

A Short Act of Contrition

O my God, because thou art so good and hatest sin, I repent with my whole heart of having offended thee; increase my sorrow.

The Mysteries of the Holy Rosary

The Joyful Mysteries

1. Our Lady is greeted by the angel.
2. Our Lady visits Elizabeth.
3. Christ is born in Bethlehem.
4. The infant Jesus is presented in the Temple.
5. The boy Jesus is found in the Temple among the doctors.

The Sorrowful Mysteries

1. Christ sweats with blood as he prays in the garden.
2. Christ is scourged at the pillar.
3. Christ is crowned with thorns.
4. Christ, condemned to death, goes to Calvary, carrying his cross.
5. Christ is nailed to the cross and dies in the presence of his Mother.

The Glorious Mysteries

1. The resurrection of Christ.
2. The ascension of Christ.
3. The coming down of the Holy Ghost on our Lady and the disciples.
4. The assumption of our Lady into heaven.
5. The coronation of our Lady and the glory of the angels and the saints.

The Litany of Loretto

I
Catechism for Little Children

The Catechism for Little Children Who Are To Be Admitted To First Communion

In Accordance With the Decree *Quam Singulari* of Pope Pius X

The Sign of the Cross.
The Our Father.
The Hail Mary.
The Apostles' Creed.
The Sacraments.[24]

1. **Who made you?**
God made me.

[24] The teacher should take pains to see that the children pronounce distinctly and devoutly the words of the Lord's Prayer, the Hail Mary, and the sign of the cross; also that they make the sign of the cross correctly. Teachers should also briefly explain to the children the meaning of the words of the Lord's Prayer and the Hail Mary and should tell them who they were who first said them. They must explain to them that the Blessed Virgin Mary, though indeed the Mother of God, is also the Mother of us all, and that she has a very tender, motherly love for us. Children should therefore be taught to love her with a childlike love, and to say often, especially at their morning and evening prayers, the Lord's Prayer and the Hail Mary, and to make the sign of the cross. It is not necessary that a child should, previous to his first Communion, learn by heart the Apostles' Creed and the act of contrition. But he must study them and understand them. Then, after his first Communion, he must continue to study them and learn them thoroughly, so as to be able to prepare himself properly for subsequent confessions and Communions.

2. **What do you mean by the word *God*?**
By the word *God*, I mean a most pure Spirit, infinite in all perfections, who created all things in heaven and earth.[25]

3. **Why did God create you?**
God created me to know him, love him, and keep his commandments in this world, that so I may be happy with him in paradise after I die.[26]

4. **How does God punish those who do not keep his commandments?**
God punishes in hell those who do not keep his commandments.[27]

5. **Where is God?**
God is in heaven, on earth, and everywhere.

6. **Has God any beginning or end?**
God has neither beginning nor end, for he is eternal.

7. **Does God see all things?**
God sees all things, even those which will come to pass by the free action of creatures, their heart's affections, and secret thoughts.

[25] The teacher should tell the children in simple fashion the story of the creation of all things out of nothing, and explain to them that God is the last end of all created things, including man. He will tell them of the fall of the angels, and try at the same time to give them some idea of what an angel is, especially of their guardian angels and of the evil spirits. He should speak of the happiness of man in paradise, or Eden, before original sin; should explain to them in what the sin of our first parents consisted and how it was transmitted to us all, except to the Blessed Virgin; how, too, it is remitted in baptism. Finally, he should tell them how, in the earthly paradise, God promised to Adam and Eve that someone would come to redeem them from their sin, namely, Jesus Christ.

[26] We know God both by reason and by revelation; we love and serve him by faithfully keeping his commandments and by doing other good works, namely, things which are not actually commanded. The teacher must be careful to explain these points.

[27] Children should be simply told what is the state of the soul in heaven and what in hell: in heaven, the soul sees God as he is, and is filled with perfect and never-ending happiness with Jesus Christ our Lord, the Blessed Virgin, and the other inhabitants of heaven; in hell, the soul, deprived of the vision of God which alone can make it happy, forever endures fire and other torments in the company of the evil spirits and the damned.

8. **Is God one?**
God is one by unity of nature in three distinct Persons, called the Father, the Son, and the Holy Ghost; these form the most Holy Trinity.

9. **Which of the divine Persons was made man?**
The second Person, that is, the Son of God, was made man.

10. **What is the name of the Son of God made man?**
The name of the Son of God made man is Jesus Christ.

11. **How was the Son of God made man?**
The Son of God was made man by the power of the Holy Ghost, taking a body and a soul in the most pure womb of the Blessed Virgin Mary.[28]

12. **Why was the Son of God made man?**
The Son of God was made man that he might free us from sin and so lead us to paradise.

13. **How did Jesus Christ free us from sin and so lead us to paradise?**
To free us from sin and so lead us to paradise, Jesus Christ suffered and died on the cross, then rose and ascended into heaven, whence he shall come to judge the living and the dead.[29]

14. **What are sacraments?**
Sacraments are means instituted by Christ to give us grace.

[28] The teacher will here tell the children how the angel Gabriel was sent to the Blessed Virgin, how Jesus Christ was born in the stable at Bethlehem, how the Magi came and adored him, how he spent thirty years in hidden life at Nazareth and gave children an example of work and of obedience to their parents.

[29] The children should learn something of the mystery of man's redemption, of the passion and death of Christ on the cross, of his resurrection and his ascension into heaven, whence he is to come again at the end of the world to judge all mankind. These things all serve to show his love for us men, a love that he has never ceased to show and that calls for a return of love on our part.

15. **What sacrament have you already received?**
The sacrament I have already received is baptism, by which I was made a Christian and able to receive the other sacraments.

16. **What sacraments do you now wish to receive?**
I now wish to receive the sacraments of confirmation, penance, and the Holy Eucharist.

17. **What is the sacrament of confirmation?**
Confirmation is a sacrament instituted by Jesus Christ to confer special grace and the gifts of the Holy Ghost by which we are made strong to profess our faith in word and deed.[30]

18. **What is the sacrament of penance?**
Penance is a sacrament instituted by Jesus Christ by which sins committed after baptism are remitted.

19. **What is needed if we are to receive the sacrament of penance rightly?**
To receive the sacrament of penance rightly, we need:
1. To examine our conscience.
2. To be sorry for our sins.
3. To have a firm purpose not to sin again.
4. To confess our sins.
5. To do the penance given us by our confessor.[31]

20. **What sins must we confess in the sacrament of penance?**
In the sacrament of penance, we must confess all mortal sins committed after baptism, and it is useful also to confess venial sins, also mortal sins which have been already directly remitted.

[30] If a child has been confirmed before making his first Communion, then Questions 15 and 16 are to be corrected in accordance with this, and Question 17 omitted.

[31] The teacher should be careful to show children how to examine their consciences, how to make their confession, to say the penance given them, and to be careful to make a resolution not to sin again. An act of contrition will be found in the note to Question 25.

21. **What is the sacrament of the Holy Eucharist?**

The Holy Eucharist is the sacrament of the body and blood of Jesus Christ.[32]

22. **Where is Jesus Christ?**

Jesus Christ, as God, is everywhere; as God made man, he is in heaven and in the Holy Eucharist.

23. **What then is Holy Communion?**

Holy Communion is to receive Jesus Christ himself, really and truly present in the sacrament of the Holy Eucharist.

24. **Why do you wish to go to Holy Communion?**

I wish to go to Holy Communion, because Jesus Christ loves me and therefore desires to come to me; and I love Jesus Christ, and so I earnestly desire to receive him.

25. **What do we need if we are to receive the sacrament of the Eucharist rightly?**

For us to receive the sacrament of the Eucharist rightly, we need:

1. To be in a state of grace, that is, of friendship with God.

[32] This supreme mystery of our faith may be thus briefly stated: at Mass, before the words of consecration, pronounced by the celebrating priest, the host is simply bread; but after the words of consecration, it is no longer bread but Jesus Christ himself, together with his soul and his Godhead, under the appearance of bread; the same should be explained of the wine. This mystery we must accept because Christ our Lord openly declared it and holy mother Church has always taught it and continues to teach it. Christ instituted the Holy Eucharist at the last supper in order that, in the Mass, the sacrifice of the cross might be renewed and presented again, also that he might be able to dwell with us men in the tabernacle, though still sitting at the right hand of the Father in heaven, and might be united to us in Holy Communion. We ought never to forget this pledge of his love which he has left us; consequently, we ought to make a point of assisting at Mass at least on the great feast days; we ought, too, to try and assist at it with the same feelings of devotion as we should have experienced had we stood on Calvary while he was dying on the cross. In the same way, we ought to pay devout visits to the Blessed Sacrament preserved in the tabernacle, and to go to Holy Communion frequently and devoutly.

2. To be fasting from midnight until the moment of Communion.
3. To make a careful preparation before Holy Communion and a good thanksgiving after it.[33]

26. **What will you promise in the presence of Jesus Christ on the day of your first Holy Communion?**

On the day of my first Holy Communion, I will promise in the presence of Jesus Christ to hear Mass every feast day, often to receive the sacraments of penance and Holy Communion, to go to the catechism class, to be obedient to my parents, and carefully to avoid bad companions.

[33] After he has explained the first and second conditions, the teacher should show the children how to make acts of preparation for and thanksgiving after Holy Communion; he should read the acts to them slowly and get them to repeat them after him. Cardinal Gennari, in his Commentary on the Decree of Pope Pius X on First Communion (see p. 7, note 9), suggests the following acts:

Before Holy Communion

An act of faith.—O good Jesus, I firmly believe all that thou hast said to me through thy Church, especially that thou art really and truly present in the consecrated host.

An act of hope.—O good Jesus, trusting in thy goodness and thy promises, I hope to receive from thee grace, all good things needful, and eternal life.

An act of charity.—Because thou art infinitely good, I love thee, Jesus, with all my heart and soul and strength.

An act of contrition.—O my God, I repent of all my sins, because they have deserved thy punishments, but especially because they have offended thy infinite goodness.

An act of humility.—O good Jesus, I am thy creature, full of misery and sin and unworthy to receive thee.

An act of desire.—O good Jesus, I earnestly desire to receive thee into my heart; come to me quickly and do not delay.

After Holy Communion

An act of adoration.—I adore thee, O good Jesus present in my soul; I humble myself before thee, I am astonished at thy wonderful goodness.

An act of gratitude.—O good Jesus, how can I thank thee properly? I offer thee all the thanksgivings of thy saints, especially of the Blessed Virgin and of all who love thee.

Appendix I

(FROM THE ACTS OF THE VATICAN COUNCIL.)

THE SCHEME OF THE CONSTITUTION ON A SHORTER CATECHISM AS RECAST IN ACCORDANCE WITH THE EMENDATIONS ACCEPTED BY THE GENERAL CONGREGATION

Pius, Bishop, Servant of the Servants of God, with the Approbation of the Sacred Council, for a Perpetual Remembrance

OF DRAWING UP AND USING A SINGLE SHORTER CATECHISM FOR THE UNIVERSAL CHURCH

Taught by the precepts and example of her spouse, our Savior Jesus Christ, holy mother Church has always devoted special care and attention to the children, to the end that, after being nourished with the milk of heavenly doctrine, they should receive in due course fuller training in the duties of their religion.

Hence the holy Synod of Trent was not content to bid the bishops see that children were carefully taught the rudiments of their faith and their duties toward God and their parents,[34] but also felt bound to provide that some definite form and method of instruction in the rudiments of their faith should be drawn up for the faithful, so that all legitimate pastors and teachers could adopt it.[35]

The holy synod itself was, however, unable to carry this into effect; the Apostolic See therefore, in accordance with the above desire,[36] published

[34] Cf. Council of Trent, Session 24, "Decree on Reformation," Ch. 4

[35] Cf. Council of Trent, Session 24, "Decree on Reformation," Ch. 7. See TCCI 7:35ff.

[36] Cf. Council of Trent, Session 25, "Decree on the Index of Books, on the Catechism," etc.

The Catechism for Parish Priests, or *Catechism of the Council of Trent*. But not content with this, and anxious to meet in the fullest manner possible the wishes of the Tridentine fathers, who desired that in future one identical method of teaching and learning the catechism should be used by all, the Apostolic See gave its approval to the *Shorter Catechism* for the instruction of children, drawn up at its request by the Ven. Cardinal Bellarmine,[37] and this catechism it warmly recommended to all ordinaries, parish priests, and others concerned.[38]

At the present time, however, much inconvenience has arisen from the large number of *Shorter Catechisms* in use in different provinces, even in different dioceses of the same province. We therefore propose, with the approbation of the sacred council—while paying special attention to the abovementioned catechism brought out by the Ven. Cardinal Bellarmine, as well as other catechisms already familiar to the faithful—to have a new catechism in Latin drawn up for general use with Our authority, so that the differing forms of the *Shorter Catechism* may fall into disuse.[39]

It will be for the patriarchs or archbishops in the various provinces, after taking council with their suffragans and then with the other archbishops of countries where the same language is spoken, to see that this Latin text is accurately translated into the vernacular.

Bishops will, of course, be perfectly free, while always retaining unaltered this *Shorter Catechism* for the elementary instruction of the faithful, to draw up fuller instructions for their more complete training, thus

[37] Editor's note: St. Robert Bellarmine's catechism spoken of here, *A Shorte Catechisme*, is included in full in Volume II of this series.

[38] Cf. Clement VII, Brief *Pastoralis*, July 15, 1598; Benedict XIV, Constitution *Etsi Minime*, Feb. 7, 1742

[39] No mention is made in this scheme of the *Shorter Catechism for Children preparing for their First Communion* which was drawn up in accordance with the decree of Pope Pius X, *Quam singulari*. Before the publication of that decree, children were generally not admitted to their first Communion before they reached a later age, which varied in different places; to prepare them for this, Bellarmine's catechism was used, or others of the same kind. But since the appearance of Pope Pius's decree, the abovementioned catechism can, as stated in our Preface, be used for teaching children who after their first Communion continue learning their Christian doctrine; but they should not be used for children who, in accordance with that decree, are preparing for their first Communion.

providing them with a defense against any particular errors prevailing in their districts. If the bishops prefer to combine the said additions with the catechism, they should be careful to keep intact and distinct the text of the catechism as We publish it.[40]

Lastly it is of little use for the faithful to commit to memory the formulas given in the catechism, unless they are taught by word of mouth to understand what these formulas mean, a fact which makes it all the more important to have one uniform method in setting before the people the doctrines of their faith, and the ordinary practices of piety. For this purpose, we very warmly recommend—as Our Predecessors have so often done—the use of the *Catechism for Parish Priests* or *Catechism of the Council of Trent.*

[40] Our Third Catechism is most suitable for this purpose, as it is prepared for grown-up and educated people, and in it the truths of Christian doctrine are explained with greater fullness. On this same Third Catechism, we have based our Second Catechism for children, and in it we have kept to the same words, so that, when a child wants later on to get a better knowledge of Christian doctrine, he can easily do so by using this Third Catechism. The bishop of the diocese can, of course, have certain doctrinal questions more fully developed according to local requirements, as we have said in the Preface.

Appendix II

DECREE OF THE SACRED CONGREGATION OF THE SACRAMENTS ON THE AGE AT WHICH CHILDREN ARE TO BE ADMITTED TO FIRST COMMUNION

The gospel clearly shows the singular love Christ had for little children when he was on earth. He delighted to be with them, was wont to lay his hands on them, to embrace them and bless them, while he indignantly rebuked his disciples when they would have driven them away. "Suffer," he said, "the little children to come to me and forbid them not, for of such is the kingdom of heaven."[41] He showed, too, the high esteem in which he held their innocence and purity of soul when he called a little child to him and said to his disciples: "Amen, I say to you, unless ye become as little children ye shall not enter the kingdom of heaven. Whosoever, therefore, shall humble himself as this little child, he is the greater in the kingdom of heaven. And he that shall receive one such little child in my name, receiveth me."[42]

Mindful of this, the Catholic Church took pains, even from the outset, to bring little children to Christ through the Holy Eucharist, which she administered to them even when babes at the breast. That this was done at their baptism we find stated in nearly all the ancient *Rituals* down to the thirteenth century; while in some places, the custom prevailed even later, and the Greek and Eastern Churches still practice it. To obviate the danger of the consecrated bread's being cast up by children at the breast, it was the custom in early days to administer the Holy Eucharist to them under the species of wine only.

Nor was this practice confined to the time of their baptism, for children were periodically admitted to this sacred banquet. Thus in some Churches it was the practice to give the Holy Eucharist to them immediately after

[41] Mk 10:14

[42] Mt 18:3-5

the clergy; in others, the fragments were given to the children after the grown-up people had received.

Later on, this practice died out in the Latin Church, and children were not admitted to the holy table until they had come to the use of reason and had some realization of what this august sacrament meant. This more modern practice, already endorsed by some provincial synods, was solemnly ratified by the Fourth Council of the Lateran, A.D. 1215, when it promulgated its celebrated Canon 21, in which sacramental confession and Holy Communion were made obligatory on the faithful after they had attained the age of reason. The words of the canon are: "All the faithful of either sex shall, after reaching years of discretion, make private confession to their own priest, of all their sins, at least once a year, and shall, according to their capacity, perform the penance imposed on them; they shall also reverently receive the sacrament of the Holy Eucharist, at least at Easter, unless on the advice of their own priest, for some reasonable cause, they defer doing so for a time."

The Council of Trent[43]—while in no sense condemning the old practice of administering the Holy Eucharist to children before they have reached the use of reason—confirmed the above decree of the Lateran Council and added an anathema against those who might think otherwise: "If any one shall deny that every individual Christian of either sex is, when he has reached years of discretion, bound each year, at least at Easter, to receive Holy Communion in accordance with the command of holy mother Church, let him be anathema."[44]

Owing, then, to this Lateran decree, which still holds good, the faithful are bound, so soon as they reach years of discretion, to approach at least once a year the sacraments of penance and the Holy Eucharist.

But in deciding what is meant by "the age of reason or discretion," there have crept in, in the course of time, many errors and deplorable abuses. For some would maintain that the age of discretion for receiving

[43] Cf. Council of Trent, Session 21, "Decree on Communion under Both Species, and the Communion of Infants," Ch. 4

[44] Council of Trent, Session 13, Can. 9; Cf. "Decree concerning the Most Holy Sacrament of the Eucharist," Ch. 8

the sacrament of penance is not the same as that for reception of the Holy Eucharist. They feel that for confession the age of discretion is reached when children can distinguish between right and wrong and so can sin; but that for receiving the Holy Eucharist a more mature age is requisite, one at which they can have a fuller knowledge of the truths of faith and may better prepare themselves. Consequently, owing to varying local practices and views, in some places, the age of ten years, in others, twelve, fourteen, or even more are required, and, until that age, children are not allowed to receive Holy Communion.

Yet this practice, which keeps people away from Holy Communion on the alleged ground of greater reverence for so august a sacrament, has been the occasion of many evils. For it has meant that children who in their state of innocence were debarred from Christ's embrace, were afforded no food for their interior life, so that, deprived in their youth of this powerful safeguard though surrounded by many temptations, they lost their innocence and fell into vicious habits before they came to make their first Communion. And even when careful and painstaking preparation for sacramental confession preceded their first Communion—though this was not always provided—no one can help bewailing the children's loss of their primitive innocence, a loss which might, had they been earlier admitted to Holy Communion, have been avoided.

No less reprehensible is the practice prevailing in several places of not admitting to confession children who have not yet made their first Communion, or at least of not giving them absolution; with the result that when they fell into grave sin, they were obliged, to their great detriment, to stay in that state for a long time.

Still worse is the case when, as happens in some places, children who have not yet made their first Communion are not allowed, even when at death's door, to be fortified by the holy viaticum, so that if they die they are buried with the rites due to infants, and are thus deprived of the prayers of the Church.

Probably those who unduly insist on extraordinary preparations for first Communion are hardly aware of the dangers just mentioned; nor, perhaps, do they realize that such precautions have their roots in Jansenism, which regarded Holy Communion as a reward rather than as a remedy for human frailty. Yet the Council of Trent certainly thought otherwise, when laying down that the Holy Eucharist was "an antidote whereby we are delivered from daily faults and preserved from mortal sin."[45] The doctrine of that council was, only recently, strongly emphasized by the Sacred Congregation of the Council, when on December 26, 1905, it declared that access to Holy Communion was free to all, old and young alike, the sole condition being that people should be in a state of grace and be determined to avoid sin.

Nor in view of the fact that of yore the remains of the sacred species were given even to children at the breast, does there seem to be any real reason why an extraordinary preparation should now be demanded of children who are in their first blissful innocence and purity of soul, and who, in the midst of all the dangers and seductions of the present time, so emphatically need the mystic food of the Holy Eucharist.

The abuses we have been condemning are due to the fact that the suggested distinction between the age of discretion for confession and that for Communion is neither wise nor sound. The Lateran Council laid down the same age for either sacrament when it brought them under a single precept. Consequently, just as we regard the age of discretion for going to confession as the time when one can distinguish between right and wrong—in other words, when a child has come to some use of reason—so we ought to say that the age required for Holy Communion is the age when a child can distinguish between the bread of the Holy Eucharist and ordinary bread, in other words, the age at which a child has arrived at the use of reason.

The contemporaries of the Lateran Council, as well as its subsequent interpreters, put no other construction on its decree. The history of the Church affords instances of several synodal and episcopal pronouncements, even from the thirteenth century, that is, shortly after the Lateran Council, admitting children to Holy Communion at the age of seven. We have, too, a testimony of the highest authority, for St. Thomas Aquinas

[45] Council of Trent, Session 13, "Decree concerning the Most Holy Sacrament of the Eucharist," Ch. 2

says: "When children begin to have some use of reason, such as enables them to form sentiments of devotion toward this sacrament of the Eucharist, then it can be administered to them."[46] On these words, Ledesma thus comments: "I say that, by common agreement, the Holy Eucharist is to be given to all who have the use of reason, and as soon as they have it, even though such a child have only a confused notion of what he is doing."[47] Vasquez comments thus: "If a child has once come to the use of reason, he is at once so bound by the divine law that the Church cannot possibly exempt him from it."[48] So, too, St. Antoninus: "When capable of deceit, that is, when he can sin mortally, a child comes under the obligation of going to confession, and consequently to Communion."[49]

The Council of Trent points to the same conclusion. For when, in Session 21, Ch. 4, it says that "children who have not the use of reason are not necessarily bound to sacramental Communion," the council alleges as its sole reason the fact that they cannot sin: "For they cannot at that age lose the grace of the sonship of God which has been given them." This shows that the mind of the council was that children came under the obligation of receiving Holy Communion when they were capable of losing grace by sin. In full agreement with this are the words of the Roman synod held under Pope Benedict XII, which laid down that the obligation to receive the Holy Eucharist begins "after boys and girls have reached the age of discretion, that is, an age when they can distinguish between this sacramental food, which is none other than the body of Jesus Christ, and the ordinary bread we use, and can understand how to receive it with fitting piety and devotion."[50] And the *Catechism of the Council of Trent* says: "At what age children are to receive the holy mysteries none can better judge than their father and the priest who is their confessor. For it is their business to try to discover by questioning the children whether they have any understanding or appreciation of this wonderful sacrament."[51]

[46] *Summa Theologiae*, III, q. 80, a. 9, rep. 3

[47] *Comment. in Summam D. Thomae*, III, q. 80, a. 9, *dub.* 6

[48] *Comment. in Summam D. Thomae*, *Disp.* 214, Ch. 4, n. 43

[49] Pt. III; Tit. 14, Ch. 2, n. 5

[50] *Instruzione por quei che debbono la prima volta amettersi alla S. Communione*, Appendix xiii, p. 11

[51] See TCCI 7:277.

From all this it is clear that the age of discretion for receiving Holy Communion is reached when a child knows the difference between the bread which is the Holy Eucharist and ordinary material bread, and can therefore approach the altar devoutly. No perfect knowledge, then, of the things of faith is called for, elementary knowledge suffices, some knowledge; not full use of reason, for incipient reason, that is to say some use of reason, suffices. The practice, then, of deferring the admission of children to Holy Communion to a later period, and insisting on a more mature age for its reception, must be absolutely repudiated, and this Apostolic See has more than once condemned it. For example, Pius IX, of holy memory, in letters written by Cardinal Antonelli on March 2, 1866, to the bishops of France, condemned in the strongest terms the practice, which had already invaded certain dioceses, of deferring children's first Communion to definitely fixed maturer years. Again, the Sacred Congregation of the Council, on March 15, 1851, corrected a declaration of the Provincial Synod of Rouen, which forbade children to make their first Communion before their twelfth year. The same thing was done by the Sacred Congregation of the Discipline of the Sacraments, March 25, 1910, for when a question had arisen at Strasburg whether children should be admitted in their twelfth or in their fourteenth year, the said Congregation answered that "boys and girls are to be admitted to the holy table when they have reached years of discretion or the use of reason."

After having carefully weighed all the above points, in a General Congregation held on July 15th, with a view to the removal of the said abuses, and in order that children may, even from their tender years, cling to Jesus Christ, live his life, and therein find a safeguard against all danger of corruption, this Sacred Congregation of the Discipline of the Sacraments decided to lay down the following principles which are to be everywhere observed regarding the first Communion of children:

1. The age of discretion, both for first confession and for first Communion, is the time when a child begins to reason, that is, approximately the age of seven years. From that time dates the obligation of fulfilling both precepts, namely, of confessing and communicating.

2. Neither for first confession nor for first Communion is full and perfect knowledge of Christian doctrine requisite. But a child ought afterward gradually to learn the entire catechism according to his capacity.

3. The knowledge of his religion which is required in a child before he can make his first Communion is such as will enable him to grasp, according to his capacity, those mysteries of the faith which are necessary as means to salvation (*necessitate medii*), and to distinguish between the bread of the Eucharist and ordinary material bread, so that he may come to the Holy Eucharist with a devotion proportionate to his years.

4. The obligation falling on children of going to confession and Communion particularly affects those who have charge of them, that is, their parents, confessor, teachers, and parish priest. It is for the father—or whoever takes his place—and for the confessor, according to the *Catechism of the Council of Trent*, to admit a child to his first Communion.[52]

5. Once in the year, if not oftener, parish priests should arrange for a general Communion of the children, and they should admit to it not only the first Communicants but also those who have, with the consent of their parents or confessors, as just said, already made their first Communion; a few days of preliminary instruction and preparation should be given to both classes of children.

6. Those who have charge of the children should be careful to see that after their first Communion they come frequently to the holy table, even daily if possible, as Jesus Christ and mother Church desire, and that they do so with a devotion proportionate to their years. They must bear in mind too the grave obligation under which they are of seeing that the children come to the public catechism classes; if they do not come, then their religious instruction must be provided for in some other way.

7. The custom of not admitting to their first confession children who have come to the use of reason, or at least of not giving them absolution, must be completely given up. The local ordinary must see that it absolutely ceases; he should, if necessary, even take proceedings against those who resist.

[52] Ibid.

8. Similarly, the abuse of not administering the viaticum and extreme unction to children who have reached the age of reason, and of burying them with the rite used for infants, is a deplorable one. The local ordinaries should severely rebuke such as refuse to give up the practice.

Our most Holy Lord, Pope Pius X, in an audience granted on the 7th day of this month of August, approved all the above decisions of this Sacred Congregation and ordered the decree to be published and promulgated. He has also bidden all the ordinaries to make known the said decree not only to their parish priests and clergy but also to the laity, and he wishes it to be read in the vernacular every year at the same time as the paschal precept is read. It will be the duty of the ordinaries to make a statement every five years regarding the observance of this decree, together with other diocesan matters.

Notwithstanding anything to the contrary.

Given at Rome from the Offices of the said Congregation, August 7, 1910.

D. Card. Ferrata, *Prefect.*
Ph. Giustini, *Secretary.*

Appendix III

ON THOSE WHO ARE IN DANGER OF DEATH

If it happens that some sick person who is baptized, whether boy or girl or grown-up person, is in danger of death, and, though ignorant of the catechism, yet desires to receive the Church's sacraments, the priest should give him a brief instruction about God, his last end and rewarder, the mysteries of the Holy Trinity and of man's redemption, the real presence of Christ in the Holy Eucharist, and the sacrament of penance. He should also urge him to beg God, through the intercession of the Blessed Virgin Mary, loving Mother of us all, to pardon the sins he has committed. The priest should then hear his confession so far as is possible, give him sacramental absolution, Holy Communion, and, if time permits, extreme unction.

If, however, the sick person is not baptized but asks for baptism, yet cannot be properly instructed, then, in order to baptize him, it is enough to instruct him about God, his last end and rewarder, and the chief mysteries of faith, as above; and it is sufficient for him to show in some way or other that he agrees with all this and promises seriously that he will keep the commandments of the Christian religion. If, however, he cannot even ask for baptism, yet has previously or at the time given any presumable indications of his intention to receive it, then he should be baptized conditionally. If he should then recover, and any doubt arises about the validity of his baptism, it should be repeated conditionally.

If there is no priest at hand and no time to call one, then let anybody, so far as he is able, instruct the sick person to prepare him for death; let him add any exhortations he can and then baptize him, as above.

II

Catechism For Children Who Have Made Their First Communion

Catechism For Children Who Have Made Their First Communion

The Sign of the Cross

(The children should make the sign of the cross correctly and say the words distinctly.)

1. **Are you a Christian?**
By the grace of God, I am a Christian.

2. **What is meant by a Christian?**
A Christian is one who has received the sacrament of baptism, which is the door of the Church of Christ.

3. **Who is a Christian in the strict and full sense of the word?**
A Christian in the strict and full sense of the word is a baptized person who makes profession of the true and entire faith of Christ—one who is, in other words, a Catholic; he is a good Christian if he also keeps the law of Christ.

4. **What is the outward sign of a Christian?**
The outward sign of a Christian is the sign of the cross.

5. **Why is the sign of the cross the sign of a Christian?**
The sign of the cross is the sign of a Christian because by it we make external profession of the principal mysteries of the Christian faith.

6. **What are the principal mysteries of the Christian faith?**

The principal mysteries of the Christian faith are:

1. The mystery of one God in three distinct Persons, the Father, the Son, and the Holy Ghost.
2. The mystery of man's redemption by the incarnation, passion, and death of Jesus Christ, the Son of God.

7. **How does the sign of the cross show forth these two mysteries of the Christian faith?**

The sign of the cross shows forth these two mysteries of the Christian faith, because the words used signify the unity of God in three distinct Persons; and the cross we make calls to mind the redemption of man accomplished by Jesus Christ on the tree of the cross.

8. **Is it a good thing to make the sign of the cross?**

It is a very good thing to make the sign of the cross often and devoutly, especially at the beginning and end of our chief occupations.

The Apostles' Creed

(The children should recite the articles of the Creed distinctly.)

THE FIRST ARTICLE OF THE CREED, IN WHICH IS SET FORTH THE DOCTRINE OF THE FIRST PERSON OF THE MOST HOLY TRINITY AND OF THE WORK OF CREATION

1) I believe in God the Father Almighty, Creator of heaven and earth.

9. **What do you mean by the words, "I believe in God"?**
By the words, "I believe in God," I mean that I firmly believe that God exists and that I strive after him as the highest and most perfect good and my last end.

10. **What do you mean by the name *God*?**
By the name *God*, I mean a most pure Spirit, infinite in understanding, will, and all perfection, one by unity of nature in three distinct Persons, the Father, the Son, and the Holy Ghost, who make up the most Holy Trinity.

11. **Why are the three Persons one God?**
The three Persons are one God, because they are consubstantial; that is, they have one and the same nature, and therefore the same perfections or attributes.

12. **What are the principal perfections or attributes of God?**
The principal perfections or attributes of God are these: God is:
   1. Eternal, because he neither has nor can have beginning or end or succession.
   2. All-knowing, because he has all things in his sight, even those things which will come to pass by the free action of creatures, their hearts' affections and secret thoughts.

3. Immeasurable, because he is in heaven, on earth, and in all places that are or can be.
4. Just, because he renders to every one according to his merits, either in this life or certainly in the next.
5. Almighty, because he can do whatever he wishes by the simple act of his will.
6. Good, because he created, preserves, and disposes all things by his infinite goodness, power, and wisdom; because the good things we enjoy come from him; and because, in his goodness, he hears the prayers of those who ask.
7. Merciful, because, desiring all men to be saved, he has redeemed them from the service of the devil, and pours out on each the means necessary for salvation; for he does not will the death of a sinner, but rather that he be converted and live.[53]

13. **What do you mean by the words, "the Father Almighty, Creator of heaven and earth"?**
By the words, "the Father Almighty, Creator of heaven and earth," I mean that God made out of nothing both spiritual and corporeal creatures—that is, the angels and this world, and finally man.

14. **Does God take care of all created things?**
God takes care of all created things, inasmuch as he preserves them, upholds them, and governs them, so that there neither is nor can be anything that happens without God's will or permission.

15. **What do you call the care that God takes of created things?**
We call the care that God takes of created things "divine providence."

16. **Which are the most excellent of God's creatures?**
Angels and men are the most excellent of God's creatures.

[53] Cf. Ez 18:23, 32; 33:11

17. **What are angels?**

Angels are pure spirits endowed with intellect and will; they were established in a state of justice and holiness, so that if they cooperated with the grace of God, they might merit glory.

18. **Did all the angels cooperate with the grace of God?**

Not all the angels cooperated with the grace of God; those who did so enjoy in heaven the beatific vision of God, and are called simply "angels"; those who did not cooperate with grace were thrust down to hell: these are called "devils" and their chief is Lucifer or Satan.

19. **Does God use the ministry of angels?**

In many ways God uses the ministry of angels, especially in his care of men, for to each of them he gives a guardian angel from the time of his birth.

20. **Does it help our spiritual life to have a special devotion to our guardian angel?**

It is very helpful to our spiritual life to have special devotion to our guardian angel, reverencing him and calling on him, especially in time of temptation, following his promptings, thanking him for his help, and never vexing his presence by sin.

21. **Why did God create man?**

God created man to know him, to love him, and to serve him, so that after death, man might, by possession of God in the beatific vision, be happy with him forever in paradise.

22. **Who were the first parents of the human race?**

The first parents of the human race were Adam and Eve, whom God made and placed in an earthly paradise, raising them to a supernatural state and heaping upon them marvelous gifts of grace and nature.

23. **How did God raise our first parents to the supernatural state?**
God raised our first parents to the supernatural state by giving them justice and holiness, intending that these gifts should become the permanent endowment of human nature.

24. **What did God forbid to our first parents in their supernatural state?**
God forbade our first parents in their supernatural state to eat the fruit of the tree of knowledge of good and evil.

25. **Did our first parents obey God's command?**
Our first parents did not obey God's command, and therefore they lost justice and holiness, owing to their grave sin of pride and disobedience, and, driven out of the earthly paradise, they became subject to concupiscence, death, and all the other pains and miseries of life.

26. **Did Adam harm his descendants by his fall?**
Adam harmed his descendants by his fall, because, by it, he transmitted to them not only concupiscence, death, and other punishments, but also a human nature deprived of justice and holiness; in this consists the original sin transmitted to his descendants.

27. **Has anyone been kept free from the stain of original sin?**
The Blessed Virgin Mary alone was, from the first instant of her conception, through the foreseen merits of Jesus Christ, by a unique privilege granted her by God, kept free from the stain of original sin; she is therefore said to have been "conceived immaculate."

28. **What does the Church hold about the death of the Blessed Virgin Mary?**
The Church holds that the body of the Blessed Virgin Mary was indeed separated from her soul, but that her soul was reunited to her incorrupt body, and that she was by the ministry of angels taken up into heaven, where she is enthroned above all the choirs of angels.

THE NEXT SIX ARTICLES OF THE CREED, IN WHICH IS SET FORTH THE DOCTRINE OF THE SECOND PERSON OF THE MOST HOLY TRINITY AND OF THE WORK OF REDEMPTION

2) and in Jesus Christ, his only Son, our Lord;
3) who was conceived by the Holy Ghost, born of the Virgin Mary;
4) suffered under Pontius Pilate, was crucified, dead, and buried;
5) he descended into hell, the third day he rose again from the dead;
6) he ascended into heaven; sitteth at the right hand of God the Father Almighty;
7) from thence he shall come to judge the living and the dead.

29. **What do we mean by the second article of the Creed, "and in Jesus Christ, his only Son, our Lord"?**
By the second article of the Creed, "and in Jesus Christ, his only Son, our Lord," we mean that the Son of God, who as man is called "Jesus Christ," is the only Son of the Father, our Lord, true God of true God.

30. **What do we mean by the third article of the Creed, "who was conceived by the Holy Ghost, born of the Virgin Mary"?**
By the third article of the Creed, "who was conceived by the Holy Ghost, born of the Virgin Mary," we mean that the Son of God, by the power of the Holy Ghost, by an act surpassing all the powers of nature, took human nature—that is, a body and soul—in the most pure womb of the Blessed Virgin Mary, and was born of her.

31. **Why was the Son of God made man?**
The Son of God was made man that he might free us from sin and so restore us to the glory of paradise.

32. **Did the Son of God cease to be God when he became man?**
The Son of God did not cease to be God when he became man, but, remaining true God, he began also to be true man.

33. **How many natures and persons are there in Jesus Christ?**
In Jesus Christ, there are two natures, the divine and the human, but only one Person—that is, the Person of the Son of God.

34. **What do we mean by the fourth article of the Creed, "suffered under Pontius Pilate, was crucified, dead, and buried"?**
By the fourth article of the Creed, "suffered under Pontius Pilate, was crucified, dead, and buried," we mean that, in order to redeem man by his precious blood, Jesus Christ suffered under Pontius Pilate, the procurator of Judaea, was nailed to the cross and died upon it, and was thence taken down and buried.

35. **What do we mean by the first words of the fifth article of the Creed, "he descended into hell"?**
By the first words of the fifth article of the Creed, "he descended into hell," we mean that the soul of Jesus Christ, separated from his body but always united to his Godhead, went down to the limbo of the patriarchs where the souls of the just were awaiting the promised and longed-for redemption.

36. **What do we mean by the other words of the fifth article of the Creed, "the third day he rose again from the dead"?**
By the other words of the fifth article of the Creed, "the third day he rose again from the dead," we mean that Jesus Christ, on the third day after his death, reunited his soul to his body by his own power, and so lived again immortal and glorious.

37. **What do we mean by the sixth article of the Creed, "he ascended into heaven; sitteth at the right hand of God the Father Almighty"?**
By the sixth article of the Creed, "he ascended into heaven; sitteth at the right hand of God the Father Almighty," we mean that Jesus Christ, forty days after his resurrection, by his own power ascended, body and soul, into heaven, where he sits at the right hand of God the Father Almighty.

38. **What do we mean by the seventh article of the Creed, "from thence he shall come to judge the living and the dead"?**

By the seventh article of the Creed, "from thence he shall come to judge the living and the dead," we mean that, at the end of the world, Jesus Christ will come from heaven with his angels to judge all men, and then will "render to every man according to his works."[54]

THE REMAINING FIVE ARTICLES OF THE CREED, CONTAINING THE DOCTRINE OF THE THIRD PERSON OF THE MOST HOLY TRINITY, AND OF THE WORK OF OUR SANCTIFICATION

8) I believe in the Holy Ghost;
9) the holy Catholic Church; the communion of saints;
10) the forgiveness of sins;
11) the resurrection of the body;
12) and life everlasting. Amen.

39. **What do we mean by the eighth article of the Creed, "I believe in the Holy Ghost"?**

By the eighth article of the Creed, "I believe in the Holy Ghost," we mean that the Holy Ghost is the third Person of the Holy Trinity, who proceeds from the Father and the Son.

40. **When did the Holy Ghost come down visibly upon the apostles, and what did he effect in them?**

The Holy Ghost came down visibly upon the apostles on the day of Pentecost; he confirmed them in their faith and filled them with the fullness of all gifts, that they might preach the gospel and spread the Church throughout the whole world.

[54] Mt 16:27

41. **What work does the Holy Ghost do in the faithful?**
The Holy Ghost, by his sanctifying grace, by the virtues he infuses, by his gifts and actual graces of every kind, sanctifies the faithful; and he enlightens and moves them, so that, if they cooperate with grace, they may attain to the possession of life everlasting.

42. **What work does the Holy Ghost do in the Church?**
The Holy Ghost perpetually gives life to the Church by his ever-present help, he unites her to himself, and, by his gifts, guides her infallibly in the way of truth and holiness.

43. **What do we mean by the first words of the ninth article of the Creed, "the holy Catholic Church"?**
By the first words of the ninth article of the Creed, "the holy Catholic Church," we mean that there is a supernatural, visible, holy, and universal society, which Jesus Christ founded while he lived on earth, and which he called his "Church."

44. **Why did Jesus Christ found the Church?**
Jesus Christ founded the Church to continue his work on earth, so that, in her and through her, the fruits of the redemption accomplished on the cross might be applied to men until the end of the world.

45. **How did Jesus Christ will the Church to be governed?**
Jesus Christ willed the Church to be governed by the authority of the apostles under Peter their head, and of their lawful successors.

46. **Who is the lawful successor of St. Peter in governing the universal Church?**
The lawful successor of St. Peter in governing the universal Church is the bishop of the city of Rome—that is, the Roman pontiff or pope—because, in the primacy of jurisdiction, he succeeds to St. Peter, who lived and died bishop of the city of Rome.

47. **Who are the lawful successors of the apostles?**

The lawful successors of the apostles are, by divine institution, the bishops; they are set over particular Churches by the Roman pontiff, and govern them by their own proper power under his authority.

48. **Which, of all the various churches which claim the name of Christian, is the true Church founded by Jesus Christ?**

Among the various churches claiming the name of Christian, the true Church founded by Jesus Christ is that which is governed by the authority of the Roman pontiff and the bishops in communion with him.

49. **What power did Christ the Lord bestow on his Church in order that she might attain the end for which she was founded?**

That she might attain the end for which she was founded, Christ the Lord bestowed on his Church the power of jurisdiction and the power of order; the power of jurisdiction includes the power of teaching.

50. **What is the power of teaching?**

The power of teaching is the right and duty of the Church to guard, hand on, and maintain the doctrine of Jesus Christ, and to preach it to every creature, independently of any human authority.

51. **Who have the power of teaching in the Church?**

The Roman pontiff and the bishops in communion with him have the power of teaching in the Church.

52. **Is the Church infallible in her office of teaching?**

The Church is infallible in her office of teaching when, either in the exercise of her ordinary and universal governance, or by a solemn pronouncement of the supreme authority, she proposes, for the acceptance of all, truths of faith or morals that are either revealed in themselves or connected with revelation.

53. **Whose peculiar function is it to pronounce a solemn judgment of this kind?**

To pronounce a solemn judgment of this kind is the peculiar function of the Roman pontiff, and of the bishops together with the Roman pontiff, especially when assembled in an ecumenical council.

54. **What does the power of jurisdiction in the Church mean?**

The power of jurisdiction in the Church means that the Roman pontiff in respect of the whole Church, and the bishops in respect of their dioceses, have the power of governing; that is, they have legislative, judicial, administrative, and punitive power, whereby to secure the Church's attainment of the objects for which she was founded.

55. **What is the power of order?**

The power of order is the power of performing sacred functions, especially of ministering at the altar; by the sacrament of holy order, this power is conferred on the sacred hierarchy, especially on the bishops, and its immediate purpose is the care and salvation of souls.

56. **Who are outside the Church founded by Jesus Christ?**

Those are outside the Church founded by Jesus Christ:

1. who are not baptized;
2. who are open apostates, heretics, schismatics, or excommunicated persons that are "to be shunned."

57. **Can those outside the Church be saved?**

Those who are outside the Church through their own fault cannot be saved; those who are outside the Church through no fault of their own can be saved if they do not die in mortal sin.

58. **What do we mean by those other words of the ninth article of the Creed, "the communion of saints"?**

By those other words of the ninth article of the Creed, "the communion of saints," we mean that between the members of the Church—in heaven, in purgatory, and on earth—there exists, by reason of their close union with one another under Christ their head, a mutual communication in spiritual riches.

59. **What do we mean by the tenth article of the Creed, "the forgiveness of sins"?**
By the tenth article of the Creed, "the forgiveness of sins," we mean that there is in the Church true power to forgive sins through the merits of Jesus Christ.

60. **What do we mean by the eleventh article of the Creed, "the resurrection of the body"?**
By the eleventh article of the Creed, "the resurrection of the body," we mean that it will come to pass at the end of the world that all the dead will be recalled to life and rise for the general judgment, and that each soul will resume the body to which in this life it was united, and will never again be separated from it.

61. **Why did God will that the bodies of the dead should rise again?**
God willed that the bodies of the dead should rise again in order that the whole man might, according to his merits, obtain an everlasting reward in heaven or everlasting punishment in hell.

62. **What do we mean by the last article of the Creed, "life everlasting"?**
By the last article of the Creed, "life everlasting," we mean that there is prepared for the elect after death a perfect and never-failing happiness in paradise, while the eternal pains of hell await the reprobate.

The Decalogue

(The children should repeat the commandments distinctly.)

THE FIRST THREE COMMANDMENTS OF THE DECALOGUE, WHICH HAVE TO DO WITH GOD

1) Thou shall not have strange gods before me.

2) Thou shalt not take the name of the Lord thy God in vain.

3) Remember thou keep holy the sabbath day.

63. **What does God forbid in the first commandment, "Thou shalt not have strange gods before me"?**
In the first commandment, "Thou shalt not have strange gods before me," God forbids us to offer to others the worship due to himself.

64. **What worship do we owe to God?**
To God, and to God alone, we owe supreme worship—that is, the worship of adoration.

65. **Should we not also offer worship to the saints and to their relics?**
We should also offer worship to the saints, especially the Blessed Virgin Mary, and to their relics—but a different and lower form of worship, namely, that of veneration, in order to show them honor and win their patronage.

66. **Should due honor and veneration be paid also to sacred images?**
Due honor and veneration should be paid also to sacred images, since the honor shown them is offered to the persons they represent.

67. **What does God forbid in the second commandment, "Thou shalt not take the name of the Lord thy God in vain"?**
In the second commandment, "Thou shalt not take the name of the Lord thy God in vain," God forbids all irreverence toward his name.

68. **Are we also forbidden to take the names of the saints in vain?**
Just as we ought to pay honor to the saints, and especially to the Blessed Virgin Mary, so, for the same reason, we are forbidden to take their names in vain.

69. **What does God command in the third commandment, "Remember that thou keep holy the sabbath day"?**
In the third commandment, "Remember that thou keep holy the sabbath day," God commands that festival days—that is, days dedicated to him—should be kept with divine worship, business and bodily toil being laid aside, as lawful authority lays down.

THE REMAINING SEVEN COMMANDMENTS OF THE DECALOGUE, WHICH REFER TO OURSELVES AND OUR NEIGHBOR

4) Honor thy father and thy mother.
5) Thou shalt not kill.
6) Thou shalt not commit adultery.
7) Thou shalt not steal.
8) Thou shalt not bear false witness against thy neighbor.
9) Thou shalt not covet thy neighbor's wife.
10) Thou shalt not covet thy neighbor's goods.

70. **What does God command in the fourth commandment, "Honor thy father and thy mother"?**
In the fourth commandment, "Honor thy father and thy mother," God bids us show due honor to our parents and those who hold their place; such honor involves love, attention, obedience, and service.

71. **Is it merely honor that we owe to our parents?**
We ought not only to honor our parents, but to afford them assistance, especially in their temporal or spiritual needs.

72. **Does this commandment insist solely on the duties of children toward parents?**
This commandment lays down not only the duties of children toward their parents, but also indirectly the duties of husband and wife to one another and to their children, the mutual rights and duties of subjects and superiors, and of workpeople and their employers.

73. **What are the duties of parents toward their children?**
The duties of parents toward their children flow from the law of nature itself; they have to see to their proper education, especially their religious and moral education, while they have, according to their means, to provide for their temporal welfare.

74. **What does God forbid in the fifth commandment, "Thou shalt not kill"?**
In the fifth commandment, "Thou shalt not kill," God forbids us to cause death either to our neighbor or to ourselves, or to inflict on him or ourselves any other harm to body or soul, or cooperate in so doing.

75. **What does God forbid in the sixth commandment, "Thou shalt not commit adultery"?**
In the sixth commandment, "Thou shalt not commit adultery," God forbids not only infidelity to one another on the part of married people, but also any other external sin against chastity, and anything that may lead to sins of impurity.

76. **What does God forbid in the seventh commandment, "Thou shalt not steal"?**
In the seventh commandment, "Thou shalt not steal," God forbids all unjust taking of another person's property or damaging it, also cooperation in so doing.

77. **What does God forbid in the eighth commandment, "Thou shalt not bear false witness against thy neighbor"?**
In the eighth commandment, "Thou shalt not bear false witness against thy neighbor," God forbids lying, false swearing, and any harm we may do to our neighbor by our words.

78. **What does God forbid in the ninth commandment, "Thou shalt not covet thy neighbor's wife"?**
In the ninth commandment, "Thou shalt not covet thy neighbor's wife," God forbids not only such unchaste desires, but also every interior thought contrary to chastity, just as the sixth commandment expressly forbids external acts.

79. **What does God forbid in the tenth commandment, "Thou shalt not covet thy neighbor's goods"?**
In the tenth commandment, "Thou shalt not covet thy neighbor's goods," God forbids all unjust and inordinate desires for another's property.

80. **What is the sum of all the commandments of the decalogue?**
The sum of all the commandments of the decalogue is: "Thou shalt love the Lord thy God with thy whole heart, and with thy whole soul, and with all thy strength,...and thy neighbor as thyself."[55]

81. **Are all people bound to the observance of the duties proper to their state in life?**
All are bound to the careful observance of the duties proper to their state of life—that is, of those duties to which they are bound in virtue of their position or office.

[55] Lk 10:27

The Precepts of the Church

(The children should repeat these precepts distinctly.)

82. **How many precepts of the Church are there?**
There are many precepts of the Church, and a Catholic is bound to keep them all; but, at the beginning of this catechism, only five are enumerated, for these more particularly concern the ordinary spiritual life of the faithful in general.

THE FIRST PRECEPT OF THE CHURCH

1) On Sundays and other days of obligation, to hear Mass and to refrain from servile works.

83. **What does the Church lay down in the first precept, "On Sundays and other days of obligation, to hear Mass and to refrain from servile works"?**
In this first precept, "On Sundays and other holy days of obligation, to hear Mass and to refrain from servile works," the Church lays down the way in which we are to sanctify Sundays and other holy days of obligation; this is done especially by hearing Mass and refraining from servile works.

84. **What works are called "servile"?**
Those works are said to be "servile" which are performed by serfs or for wages; they are more particularly such as involve bodily labor and are concerned mainly with bodily gain.

85. **Are any servile works permitted on Sundays and other holy days of obligation?**
Those servile works are permitted on Sundays and other holy days of obligation which particularly concern the service of God or the ordinary necessities of domestic and public life; also such as are demanded by charity,

or such as could not be omitted without grave inconvenience; such, too, as approved custom allows.

86. **How, in addition to hearing Mass, ought a Christian to occupy himself on Sundays and other holy days of obligation?**
In addition to hearing Mass, it is only fitting that a Christian should on Sundays and other holy days of obligation devote himself to works of piety and religion so far as he can, especially by assisting at the ceremonies of the Church, hearing sermons, and attending catechism classes.

THE SECOND PRECEPT OF THE CHURCH

2) On days appointed by the Church, to fast and abstain from flesh meat.

87. **What does the Church lay down in the second precept, "On days appointed by the Church, to fast and abstain from flesh meat"?**
In the second precept, "On days appointed by the Church, to fast and abstain from flesh meat," the Church lays down that, on days appointed by her, we are either to fast only, or to abstain from flesh meat only, or both to fast and abstain from flesh meat as well.

88. **What does the law of fasting command?**
The law of fasting commands that there should be only one full meal in the day, but it does not forbid us to take a small quantity of food in the morning and evening, if we keep to the local custom regarding its quantity and quality.

89. **What does the law of abstinence from flesh meat forbid?**
The law of abstinence from flesh meat forbids us to eat meat or soup made from meat, but it does not forbid the use of eggs, milk-foods, or any condiments made from animal fats.

90. **On what days do these laws bind?**
Unless there is a dispensation granted by lawful authority,

1. the law of abstinence binds on every Friday;
2. the law of fasting and abstinence binds on Ash Wednesday, the Fridays and Saturdays of Lent, the Ember days, the Vigils of Pentecost, of the Assumption of Our Blessed Lady, and of All Saints, and on Christmas Eve;
3. the law of fasting binds on every day of Lent, except the Sundays.

91. **Are there certain days when these laws do not bind?**
On Sundays and other holy days of obligation, and on Holy Saturday after midday, the laws of abstinence only, or of fasting and abstinence combined, or of fasting only, do not bind, except when the day of obligation falls during Lent; vigils are not anticipated.[56]

92. **Who are bound to keep the laws of fasting and abstinence?**
Unless lawfully excused or dispensed, all who are of sane mind and have completed their seventh year are bound to abstain, while all who have completed their twenty-first year are bound to fast, until they begin their sixtieth year.

THE THIRD AND FOURTH PRECEPTS

3) To confess our sins at least once a year.
4) To receive the sacrament of the Holy Eucharist at least at Easter.

93. **What does the Church lay down in the third precept, "To confess our sins at least once a year"?**
In the third precept, "To confess our sins at least once a year," the Church lays down that, as soon as they have come to the age of discretion, the faithful must, at least once a year, confess all mortal sins not directly remitted in previous confessions.

[56] *Codex Juris Canonici*, Can. 1252, p. 4

94. **What does the Church lay down in the fourth precept, "To receive the sacrament of the Holy Eucharist at least at Easter"?**
In the fourth precept, "To receive the sacrament of the Holy Eucharist at least at Easter," the Church lays down that all the faithful who have reached the age of discretion shall receive the Holy Eucharist at least at Easter or thereabouts.

95. **Why does the Church add to the third and fourth precepts the words *at least*?**
The Church adds to these two precepts the words *at least* to teach us that it is most fitting and in accordance with her wishes that the faithful—even those conscious of only venial sin or of mortal sins already directly remitted—should often go to confession, and that they should frequently, even every day, devoutly receive Holy Communion.

96. **Does the obligation of receiving Holy Communion cease if it has not been fulfilled during Easter time?**
The obligation of receiving Holy Communion, if not fulfilled during Easter time, does not cease, and must be obeyed within the same year at the first opportunity.

97. **Is the obligation of yearly confession and Easter Communion fulfilled by a sacrilegious confession or Communion, or by a deliberate bad confession?**
The obligation of yearly confession and Easter Communion is fulfilled neither by a sacrilegious confession and Communion nor by a deliberate bad confession; in fact, owing to the presence of a fresh sin, the obligation is only increased.

THE FIFTH PRECEPT OF THE CHURCH

5) To relieve the necessities of the Church and her clergy.

98. **What does the Church lay down in the fifth precept, "To relieve the necessities of the Church and her clergy"?**
In the fifth precept, "To relieve the necessities of the Church and her clergy," the Church urges on the faithful a divine command, namely, to relieve the temporal necessities of the Church and her clergy according to local regulations and accepted custom.

99. **Why is this enjoined?**
This is enjoined because it is but just that the faithful should provide for the sacred ministers who work for their salvation, so that they may be able to meet the expenses of divine worship, and support themselves decently.

Grace

100. **What is grace?**
Grace is a supernatural gift, freely bestowed by God on rational creatures, so that they may attain to eternal life.

101. **How many kinds of grace are there?**
There are two kinds of grace—habitual (also called "sanctifying grace"), and actual.

102. **What is habitual grace?**
Habitual grace is a supernatural quality dwelling in the soul by which man is made a partaker in the divine nature, a temple of the Holy Ghost,

a friend of God, his adopted son, and heir to the glory of heaven, and so capable of performing acts meriting eternal life.

103. **Is habitual grace necessary for obtaining eternal life?**
Habitual grace is absolutely necessary for all, even infants, if they would obtain eternal life.

104. **How is habitual grace lost?**
Habitual grace is lost by any mortal sin.

105. **What is actual grace?**
Actual grace is a supernatural help from God, by which he enlightens our minds and moves our wills to do good and shun evil for the sake of eternal life. Unlike habitual grace, actual grace is not a quality dwelling in the soul, but a divine impulse from without, moving a person to perform acts beyond his natural powers, such as an act of contrition.

106. **Is actual grace necessary for us?**
Actual grace is absolutely necessary for us if we would do good and shun evil for the sake of eternal life.

Prayer

(The children should repeat distinctly the Our Father and Hail Mary.)

PRAYER IN GENERAL

107. **What is prayer?**
Prayer is the devout raising up of the soul to God, to adore him, to thank him for benefits received, to beg his pardon for our sins, and to ask him for other things necessary or useful for ourselves or for others.

108. **Is it necessary for us to pray?**
It is necessary for us to pray, because God so wills, and because God does not as a rule give the aid we always need, except to those who ask him for it.

109. **To whom is prayer addressed?**
All prayer is addressed to God, who alone can give us what we ask; but, that they may intercede for us with God, we pray also to all the blessed in heaven, especially the Blessed Virgin Mary, and even to the souls in purgatory.

110. **How ought we to pray so that our prayers may be heard?**
That our prayers may be heard, they should be offered in the name of Jesus Christ, on whose merits they depend; they should be devout, full of faith and humility, also persevering.

111. **Which is the most perfect of all prayers?**
The most perfect of all prayers is the Lord's Prayer or Our Father, to which is usually added the Angelic Salutation or Hail Mary.

THE OUR FATHER AND HAIL MARY

The Our Father

Our Father who art in heaven,

1. hallowed be thy name,
2. thy kingdom come,
3. thy will be done, on earth as it is in heaven.
4. Give us this day our daily bread,
5. and forgive us our trespasses as we forgive them that trespass against us,
6. and lead us not into temptation,
7. but deliver us from evil. Amen.

112. **Why is the Our Father called the "Lord's Prayer"?**
The Our Father is called the "Lord's Prayer," because our Lord Jesus Christ himself taught it to us.

113. **Whom do we invoke by the words, "Our Father"?**
By the words, "Our Father," we invoke God as a most loving Father, to show our love and trust in him, and to incline his goodness and mercy toward us.

114. **What do we ask in the first petition, "hallowed be thy name"?**
In the first petition, "hallowed be thy name," we ask that the holy name of God may become known to all men and be praised by all in thought, word, and deed.

115. **What do we ask in the second petition, "thy kingdom come"?**
In the second petition, "thy kingdom come," we ask that God may reign on earth over us and over all men by his grace, and over all society and every nation by his law, so that at last we may be made partakers of his eternal glory in heaven.

116. **What do we ask in the third petition, "thy will be done, on earth as it is in heaven"?**
In the third petition, "thy will be done, on earth as it is in heaven," we ask that, as all the blessed in heaven and the souls in purgatory always and in all things lovingly do the will of God, so men may do it on earth.

117. **What do we ask in the fourth petition, "Give us this day our daily bread"?**
In the fourth petition, "Give us this day our daily bread," we ask that God may give us both spiritual bread—that is, all things necessary for the spiritual life of the soul, especially the bread of the Holy Eucharist—and also the body's bread—that is, all things needful for the support of the body.

118. **What do we ask in the fifth petition, "and forgive us our trespasses as we forgive them that trespass against us"?**
In the fifth petition, "and forgive us our trespasses as we forgive them that trespass against us," we ask God to pardon the sins we have committed against him and remit the punishments we have deserved for them, as we ourselves forgive men the offenses they commit against us.

119. **What do we ask in the sixth petition, "and lead us not into temptation"?**
In the sixth petition, "and lead us not into temptation," acknowledging our own weakness, we turn to God, praying him to deliver us from temptations, or at least to grant us the help of his grace to overcome them.

120. **What do we ask in the seventh petition, "but deliver us from evil"?**
In the seventh petition, "but deliver us from evil," we ask especially that God may deliver us from spiritual evil, or sin, and therefore from the devil who induces us to sin, also from other evils, at least those that can give us occasion to sin.

The Hail Mary

Hail Mary, full of grace, the Lord is with thee; blessed art thou among women and blessed is the fruit of thy womb, Jesus.

Holy Mary, Mother of God, pray for us sinners now and at the hour of our death. Amen.

121. **Who spoke the words, "Hail [Mary], full of grace, the Lord is with thee; blessed art thou among women"?**
The archangel Gabriel spoke the words, "Hail [Mary], full of grace, the Lord is with thee; blessed art thou among women," when he declared to the Blessed Virgin Mary the mystery of the incarnation; hence this prayer is called the "Angelic Salutation."

122. **Who spoke the words, "blessed is the fruit of thy womb," and what do they mean?**
St. Elizabeth spoke the words, "blessed is the fruit of thy womb," when she welcomed the Blessed Virgin Mary as her guest; they mean that Christ the Lord, Son of the Blessed Virgin Mary, is blessed above all things forever.

123. **Whose are the words, "Holy Mary, Mother of God, pray for us sinners now and at the hour of our death," and what do we ask by them?**
The words, "Holy Mary, Mother of God, pray for us sinners now and at the hour of our death," were added by the Church; by them we ask for the protection of the Blessed Virgin Mary in all our needs, but especially at the hour of our death.

124. **Is the Blessed Virgin Mary really the Mother of God?**
The Blessed Virgin Mary is really the Mother of God, because she conceived and bore, according to his human nature, Jesus Christ our Lord, who is true God and true man.

125. **Is the Blessed Virgin Mary, Mother of God, also our Mother?**
The Blessed Virgin Mary, Mother of God, is also our Mother by that adoption which makes us brothers of her Son; and this Jesus Christ himself confirmed at his death on the cross.

126. **What reward do they receive who honor the Blessed Virgin Mary with loving devotion?**
Those who honor the Blessed Virgin Mary with loving devotion receive this great reward: that they are in their turn loved and protected by her with a special motherly love.

The Sacraments

(The children should give the list of the sacraments of the new law.)

THE SACRAMENTS IN GENERAL

Baptism, confirmation, Holy Eucharist, penance, extreme unction, holy order, matrimony.

127. **What is meant by a "sacrament of the new law"?**
By a "sacrament of the new law" is meant an outward sign instituted by Jesus Christ, to signify grace and confer it on those who worthily receive the sacrament.

128. **What grace do the sacraments confer on us?**
The sacraments confer on us sanctifying grace or an increase of it, also sacramental grace or the right to special assistance whereby we may attain the effect intended by each sacrament.

129. **Which are the sacraments of the dead, and which the sacraments of the living?**
The sacraments of the dead are baptism and penance, the rest are sacraments of the living.

130. **Why are baptism and penance called "sacraments of the dead," and the rest "sacraments of the living"?**
Baptism and penance are called "sacraments of the dead," because they were instituted primarily for those who, through sin actual or original, have no supernatural life, in other words, no sanctifying grace; the rest are called "sacraments of the living," because they are received lawfully only by those who already have supernatural life.

131. **What sin do they commit who approach the sacraments of the living in conscious mortal sin?**
They who approach the sacraments of the living in conscious mortal sin not only receive no grace, but commit a grave sin of sacrilege.

132. **Which sacraments can be received only once?**
The sacraments that can be received only once are baptism, confirmation, and holy order, for these stamp an indelible character on the soul.

INDIVIDUAL SACRAMENTS

Baptism

133. **What is the sacrament of baptism?**
The sacrament of baptism is a sacrament of cleansing instituted by Jesus Christ; by it, the person baptized is made a member of the mystical body of Christ or the Church, obtains remission of original sin and of all actual sins if he has committed any, with all the punishment due to them, and becomes capable of receiving the other sacraments.

134. **What is the duty of a baptized person?**
The duty of a baptized person is to make profession of his faith in Christ in the Catholic Church, and to keep the commandments of Christ and of the Catholic Church.

135. **Is baptism necessary to all for salvation?**
Baptism is necessary to all for salvation, for Jesus Christ said: "Unless a man be born again of water and the Holy Ghost, he cannot enter into the kingdom of God."[57]

136. **Who can confer baptism in case of necessity?**
In case of necessity, anyone can confer baptism without the ceremonies, by pouring a little ordinary water on the head of the person to be baptized, saying at the same time: "I baptize thee in the name of the Father and of the Son and of the Holy Ghost."

Confirmation

137. **What is the sacrament of confirmation?**
The sacrament of confirmation is a sacrament instituted by Jesus Christ to confer special grace and the gifts of the Holy Ghost, that by them the person confirmed may be strengthened, so as to enable him, as a perfect soldier of Christ, to make profession of his faith by word and deed.

138. **Besides being baptized and in a state of grace, what is required in those who receive confirmation?**
Besides being baptized and in a state of grace, those who receive confirmation must, if they have the use of reason, know the chief mysteries of faith and other truths regarding this sacrament.

139. **Is confirmation absolutely necessary for salvation?**
Confirmation is not absolutely necessary for salvation, but it is wrong to neglect it, because it is a means for attaining salvation more easily and fully.

[57] Jn 3:5

The Holy Eucharist

140. **What is the Holy Eucharist?**

The Holy Eucharist ("good grace" or "thanksgiving") is the most divine gift of our Redeemer, the mystery of faith; in it, under the appearances of bread and wine, Jesus Christ himself is contained, offered, and received. It is the sacrifice as well as the sacrament of the new law.

The Real Presence of Jesus Christ in the Holy Eucharist

141. **When did Jesus Christ institute the Holy Eucharist?**

Jesus Christ instituted the Holy Eucharist at the last supper when, before he suffered, taking bread, he gave thanks and gave to his disciples, saying: "Take ye and eat, this is my body," and, taking the chalice, he gave it them saying: "Drink, this is my blood," adding: "Do this in commemoration of me."[58]

142. **What took place when Jesus Christ pronounced the words of consecration over the bread and wine?**

When Jesus Christ pronounced the words of consecration over the bread and wine, there took place a wonderful and unique change of the whole substance of the bread into the body, and of the whole substance of the wine into the blood of Jesus Christ, although the appearances of bread and wine remained.

143. **What did Jesus Christ intend by the added words, "Do this in commemoration of me"?**

By the added words, "Do this in commemoration of me," Jesus Christ made his apostles priests of the new covenant, and commanded them and their successors in the priesthood, in like manner, to consecrate, offer, and administer his body and blood under the appearances of bread and wine.

[58] Lk 22:19-20; Cf. 1 Cor 11:23-25

144. **When do priests exercise this power and carry out this command?**
Priests exercise this power and carry out this command when, acting in the Person of Jesus Christ, they offer the Sacrifice of the Mass.

145. **What happens, then, when at Mass the priest pronounces the words of consecration over the bread and wine?**
When the priest in the Mass pronounces the words of consecration over the bread and wine, the body and blood of our Lord Jesus Christ, together with his soul and his Godhead, become truly, really, and substantially present under the appearances of bread and wine.

146. **What is the proper matter, and what are the words that must necessarily be used in consecrating the Holy Eucharist?**
The proper matter for the Holy Eucharist is wheaten bread and wine of the grape; the words that must necessarily be used are the very words that Christ the Lord pronounced over the bread and wine at the last supper.

The Sacrifice of the Mass

147. **Is the Mass the true and especial sacrifice of the new law?**
The Mass is the true and especial sacrifice of the new law; in it, Jesus Christ, by the ministry of the priest, offers his body and blood to God the Father under the appearances of bread and wine, by a mystical immolation in an unbloody manner for a renewal and a memorial of the sacrifice of the cross.

148. **Is the Sacrifice of the Mass one and the same sacrifice as the sacrifice of the cross?**
The Sacrifice of the Mass is one and the same sacrifice as the sacrifice of the cross which is renewed, for the victim is one and the same, now offering himself through the ministry of his priests as he then offered himself on the cross, only the manner of offering being different.

149. **How are the fruits of the sacrifice of the cross applied to us in the Sacrifice of the Mass?**
The fruits of the sacrifice of the cross are applied to us in the Sacrifice of the Mass in that God, appeased by this immolation, bestows on us the graces that Jesus Christ merited for us at the price of his blood.

150. **What is the best way of assisting at Mass?**
The best way of assisting at Mass is for the faithful who are present to join with the priest in offering the divine victim to God, calling to mind the sacrifice of the cross, and uniting themselves to Jesus Christ by sacramental or at least spiritual Communion.

The Sacrament of the Holy Eucharist

151. **What is the sacrament of the Holy Eucharist?**
The sacrament of the Holy Eucharist is a sacrament instituted by Jesus Christ wherein Jesus Christ himself, the author of grace, is truly, really, and substantially contained under the appearances of bread and wine, for the spiritual refreshment of our souls.

152. **In order to receive the Holy Eucharist worthily, what is required?**
In order to receive the Holy Eucharist worthily, in addition to being baptized (for baptism is requisite for the reception of any other sacrament) and in a state of grace (which is requisite for the reception of all sacraments of the living), we must also, under pain of grave sin, keep the natural fast.

153. **What does the "natural fast" mean?**
The "natural fast" means that from midnight until the time of receiving Holy Communion, we take nothing by way of food or drink, or even medicine.

154. **What sin do we commit if we receive Holy Communion not fasting?**
If we receive Holy Communion not fasting, we commit a grave sin of sacrilege.

155. **When is Holy Communion allowed without fasting?**
Holy Communion is allowed without fasting when there is danger of death, or when it is necessary in order to prevent some irreverence to the Blessed Sacrament.

156. **Are any invalids allowed to receive Holy Communion not fasting?**
Invalids who have been ill in bed for a month and have no certain hope of quick recovery are allowed, with the prudent advice of their confessor, to receive Holy Communion once or twice a week even though they have taken medicine or something to drink beforehand.

157. **What is necessary for receiving Holy Communion devoutly?**
For receiving Holy Communion devoutly, it is necessary to make a careful preparation and also fit thanksgiving according to our capacity, condition, and duties.

158. **In what does preparation for Holy Communion consist?**
Preparation for Holy Communion consists in meditating attentively and devoutly for a while on what we are about to receive, and in making diligent acts of faith, hope, charity, and contrition.

159. **In what does thanksgiving after Holy Communion consist?**
Thanksgiving after Holy Communion consists in meditating attentively and devoutly for a while on what we have received, and in making acts of faith, hope, and charity, with good resolutions, acts of gratitude, and petitions.

160. **What effects does Holy Communion produce in those who receive it worthily and devoutly?**
In those who receive it worthily and devoutly, Holy Communion produces these effects:

1. It increases sanctifying grace and the fervor of charity.
2. It remits venial sins.

3. It does much to secure final perseverance by lessening concupiscence, preserving them from mortal sin, and strengthening them in the practice of good works.

Penance

161. **What is the sacrament of penance?**
The sacrament of penance is a sacrament instituted by Jesus Christ for the faithful, so that, as often as they fall into sin after baptism, they may be reconciled to God.

162. **When did Jesus Christ institute this sacrament?**
Jesus Christ instituted this sacrament more especially when, after his resurrection, he breathed on his assembled disciples and said: "Receive ye the Holy Ghost; whose sins ye shall forgive they are forgiven, and whose sins ye shall retain they are retained."[59]

163. **Who is the lawful minister of the sacrament of penance?**
The lawful minister of the sacrament of penance is a priest duly approved for hearing confessions.

164. **What sins form the matter of this sacrament?**
The matter of this sacrament is all mortal sins committed after baptism and not already directly forgiven by the power of the keys; but we can usefully confess venial sins, and mortal sins already directly forgiven.

165. **What are the parts of this sacrament?**
The parts of this sacrament are the acts of the penitent, constituting its matter, and the absolution given by a lawful minister, which is its form.

[59] Jn 20:22-23

The Acts of the Penitent

166. **What is necessary on the part of the penitent for worthy reception of the sacrament of penance?**

For worthy reception of the sacrament of penance, there are required on the part of the penitent:

a) an examination of conscience;
b) contrition for sins committed, with a firm purpose of amendment;
c) confession of his sins;
d) satisfaction.

EXAMINATION OF CONSCIENCE

167. **What is examination of conscience?**

Examination of conscience means recalling as carefully as possible the sins committed since the last good confession.

168. **How is this examination of conscience to be made?**

In examining his conscience, the penitent first asks for the help of God, and then carefully calls to mind any mortal sins committed by thought, word, deed, or omission against the commandments of God and the Church, and against the special duties of his state.

169. **What should we try to recall in examining our conscience?**

In examining our conscience, we should try to recall the number of our sins and their character, and any circumstances that may alter their character.

CONTRITION AND FIRM PURPOSE OF AMENDMENT

170. **What is contrition for sin?**

Contrition for sin is heartfelt sorrow for the sins we have committed, with hatred of them and a firm purpose of amendment.

171. **What is a firm purpose of amendment?**

A firm purpose of amendment is a resolution not to commit sin again, and to avoid as far as possible the proximate occasions of sin.

172. **What kind of contrition for sin ought we to have?**

Contrition for sin ought to be:

a) inward, or from the heart;
b) supernatural, or from supernatural motives;
c) profound, so that we hate sin above all evils;
d) universal, or including all mortal sins committed since baptism and not directly remitted by the power of the keys.

173. **What if the penitent has only venial sins of which to accuse himself, or mortal sins already directly remitted?**

If the penitent has only venial sins of which to accuse himself, or mortal sins already directly remitted, then he should make an act of sorrow for some, or at least one, of them, and this suffices.

174. **How many kinds of contrition are there?**

Contrition can be either perfect—and this is usually called simply "contrition"—or imperfect—and this is called by the special name of "attrition."

175. **What is perfect contrition?**

Perfect contrition is a sorrow and hatred for sin, springing from charity, inasmuch as sin is an offense against God, who is supremely good and worthy to be loved above all things.

176. **What is the effect of perfect contrition?**

Perfect contrition immediately washes away sin, and reconciles man to God even apart from the sacrament of penance; yet such contrition implies the desire of receiving the sacrament of penance.

177. **What is imperfect contrition?**
Imperfect contrition is that supernatural sorrow and hatred for sin which is aroused either by reflection on the baseness of sin or by fear of hell and its torments.

178. **What kind of contrition is sufficient for the valid reception of the sacrament of penance?**
Imperfect contrition is sufficient for the valid reception of the sacrament of penance, though we should try to have perfect contrition.

179. **What kind of sin does a person commit who goes to confession knowing well that he has no contrition?**
A person who goes to confession knowing well that he has no contrition, not only does not obtain forgiveness of his sins, but also commits a grave sin of sacrilege.

Confession

180. **What is confession of sins?**
Confession is to accuse oneself of one's sins to a priest lawfully approved, in order to obtain sacramental absolution.

181. **What kind of confession is necessary for the valid reception of the sacrament of penance?**
For the valid reception of the sacrament of penance, confession must be vocal or at least the equivalent of vocal, and integral or complete.

182. **When is a confession integral or complete?**
A confession is integral or complete when the penitent confesses all mortal sins not already directly forgiven, of which, after careful examination, he is conscious, with their number and character, and the circumstances that alter their character.

183. **What ought a person to do if he cannot remember the number of his mortal sins?**

If a person cannot remember the number of his mortal sins, he should state their probable number and add "about."

184. **What if a person omits a mortal sin in confession, through no fault of his own?**

If a person through no fault of his own omits a mortal sin in confession, the sacrament is validly received and the sin forgotten is indirectly forgiven; but when he remembers it, the penitent is bound to accuse himself of it in his next confession.

185. **What sin does a person commit who culpably keeps back a mortal sin in confession?**

A person who culpably keeps back a mortal sin in confession not only gains nothing by his confession, but adds a grave sin of sacrilege.

186. **Is anything else required for the lawful reception of the sacrament of penance?**

For the lawful reception of the sacrament of penance, the confession should also be humble and devout; that is, the penitent should briefly, clearly, and modestly, without useless words, humbly confess his sins, without excusing, minimizing, or exaggerating them, and accept the admonitions of the confessor.

Satisfaction

187. **What is satisfaction?**

Satisfaction is the penance imposed on the penitent by the confessor for the sins made known to him in confession; this penance has, by the merits of Jesus Christ which are applied through the sacrament, special virtue for the payment of the debt of temporal punishment due to sin.

188. **Why does the confessor impose a penance?**
The confessor imposes a penance not only as a help to the penitent in leading a new life, and as a remedy for his weakness, but also as a penalty and a correction for his past sins now forgiven.

189. **When should the penitent perform the penance given him by the confessor?**
The penitent should perform the penance given him by the confessor as soon as possible, unless the latter appoints some particular time for its fulfillment.

Sacramental Absolution

190. **What is sacramental absolution?**
Sacramental absolution is the act whereby the confessor, in the name of Jesus Christ, by pronouncing the proper form of words, remits the sins duly and with true sorrow confessed by the penitent.

191. **Is the confessor bound by the seal of confession?**
The confessor is bound by an inviolable sacramental seal; not only is he forbidden to reveal sins heard in confession, but he must take great care not to betray the sinner for any reason, by word or sign or in any other way.

192. **When absolution has been given and the penance performed, is the whole debt of temporal punishment for sin always paid?**
When absolution has been given and the penance performed, the whole debt of temporal punishment for sin is not always paid; but it may be paid by other voluntary penances, especially by gaining indulgences.

193. **What do we mean by an "indulgence"?**
By an "indulgence," we mean the remission by God of the temporal punishment due to sins whose guilt has already been forgiven; such remission the Church grants apart from the sacrament of penance.

Extreme Unction

194. **What is the sacrament of extreme unction?**

The sacrament of extreme unction is a sacrament instituted by Jesus Christ, whereby spiritual assistance is bestowed on people who have come to the age of reason, who are sick and in grave danger; this assistance is most profitable when death is imminent, and even sometimes affords relief from bodily ailments.

195. **Is this sacrament necessary for salvation?**

This sacrament is not absolutely necessary for salvation, but it is wrong to neglect it; indeed we ought to be most careful, when a sick person begins to be in danger of death, to see that he receives this sacrament as soon as possible, and while still in possession of his senses.

Holy Order

196. **What is the sacrament of holy order or ordination?**

The sacrament of holy order or ordination is a sacrament instituted by Jesus Christ for providing the Church with bishops, priests, and other ministers, each receiving power and grace for the due fulfillment of the sacred duties belonging to the degree conferred on him.

197. **Of what kind is the dignity of the priesthood?**

The dignity of the priesthood is very great, for the priest is the minister of Christ and "the dispenser of the mysteries of God";[60] he is a mediator between God and man, with power over the real, as well as over the mystical body of Christ. Christ is the "one mediator of God and men";[61] that is, he alone is the mediator of redemption; but the priest, acting in the Person of Christ, applies to men the fruits of that redemption; and is thus rightly called a "mediator."

[60] 1 Cor 4:1
[61] 1 Tm 2:5

Matrimony

198. **What is the sacrament of matrimony?**
The sacrament of matrimony is marriage between Christians—that is, all who are baptized—validly entered upon; it was raised by Jesus Christ to the dignity of a sacrament whereby grace is bestowed on husband and wife, that they may rightly fulfill their duties to one another and to their children.

199. **Can there be a valid marriage between Christians without its being a sacrament?**
There cannot be a valid marriage between Christians without its being necessarily a sacrament, for Jesus Christ deigned to raise such marriage to the dignity of a sacrament.

200. **What are the essential qualities of matrimony?**
The essential qualities of matrimony are unity and indissolubility, which in Christian marriage are rendered peculiarly stable owing to the sacrament.

201. **By what law is Christian marriage governed?**
Christian marriage is governed by the law of God and of the Church, saving the authority of the state as regards purely civil effects.

The Virtues

202. **What is a virtue?**
A virtue is a habit or permanent disposition leading a person to do good and avoid evil.

203. **How are virtues divided?**
Virtues fall into two classes, theological and moral, according to their subject matter.

THE THEOLOGICAL VIRTUES

204. **What is a theological virtue?**

A theological virtue is one whose immediate object is man's supernatural end—namely, God, to whom it directly leads him.

205. **How many theological virtues are there?**

There are three theological virtues—faith, hope, and charity.

206. **Are the theological virtues necessary for salvation?**

The theological virtues are absolutely necessary for salvation, for without them the right direction of mind and will toward our supernatural goal is impossible.

207. **Which is the greatest of the theological virtues?**

The greatest of the theological virtues is charity, which is "the perfection of the law,"[62] and will not cease even in heaven.

208. **What is faith?**

Faith is a supernatural virtue whereby, through the inspiration and help of God's grace, we believe that what God has revealed and taught us through the Church is true, because of the authority of God who reveals it, for he can neither deceive nor be deceived.

209. **Must we believe all revealed truths?**

We must believe all revealed truths at least implicitly; for example, "I believe whatever holy mother Church believes." Explicitly we must believe that God exists and will reward us; also, in the mysteries of the most Holy Trinity, the incarnation, and the redemption.

[62] Rom 13:10

210. **How do we show our faith?**
We show our faith by professing it in word and deed, even, if necessary, giving our lives for it.

211. **What is hope?**
Hope is a supernatural virtue whereby, because of the merits of Jesus Christ, and relying on the goodness, omnipotence, and faithfulness of God, we look for eternal life and the graces necessary to obtain it, because God has promised it to those who do good works.

212. **How do we show our hope?**
We show our hope not only in word but also in deed, when, by putting wholehearted trust in the divine promises, we bear the hardships and afflictions, and even the persecutions of this life with patience.

213. **What is charity?**
Charity is a supernatural virtue whereby we love God above all things for his own sake, and ourselves and our neighbor for the sake of God.

214. **How do we show our love for God?**
We show our love for God by faithfully keeping his commandments, and by doing other good works which, though not commanded by him, are acceptable to him.

215. **How ought we to love ourselves?**
We ought to love ourselves by seeking in all things the glory of God and our own eternal salvation.

216. **How ought we to love our neighbor?**
We ought to love our neighbor by inward and outward acts—that is, we ought to pardon his offenses, avoid causing him loss, injury, or scandal, and help him in his needs so far as we can, especially by the corporal and spiritual works of mercy.

217. **What are the spiritual works of mercy?**

The spiritual works of mercy are:

1. To counsel the doubtful.
2. To instruct the ignorant.
3. To convert the sinner.
4. To comfort the sorrowful.
5. To forgive injuries.
6. To bear wrongs patiently.
7. To pray for the living and the dead.

218. **What are the corporal works of mercy?**

The corporal works of mercy are:

1. To feed the hungry.
2. To give drink to the thirsty.
3. To clothe the naked.
4. To harbor the harborless.
5. To visit the sick.
6. To visit the imprisoned.
7. To bury the dead.

219. **Does charity toward our neighbor also extend to our enemies?**

Charity toward our neighbor extends also to our enemies, for they too are our neighbors, and Christ himself has given us a commandment and an example on this subject.

THE MORAL VIRTUES

220. **What is a moral virtue?**

A moral virtue is one whose immediate object is good actions done in accordance with right reason.

221. **Which are the principal moral virtues, and how many are there?**

The principal moral virtues are four—prudence, justice, fortitude, and temperance. These are also called "cardinal" virtues.

222. **Why are these virtues called "cardinal"?**
These virtues are called "cardinal," because they are, as it were, the hinges (*cardines*) on which turns the whole structure of the moral life; to them the other moral virtues are reducible.

Actual or Personal Sins

223. **How many kinds of sin are there?**
There are two kinds of sin: original sin and actual or personal sin.

224. **What is actual sin?**
Actual sin is a conscious and deliberate breach of God's law.

225. **In how many ways can actual sin be committed?**
Actual sin can be committed by thought, word, and deed, whether of commission or omission, against either God, or ourselves, or our neighbor, according as the law we break is directly concerned with God, or ourselves, or our neighbor.

226. **How is actual sin divided?**
Actual sin is divided into mortal sin and venial sin.

227. **What is mortal sin?**
Mortal sin is a conscious and deliberate breach of God's law by one who is aware of the grave obligation involved.

228. **Why is this sin called "mortal"?**
This sin is called "mortal," because it turns away the soul from its final end, robs it of its supernatural life or sanctifying grace, makes it deserving of eternal death in hell, and destroys all merits acquired, so that they no

longer avail for salvation, until they revive by the recovery of grace; it also prevents us from performing works meriting eternal life.

229. **What is venial sin?**

Venial sin is a conscious and deliberate breach of God's law by one who is aware of the lesser obligation involved.

230. **Why is this sin called "venial"?**

This sin is called "venial" because, since it does not turn away the soul from its final end or cause its supernatural death, it can be more easily pardoned, even without sacramental confession; it is a weakness of the soul that can of its very nature be easily cured.

231. **What are the chief effects of venial sin?**

The chief effects of venial sin are that it lessens the fervor of charity, and makes it easier to sin mortally; by it, too, a person incurs a debt of temporal punishment which has to be paid either in this world or in the next.

232. **Ought we to avoid not only sin but also the occasions of sin?**

We ought to avoid not only sin but also, so far as we can, proximate occasions of sin, namely, those in which a person exposes himself to grave danger of sin.

The Last Things

233. **What is meant by "the last things"?**

By "the last things," we mean the things that will befall men at the last—death, judgment, hell, and heaven (though, between judgment and heaven, purgatory may intervene).

234. **What should be our principal reflections on death?**
Our principal reflections on death should be that it is a punishment for sin; that it is the moment on which our eternity hangs, so that after death there is no further room for repentance and merit; also that its time and circumstances are uncertain.

235. **What happens to the soul immediately after death?**
Immediately after death, the soul stands before the tribunal of Christ, to face the particular judgment.

236. **About what things will the soul be judged at the particular judgment?**
At the particular judgment, the soul will be judged about every single thing—its thoughts, words, deeds, and omissions. The sentence then passed on the soul will be ratified at the general judgment when it will be made publicly manifest.

237. **What will happen to the soul after the particular judgment?**
After the particular judgment, the soul, if, owing to mortal sin, it is not in the grace of God, will be at once consigned to the punishment of hell; if it is in a state of grace and free from all venial sin and all debt of temporal punishment, it will at once be taken up into the glory of heaven; if it is in a state of grace but with some venial sin or with some debt of temporal punishment still unpaid, it will be detained in purgatory until it shall have fully satisfied God's justice.

238. **What will be the state of the damned in hell?**
In hell, the devils—and with them the damned (their souls only, before the general judgment, their bodies too thereafter)—are deprived forever of the beatific vision of God and are tormented with real fire and other most grievous pains.

239. **What will be the state of the soul in purgatory?**
In purgatory, the soul pays any debt of temporal punishment due to sin not fully paid in this life, by being deprived of the beatific vision of God

and suffering other grievous pains until it has fully satisfied God's justice and so can be admitted to heaven.

240. **What will be the state of the souls of the just in heaven?**
In heaven, the souls of the just, separated from their bodies before the general judgment but united with them after it, enjoy forever the beatific vision of God, and with it all good things, without the presence or fear of any evil, in the company of our Lord Jesus Christ, the Blessed Virgin Mary, and all the inhabitants of heaven.

Appendix IV

DECREE ON INDULGENCES GRANTED TO SUCH AS DEVOTE THEMSELVES EITHER TO TEACHING OR TO LEARNING CHRISTIAN DOCTRINE

POPE PIUS XI
FOR PERPETUAL REMEMBRANCE

In a *Motu proprio* issued by Us on June 29, 1923, We set up in the Sacred Congregation of the Council a special Commission whose duty should be to provide for and promote catechetical teaching in the Church. Now this Catechetical Commission of the said Congregation has repeatedly asked Us, with a view to furthering still more the work of teaching and giving religious instruction to the faithful, to grant certain indulgences to such as devote themselves either to teaching or to learning the catechism. Our Predecessors indeed, Popes Paul IV and Clement XIII, conceded such indulgences as were then fitting, but we think that these now need to be increased and made more suitable to the needs of the present time. Consequently, We abrogate all indulgences granted for this purpose in the past by the aforesaid pontiffs, and, after taking counsel with our beloved son, the Cardinal Penitentiary of the holy Roman Church, We, trusting in the mercy of Almighty God and relying on the authority of the blessed apostles Sts. Peter and Paul, grant to each and all of the faithful who shall for approximately half an hour or not less than twenty minutes devote themselves to learning or teaching the catechism at least twice in the month, a plenary indulgence which they can gain twice a month on any day they choose, provided that, being truly penitent, they have been to confession and Communion, and have visited some church or public oratory, and there prayed for Our, that is to say, the Roman pontiff's intention.

Moreover, We grant to the same members of the faithful a partial indulgence of one hundred days as often as, for the abovementioned space of time, they teach or learn the catechism—provided always that they are sorry for their sins. The present concessions to hold good for the future notwithstanding anything to the contrary.

Given at St. Peter's, Rome, under the Seal of the Fisherman.

March 12, 1930, the ninth year of Our Pontificate.

E. CARD. PACELLI, *SECRETARY OF STATE.*

Appendix V

AN EPITOME OF THE HISTORY OF DIVINE REVELATION[63]

The Creation of the World and of Man

1. In the beginning, there was nothing but God. And he, since infinitely perfect and happy of himself, needed no person or thing; but, led only by his own goodness, he created what things he would, that is, he made out of nothing all things contained in heaven and on earth, visible and invisible.

2. All created things are part of a wonderful harmony; the last to be created, namely man, as the completion of the whole creation, was made to the image and likeness of God.

3. God called the first man Adam, and to him he gave Eve as his companion when he had formed her out of one of Adam's ribs; from these two sprang the whole human race.

The Fall of Man and the Promise of Redemption

4. Man, made the king of the whole earth, was placed in a most beautiful spot, an earthly paradise, where he enjoyed good things of every kind. But

[63] Taken from the *Catechism of Pope Pius X.*

to help him to recognize the full authority of his Creator, God commanded him not to eat of the tree of the knowledge of good and evil.

5. Yet Eve, who believed the serpent rather than God, and Adam, who gave in to her, miserably broke God's command; and through their fault came to pass what God decreed, namely, that not only they two but all men from then onward were deprived of grace and eternal happiness, as well as of other gifts meant to remedy the defects of human nature. Thus they became subject to the service of the devil, to evil desires, to all sorts of troubles, even to death itself; and, at the same time, they forced us too into the danger of losing eternal happiness.

6. But though he had driven them out of the paradise of pleasure and had condemned them to toil and bodily death, God did not deprive them of all hope of eternal salvation. On the contrary, he promised that the devil's cruel tyranny over them should be destroyed by himself through the Messias, that is, the Christ, who should come in the fullness of time. Relying on this hope and confidence, man might live again by obeying the moral law graven in his heart.

The Corruption of Mankind; the Flood; the Chosen People

7. Yet, beginning with Cain, who through jealousy slew his brother Abel, sin multiplied on the earth as the human race increased, so that all became wholly corrupt. God therefore sent a flood upon the earth and in it all perished except a just man called Noe with his family, for God preserved them by putting them into the ark, which was a large kind of a ship he had told Noe to make. When the flood was over, Noe offered a sacrifice to God on an altar to thank him for his great mercy.

8. But the other nations which had sprung from Sem, Cham, and Japheth, sons of Noe, went so far astray that in the course of time they all forgot God and worshipped idols. Out of the few children of Sem who had remained faithful, God chose Abraham the Chaldean; he called him out of his own country and promised him that, if he and his descendants would but be faithful, he would be their God, also that he would not only give them great increase in numbers and make them owners of the land of

Chanaan or Palestine, but that all nations should be blessed in their seed. This same promise was renewed to Isaac, the son of Abraham and to Jacob or Israel, son of Isaac.

9. Thus were the descendants of Abraham and Israel made the chosen people, that they might keep safe the true religion and belief, and hand down to their children the promise of a Redeemer.

The Exile of the Hebrews in Egypt; God Delivers Them through the Hand of Moses

10. Jacob died in Egypt, whither he and his sons had, during a heavy famine, gone for help to Joseph, his beloved son. His brethren had through jealousy sold Joseph to the Egyptians as a slave, but Pharao, Egypt's king, struck by Joseph's gift of prophecy and his prudence and fidelity, advanced him to the highest dignities in the kingdom. When, however, the Jews in Egypt grew numerous and prosperous, a later Pharao, fearing their power, tried to crush them out of existence by reducing them to slavery, also by commanding that all their male children should be drowned in the river Nile as soon as they were born.

11. But God came to the rescue of his people. For Moses—the future deliverer of the people—was rescued from the river by Pharao's daughter, who had him brought up in her palace. Later on, God, through Moses, bade Pharao let his people go. On his refusal, God struck his kingdom with ten plagues, called the "plagues of Egypt," the last of which was the destruction by an angel in the night of the firstborn children of the Egyptians; but the angel spared the houses of the Hebrews, where he found that they had sprinkled them with the blood of a lamb.[64]

12. When Pharao at length gave in to their demands, Moses and the people immediately departed and crossed the Red Sea, which was miraculously divided before them. But when the Egyptians repented of having let them go and entered the sea in pursuit, the divided waters reunited and

[64] From the fact that the destroying angel "passed over" the houses of the Hebrews, which were marked by the blood of the lamb, came the name *Passover* (cf. Ex 12:7, 12-13, 23).

they all perished. Thus took place the passing over of the Hebrews; as a reminder of this marvelous deliverance,[65] the feast of the Passover was celebrated every year until the coming of Jesus Christ, by whom the human race was redeemed from the far graver captivity of sin.

The Hebrews in the Wilderness; the Giving of the Law; Josue; the Promised Land

13. As he led the Hebrews through the wilderness, God gave them on Mount Sinai, with great solemnity and amidst thunder and lightning, the decalogue or ten commandments, graven on two tablets of stone. To these he added certain ceremonial and social laws which they were to observe until the coming of Christ (or the "Messias"), and so deserve the fulfillment of God's promises.

14. This was the old testament or covenant which God made with his chosen people. This old or Mosaic law, which contained many minute and burdensome precepts, was to be a safeguard of their belief in and worship of the one true God whom the heathen did not know, and a preparation for the new testament, or new law of Christ, which far excelled the old testament. On the foundation of this old covenant, the nation of the Hebrews was to be built up by Moses.

15. But though God by this covenant had given to the Hebrews a most exalted position and had wonderfully supported them in the desert, yet through their own fault they retarded their entrance into the promised land. Moses himself died on its borders; but Josue, who succeeded him, captured Palestine forty years after they had begun their wanderings, and divided it among the twelve tribes descended from the twelve sons of Jacob.

The Judges; the Kings; David and Solomon; the Temple; the Kingdom of Juda

16. After the death of Josue, judges, or men raised up by God whenever grave necessities demanded it, ruled the people. Then came kings, of whom

[65] Cf. Ex 12:17

Saul was the first. When God rejected him, David, of the tribe of Juda, became king. He was a man full of zeal and faithful to God; the kingdom was to be hereditary in his family and of it was to be born at last the Christ "of whose kingdom there shall be no end."[66]

17. Solomon, David's son and the wisest of men, built at Jerusalem a great and splendid Temple for the Lord; but, in his old age, he fell into vice and idolatry. Because of this sin, and because of the hardness of heart of his son Roboam, who succeeded him, ten tribes separated off from the house of David; out of these, Jeroboam, the author of this schism, made the kingdom of Israel, which soon fell into idolatry and was therefore rejected by God and carried away by the Assyrians.

18. Meanwhile, the tribes of Juda and Benjamin, which made up the kingdom of Juda and which alone remained to the successors of David, frequently fell into sin, though the prophets, especially in the time of their wicked kings Achaz and Manasses, sternly rebuked them for it. Consequently, Nabuchodonosor, the king of Babylon, came and destroyed the Temple at Jerusalem and carried the people into captivity.

The Babylonian Captivity; the Return of the People to Their Fatherland; the Rebuilding of the Temple

19. In the miseries of their captivity, the Hebrews, stirred up by the prophets, changed their lives and once more asserted their belief in God and in the delivery of Israel, which was to be accomplished by the Christ or Messias.

20. When, then, after seventy years, Cyrus, the king of the Persians, who had captured Babylon, gave the people leave—in accordance with the wonderful predictions of Isaias the prophet—to return to their own country, the city of Jerusalem was, under the leadership of Zorobabel and Nehemias, rebuilt amid immense enthusiasm. The Temple, too, was rebuilt, though not so splendidly as before; it was later on to be glorified by the presence there of the expected Lord and angel of the new covenant. The

[66] Lk 1:33

worship of God was publicly restored, and, under Esdras the priest, the people again obeyed the law which was publicly read out to them with appropriate explanations.

21. Then, in the course of time, though the civil liberties, as well as the power and wealth of the people of Israel, were much lessened, yet, despite the fact that many fell away from their early principles, their zeal for the law of God and their expectation of the coming of the Savior of the human race, of whose coming the prophets spoke evermore and more clearly, did not lessen but rather grew stronger, until Jesus of Nazareth appeared, in whom were divinely fulfilled all the prophecies.[67]

The Life, Preaching, Death, Resurrection, and Ascension of Jesus Christ

22. Jesus was born in Bethlehem of the Virgin Mary, the spouse of Joseph, of the house of David. As the angel Gabriel had declared to her, the Holy Spirit overshadowed her; hence, while remaining a Virgin, she became the Mother of the Word of God, who took flesh of her.

23. In accordance with the law, he was circumcised and called *Jesus*—that is, "Savior." After the sojourn in Egypt caused by Herod's persecution, he lived at Nazareth, subject to Mary and Joseph, growing day by day "in wisdom, age, and grace, before God and men."[68] When he was thirty years old, he received the baptism of penance at the hands of John the Baptist in the river Jordan and began throughout Judaea and Galilee to preach the gospel, or good tidings, that is, the remission of sin, and eternal life to all who should believe in him and obey his commandments; this divine teaching and mission he confirmed by many miracles.

24. Many believed in him, especially his twelve apostles, or "men sent"; these he chose for the purpose of founding his Church, of which he appointed Peter to be the head and, as it were, the foundation. But the chief priests, the Pharisees, and the teachers of the law stirred up hatred and envy against him; for they envied his power and took in bad

[67] See the Third Catechism, q. 80ff, below.

[68] Lk 2:52

part his reproval of their errors and hypocrisy. Owing to this hatred, the Sanhedrin, or supreme tribunal of the nation, condemned to death the Redeemer for whom the nations were waiting, and preferred the robber Barabbas to him when Pilate, the Roman governor, but a coward, tried to save his life on the plea that the Passover was approaching.

25. Then, after the most cruel torments—for he was scourged, crowned with thorns, and crucified between two robbers on Calvary, a spot near Jerusalem—he bowed his head as he hung upon the cross, and, when dying, he not only forgave his enemies but asked pardon for them from God. In this way he completed the work of our redemption by offering to his eternal Father full satisfaction for us.

Thus was completed the old testament, or the covenant God had made with an unmindful and ungrateful people; they rejected and cruelly put to death the Redeemer of all mankind, but he thus consecrated a new and eternal covenant in his precious blood.

26. When the body of Jesus was buried, his soul descended into hell to set free the souls of the just there awaiting redemption. But on the third day, as he had repeatedly foretold, he rose from the dead and then appeared to the holy women, to Peter, to the two disciples on their way to Emmaus, and to the other apostles, who were still doubting the truth, but on seeing his glorious wounds became certain of Christ's resurrection. Then when he had instructed them in the kingdom of God and had given them power to remit or retain sins, he sent them out into the whole world to teach and baptize, promising that he would send them his Holy Spirit and that he himself would be with them unto the consummation of the world. Finally, on the fortieth day after his resurrection, he was, before their eyes, taken up to heaven where he sits at the right hand of the Father, endowed with all power in heaven and on earth.

The Descent of the Holy Spirit; the Catholic Church

27. Ten days later, on the feast of Pentecost, the Holy Spirit promised by Christ descended on the apostles and on the infant Church, never again to be separated from it. Thus was the kingdom of God, with the apostles

as its rulers and propagators, established and perfected. Furnished, too, with supernatural assistance in the shape of God's teaching given by word of mouth or in writing, with the sacraments—of which the chief is the Holy Eucharist, under whose veils Christ, unceasingly present with us, lies hidden—and with the gifts of the Holy Spirit, the Church, now wholly distinct from the synagogue, began its own peculiar task of ministering to the salvation of the human race. Whence it came to pass that the heathen, in spite of terrible persecutions at the hands of the Roman Empire, were by degrees recalled from the idolatry and corruption into which they had fallen, and very many of them, when once they had embraced the Catholic faith, became glorious examples of every virtue.

28. Shortly afterward, Jerusalem, with its Temple, was destroyed, and the Jews scattered to all parts of the earth. The ancient world, eaten up by its vices, had fallen into decay; kingdoms and empires have worn out and perished; but the Church abides, and, through the civilization she has introduced, helps on ever more and more the salvation of human society, even though the most powerful nations have, through heresy and schism, quitted their mother's breast, and those who hate Christianity still wage—as they have always done—unceasing war against her.

"The gates of hell shall not prevail against her":[69] that is the divine promise; relying on it, Christ's soldiers know no fear, but with holy mother Church they pray, toil, and bear in patience every trial, looking forward to that last day when Christ, the glorious judge of the living and the dead, shall come again—he who, though he predicted hatred, persecutions, and apostasies, strengthened and encouraged the spirits of all his disciples by saying: "If the world hates you, know that it hated me before;...if they persecute me, they will also persecute you...Have confidence: I have overcome the world."[70]

[69] Mt 16:18

[70] Jn 15:18, 20; 16:33. For the proofs of the Godhead of Christ, see the Third Catechism, q. 82, below.

III
Catechism For Adults

ARRANGEMENT

OF THE CHAPTERS ON CHRISTIAN DOCTRINE IN THE CATECHISM FOR ADULTS

Chapter 1 will deal with the sign of the cross, the hallmark of a Christian.

Chapter 2 will deal with divine revelation. This chapter may be termed the "door" by which we enter the catechism, for we are here shown how we are to learn about God and the things of eternity.

And since for the attainment of salvation, which is "the one thing necessary"[71] and man's final end, we must first of all believe, Chapter 3 will deal with the Apostles' Creed, in which the truths of faith are contained.

Since, too, good works should follow on faith, Chapter 4 will treat of the decalogue or ten commandments; Chapter 5 with the precepts of the Church; Chapter 6 with the evangelical counsels.

Then, since we need divine grace to carry out what has been taught in the foregoing chapters, Chapter 7 will treat of grace.

And since we obtain grace more particularly by prayer and the sacraments, Chapter 8 will deal with prayer; and Chapter 9 with the sacraments.

Further, since by justification we obtain, in addition to the remission of our sins, the infused virtues and the gifts of the Holy Spirit, whence flow the beatitudes of the gospel and the fruits of the Holy Spirit, Chapter 10 will treat of the theological virtues, the moral virtues, the gifts of the Holy Spirit, the beatitudes, and the fruits of the Holy Spirit.

But we can always resist the grace so mercifully given us and deliberately break God's law and so commit sin; Chapter 11 will therefore deal with sin.

Finally, since reflection on the last things helps us, as holy scripture says, to avoid sin, Chapter 12 will treat of the last things.

[71] Lk 10:42

Catechism For Adults Who Desire To Have A Fuller Knowledge Of Catholic Doctrine

The Sign of the Cross

1. **Are you a Christian?**
By the grace of God, I am a Christian.

2. **What is meant by a Christian?**
A Christian is one who has received the sacrament of baptism, which is the door of the Church of Christ.[72]

3. **Who is a Christian in the strict and full sense of the word?**
A Christian in the strict and full sense of the word is a baptized person who makes profession of the true and entire faith of Christ—one who is, in other words, a Catholic; he is a good Christian if he also keeps the law of Christ.

4. **What is the outward sign of a Christian?**
The outward sign of a Christian is the sign of the cross.[73]

[72] Cf. Council of Florence, Session 8 (November 22, 1439), "Bull of Union with the Armenians"; Council of Trent, Session 6, Can. 28; Benedict XV, Encyclical *Ad beatissimi*, Nov. 1, 1914; *Codex Juris Canonici*, Can. 87

[73] Cf. Augustine, *Tractate 118 on John*, n. 5

5. **How do we make the sign of the cross?**
We make the sign of the cross by touching the forehead with the right hand, saying, "In the name of the Father," then the breast, adding, "and of the Son," and then from the left shoulder to the right, while saying, "and of the Holy Ghost. Amen."[74]

6. **Why is the sign of the cross the sign of a Christian?**
The sign of the cross is the sign of a Christian, because by it we make external profession of the principal mysteries of the Christian faith.

7. **What is a mystery?**
A mystery is a truth which of its very nature so exceeds created reason that it could not be known unless it were revealed.[75]

8. **What are the principal mysteries of the Christian faith?**
The principal mysteries of the Christian faith are:
   1. The mystery of one God in three distinct Persons, the Father, the Son, and the Holy Ghost.
   2. The mystery of man's redemption by the incarnation, passion, and death of Jesus Christ, the Son of God.[76]

9. **How does the sign of the cross show forth these two mysteries of the Christian faith?**
The sign of the cross shows forth these two mysteries of the Christian faith, because the words used signify the unity of God in three distinct Persons;

[74] If in any place the sign of the cross is made in different fashion, any approved custom may be observed (Innocent III, *De Sacro Altaris Mysterio*, Bk. II, n. 45).

[75] Cf. 1 Cor 2:6-13; First Vatican Council, Constitution *Dei Filius*, Ch. 4; Pius IX, Epistle *Tuas libenter*, Dec. 21, 1863, to the archbishop of Munich. Unbelievers and opponents of the Catholic religion deceive themselves when they repudiate all mysteries of the supernatural order; for, as a matter of fact, they have to admit the presence of many mysteries in the natural order itself; these mysteries baffle the human reason and can only be inadequately explained.

[76] These mysteries of the faith are more fully set out under q. 33ff, below.

and the cross we make calls to mind the redemption of man accomplished by Jesus Christ on the tree of the cross.

10. **Is it a good thing to make the sign of the cross?**
It is a very good thing to make the sign of the cross often and devoutly, especially at the beginning and end of our chief occupations.

11. **Why is it a good thing to make the sign of the cross often and devoutly?**
It is a very good thing to make the sign of the cross, because this sign, rightly made, is an outward sign of our inward faith, and has therefore power to stir up our faith, overcome human respect, drive away temptations, avert occasions of sin, and obtain other graces from God.[77]

Divine Revelation

12. **Can we know and prove the existence of God by the light of natural reason?**
By the light of natural reason, we can certainly know and prove from created things the existence of the one true God, the beginning and end of all things, our Creator and Lord—arguing, that is, from created things to the Creator, from effect to cause.[78]

13. **Can we know God in any other way than by the natural light of reason?**
Besides the natural light of reason, there is another way of knowing God, namely, by faith; because it has pleased his wisdom and goodness to make known to men both himself and the everlasting decrees of his will by supernatural revelation.[79]

[77] Cf. Canisius, *De Fide et Symbolo*, i, 12

[78] Cf. Ps 13:2; Ws 13:1-5; Rom 1:20; First Vatican Council, Constitution *Dei Filius*, Ch. 2; "On Revelation," Can. 1; Pius X, Motu proprio *Sacrorum Antistitum*, Sept. 1, 1910; Irenaeus, *Against Heresies*, Bk. 2, Ch. 9, n. 1; Augustine, *Sermon 141*, n. 2

[79] Cf. Heb 1:1; First Vatican Council, Constitution *Dei Filius*, Ch. 2

14. **What do you mean by "supernatural revelation"?**
By "supernatural revelation," I mean both the word of God, whereby in order to instruct us in the doctrine of eternal salvation he has made manifest to men certain truths, and also the truths themselves thus revealed.[80]

15. **What follows from this notion of supernatural revelation?**
From this notion of supernatural revelation, it follows that it is wholly free from all error, since God, who is the supreme truth, can neither deceive nor be deceived.

16. **What truths are contained in divine revelation?**
In divine revelation are contained not only mysteries beyond created understanding, but also many truths that human reason could discover.

17. **Why did God deign to reveal to man truths that are not in themselves beyond human reason?**
God deigned to reveal to man truths that are not in themselves beyond human reason so that these truths might, even in the present state of mankind, be easily known by all with full certainty and without any admixture of error.[81]

18. **What external arguments for his revelation has God chosen to give, that the obedience of our faith may be in accordance with reason?**
That the obedience of our faith may be in accordance with reason, God has chosen to give us, in addition to the inward assistance of his grace, external arguments for his revelation, namely, certain divine works, especially miracles and prophecies; these are most certain signs of divine revelation and suited to the understanding of everyone, for they clearly show the omnipotence and infinite knowledge of God.[82]

[80] Cf. 1 Cor 2:10; Heb 1:1

[81] Cf. First Vatican Council, Constitution *Dei Filius*, Ch. 2

[82] Cf. Is 41:23; Jn 10:25, 37-38; 15:24; 2 Pt 1:19; First Vatican Council, Constitution *Dei Filius*, Ch. 3; Origen, *Contra Celsum*, Bk. 6, Ch. 10

19. **What is a miracle?**
A miracle is something produced by God outside the order of the whole of created nature.[83]

20. **What is prophecy?**
Prophecy is in its strict sense a certain prediction of some future event that could in no way be known through natural causes.[84]

21. **Where are the truths revealed by God to be found?**
The truths revealed by God are to be found in holy scripture and tradition.[85]

22. **What do you mean by "holy scripture"?**
By "holy scripture," I mean the books of the old and new testaments, which, being written under the inspiration of the Holy Ghost, have God for their author, and, as such, have been given to the Church by God himself.[86]

23. **In what does the inspiration of the Holy Ghost consist?**
The inspiration of the Holy Ghost consists in this: that the Holy Ghost so stimulated and moved men to write, so stood by them as they wrote, that all those things, and only those things, which he commanded they rightly conceived in their minds, sought faithfully to commit to writing, and aptly expressed with infallible truth.[87]

24. **What do you mean by the "old and new testaments"?**
By the "old testament," I mean the books of the Bible written before the coming of Jesus Christ; by the "new testament," the books written after his coming.

[83] Cf. *Summa Theologiae*, I, q. 110, a. 4

[84] Cf. *Summa Theologiae*, II-II, q. 171, a. 3

[85] Cf. Theophilus of Antioch, *To Autolycus*, Bk. 3, Ch. 12; Epiphanius, *Adversus Haereses*, Heresy 61, Ch. 6

[86] Cf. 2 Tm 3:15-16; 2 Pt 1:20-21

[87] Cf. Council of Trent, Session 4, "Decree concerning the Canonical Scriptures"; First Vatican Council, Constitution *Dei Filius*, Ch. 2; Leo XIII, Encyclical *Providentissimus Deus*, Nov. 18, 1893

25. **What do you mean by *tradition*?**
By *tradition*, I mean that body of revealed truths, received by the apostles from the lips of Christ himself or told them by the Holy Ghost, that has come down to us, delivered to us as it were by hand, and preserved in the Catholic Church by unbroken succession.[88]

26. **What is the body of all revealed truth called?**
The body of all revealed truth is called the "deposit of faith."

27. **To whom did Jesus Christ choose to entrust the deposit of faith?**
Jesus Christ chose to entrust the deposit of faith to the Church, that she, by the assistance of the Holy Ghost, might guard this revealed doctrine inviolably and faithfully expound it.[89]

28. **What is primarily necessary for us if we would attain eternal life?**
To attain eternal life, it is first of all necessary for us to believe those truths which God has revealed and which the Church proposes for our belief.[90]

29. **Where are the truths which God has revealed, and which the Church proposes for our belief, principally to be found?**
The truths which God has revealed and the Church proposes for our belief are to be found principally in the Apostles' Creed.[91]

[88] Cf. Mt 28:19-20; Jn 14:26; 16:13; 20:30; 21:25; Acts 1:3; 2 Thes 2:15; Council of Trent, Session 4, "Decree concerning the Canonical Scriptures"; First Vatican Council, Constitution *Dei Filius*, Ch. 2

[89] Cf. Mt 28:20; Jn 14:16; 16:13; First Vatican Council, Constitution *Dei Filius*, Ch. 4; Constitution *Pastor Aeternus*, Ch. 4; Irenaeus, *Against Heresies*, Bk. 3, Ch. 3, n. 1ff

[90] Cf. Mk 16:16; Jn 3:18; Heb 11:6

[91] The truths of the faith are said to be discoverable mainly in the Creed, because there are several other truths of the faith which are presented to us outside the Creed, for example, in the catechism. The virtue of faith will be found explained under q. 515ff, below.

The Apostles' Creed

30. **Why is this collection of the truths of faith called the "Apostles' Creed"?**
This collection of the truths of faith is called the "Apostles' Creed," because it contains a summary of the principal truths handed down by the apostles, and was in use from the earliest ages of the Church as the hallmark of a Christian.

31. **What do the twelve articles of the Creed contain?**
The twelve articles of the Creed contain the mystery of one God in three distinct Persons, Father, Son, and Holy Ghost, together with the operations that are, for some particular reason, attributed to each Person.[92]

32. **How is the doctrine of this mystery set forth in the Apostles' Creed?**
In the Apostles' Creed, the doctrine of this mystery is so set forth in its three main parts that the first tells of the first Person of the divine nature and the work of creation; the next of the second Person and the work of redemption; and the third of the third Person and the work of our sanctification, begun here by grace and completed hereafter by glory.[93]

[92] Cf. Canisius, *De Fide et Symbolo*, i, 7; TCCI 7:45-47

[93] As the *Catechism of the Council of Trent* says: "As our fathers before us who have carefully studied this question have pointed out, the mystery of the Holy Trinity may be considered under three aspects: under the first, the first Person of the Godhead is set before us and the wonders of the work of creation; under the second comes the second Person and the mystery of our redemption; under the third comes the third Person, the fount and source of our sanctification" (see TCCI 7:47).

THE FIRST ARTICLE OF THE CREED, IN WHICH IS SET FORTH THE DOCTRINE OF THE FIRST PERSON OF THE MOST HOLY TRINITY AND OF THE WORK OF CREATION

God, One in Three Persons

33. **What do you mean by the words, "I believe"?**
By the words, "I believe," I mean that I firmly assent to the truths set forth in the Creed, on the authority of God who has revealed them.

34. **What do you mean by the words, "I believe in God"?**
By the words, "I believe in God," I mean that I firmly believe that God exists, and that I strive after him as the highest and most perfect good and my last end.[94]

35. **What do you mean by the name *God*?**
By the name *God*, I mean a most pure Spirit—that is to say, a spiritual being, absolutely simple and unchangeable, infinite in understanding, will, and all perfections, in himself and of himself most blessed.

36. **What are the principal perfections or attributes of God?**
The principal perfections or attributes of God are these: God is:
    1. Eternal, because he neither has nor can have beginning, or end, or succession.
    2. All-knowing, because he has all things in his sight, even those things which will come to pass by the free action of creatures, their hearts' affections and secret thoughts.
    3. Immeasurable, because he is in heaven, on earth, and in all places that are or can be.
    4. Just, because he renders to everyone according to his merits, either in this life, or certainly in the next.

[94] Cf. TCCI 7:48-54

5. Good, because he created, preserves, and disposes all things by his infinite goodness, power, and wisdom; because the good things we enjoy come from him, and because, in his goodness, he hears the prayers of those who ask.
6. Merciful, because, desiring all men to be saved, he has redeemed them from the slavery of the devil, and pours out on each the means necessary for salvation; for he does not will the death of a sinner, but rather that he be converted and live.[95]

37. **Is God distinct from the world?**
God is really and essentially distinct from the world, and immeasurably above all things that exist or can be thought of apart from himself.[96]

38. **Is God one?**
God is one by unity of nature, yet in three really distinct Persons, Father, Son, and Holy Ghost, who make up the most Holy Trinity.

39. **How are Father, Son, and Holy Ghost distinguished from each other?**
Father, Son, and Holy Ghost are distinguished from each other by the opposite relations of the Persons, inasmuch as the Father begets the Son, and from both Father and Son proceeds the Holy Ghost.[97]

40. **Does any one of the three Persons precede the others in time?**
No one of the three Persons precedes the others in time, but all are equally eternal because they neither have nor can have beginning or end.

[95] Cf. Ez 18:23, 32; 33:11; Ps 7:10; 37:10; 43:22; 138:1-12; Jn 4:24; Acts 18:25; 1 Tm 1:17; Apoc 1:8; 4:8, 11; Fourth Lateran Council, Const. 1; First Vatican Council, Constitution *Dei Filius*, Ch. 1; Cyril of Jerusalem, *Catechetical Lecture* 4, n. 5

[96] Cf. Acts 17:24-25; Heb 1:10-12; First Vatican Council, Constitution *Dei Filius*, Ch. 1

[97] Cf. Fourth Lateran Council, Const. 2; Second Council of Lyons, *De Processione Spiritus Sancti*; Council of Florence, Session 6 (July 6, 1439), "Decree for the Greeks"; Augustine, *On the Trinity*, Bk. 1, Ch. 4, n. 7; Epiphanius, *Ancoratus*, Ch. 8; John Damascene, *An Exposition of the Orthodox Faith*, Bk. 1, Ch. 12. The Greek fathers describe this eternal procession of the Holy Spirit by means of the formula: "from the Father through the Son."

41. **Why are the three Persons one God?**
The three Persons are one God because they are consubstantial—that is, they have one and the same divine nature, and therefore the same perfections or attributes and external works.[98]

42. **Does not holy scripture ascribe power to the Father, wisdom to the Son, and goodness to the Holy Ghost?**
Although all the divine attributes are common to each of the three Persons, yet holy scripture ascribes: power to the Father, because he is the fount whence all things spring; wisdom to the Son, because he is the Word of the Father; goodness and holiness to the Holy Ghost, because he is the love of the other two Persons.[99]

43. **What form of praise to the Holy Trinity do the faithful generally make use of, especially at the close of their prayers?**
The form of praise to the Holy Trinity that the faithful generally make use of at the end of their prayers is: "Glory be to the Father and to the Son and to the Holy Ghost, as it was in the beginning, is now, and ever shall be, world without end. Amen."

44. **What does the word *Almighty* mean?**
The word *Almighty* means that God can, by the simple act of his will, do whatever he wishes.[100]

[98] Cf. Council of the Lateran under Martin I, Can. 1; Fulgentius, *De Fide*, Ch. 1, n. 4; Ephraem, *Hymnus de defunctis et Trinitate*, n. 11-12; Gregory Nazianzen, *Oration 33*, n. 16; TCCI 7:52ff. The external works of God (*ad extra*) are all those produced by God outside himself, whether in the natural or in the supernatural order; they are so called in order to distinguish them from those immanent actions of God which constitute the inner life of the Godhead.

[99] Cf. TCCI 7:60, 116

[100] Cf. Ps 113:11; Lk 1:37

THE CREATION OF THE WORLD; DIVINE PROVIDENCE

45. **What do you mean by the words, "Creator of heaven and earth"?**
By the words, "Creator of heaven and earth," I mean that God, by his own free decree, simultaneously in the beginning of time, made creatures out of nothing both spiritual and corporeal—that is, the angels and this world, and finally man, who belongs, as it were, to both, being composed of spirit and body.

46. **Why did God deign to create all these things?**
God, in his goodness and almighty power, deigned to create all these things, not to increase his own happiness thereby, nor to acquire any perfection, but to manifest his own perfection by the good things he bestowed on his creation.[101]

47. **Does God take care of all created things?**
God takes care of all created things, inasmuch as he preserves them, upholds them—otherwise they would at once return to nothingness—and governs them, so that there neither is nor can be anything that happens without God's will or permission.[102]

48. **What do you call the care that God takes of created things?**
We call the care that God takes of created things "divine providence."[103]

49. **Why then does God not prevent sin?**
God does not prevent sin because he has conferred freedom on man, as well as the help of his grace, so that man himself may be the author of his blessedness or perdition, in proportion, that is, as he corresponds with grace or resists it; but from man's very abuse of freedom, God marvelously

[101] Cf. Gn 1:1; Ps 134:6; Heb 1:10; Fourth Lateran Council, Const. 1; First Vatican Council, Constitution *Dei Filius*, Ch. 1; TCCI 7:60-61

[102] Cf. Ws 11:26; Mt 6:30; Lk 12:6-7; Acts 17:25; Rom 8:30; Heb 1:3; First Vatican Council, Constitution *Dei Filius*, Ch. 1; TCCI 7:63-64

[103] Cf. Chrysostom, *Contra Anomaeos*, Ch. 12, n. 4

draws good, so that his justice and mercy may shine forth always and everywhere.[104]

50. **Why does God will or permit all those physical evils whereby we are afflicted in this mortal life?**

God wills or permits all those physical evils whereby we are afflicted in this mortal life, either as a punishment of sin, or to bring back sinners to himself, or to prove the just and make them worthy of everlasting reward, or because he knows of some greater good which will result from them.[105]

51. **Which are the most excellent of God's creatures?**

Angels and men are the most excellent of God's creatures.

The Creation of the Angels

52. **What are angels?**

Angels are pure spirits endowed with intellect and will; they were established in a state of justice and holiness, so that, if they cooperated with the grace of God, they might merit glory.[106]

53. **Did all the angels cooperate with the grace of God?**

Not all the angels cooperated with the grace of God. Those who did so enjoy in heaven the beatific vision of God; these are called simply "angels" and form the nine choirs of angels. Those who did not cooperate with grace were thrust down to hell because of their sin of pride; these are called "devils" and their chief is Lucifer or Satan.[107]

[104] Cf. Augustine, *On the Spirit and the Letter*, Ch. 58

[105] Cf. Gn 3:16-19; Tb 2:12; Jb 2:6-7; Jn 9:3; Ephraem, *Carmina Nisibena*, Hymn 3, n. 8-10; *Summa Theologiae*, I, q. 19, a. 9; q. 49, a. 2

[106] Cf. Mt 18:10; Heb 1:7, 14; John Damascene, *An Exposition of the Orthodox Faith*, Bk. 2, Ch. 3

[107] Cf. Is 14:12-15; Jb 4:18; 2 Pt 2:4; Jude 6; Athanasius, *De Virginitate*, n. 5; Gregory the Great, *On the Gospels*, Bk. 2, Homily 34, n. 7-9

54. **Does God use the ministry of angels?**
In many ways God uses the ministry of angels, especially in his care of men, for to each of them he gives a guardian angel from the time of his birth.[108]

55. **What does our guardian angel do for us?**
Our guardian angel protects us, especially in time of temptation; he suggests to us good thoughts; he offers our prayers to God; and he himself prays for us.[109]

56. **Does it help our spiritual life to have special devotion to our guardian angel?**
It is very helpful to our spiritual life to have special devotion to our guardian angel, reverencing him and calling on him, especially in time of temptation, following his promptings, thanking him for his help, and never vexing his presence by sin.

57. **What prayer to our guardian angel should we often make use of?**
We should often pray to our guardian angel by saying: "O angel of God, my guardian, enlighten, guard, rule, and govern me, who have been committed to thy care by the Divine Majesty."

58. **What can the devils do against man?**
The devils can, by God's just permission, do harm to man in external things and even to his person, by taking possession of his body, and by tempting him to sin; but they cannot prejudice his eternal salvation without his free consent.[110]

[108] Cf. Tb 5:15; Ps 90:11; Mt 2:13, 19; 18:10; Lk 1:26, 28; Heb 1:14; Jerome, *On Matthew*, Ch. 18; TCCI 7:516-518

[109] Cf. Ex 23:20-23; Tb 3:25; 12:12-13

[110] Cf. Jb 1:12; 2:6; Lk 22:3, 31; Jn 13:27; 1 Pt 5:8; Irenaeus, *Against Heresies*, Bk. 5, Ch. 24, n. 3-4

The Creation of Man; Original Sin

59. **What is man?**

Man is a creature, made up of a rational soul and an organic body.[111]

60. **What is a rational soul?**

A rational soul is a spiritual substance, endowed with intellect and free will, and immortal; it is so intimately united to the body that it is the principle of all life in a man.[112]

61. **Why did God create man?**

God created man to know him, to love him, and to serve him, so that after death man might, by possession of God in the beatific vision, be happy with him forever in paradise.[113]

62. **In what does the beatific vision of God consist?**

The beatific vision of God consists in the vision of the very essence of God, who manifests himself directly, clearly, and openly to the soul which, however, is only able to exercise this vision by the help of the light of glory; from this vision and possession, man gains true, full, and never-failing happiness—that is, eternal life.[114]

[111] Cf. Gn 2:7

[112] Cf. Fifth Lateran Council, Session 8; Pius IX, Epistle *Dolore haud mediocri*, April 30, 1860, to the bishop of Wratislavia; John Damascene, *An Exposition of the Orthodox Faith*, Bk. 2, Ch. 12

[113] Cf. Dt 6:13; Jn 17:3; 1 Jn 3:2

[114] Cf. Benedict XII, Constitution *Benedictus Deus*, January 29, 1336; John Damascene, *An Exposition of the Orthodox Faith*, Bk. 4, Ch. 27; TCCI 7:166-168

63. **Is the beatific vision man's natural right?**
The beatific vision is not man's natural right, but is something supernatural, wholly beyond created nature, and freely granted by the pure goodness of God to rational creatures.[115]

64. **Who were the first parents of the human race?**
The first parents of the human race were Adam and Eve, whom God made and placed in an earthly paradise, raising them to a supernatural state and heaping upon them marvelous gifts of grace and nature.[116]

65. **How did God make man's first parents?**
God made the body of Adam out of the slime of the earth and the body of Eve from a rib taken from Adam, but the souls of both he created out of nothing, joining them to their respective bodies in a wonderful union of substance.[117]

66. **What does holy scripture mean when it says that God made man "to his own image and likeness"?**
Holy scripture says that God made man "to his own image and likeness," because, in making man, God endowed him with intellect and free will,

[115] That perfect happiness at which all men aim by nature can be attained only in the next life by the possession of God through perfect intellectual knowledge of him, followed by love on the part of the will, or, as St. Augustine expresses it: "Thou hast made us, O Lord, for thee; and our souls are not at ease till they find rest in thee" (*Confessions*, Bk. 1, Ch. 1, n. 1). Now, God has, through his infinite goodness, deigned to raise mankind to that perfect supernatural happiness which is attained in the possession of God, by seeing as he is him in whom our eternal life consists (see 1 Cor 2:9-10; Pius V, Constitution *Ex omnibus afflictionibus*, against the errors of Baius, Oct. 1, 1567, the first through the tenth condemned Propositions; Clement XI, Constitution *Unigenitus*, against the errors of Quesnel, Sept. 8, 1713, the thirty-fifth condemned Proposition; Pius VI, Constitution *Auctorem Fidei*, against the errors of the Synod of Pistoia, Aug. 28, 1794, the sixteenth condemned Proposition).

[116] Cf. Gn 2:7ff. God subordinated to man—who was made to his own image and likeness—the animals of the earth which he was to use, like its herbs and fruits, for his own advantage. We should therefore be careful not to maltreat animals, but to use them well. For if we are unreasonably angry with them, we are acting contrary to that spirit of meekness which befits a Christian.

[117] Cf. Gn 2:7ff; Chrysostom, *Homily 13 on Genesis*, Ch. 1

whereby in a very special way man imitates the nature of God, who at the same time raised him to a supernatural state.[118]

67. **What difference is there, in the purely natural order, between the creation of our first parents and the origin of their posterity, who descend from them by generation?**
In the purely natural order, the only difference lies in the forming of the bodies of Adam's posterity, which are produced by generation; but the souls of every one of Adam's descendants are created immediately by God and substantially united to the body.

68. **What gifts did God bestow upon our first parents in the earthly paradise?**
The gifts that God bestowed upon our first parents in the earthly paradise were these:
1. He made them perfect in soul and body, with a knowledge fitting their estate.[119]
2. He destined them for a supernatural end, and therefore bestowed on them justice and holiness, as well as an integrity of nature which made all their lower powers subordinate to their reason. He also rendered them immune from death and the other pains and miseries of this life.[120]

69. **With what object did God give to our first parents justice, holiness, and the other gifts?**
God's purpose in giving to our first parents justice, holiness, and the other gifts was to make those gifts the permanent possession of human nature—a gift divinely bestowed on all mankind, one that Adam, the

[118] Cf. Gn 1:26-27; Ws 2:23; Ps 8:5-8; Ephraem, *On Genesis*, Ch. 2; Basil, *Sermo asceticus*, Ch. 1; Augustine, *On Psalm 49*, n. 2; *Summa Theologiae*, I, q. 93. This image and likeness of God becomes more and more perfect by the addition of sanctifying grace, whereby man becomes a sharer in the divine nature, a temple of the Holy Spirit, a friend of God and his adopted son, heir to eternal glory (see below, q. 280).

[119] Cf. Ecclus 17:1-12

[120] Cf. Gn 1:28; 2:17, 25; 3:3, 7, 19; Ws 1:13; 2:23; Ecclus 25:33; Rom 5:12-19; 1 Cor 15:45-49

father of the human race, was by generation to transmit to his descendants together with their nature.[121]

70. **What did God forbid to our first parents in their supernatural state?**
God forbade our first parents in their supernatural state to eat the fruit of the tree of knowledge of good and evil.[122]

71. **Did our first parents obey God's command?**
Our first parents did not obey God's command, and therefore they lost justice and holiness owing to their grave sin of pride and disobedience, and, driven out of the earthly paradise, they became subject to concupiscence, death, and all the other pains and miseries of life.[123]

72. **Did Adam harm his descendants by his fall?**
Adam harmed his descendants by his fall, because by it he transmitted to them not only concupiscence, death, and other punishments for sin, but sin itself, or the loss of justice and holiness.

73. **How did Adam transmit sin to his descendants?**
Adam transmitted sin to his descendants in that he transmitted to them a nature deprived of that justice and holiness which God wished them to have; this privation is the habitual sin of our nature; in Adam it was but one sin, by propagation it was multiplied.

74. **What is this sin thus transmitted to Adam's posterity called?**
This sin thus transmitted to posterity is called "original sin."[124]

[121] Cf. *Summa Theologiae*, I-II, q. 81, a. 2

[122] Cf. Gn 2:17; 3:3

[123] Cf. Gn 2:17; 3:1-24; Rom 5:19

[124] Cf. Jb 14:4; Ps 50:6; Jn 3:5; 1 Tm 2:6; Rom 5:12-14, 18-19; Second Council of Carthage, A.D. 418, Can. 2; Second Council of Orange, Can. 1-2; Council of Trent, Session 5, "Decree concerning Original Sin"; Pius IX, Allocution *Singulari quadam*, Dec. 9, 1854; Cyril of Alexandria, *On Romans*, Ch. 5, n. 18.

What has been said above may be thus briefly set out: the first man was created in a state of perfection not only with regard to his body, so that he could immediately

75. Has anyone been kept free from the stain of original sin?

The Blessed Virgin Mary alone was from the first instant of her conception, through the foreseen merits of Jesus Christ, by a unique privilege granted her by God, kept free from the stain of original sin; she is therefore said to have been "conceived immaculate."[125]

propagate other men, but also with regard to his soul, so that he was able to instruct and direct others with all such knowledge of the natural order as was necessary. This knowledge was bestowed on both our first parents, but particularly on Adam whose especial duty it was to instruct and direct others; but it was not meant to pass to the children whom he might have during his state of innocence. Yet even these latter would in the course of time have without difficulty acquired all such knowledge as was requisite, either by learning it or by discovering things for themselves (see *Summa Theologiae*, I, q. 94, a. 3; q. 101, a. 1-2).

Further, since God had destined our first parents for a supernatural state, revealing to them truths touching that state, which truths Adam was to transmit to his children, he also bestowed on our first parents righteousness, holiness, and other gifts. By his fall, Adam, and with him his descendants, lost all those gifts; yet he did not thereby lose his natural knowledge, nor his knowledge of revealed truths. But his loss of righteousness and holiness, and more particularly of the integrity of his nature, marked the beginning of that conflict between man's lower powers and his reason of which St. Paul says: "The flesh lusteth against the spirit and the spirit against the flesh, for these are contrary one to another," (Gal 5:17). Owing, then, to the fault of our first parent, a cruel and a bitter wound was inflicted in our human nature, for our minds became dulled and our wills prone to evil (see Pius IX, Allocution *Singulari quadam*, also *Summa Theologiae*, I-II, q. 85, a. 3, 5).

When God, in his infinite mercy, promised that there should come a Redeemer for the human race, our first parents, as well as many of their descendants, through their faith in that Redeemer and his merits, were, by the help of God's grace, freed during their lifetime from all sin whether original or actual, also from the debt of punishment due to their actual sins, not however from the debt of punishment due to original sin, for that sin shut them out from the glory of the next world so long as the price of their redemption remained unpaid (see *Summa Theologiae*, III, q. 52, a. 5, rep. 2).

At the same time, many of their posterity lost, either in whole or in part, their knowledge of the truth regarding faith and morals, or at least they retained it only in a very corrupt form. From all this it will be evident how far removed from the truth are the prevalent notions that man was originally in a purely savage condition, or that he has evolved from an ape and so arrived at his present more perfect state; all such notions will be instinctively repudiated by those imbued with Catholic faith. The state of savagery and ferocity in which so many men have lived in the past, and in which so many live even today, is merely a decay from the primitive state of man and is simply due to sin.

[125] Cf. Gn 2:15; Lk 1:28; Council of Trent, Session 5; Sixtus IV, Constitution *Cum praeexcelsa*, Feb. 28, 1476; Pius IX, Constitution *Ineffabilis Deus*, Dec. 8, 1854; Ephraem, *Carmina Nisibena*, Hymn 27, n. 8; Augustine, *On Nature and Grace*, Ch. 42

76. **What does the immaculate conception of the Blessed Virgin Mary mean?**
The immaculate conception of the Blessed Virgin Mary means that, from the first moment of her conception, the Blessed Virgin Mary possessed justice and holiness—that is, sanctifying grace, even the fullness of grace, with the infused virtues and gifts of the Holy Ghost, and with integrity of nature; yet she remained subject to death and other pains and miseries of life that her Son himself willed to undergo.

77. **What does the Church hold about the death of the Blessed Virgin Mary?**
The Church holds that the body of the Blessed Virgin Mary was separated from her soul (for that is the meaning of death), but that her soul was reunited to her incorrupt body, and that she was, by the ministry of angels, taken up into heaven, where she is enthroned above all the choirs of angels.

78. **Did God leave mankind in a state of original sin?**
God did not leave mankind in a state of original sin, but, moved by his infinite mercy, he immediately promised, and in his own time gave, a Redeemer, who is Jesus Christ, the Son of God made man; so that men by their belief in him and his merits, being united to him through faith and charity, might obtain salvation even before his coming on earth.[126]

[126] Cf. Gn 3:15; Mt 9:13; 1 Tm 1:15

THE NEXT SIX ARTICLES OF THE CREED, DEALING WITH THE DOCTRINE OF THE SECOND PERSON OF THE MOST HOLY TRINITY AND WITH THE WORK OF REDEMPTION

Jesus Christ and His Godhead

79. **What do we mean by the second article of the Creed, "and in Jesus Christ, his only Son, our Lord"?**

By the second article of the Creed, "and in Jesus Christ, his only Son, our Lord," we mean that the Son of God, who, as man, is called "Jesus Christ," is the only Son of the Father, our Lord, true God of true God, and in him we believe as we do in the Father.[127]

80. **Why do we believe in Jesus Christ as we believe in God the Father?**

We believe in Jesus Christ as we believe in God the Father, because he is true God as the Father is true God, being one God with the Father.[128]

81. **How can it be shown that Jesus is the Messias or Redeemer of the human race promised by God in the old testament?**

That Jesus is the Messias or Redeemer of the human race promised by God in the old testament can be shown mainly from the prophecies regarding that Redeemer, which find their complete fulfillment in Jesus; it can also be shown by the witness of Jesus himself.[129]

[127] Cf. Jn 1:1, 14, 18; Eph 1:20-23; Col 1:13-20; 1 Tm 6:15-16

[128] Cf. Jn 1:1; 10:30

[129] The prophets foretold that the Messias would be born in the town of Bethlehem (Mi 5:2); of a virgin (Is 7:14); of the stock of David (Is 11:1); that he would be a great teacher (Is 61:1); that he would work miracles (Is 35:5-6); that he would endure the most cruel sufferings (Is 50:6; 53:1-12; Ps 68:22); that he would die (Ps 21:1ff), would rise again (Ps 15:10); ascend into heaven (Ps 109:1; Acts 2:24). These, and many similar things which the prophets had foretold, were perfectly fulfilled in Jesus Christ, and to this we can add his own testimonies (e.g., Mt 11:3-6; 16:13-19; 26:63-64; Mk 8:27-29; 14:61-62; Lk 7:20-23; 9:18-20; 24:26; Jn 4:25-26; 11:25; 14:9-10; 16:15).

82. **What are the main arguments that lead us to believe in the Godhead of Christ?**

The main arguments that lead us to believe in the Godhead of Christ are:

1. The unchanging teaching of the Catholic Church on the point.
2. The prophecies of the old testament, wherein the promised Redeemer is exhibited as God.[130]
3. The witness of God the Father when he said, "This is my beloved Son in whom I am well pleased, hear ye him."[131]
4. The witness of Christ himself, confirmed by the holiness of his life, by his prophecies and miracles, especially by the miracle of his resurrection.[132]
5. The teaching of the apostles on the point, confirmed too by miracles.[133]
6. The testimony of so great a number of martyrs.
7. The amazingly rapid spread of the Church and her equally marvelous preservation.

83. **Why was the Son of God made man called "Jesus"?**

The Son of God made man was called "Jesus" or "Savior" by the will of God, because, by his passion and death, he saved us from sin and eternal damnation.[134]

84. **Why is Jesus also called "Christ"?**

Jesus is also called "Christ" in Greek and "Messias" in Hebrew (in Latin *unctus* or "anointed"), because the kings, priests, and prophets of old were anointed, and Jesus is King, priest, and prophet.[135]

[130] Cf. Ps 2:7; 44:7; 109:3; Is 9:6-7; 40:3-11

[131] Mt 17:5; Cf. Mt 3:17; Mk 1:11

[132] Cf. Mt 11:25-27; 16:13-19; 26:63-65; Lk 22:66-71; Jn 5:18-19, 23; 10:30

[133] Cf. Jn 20:31; 1 Jn 4:15; 5:20; Rom 9:5; Phil 2:6-7; Heb 1:2

[134] Cf. Mt 1:21; Phil 2:8-11; TCCI 7:67-68

[135] Cf. Ex 30:30; 1 Kgs 9:16; 16:3; 3 Kgs 19:16; Acts 10:38; Heb 1:9; TCCI 7:68-70

85. **Why is Jesus Christ called "our Lord"?**
Jesus Christ is called "our Lord," because, as God, he is the Creator and preserver of all creatures, having supreme power over them; and, as God made man, he is the Redeemer of all mankind; wherefore he is rightly hailed and worshipped as "King of kings and Lord of lords."[136]

86. **Why is the second Person of the Blessed Trinity called the "Word" of the Father?**
The second Person of the Blessed Trinity is called the "Word" of the Father, because, just as an idea conceived in our minds is called the "word" or concept of the mind, so the Son, or the second Person of the Trinity, proceeds from the Father as the concept of the Father's mind by his act of understanding.[137]

The Incarnation and Birth of the Son of God

87. **What do we mean by the third article of the Creed, "who was conceived by the Holy Ghost, born of the Virgin Mary"?**
By the third article of the Creed, "who was conceived by the Holy Ghost, born of the Virgin Mary," we mean that the Son of God, by the power of the Holy Ghost, by an act surpassing all the powers of nature, took human nature—that is, a body and a soul—in the most pure womb of the Blessed Virgin Mary, and was born of her.[138]

88. **What is this mystery called whereby the Son of God became man?**
This mystery whereby the Son of God became man is called the "incarnation."

[136] Cf. Mt 25:34; 28:18; Jn 18:37; Phil 2:6-11; Col 1:12-20; 1 Tm 6:15; Apoc 1:53; 19:16; Pius XI, Encyclical *Quas primas*, Dec. 11, 1925; TCCI 7:72-73

[137] Cf. Jn 1:1ff; 1 Jn 1:1; Apoc 19:13; *Summa Theologiae*, I, q. 34, a. 1-2

[138] Cf. Mt 1:20-21; Lk 1:31, 35. Jesus Christ, true God and true man, willed to be born at Bethlehem of Juda, and because there was no room for them in the inn, he was laid by the Blessed Virgin in the manger, so that, even from his cradle, he might afford us men an example of humility, and teach us to flee the honors and pleasures of this world.

89. **Did the Son of God cease to be God when he became man?**
The Son of God did not cease to be God when he became man, but, remaining true God, he began also to be true man.[139]

90. **How many natures and persons are there in Jesus Christ?**
In Jesus Christ, there are two natures, the divine and the human, but only one Person—that is, the Person of the Son of God.[140]

91. **Why did the Son of God condescend to take our human nature?**
The Son of God condescended to take our human nature "for us men and for our salvation," so that he might offer to God a fitting sacrifice for sin, might by his preaching and example teach us men the way of salvation, and might by his passion and death redeem them from the slavery of sin, restore them to the grace of God, and so bring them to the glory of paradise.[141]

[139] Cf. Ephraem, *In Hebdomadam Sanctam*, vi, 9

[140] Cf. Council of Chalcedon, "Definition on the two natures of Christ"; Third Council of Constantinople, "Definition of the two wills in Christ"; Fourth Lateran Council, Const. 1; Leo IX, *Symbolum Fidei*. As the Athanasian Creed says, "as a rational soul and human flesh make one man, so is the one Christ God and man." [Editor's note: The Athanasian Creed, or *Quicumque Vult*, is included in full in Volume VI of this series, p. 4-5.]

[141] Jesus Christ, the Redeemer of the human race, willed that by the merits of his passion and death man should be restored to that righteousness and holiness in which he had been first established, but did not mean thereby to restore the primitive integrity of his nature. Hence by baptism is blotted out all that can be called sin, but the tinder of concupiscence remains; for since it is allowed to remain in order that we may combat it, it can do no harm to such as do not consent to it but manfully fight against it by the grace of Jesus Christ; on the contrary, "he who shall have striven lawfully shall be crowned" (Council of Trent, Session 5). Further, the Redemption did not restore to human nature immunity from death and the other pains of this life; to these even our divine Redeemer willed to be subject, and his most holy Mother was liable to them (cf. Epiphanius, *Ancoratus*, n. 93).

92. **Was the incarnation of the Son of God necessary if fitting satisfaction was to be made for sin?**
The incarnation of the Son of God was necessary if fitting satisfaction was to be made for sin, because no mere creature could of itself make fitting or adequate satisfaction for sin.

93. **Why could not a mere creature make fitting or adequate satisfaction for sin?**
No mere creature could make fitting or adequate satisfaction for sin, because mortal sin is in a sense infinitely grievous, owing to the infinite majesty of God which is offended thereby.[142]

94. **Why is the incarnation attributed to the Holy Ghost?**
The incarnation is attributed to the Holy Ghost because, although the Son of God alone took flesh, and although this work of the incarnation, like all other outward works of God, belongs to all three Persons of the Holy Trinity, yet the Holy Ghost is the mutual love of Father and Son, and the incarnation shows forth God's amazing and boundless love for us.[143]

95. **Is the Blessed Virgin Mary really the Mother of God?**
The Blessed Virgin Mary is really the Mother of God, because she conceived and bore in his human nature Jesus Christ, who is true God and true man.[144]

[142] "A sin committed against God has a certain infinity owing to the infinity of the Divine Majesty; for the greater the dignity of the person against whom we sin, the greater the offense; hence, for condign satisfaction, the act of him who would make satisfaction should have an infinite efficacy" (*Summa Theologiae*, III, q. 1, a. 2, rep. 2).

[143] Cf. 1 Tm 3:16; Leo XIII, Encyclical *Divinum illud munus*, May 9, 1897; TCCI 7:75-77

[144] Cf. Lk 1:31, 35; 2:7; Council of Ephesus, the "Anathemas of Cyril," Can. 1; Second Council of Constantinople, "The Three Chapters," Can. 6; Third Council of Constantinople, "Definition of the two wills in Christ"; Gregory Nazianzen, *Epistle 101*; John Damascene, *Oratio prima de Virginis Mariae Nativitate*, n. 4. The *Catechism of the Council of Trent* thus briefly states the mysteries of the divine incarnation of Jesus Christ and of the divine maternity of the Blessed Virgin Mary: "So soon as the Blessed Virgin Mary expressed her assent to the angel's words by saying 'Behold the handmaid of the Lord, be it done unto me according to thy word,' then immediately, that is, in the very

96. **Was St. Joseph the father of Jesus Christ?**
St. Joseph was not the father of Jesus Christ by generation, but he is called his "father" because, as the true spouse of the Blessed Virgin, he exercised toward her Son the rights and duties of a father since he was the head of that family which was directly designed to receive, protect, and care for Christ.[145]

97. **Was our Lady always a Virgin?**
Our Lady was always a Virgin, but, in her case, perpetual virginity was marvelously combined with the divine motherhood.[146]

The Work of Man's Redemption

98. **What do we mean by the fourth article of the Creed, "suffered under Pontius Pilate, was crucified, dead, and buried"?**
By the fourth article of the Creed, "suffered under Pontius Pilate, was crucified, dead, and buried," we mean that, in order to redeem man by his precious blood, Jesus Christ suffered under Pontius Pilate, the procurator of Judaea, was nailed to the cross, died upon it, and was thence taken down and buried.

first instant, the most holy body of Christ was, by the power of the Holy Spirit, formed of the most pure womb of the Blessed Virgin Mary, a human soul created out of nothing was joined to that body, and the Godhead joined to the body and the soul. Whence it came to pass that, in the same instant of time, there existed perfect God and perfect man, so that the Blessed Virgin Mary could be truly and rightly called Mother of God and of man, for, in that same instant, she conceived a man who was God" (see TCCI 7:76).

[145] Cf. Lk 3:23. "Go to Joseph," says the Church to those who need favors, just as of old the Pharaoh said to the Egyptians who were starving when he sent them to that other Joseph (Gn 41:55). Nor can we doubt that St. Joseph always mercifully hears the prayers of his servants, especially at the hour of their death. Nor can it be possible that the Blessed Virgin, whose devoted spouse he was, nor Jesus Christ whose faithful and watchful guardian he was, would ever refuse him anything (cf. Leo XIII, Encyclical *Quamquam pluries*, Aug. 15, 1889).

[146] Cf. Is 7:14; Mt 1:23; Lk 1:27; Leo the Great, *Epistle to Flavian, Archbishop of Constantinople*; Ephraem, *Oratio ad Sanctissimam Dei Matrem*; Didymus of Alexandria, *De Trinitate*, Bk. 3, Ch. 4; Epiphanius, *Adversus Haereses*, Heresy 78, Ch. 6; Jerome, *The Perpetual Virginity of Blessed Mary*, against Helvidius, n. 21

99. **In what does the redemption wrought by Jesus Christ consist?**

The redemption wrought by Jesus Christ consists in this: "By reason of the exceeding charity wherewith he loved us, and through his most sacred passion on the tree of the cross, he merited for us justification, and for us made satisfaction to God the Father."[147]

100. **Did Jesus Christ suffer and die as God or as man?**

Jesus Christ suffered and died as man—for though as God he could neither suffer nor die, in the human nature that he, the second Person of the most Holy Trinity, had taken he did experience that separation of body and soul which we call death—but, on account of his divine personality, his very incarnation and all his sufferings, even the least of them, were of infinite value.[148]

101. **Why, then, did Jesus Christ choose to undergo so bitter and shameful a passion and death?**

Jesus Christ chose to undergo so bitter and shameful a passion and death in order to satisfy the divine justice to the full, to show more clearly his love for us, to rouse in us a greater hatred of sin, and to give us strength to bear trials and difficulties.

102. **For whom did Jesus Christ suffer and die?**

Jesus Christ suffered and died for all men without exception.[149]

[147] Council of Trent, Session 6, "Decree on Justification," Ch. 7

[148] Cf. Athanasius, *Epistle 59, to Epictetus*, n. 6. The *Catechism of the Council of Trent* aptly says: "Man dies when his soul is separated from his body; when, then, we say that Jesus died, we mean that his soul was separated from his body, but we do not mean that the Godhead was separated from his body; on the contrary, we firmly believe and profess that, on the separation of his soul from his body, his Godhead remained everjoined to his body in the tomb and to his soul in limbo" (see TCCI 7:86-87).

[149] Cf. Is 53:4-6; 2 Cor 5:15; 1 Tm 2:6; 4:10; Innocent X, Constitution *Cum occasione*, against the errors of Jansensius, May 31, 1653, the fifth condemned Proposition; Ambrose, *Epistle 41*, n. 7. Such a wondrous proof of overwhelming love should never be allowed to fade from our minds, we ought with our whole heart to love him who, through no compulsion nor against his will, but impelled solely by love of us, suffered so cruel a death. "If it was before irksome to love," says St. Augustine, "it should not now be irksome to repay love with love; for there is no greater inducement to love than

103. **Are all men therefore saved?**

Not all men are saved, but those only who make use of the means provided by our Redeemer for communicating to us the merits of his passion and death.[150]

104. **Did Jesus Christ, when dying on the cross, offer himself to God as a real and true sacrifice?**

Jesus Christ, when dying on the cross, offered himself to God as a real and true sacrifice of infinite worth for the redemption of men, offering for them to the divine justice a satisfaction of infinite value.[151]

105. **What do we mean by the first words of the fifth article of the Creed, "he descended into hell"?**

By the first words of the fifth article of the Creed, "he descended into hell," we mean that the soul of Jesus Christ, separated from his body but always united to his Godhead, went down into hell.[152]

106. **What is meant by the words, "into hell"?**

By the words, "into hell," we do not mean the hell of the damned, nor purgatory, but the "limbo of the patriarchs," where the souls of the just were awaiting the promised and longed-for redemption.[153]

107. **Why did Christ descend into limbo?**

Christ descended into limbo to fill the souls of the just with immeasurable joy by announcing to them his accomplishment of their redemption; he

to be the first to love; that heart is very hard which will not merely not love but refuses to repay love" (*On the Catechizing of the Uninstructed*, Ch. 4, n. 7).

[150] Cf. Council of Trent, Session 6, "Decree of Justification," Ch. 3. These means of salvation are given under q. 178, below.

[151] Cf. Heb 9:11-28; Council of Trent, Session 6, "Decree on Justification," Ch. 7; Leo XIII, Encyclical *Tanetsi futura*, Nov. 1, 1900; Ignatius of Antioch, *Epistle to the Smyrnaeans*, Ch. 2; Chrysostom, *Homily 17 on Hebrews*, Ch. 2; TCCI 7:89-94

[152] Cf. 1 Pt 3:19; TCCI 7:89-94

[153] Cf. Cyril of Jerusalem, *Catechetical Lecture* 4, n. 11

also made them partakers of the beatific vision of God, and was afterward to lead them with him into heaven.[154]

108. **What do we mean by the other words of the fifth article of the Creed, "the third day he rose again from the dead"?**
By the other words of the fifth article of the Creed, "the third day he rose again from the dead," we mean that Jesus Christ, on the third day after his death, reunited his soul to his body by his own power, as he had foretold, and so lived again immortal and glorious.[155]

109. **Why and for how long did Christ remain on this earth after his resurrection?**
Christ remained on this earth after his resurrection for forty days, in order to confirm his apostles' belief in his resurrection, to complete his teaching and the work of founding his Church.[156]

The Ascension of Jesus Christ into Heaven, and His Coming at the End of the World for the General Judgment

110. **What do we mean by the first words of the sixth article of the Creed, "he ascended into heaven"?**
By the first words of the sixth article of the Creed, "he ascended into heaven," we mean that Jesus Christ, forty days after his resurrection, when he had completed and perfected the work of our redemption, by his own power ascended, body and soul, into heaven.[157]

[154] Cf. TCCI 7:95ff. The limbo of the fathers came to an end when the redemption had been wrought.

[155] Cf. TCCI 7:99ff

[156] Cf. Acts 1:3

[157] Cf. Fourth Lateran Council, Const. 1; Leo IX, *Symbolum Fidei*; Leo the Great, *Sermons 73 and 74 de Ascensione Domini*; Irenaeus, *Against Heresies*, Bk. 1, Ch. 10, n. 1

111. **What do those other words of this article mean, "sitteth at the right hand of God, the Father Almighty"?**

Those other words of this article, "sitteth at the right hand of God the Father Almighty," mean the everlasting glory of our Redeemer in heaven, where Christ, as God, is equal to the Father, and, as man, possesses in a way surpassing all other created beings the good things promised by God.[158]

112. **What do we mean by the seventh article of the Creed, "from thence he shall come to judge the living and the dead"?**

By the seventh article of the Creed, "from thence he shall come to judge the living and the dead," we mean that, at the end of the world, Jesus Christ will come from heaven with his angels to judge all men, both those still living at the last day and those already dead, when "he will render to every man according to his works."[159]

113. **What sentence will be pronounced at the general judgment?**

The sentence pronounced on the just at the general judgment will be: "Come, ye blessed of my Father, possess ye the kingdom prepared for you from the beginning of the world"; and on the wicked: "Depart from me, ye cursed, into everlasting fire, which was prepared for the devil and his angels."[160]

[158] Cf. Dn 7:13-14; Mk 16:19; Jn 5:27; Rom 7:34; Heb 8:1; Gregory Nazianzen, *Oration 45*; *Summa Theologiae*, III, q. 58, a. 4. *Catechism of the Council of Trent*: "*To sit* does not here denote any position or bodily form, but simply asserts that firm and lasting possession of kingly and supreme power and glory which Jesus Christ received from the Father" (see TCCI 7:108).

[159] Mt 16:27; Cf. Mt 21:30; 25:31-46; Acts 10:42; Heb 9:28; Fourth Lateran Council, Const. 1; Leo IX, *Symbolum Fidei*; Benedict XII, Constitution *Benedictus Deus*, January 29, 1336; Chrysostom, *Homily 42 on First Corinthians*, n. 3; Canisius, *De Fide et Symbolo*, 15; TCCI 7:112ff

[160] Mt 25:34-41. St. Bonaventure: "O my soul, may the words 'Depart from me ye cursed, into everlasting fire…Come, ye blessed, receive the kingdom,' never fade from your memory. What more pitiable, more awe-inspiring than that 'Depart'? What more glorious than that 'Come'! Only two words, yet what more horrifying than the one, more sweet-sounding than the other" (*Soliloq*. 3, n. 5).

114. **Will there be any other judgment besides the general judgment at the end of the world?**
Besides the general judgment at the end of the world, there will be a particular judgment for each one of us immediately after death.[161]

115. **Why did God decree that there should be a general judgment in addition to the particular judgment?**
God decreed that there should be a general judgment in addition to the particular judgment to show forth his own glory as well as that of Christ and of the just; also to put the wicked to shame, and that man might receive, both in body and soul, sentence of reward or punishment, in the presence of all.[162]

116. **Why is the power to judge all men attributed to Jesus Christ?**
Although the power to judge all men belongs to all three Persons of the Holy Trinity, yet, for a special reason, it is attributed to Jesus Christ both as God and as man because he is "King of kings and Lord of lords," and among the prerogatives of a king is included the power of judgment, which implies rendering to each reward or punishment in accordance with his merits.[163]

[161] Cf. Heb 9:27. For the particular judgment and the last things, see below, q. 580ff.

[162] Cf. Ws 5:1ff; Mt 25:31-46; TCCI 7:113ff. God is indeed infinitely just, yet he does not in this present life always render to every man according to his deserts, but after death in the particular and the general judgment. Those, then, are clearly deceived who, when they see that the wicked prosper and the good suffer, do not hesitate to accuse God of injustice. Nor should it be supposed that the wicked are really perfectly happy, for their consciences feel remorse for their sins, also fear of God's vengeance. On the other hand, the afflicted condition of good people is not without its consolations, for their consciences are at peace and they have the refreshing hope of everlasting reward. And, when death shall come, there will be no merits without their due reward, no sins without their due punishment.

[163] "And he (the Father) hath given him (the Son) power to do judgment, because he is the Son of man" (Jn 5:27). Cf. Pius XI, Encyclical *Quas primas*, Dec. 11, 1925; TCCI 7:116-117

THE REMAINING FIVE ARTICLES OF THE CREED, CONTAINING THE DOCTRINE OF THE THIRD PERSON OF THE MOST HOLY TRINITY, AND OF THE WORK OF OUR SANCTIFICATION, BEGUN HERE ON EARTH BY GRACE AND COMPLETED IN HEAVEN BY GLORY

The Holy Ghost and His Work among the Faithful and in the Church

117. **What do we mean by the eighth article of the Creed, "I believe in the Holy Ghost"?**
By the eighth article of the Creed, "I believe in the Holy Ghost," we mean that the Holy Ghost is the third Person of the most Holy Trinity, who proceeds from the Father and the Son.[164]

118. **Why do we believe in the Holy Ghost as we believe in the Father and the Son?**
We believe in the Holy Ghost as we believe in the Father and the Son, because the Holy Ghost is true God as are the Father and the Son, and is one God with the Father and the Son.[165]

119. **Why does holy scripture reserve the name "Holy Ghost" for the third Person of the most Holy Trinity?**
Holy scripture reserves the name "Holy Ghost" for the third Person of the most Holy Trinity, because he proceeds from the Father through the Son by a single movement of love; moreover, he is the first and supreme love, who directs and moves the soul to that holiness which is to be found in the love of God.[166]

[164] Cf. Mt 27:19; Jn 15:26; 16:13-15

[165] Cf. Mt 28:19; 1 Jn 5:7

[166] Cf. Second Council of Lyons, *De processione Sancti Spiritus*; Leo XIII, Encyclical *Divinum illud munus*, May 9, 1897; Augustine, *City of God*, Bk. 11, Ch. 24; *Summa Theologiae*, I, q. 36, a. 1

120. **When did the Holy Ghost come down visibly on the apostles and what did he effect in them?**
The Holy Ghost came down visibly upon the apostles on the day of Pentecost; he confirmed them in their faith and filled them with the fullness of all gifts, that they might preach the gospel and spread the Church throughout the whole world.[167]

121. **What work does the Holy Ghost do in the faithful?**
The Holy Ghost, by his sanctifying grace, by the virtues he infuses, by his gifts and actual graces of every kind, sanctifies the faithful; and he enlightens and moves them, so that, if they cooperate with grace, they may attain to the possession of life everlasting.[168]

122. **How is the Holy Ghost in the Church and what does he effect in her?**
The Holy Ghost is, as it were, the soul of the Church, inasmuch as he perpetually gives life to her by his ever-present help, unites her to himself, and, by his gifts, guides her infallibly in the way of truth and holiness.[169]

The True Church of Christ

123. **What do we mean by the first words of the ninth article of the Creed, "the holy Catholic Church"?**
By the first words of the ninth article of the Creed, "the holy Catholic Church," we mean that there is a supernatural, visible, holy, and universal society, which Jesus Christ founded while he lived on earth, and which he called his "Church."[170]

[167] Cf. Acts 2:1-4

[168] Cf. Jn 14:16-17; Rom 8:26; 1 Cor 3:16; Basil, *Epistle* 38, n. 4. For grace, see below, q. 278ff. For the virtues and the other gifts of the Holy Spirit, see below, q. 506ff and 543ff.

[169] Cf. Jn 14:16, 26; 16:13; Leo XIII, Encyclical *Divinum illud munus*, May 9, 1897; *Summa Theologiae*, III, q. 8, a. 1, rep. 3

[170] The *Catechism of the Council of Trent* accurately remarks: "The formula is here changed and we make profession of belief not 'in the holy Catholic Church' but simply 'the holy Catholic Church' (that is, without the preposition), so as, by this change, to express the distinction between God the Maker of all things and the things he has created, also to show that we refer all the wondrous benefits which he has bestowed

124. **How does the first part of the ninth article follow upon the eighth article?**
The first part of the ninth article follows upon the eighth article, because, although Jesus Christ her founder always abides with his Church, yet it is by the Holy Ghost that she is endowed with holiness, for he is the source and dispenser of all holiness.[171]

The Founding of the Church, and Her Constitution

125. **Why did Jesus Christ found the Church?**
Jesus Christ founded the Church to continue his work on earth, so that in her and through her the fruits of the redemption accomplished on the cross might be applied to men until the end of the world.[172]

126. **How did Jesus Christ will the Church to be governed?**
Jesus Christ willed the Church to be governed by the authority of the apostles under Peter their head, and of their lawful successors.[173]

upon his Church to his divine goodness" (see TCCI 7:141). For the fuller understanding of this article of the Creed, it should be pointed out that theologians distinguish three parts of the Church: the Church triumphant, militant, and suffering—though these three form but one Church of Christ; for there is but one head, Jesus Christ, one spirit which quickens and unites it, one goal, namely, eternal life, which some already enjoy while others hope to enjoy it. But, in the Creed, we treat simply of the Church militant.

[171] Cf. TCCI 7:128

[172] Cf. Mt 28:18-20; First Vatican Council, Constitution *Pastor aeternus*, at the beginning

[173] Cf. Council of Ephesus, Act 3; First Vatican Council, Constitution *Pastor aeternus*, Ch. 1; Innocent X, Decree of the Congregation of the Holy Office, Jan. 24, 1647; Ephraem, *In Hebdomadem Sanctum*, iv, 1. Before his passion, Jesus Christ promised to St. Peter the primacy over his Church: "Thou art Peter and upon this rock I will build my church, and the gates of hell shall not prevail against it. And to thee I will give the keys of the kingdom of heaven. And whatsoever thou shalt bind upon earth it shall be bound also in heaven; and whatsoever thou shalt loose upon earth it shall be loosed also in heaven" (Mt 16:18-19). This he confirmed after his resurrection when he conferred that primacy on St. Peter, saying: "Feed my lambs…feed my sheep" (Jn 21:15-17); that is, "Rule my entire flock, my whole Church." And since he instituted a Church which, in its head, was to last forever (cf. Mt 28:19-20), this primacy of St. Peter had to pass to his legitimate successors; holy scripture also plainly shows that the mission of the apostles was under the headship of Peter (e.g., Mt 28:19-20; Mk 16:14-15; Acts 1:8; 15:6-7; 20:28; Ti 1:5; 1 Cor 12:28).

127. **Who is the lawful successor of St. Peter in governing the universal Church?**
The lawful successor of St. Peter in governing the universal Church is the bishop of the city of Rome—that is, the Roman pontiff or pope—because, in the primacy of jurisdiction, he succeeds to St. Peter, who lived and died bishop of the city of Rome.[174]

128. **Who is the true head of the Church?**
The true head of the Church is Jesus Christ himself, who invisibly abides in and governs the Church, and in himself unites her members together.[175]

129. **Why is the Roman pontiff called the "visible head of the Church" and the "vicar of Christ on earth"?**
The Roman pontiff is called the "visible head of the Church" and the "vicar of Christ on earth," because, since a visible society needs a visible head, Jesus Christ made Peter, and each successor of his, to the end of the world, the visible head and the vicegerent of his own power.[176]

130. **What power, then, has the Roman pontiff over the Church?**
By divine right, the Roman pontiff has over the Church a primacy not only of honor but of jurisdiction, and this both in things concerning faith and morals and in discipline and government.

[174] Cf. Council of Ephesus, Act 3; First Vatican Council, Constitution *Pastor aeternus*, Ch. 2. On earth there is no greater authority, no more solidly established teaching office, no fatherly authority more lofty and extensive than that of the Roman pontiff who, in the name of Jesus Christ and as his vicar, governs men so as to lead them to eternal salvation, and, without fear of being deceived, teaches them what has been divinely revealed. We ought, then, to strive to show to the supreme pontiff obedience, reverence, and love; we ought not merely to obey his commands, but to attend to his wishes and his counsels and, mindful of his august office, to pray to God for his intentions.

[175] Cf. Mt 28:18ff; Jn 1:33; 1 Cor 4:1; Eph 1:22. "And he is the head of his body which is the church" (Col 1:18). Cf. also TCCI 7:134

[176] Cf. Mt 16:18; Lk 22:32; Jn 21:15-17; Eph 1:22; TCCI 7:134-136

131. **What kind of power has the Roman pontiff?**
The Roman pontiff has supreme, full, ordinary, and immediate power both over each and every Church, and over each and every pastor and his flock.[177]

132. **Who are the lawful successors of the apostles?**
The lawful successors of the apostles are, by divine institution, the bishops; they are set over particular churches by the Roman pontiff, and govern them by their own proper power under his authority.[178]

133. **What, then, is the Church founded by Jesus Christ?**
The Church founded by Jesus Christ is the visible society of people who are baptized, and who, joined together by professing the same faith and by a mutual fellowship, strive to attain the same spiritual end under the guiding authority of the Roman pontiff and of the bishops in communion with him.[179]

134. **What is meant by the "body of the Church"?**
By the "body of the Church" is meant what is visible in the Church and makes the Church herself visible—namely, the faithful themselves insofar as they are one body, also external forms of government, external authority, outward profession of faith, the administration of the sacraments, ritual worship, etc.

[177] Cf. Second Council of Lyons, *Profession of Faith by Michael Palaeologus*; Council of Florence, Session 6 (July 6, 1439), "Decree for the Greeks"; First Vatican Council, Constitution *Pastor aeternus*, Ch. 3; Leo IX, Epistle *In terra pax hominibus*, Sept. 2, 1053; Boniface VIII, Bull *Unam sanctam*, Nov. 18, 1302. The power of the Roman pontiff is said to be "ordinary," because it is not delegated to him by someone else but is inherent in his primacy, also because it can be exercised always and everywhere. Thus it is distinguished from "extraordinary" power, for this latter is only exercised in particular cases, e.g., when some lesser pastor of souls is unable to fulfill his task.

[178] Cf. Acts 20:28; Ignatius of Antioch, *Epistle to the Smyrnaeans*, Ch. 8; Irenaeus, *Against Heresies*, Bk. 3, Ch. 3, n. 1. Patriarchs, archbishops, and other prelates are of ecclesiastical institution.

[179] Cf. Pius XI, Encyclical *Mortalium animos*, Jan. 6, 1928

135. **What is meant by the "soul of the Church"?**
By the "soul of the Church" is meant the invisible principle of the spiritual and supernatural life of the Church—namely, the ever-present assistance of the Holy Ghost, the principle of authority, inward obedience to rule, habitual grace, and the infused virtues, etc.[180]

136. **Why is the Church of Christ said to be the "way," or the "necessary means to salvation"?**
The Church of Christ is said to be the "way" or the "necessary means to salvation," because Jesus Christ instituted the Church so that in her and by her the fruits of redemption might be applied to men. Hence none of those who are outside can obtain eternal salvation, in accordance with the axiom: "Outside the Church no salvation."[181]

137. **How is the Church founded by Jesus Christ distinguished from other churches which claim the name of Christian?**
The Church founded by Jesus Christ is distinguished from other churches which claim the name of Christian by its unity, holiness, catholicity, and apostolicity, which, conferred by Jesus Christ on his Church, are to be found only in the Catholic Church, whose head is the Roman pontiff.[182]

[180] Cf. Rom 12:4-5; Eph 4:16

[181] Cf. Mk 16:15-16; Fourth Lateran Council, Const. 1; Council of Florence, Session 11 (Feb. 4, 1442), "Decree for the Jacobites"; Innocent III, Epistle *Ejus exemplo*, Dec. 18, 1208, to the archbishop of Tarragona; Boniface VIII, Bull *Unam sanctam*, Nov. 18, 1302; Pius IX, Allocution *Singulari quadam*, Dec. 9, 1854; Leo XIII, Encyclical *Satis cognitum*, June 29, 1896; Cyprian, *On the Unity of the Church*, n. 6; Jerome, *Epistle 15 to Damasus*, n. 2; Augustine, *Sermo ad Caesariensis Ecclesiae plebem*, n. 6. The above axiom is more fully set out under q. 162ff, below.

[182] By the term "notes of the Church," we mean the visible and permanent characteristics of the Church founded by Jesus Christ. Though there are many such, yet, in the Creed of Constantinople, the four following are enumerated. 1. The Church of Christ was, by the will of its divine founder, to be one in government, faith, and unity of fellowship, whereby all its members make one social body, that is, the mystical body of Christ, and this despite diversities of rites (cf. Jn 10:16; Rom 12:5-6; 1 Cor 1:10; 12:12-13; Eph 4:2-16). 2. Holy, by the holiness of the goal at which it aims, namely, the salvation of souls; also by the holiness of its teaching, both speculative and practical, whence comes the holiness of so many members of the Church, a sanctity at times heroic and approved by miracles (cf. Jn 17:17-19; Eph 5:25-27; Ti 2:14). 3. Catholic or universal, that is, by its destination or mission to all peoples of the

138. **Is it possible to distinguish the true Church from other churches in some shorter and more simple way?**
It is possible to distinguish the true Church from other churches in a shorter and more simple way, namely, by the essential and visible head of that Church, in accordance with the ancient principle of the fathers: "Where Peter is, there is the Church."[183]

139. **How can this be deduced from that principle?**
It can be deduced from that principle because, since Jesus Christ "built his Church," which was to last for all time, "on Peter," it follows that that only is the true Church of Christ which is ruled and governed by the lawful successor of Peter, namely, by the Roman pontiff.

The Power of the Church

140. **What power did Christ the Lord bestow on his Church in order that she might attain the end for which she was founded?**
That she might attain the end for which she was founded, Christ the Lord bestowed on his Church the power of jurisdiction and the power of order; the power of jurisdiction includes the power of teaching.[184]

earth, whence that marvelous propagation of the Church which began even in the days of the apostles and has never ceased despite all sorts of difficulties; yet, the actual spread of the Church depends on human means of propagation accompanied by God's help, whence it comes that this spread of the Church admits of successive growth (cf. Mt 28:19-20; Lk 24:47; Acts 1:8; Pius XI, Encyclical *Rerum Ecclesiae*, Feb. 28, 1926). 4. Apostolic in origin, founded, that is, on the foundation of the apostles, especially of St. Peter, it is ruled and governed by their legitimate successors in unbroken succession (cf. Eph 2:20; Apoc 21:14).

Now, it is certain that these characteristics are to be found in the Catholic Church, the head of which is the Roman pontiff, also that they are not to be discovered in other and false religions, though they claim the title of "Christian" (cf. Augustine, *Against the Fundamental Epistle of Manichaeus*, Ch. 4, n. 5; *A Sermon to Catechumens on the Creed*, Ch. 14; TCCI 7:145ff).

183 Ambrose, *On Psalm 40*, n. 30; Cf. Cyprian, *Epistle 39*, n. 5

184 For the power of teaching, see Mt 28:19-20; Mk 16:15-16. For jurisdiction, see Mt 16:19; 28:18-19; Jn 21:15-17; Acts 20:28. For the power of order, see Jn 20:22-23; Mt 18:18; Mk 16:16; Acts 8:15-17. From all this it follows that the Church is a society in which there are various grades.

141. **What is the power of teaching?**

The power of teaching is the right and duty of the Church to guard, hand on, and maintain the doctrine of Jesus Christ, and to preach it to every creature, independently of any human authority.[185]

142. **Does the exercise of this power of teaching affect in the same way those who are baptized and those who are not baptized?**

The exercise of this power of teaching affects the baptized and the unbaptized differently; for, in the case of those who are baptized, the Church not only states her doctrine, but imposes it on them as obligatory, with the result that they are bound to accept it, not only because God commands it, but also in obedience to the authority that the Church has over her subjects; whereas, in the case of those who are not baptized, the Church simply sets her teaching before them in the name of God, with the consequence that they are bound to study it and embrace it, not because the Church imposes it on them, but because God commands it.

143. **Who have the power of teaching in the Church?**

The Roman pontiff and the bishops in communion with him have the power of teaching in the Church, and are therefore called the "Church teaching" (*Ecclesia docens*).[186]

144. **Is the Church infallible in her office of teaching?**

The Church is infallible in her office of teaching, owing to the perpetual assistance of the Holy Ghost promised to her by Christ, when, either in the exercise of her ordinary and universal governance or by a solemn pronouncement of the supreme authority, she proposes, for the acceptance

[185] Cf. Mt 28:18-20; Mk 16:15-16; *Codex Juris Canonici*, Can. 1322, sect. 2

[186] The pastors of the Church have the right and the duty of preaching the gospel to every creature, and it is the duty of good children of the Church to assist them in this holy and salutary task. We ought, therefore, to help the work of Catholic missions by prayers, alms, and active work according to our capacity. By so doing, we shall be performing a spiritual as well as a corporal work of mercy toward our brethren who "sit in darkness and the shadow of death" (Lk 1:79); we shall be workers, too, for the glory of God and performing a task warmly recommended by the Church and the Roman pontiffs.

of all, truths of faith or morals that are either revealed in themselves or connected with revelation.[187]

145. **Whose peculiar function is it to pronounce a solemn judgment of this kind?**
To pronounce a solemn judgment of this kind is the peculiar function of the Roman pontiff, and of the bishops together with the Roman pontiff, especially when assembled in an ecumenical council.

146. **What is an ecumenical council?**
An ecumenical or general council is an assembly of the bishops of the entire Catholic Church called together by the Roman pontiff; over such an assembly he himself presides either personally or by his legates, and it belongs to him authoritatively to confirm the decrees of such a council.[188]

147. **When does the Roman pontiff exercise his prerogative of personal infallibility?**
The Roman pontiff exercises his prerogative of personal infallibility when he speaks *ex cathedra*—that is, when, in the exercise of his office as shepherd and teacher of all Christians, he defines a doctrine concerning faith or morals to be held by the whole Church.[189]

148. **What obligation do we incur when the Church proposes, for acceptance by all the faithful, truths concerning faith or morals as divinely revealed?**
We are bound to believe, with divine and Catholic faith, truths concerning faith or morals that the Church proposes for acceptance by all the

[187] Cf. Mt 16:18; 28:19-20; Lk 22:32; Jn 14:16-26; 16:13; Acts 15:28; Adamantius, *Dialogus*, Pt. 5, n. 28; Cyprian, *Epistle 54*, n. 14, *inter Sti. Cornelii Epistolas*; Peter Chrysologus, *Ep. ad Eutychen*, Ch. 2

[188] Cf. *Codex Juris Canonici*, Can. 222

[189] Cf. First Vatican Council, Constitution *Pastor aeternus*, Ch. 4. Jesus Christ patently promised the gift of infallibility to Peter and his successors in the primacy when he said to Simon Peter: "I have prayed for thee that thy faith fail not; and thou, being once converted, confirm thy brethren" (Lk 22:32).

faithful, whether by her ordinary and universal authority or by some solemn pronouncement.[190]

149. **What do we call truths thus defined?**
A truth thus defined is called a "dogma of the faith"; denial of it is called "heresy."

150. **What do you mean by "truths not in themselves revealed but connected with revelation"?**
Truths not in themselves revealed but connected with revelation are principally dogmatic facts and censures of such propositions as are proscribed and prohibited by the Church.[191]

151. **Are we also bound to accept truths, not in themselves revealed but connected with revelation, that the Church proposes in the same way for universal acceptance?**
We are also bound to accept with our hearts as well as with our lips truths not in themselves revealed but connected with revelation and proposed in the same way by the Church for universal acceptance, owing to the Church's infallibility, which extends to these truths also.[192]

[190] Cf. First Vatican Council, Constitution *Dei Filius*, Ch. 3

[191] Cf. First Vatican Council, Constitution *Dei Filius*, Ch. 4. By "dogmatic facts," we mean facts defined by the Church, not as being in themselves revealed, yet as having a connection with some dogma which has to be safeguarded, or applied, or correctly explained. The chief dogmatic facts are: that in such and such a book are contained or are not contained propositions opposed to the deposit of faith; that people canonized by a definite pronouncement of the Church are verily saints and are in the enjoyment of eternal glory; that a certain council was or was not a legitimate one; that such and such an edition or version of holy scripture is or is not conformable to the text of scripture.

[192] Cf. First Vatican Council, Constitution *Dei Filius*, Ch. 4, at the close; Alexander VII, Constitution *Regiminis Apostolici*, Feb. 15, 1664; Clement XI, Constitution *Vineam Domini Sabaoth*, July 16, 1705; Pius X, Decree *Lamentabili sane*, July 3, 1907, the seventh condemned Proposition. From this it follows that the Church has the right of prohibiting books and forbidding the faithful either to read them or keep them.

152. **What attitude is to be adopted toward other doctrinal decisions regarding faith and morals which the Apostolic See publishes either directly or through the Roman Congregations?**

We are bound in conscience to receive other doctrinal decrees concerning faith or morals that are issued by the Apostolic See either directly or through the Roman Congregations, because of the obedience we owe to the Apostolic See, which in this way too exercises an authority given to it by Christ.[193]

153. **What powers and duties arising from their power of teaching have bishops in their own dioceses?**

By reason of their power of teaching, bishops can and ought, as opportunity offers, to teach and inculcate in their own dioceses, whether personally or through others, truths concerning faith or morals received in the Church; it is for them to repress dangerous novelties in doctrine, and, if necessary, bring them to the notice of the supreme authority in the Church.[194]

154. **What does the power of jurisdiction in the Church mean?**

The power of jurisdiction in the Church means that the Roman pontiff in respect of the whole Church, and the bishops in respect of their dioceses, have the power of governing—that is, they have legislative, judicial, administrative, and punitive power, whereby to secure the Church's attainment of the objects for which she was founded.[195]

155. **What is the power of order?**

The power of order is the power of performing sacred functions, especially of ministering at the altar; by the sacrament of holy order, it is conferred on the sacred hierarchy, especially on the bishops. Since this power has for its main object the sanctification of men's souls through divine worship

[193] Cf. Pius IX, Epistle *Tuas libenter*, Dec. 21, 1863, to the archbishop of Munich and Freisingen; Pius X, Decree *Lamentabili sane*, July 3, 1907, the eighth condemned Proposition

[194] Cf. *Codex Juris Canonici*, Can. 336, 343

[195] Cf. *Codex Juris Canonici*, Can. 335

and the administration of the sacraments, it comprises what is generally known as "the care of souls."[196]

156. **Who are the bishops' assistants in the care of souls?**
The bishops' assistants in the care of souls are the priests, especially the parish priests, who are subject to the bishops according to the provisions laid down in canon law.[197]

The Members of the Church

157. **Who are members of the Church founded by Jesus Christ?**
Those are members of the Church founded by Jesus Christ who have been baptized and are joined together in the bonds of unity, faith, and Catholic fellowship.

158. **Who are outside the Church founded by Jesus Christ?**
Those are outside the Church founded by Jesus Christ:
1. who are not baptized;
2. who are open apostates, heretics, schismatics, or excommunicated persons that are "to be shunned."[198]

[196] The power of order is, for its legitimate exercise, subordinated to the power of jurisdiction.

[197] The laity of either sex can most effectively help the Church in her ministry as well by their own personal influence which may affect the spiritual goods of their neighbors, as also by what is termed "Catholic action," so earnestly recommended by the supreme pontiff, and so clearly referred to by St. Paul (cf. Phil 4:3). The laity should, if they can, join in "Catholic action," for by such loyal cooperation with their bishops on the lines laid down by the Apostolic See, they will be materially forwarding the ideal set before us by the Church, in other words, the triumph of the kingdom of Christ and the salvation of the human race.

[198] Cf. Augustine, *Of Faith and the Creed*, Ch. 10, n. 21; *Codex Juris Canonici*, Can. 87; TCCI 7:133. An unbaptized person is, simply-speaking, outside the Church, though he may by God's grace be able through charity to belong to the soul of the Church. But a baptized person is, by valid reception of baptism, united to the mystical body of Christ which is the Church, and such union is perpetual and indicated by the indelible character of baptism. Hence a baptized person always in some sense belongs to the Church. But he can cut himself off from the Church by breaking the bond of union and communion through apostasy, heresy, or schism. He can also, for very grave sin, be deprived of all

159. **What do you mean by "apostates, heretics, schismatics, or excommunicated persons that are to be shunned"?**

Apostates are baptized persons who have wholly given up the Christian faith; heretics are those who obstinately deny or call in question a dogma of faith; schismatics are those who refuse submission to the Roman pontiff, or decline to hold communion with the members of the Church, who are his subjects; excommunicated persons that are to be shunned (*vitandi*) are those who come under this particular censure fulminated by canon law.[199]

160. **Do all these remain bound by the Church's laws?**

All these, since they are subjects of the Church—though rebellious ones—remain bound by the Church's laws, unless she either expressly or tacitly exempts them from their application.

161. **Are "tolerated" excommunicated persons members of the Church?**

Tolerated excommunicated persons are members of the Church, but they are excluded from sharing in those effects of the communion of the faithful which are set forth in canon law, nor can they regain a share in them until they cease to be contumacious and are absolved from this grave penalty.

162. **Can an adult person who dies unbaptized be saved?**

An adult person who dies unbaptized can be saved not only

1. if he has faith at least as regards those truths which must of necessity be believed, since they are the necessary means of salvation, and that charity which supplies the place of baptism; but also

the rights of the faithful by the supreme ecclesiastical authority, and thus wholly cut off from communion with the faithful. He will then be really placed outside the Church, though under the obligation of returning to it, and securing reconciliation by laying aside his contumacy. He always remains a subject of the Church. So, too, a deserter from the army is really outside the army, but is bound to return to it and, although deprived of the privileges which other soldiers enjoy, he still remains subject to his officers and can be punished by them.

[199] Cf. *Codex Juris Canonici*, Can. 2257ff, Can. 1325, sect. 2

2. if, through the operation of God's light and grace, he is—despite his invincible ignorance of the true religion—prepared to obey God and has been careful to keep the natural law.[200]

163. **Can an adult person who has been validly baptized but, through no fault of his own, belongs to a heretical or schismatical body be saved?**
An adult person who has been validly baptized but, through no fault of his own, belongs to a heretical or schismatic body can be saved, provided he has not lost the grace received in baptism, or if, after losing it by sin, he regains it by due repentance.[201]

164. **What of those who, while recognizing the truth of the Church of Christ, yet willfully remain outside her?**
Those who, while recognizing the truth of the Church of Christ, yet willfully remain outside her, commit grave sin; consequently, if they persist in such a state, they cannot be saved.

165. **What are those bound to do who are outside the Church, but are in doubt about their state?**
Those who are outside the Church but are in doubt about their state are in duty bound sincerely to seek the truth "in the Lord," to learn as far as they can Christ's teaching set before them, and—when they have recognized which is the true Church of Christ—to enter her.

[200] St. Thomas says of those who, being brought up in a savage state, have, through no fault of their own, never attained any knowledge of the true Church: "It belongs to divine providence to provide for each what is necessary for their salvation, so long as they on their part put no obstacle in the way. Consequently, were a person thus brought up in a savage state to follow the guidance of his natural reason in pursuing good and avoiding evil, we must most certainly hold that God would reveal to him by interior inspiration what it was necessary for him to believe, or would send him some preacher of the faith—as he sent Peter to Cornelius" (*Disputed Questions, De Veritate*, q. 14, a. 11, rep. 1; cf. Innocent II, Epistle *Apostolicam Sedem*, to the bishops of Cremona; Pius IX, Epistle *Quanto conficiamur*, Aug. 10, 1863, to the bishops of Italy).

[201] Cf. Pius IX, as in the previous note. This repentance will either be perfect contrition with the desire—which is included in it—of entering the true Church and receiving the sacrament of penance, or imperfect contrition combined with the reception of the said sacrament.

The Difference between the Church and the State and the Respective Powers of These Two Societies

166. **Is the Church instituted by Christ distinct from the state?**

The Church instituted by Christ is distinct from the state; yet the state neither is nor can be lawfully separated from the Church, though, in peculiar and grave circumstances, such a separation may be tolerated or even preferred.[202]

[202] From various documents emanating from the Roman pontiffs—especially from Leo XIII, Encyclical *Immortale Dei*, Nov. 1, 1885; Encyclical *Au milieu*, Feb. 16, 1892; Epistle *Longinqua Oceani*, Jan. 6, 1895—the doctrine regarding the mutual relations of Church and state can be summarily set forth as follows:

The immediate goal and object of the Church is the supernatural sanctification of the souls of men, for that is the necessary condition and the norm for attaining eternal happiness in heaven. But the immediate goal and object of the state is the common temporal good of men, even in the moral order, and this is to be obtained by adhering to the principles of justice and supplying for the deficiencies of individual people and families. Hence, although the Church is directly only concerned with the sanctification of men's souls, yet at the same time it so truly and effectively promotes temporal advantages, whether public or private, that it could hardly do more had it direct charge of them; see, for example, the way in which it insists on everybody fulfilling the duties of their state of life. Conversely, the state, while having direct charge over temporal concerns, does by that very fact work indirectly for the sanctification of souls. Since, then, societies are differentiated by their immediate goal, and the goal of the Church is distinct from that of the state, it follows that these two societies are quite distinct, the Church being a supernatural and spiritual society, the state a natural and temporal society; while each is in its own order a perfect society endowed with full powers, since each possesses in itself the requisite means for the attainment of its own peculiar goal. At the same time, this distinction between the two societies does not mean that the state can, as though wholly separate from the Church, behave as though there were no God and repudiate all responsibility for religion as being something alien to itself and of no importance. Nor out of the various forms of religion can it choose anyone it likes. For the state, no less than individual citizens, is bound to worship God according to that form of religion which he has himself commanded, and the truth of which he has established by proofs that are certain and leave no room for doubt; that form of religion is the only true Church of Christ. Juridical separation between Church and state can only be tolerated under certain peculiarly grave circumstances, when, that is, by such separation, greater evils will be avoided and full liberty of life and action conceded to the Church. Consequently, since the spiritual and supernatural society is more excellent and of higher standing than the temporal society—for its goal is a higher one—the state must, since it is meant simply for the common advantage—so work for the temporal advantage of its citizens as to put no hindrance to the Church in its task, rather should it afford to the Church every assistance it possibly can.

167. **On what principles are the respective powers of each society to be defined?**
The principles for defining the respective powers of each society are:
1. Whatever concerns the salvation of souls and the worship of God comes under the power of the Church.
2. Other matters concerning civil and political affairs fall under the state.
3. But in matters affecting both Church and state alike, there is naturally, as well as in the counsels of God, room for harmony between these two authorities, so that strife which would prove disastrous to both is avoidable.[203]

168. **Can the Church pass judgment on civil and political affairs?**
The Church can pass judgment on civil and political affairs when they are connected with faith or morals and therefore with the salvation of souls.

169. **Whose function is it to decide whether such a connection exists?**
It is the function of the Church to decide whether such a connection exists, and no Catholic can refuse dutiful obedience to her teaching authority.[204]

The Communion of Saints

170. **How is the second part of the ninth article of the Creed, "the communion of saints," connected with the first?**
The second part of the ninth article of the Creed, "the communion of saints," is connected with the first part as in some sort explaining it, for it teaches us what benefit the members of the Church may gain from the holiness obtained in and through the Church.[205]

171. **What do we mean by this second part of the ninth article of the Creed?**
By this second part of the ninth article of the Creed, we mean that between the members of the Church—in heaven, in purgatory, and on

[203] Cf. Leo XIII, Encyclical *Diuturnum illud*, June 29, 1881; Encyclical *Immortale Dei*; Pius X, Encyclical *Vehementer*, Feb. 11, 1906

[204] Cf. Pius IX, Epistle *Gravissimas inter acerbitates*, Dec. 11, 1862, to the archbishop of Munich and Freisingen; Leo XIII, Encyclical *Immortale Dei*, Nov. 1, 1885

[205] Cf. TCCI 7:141-144

earth—there exists, by reason of their close union with one another under Christ their head, a mutual communication in spiritual riches.[206]

172. **Do all the Church's members fully enjoy this fellowship?**
Not all the Church's members fully enjoy this fellowship, but those only who are in a state of grace, wherefore this fellowship is called "the communion of saints."

173. **Are those in mortal sin excluded from this communion of saints?**
Those in mortal sin are not wholly excluded from this communion of saints, for both by the public prayers of the Church and the petitions and good works of those in a state of grace, they can be helped to recover the grace of God.

174. **Is there fellowship with the blessed in heaven?**
There is fellowship with the blessed in heaven; for while we pay them honor and humbly invoke their assistance, they pray to God on our behalf.[207]

175. **Is there also communion with the souls detained in purgatory?**
There is also communion with the souls detained in purgatory, inasmuch as we can help them by our suffrages, that is, by the Sacrifice of the Mass, by gaining indulgences, by prayers, almsdeeds, and other works of piety and penance; and they in their turn help us by their prayers before God.[208]

[206] Cf. Rom 12:4-5; 1 Cor 12:11-13; Eph 4:4-13; TCCI 7:141-144. The spiritual goods of the Church in general are the infinite merits of Jesus Christ, the superabundant merits of the Blessed Virgin Mary and the saints, indulgences, prayers and good works performed by the members of the Church, the sacraments and the Sacrifice of the Mass, also public prayers and external rites which serve to bind the faithful to Christ and to one another by a species of sacred tie.

[207] Cf. Tb 12:12; Ecclus 44:1; Dn 3:35; 2 Mac 15:14; Apoc 5:8; 8:3; Council of Trent, Session 25, "On the Invocation, Veneration, and Relics of Saints, and on Sacred Images"; Jerome, *Against Vigilantius*, Ch. 6

[208] Cf. Cyril of Jerusalem, *Catechetical Lecture 23*, n. 9; Augustine, *City of God*, Bk. 20, Ch. 9

176. **What prayers do the faithful generally say for the souls in purgatory?**
The prayers for the souls in purgatory generally used are: the psalm "Out of the depths…", and the brief petition: "Eternal rest give unto them, O Lord, and let perpetual light shine upon them. May they rest in peace. Amen."[209]

The Forgiveness of Sins

177. **What do we mean by the tenth article of the Creed, "the forgiveness of sins"?**
By the tenth article of the Creed, "the forgiveness of sins," we mean that there is in the Church true power to forgive sins through the merits of Jesus Christ.[210]

178. **By what means do we obtain in the Church the forgiveness of our sins?**
In the Church we obtain the remission of mortal sins through the sacraments instituted by Christ for that purpose, also by an act of perfect contrition accompanied by a desire of receiving those sacraments. The forgiveness of our venial sins we can obtain by other devout acts, but the debt of temporal punishment remains and has to be paid either in this life or in the next, that is, in purgatory.[211]

[209] "It is a holy and a wholesome thought to pray for the dead" (2 Mc 12:46).

It is certainly a most holy act of charity to help by our prayers the souls detained in purgatory, more especially when it is question of those who are our relatives or to whom we are bound by ties of gratitude. For ourselves, too, it is "a wholesome" thing, for by such an act of charity toward those souls who are so dear to God, we win God's mercy for ourselves as well as the gratitude of the holy souls themselves.

[210] Cf. Mt 16:19; 18:18; Jn 20:23; Fourth Lateran Council, Const. 1; Council of Trent, Session 14, "Doctrine on the Sacrament of Penance," Ch. 1; "On the Most Holy Sacrament of Penance," Can. 1; Leo IX, Epistle *Congratulamur vehementer*

[211] For a just man to obtain the forgiveness of his venial sins, any act springing from the grace of God suffices, provided it contains at least implicitly a detestation of his faults. Hence the forgiveness of one's venial sins can be obtained not only through the sacraments whereby grace is conferred, but by any acts which include a detestation of sin, for example, by saying the *confiteor* or the Lord's Prayer, or by beating one's breast, or again by any acts indicating reverence for God or holy things, such as getting a priest's blessing, using holy water, any sacramental anointing, prayer in a church (see *Summa Theologiae*, III-Sup., q. 87, a. 3).

The Resurrection of the Dead; Eternal Life

179. **What do we mean by the eleventh article of the Creed, "the resurrection of the body"?**

By the eleventh article of the Creed, "the resurrection of the body," we mean that it will come to pass, at the end of the world, that all the dead will be recalled to life and rise for the general judgment, and that each soul will resume the body to which in this life it was united, and will never again be separated from it.[212]

180. **By what power will this resurrection of the body take place?**

The resurrection of the body will take place by the divine power of Jesus Christ, for just as he raised his own body from the dead, so at the end of the world will he raise up the bodies of those whom he is going to judge.[213]

181. **Why did God will that the bodies of the dead should rise again?**

God willed that the bodies of the dead should rise again in order that the whole man might, according to his merits, obtain an everlasting reward in heaven or an everlasting punishment in hell.

182. **Will the bodies of all the dead rise in the same way?**

The bodies of all the dead will rise immortal, but only the bodies of the elect will—in the likeness of the body of Christ—rise endowed with the qualities of a glorified body.[214]

[212] Cf. Jb 19:25-27; Mt 13:40-43; Jn 5:28-29; 6:39-40; Acts 24:15; 1 Cor 15:12ff; Fourth Lateran Council, Const. 1; Leo IX, Epistle *Congratulamur vehementer*; Innocent III, Epistle *Ejus exemplo*, Dec. 18, 1208, to the archbishop of Tarragona; Cyril of Alexandria, *On John*, Ch. 8, n. 51; Chrysostom, *De resurrectione mortuorum*, n. 8; TCCI 7:151ff

[213] Cf. Jn 5:28-29; Chrysostom, *De resurrectione mortuorum*, n. 7; *Summa Theologiae*, III, q. 56, a. 1

[214] Cf. 1 Cor 15:52; Phil 3:21; Apoc 20:12-13; Cyril of Jerusalem, *Catechetical Lecture 18*, n. 18-19

183. **What are the qualities of a glorified body?**

Four qualities of the glorified body are commonly enumerated—impassibility, clarity, agility, and subtlety.[215]

184. **What do we mean by the last article of the Creed, "life everlasting"?**

By the last article of the Creed, "life everlasting," we mean that there is prepared for the elect after death a perfect and never-failing happiness in paradise, while the eternal pains of hell await the reprobate.[216]

185. **What is meant by the word *Amen* at the end of the Creed?**

The word *Amen* at the end of the Creed means that every one of the articles contained in the Creed are true, and that we believe them and make profession of them unhesitatingly.

186. **Is it sufficient to believe what is proposed for our belief if we would obtain eternal life?**

It is not sufficient to believe what is proposed for our belief if we would obtain eternal life; it is also necessary to keep the commandments that God and his Church have given us.[217]

[215] Cf. 1 Cor 15:42-44; *Catechism of the Council of Trent* says: "*Impassibility* will preclude the glorified body from any suffering or inconvenience. *Clarity* is a corollary to impassibility, for it is a certain radiance flowing over on to the body from the supreme blessedness enjoyed by the soul, in some sort a sharing of the bliss the soul enjoys. *Agility* is combined with clarity, by it the body can be moved with the greatest ease whithersoever the soul wishes. To these is to be added *subtlety*, whereby the body will be subordinated to the soul, be its servant, and always at its beck and call" (see TCCI 7:159-161; see also *Summa Theologiae*, III-Sup., q. 82ff).

[216] Cf. Mt 25:46. St. Peter Canisius says: "For the sake of obtaining that eternal life, no works of piety ought to seem too hard to a true believer, no toil too heavy, no pain too bitter, no time spent in labor and suffering too long or too wearisome. For if nothing is sweeter or more desirable than this present life which is so full of calamities, how much more desirable must that other life be deemed which is so far removed from all sense of evil or fear of it, which will in every conceivable way always abound in the unspeakable and unending joys, delights, and happiness of heaven" (*De Fide et Symbolo fidei*, xxi).

[217] Cf. Mt 5:16; 7:26-27; 9:15; 25:35ff; Jas 2:14ff

The Ten Commandments, or Decalogue[218]

187. **What does the word *decalogue* mean?**
The word *decalogue* means the ten words or commandments, which God gave to Moses on Mount Sinai and which Jesus Christ confirmed in the new law.[219]

188. **How are the ten commandments of the decalogue divided?**
The ten commandments of the decalogue are so divided that the first three are concerned with God, while the remaining seven refer to ourselves and to our neighbor.

189. **Why did God prefix to the decalogue the words, "I am the Lord thy God"?**
God prefixed to the decalogue the words, "I am the Lord thy God," to warn us that he, as God and Lord, has the right to lay commands upon us which we are bound to obey.[220]

[218] All ought to learn and carefully observe the ten commandments solemnly promulgated by God himself on Mount Sinai, and explained and confirmed by Christ under the new law. For these commandments do not merely serve as guides to individual men in their journey toward eternity, but are the very foundation of all civil society.

[219] Cf. Ex 20:2-17; Mt 5:17-18; 19:17-20. God gave these commandments, written on two tables, to Moses. The first three are termed the "commandments of the first table," the rest the "commandments of the second table" (see TCCI 7:379ff, 428).

[220] Cf. Ex 20:2-6; Lv 26:1; Dt 5:6ff; TCCI 7:388; Council of Trent, Session 6, "Decree on Justification," Ch. 11

THE FIRST THREE COMMANDMENTS OF THE DECALOGUE, WHICH HAVE TO DO WITH GOD

The First Commandment of the Decalogue

190. **What does God forbid in the first commandment, "Thou shalt not have strange gods before me"?**
In the first commandment, "Thou shalt not have strange gods before me," God forbids us to offer to others the worship due to himself.[221]

191. **What worship do we owe to God?**
To God, and to God alone, we owe supreme worship—that is, the worship of adoration.

192. **Why ought we to worship and adore God?**
We ought to worship and adore God because he is our Creator, because, by his providence, he takes care of us, and because he is our last end.

193. **How ought we to worship and adore God?**
We ought to worship and adore God as the Creator of all things, as their preserver by his providence, as their first beginning and last end, by both interior and exterior acts of religion, such as our nature itself and still more revelation suggests to us; the chief of these acts is sacrifice, which should be offered to no created thing.

194. **How do we sin against the first commandment?**
We sin against the first commandment:
   1. By superstition—that is, by idolatry, divination, vain observances, and by spiritism, which last is included under divination and vain observances.

[221] Cf. Ex 20:2-6; Lv 26:1; Dt 10:6ff; TCCI 7:388-402

2. By irreligion—that is, by the omission of those acts of worship which we ought to make, also by sacrilege and simony.[222]

195. **Should we not also offer worship to the saints?**
We should also offer worship to the saints, especially to the Blessed Virgin Mary, but only a different and lower form of worship, namely, that of veneration, in order to show them honor and win their patronage.[223]

196. **What do we call the worship we pay to God, to the saints, and to the Blessed Virgin Mary?**
We call the worship we pay to God *latria* or "adoration"; that offered to the saints we call *dulia* or "veneration"; that offered to the Blessed Virgin Mary *hyperdulia* or a "more excellent form of veneration."[224]

[222] By *idolatry*, we mean that form of superstition whereby divine worship is offered to some image of the Godhead, or to some creature or demon. *Divination* is that form of superstition which seeks to learn hidden or future things by open or implied invocation of demons. By *vain observances*, we mean that form of superstition whereby people make use of unworthy means for producing some effect, and openly or tacitly invoke the aid of demons. *Spiritism* in England, commonly called "spiritualism," is a superstitious practice whereby people hold communication with evil spirits, and seek through their aid to learn what is hidden from us. *Sacrilege* is the unbecoming handling of sacred persons or things, also of any place dedicated to God or divine worship. *Simony* is a contract concerning spiritual matters or things connected with spiritual matters, or about temporal things under the guise of religion; it is forbidden alike by the natural law, the divine law, and the canon law.

[223] Cf. TCCI 7:391ff

[224] The worship known as *latria* is that due to God alone; by it, a man expresses his sense of service due to God who has full and chief dominion over all his creation. The worship known as *dulia* is that whereby we venerate and worship the saints as created by God and most dear to him as his children and friends, as members of the body of Christ, and as intercessors for us with God. But since the Blessed Virgin Mary, though but a creature, is, as being true Mother of God, joined, above all other creatures, to God in the most special manner, she is worshipped with a special cult called *hyperdulia* (see John Damascene, *De Imaginibus*, Oration 2, n. 5; Oration 3, n. 41).

197. **Should we not also venerate the relics of the martyrs and of other saints reigning with Christ?**
We should also venerate the relics of the martyrs and of other saints reigning with Christ, for their bodies were once the living members of Christ and the temples of the Holy Spirit, and are one day to be raised up by him to enjoy eternal life and glory; moreover, through the medium of their relics, God bestows many blessings on men.[225]

198. **Should not due honor and veneration be paid also to sacred images?**
Due honor and veneration should be paid also to sacred images, since the honor shown them is offered to the persons they represent, so that, by the reverence we exhibit, we adore Christ himself and venerate the saints whose images they are.[226]

199. **Why, then, did God in the old testament forbid graven things or images?**
God did not in the old testament entirely forbid graven things or images, but he forbade them to be introduced for purposes of adoration after the manner of the heathen, lest, by the worship of graven things as gods, the worship of the true God should be diminished.[227]

The Second Commandment of the Decalogue

200. **What does God forbid in the second commandment, "Thou shalt not take the name of the Lord thy God in vain"?**
In the second commandment, "Thou shalt not take the name of the Lord thy God in vain," God forbids all irreverence toward his name.[228]

[225] Cf. 4 Kgs 2:14; 13:21; Mt 9:20-22; 14:36; Acts 5:15; 19:12; Second Council of Nicea, *De Sacris Imaginibus*, Act 7; Council of Trent, Session 25, "On the Invocation, Veneration, and Relics of Saints, and on Sacred Images"

[226] Cf. Second Council of Nicea and Council of Trent, as in the previous note; Cyril of Alexandria, *On Psalm 113*, n. 16

[227] Cf. Ex 20:4-5; Dt 4:15-193; *Summa Theologiae*, III, q. 25, rep. 3

[228] Cf. Ex 20:7; Lv 19:12; Dt 5:11

201. **Who are guilty of such irreverence?**

Those are guilty of such irreverence who pronounce the name of God without good reason or due reverence, or who break vows they have made, or indulge in false, rash, and unjust oaths, more especially if they blaspheme.[229]

202. **Are we also forbidden to take the names of the saints in vain?**

Just as we ought to pay honor to the saints, and especially to the Blessed Virgin Mary, so for the same reason we are forbidden to take their names in vain.

The Third Commandment of the Decalogue

203. **What does God command in the third commandment, "Remember that thou keep holy the sabbath day"?**

In the third commandment, "Remember that thou keep holy the sabbath day," God commands that festival days—that is, days dedicated to him—should be kept with divine worship, business and bodily toil being laid aside.[230]

[229] Cf. Lv 19:12; 24:11-16; 4 Kgs 19:6ff. A vow is a promise deliberately made to God of some better thing. An oath is calling on the name of God in witness of what one has said or in confirmation of a promise. An oath is said to be "false" if the statement is contrary to known truth; "rash" if it is made without the person who makes it being certain of his facts; "unjust" if the assertion coupled with it is wicked, or if the thing promised under oath is bad. Blasphemy is the uttering of profane speech about God. Pius XI in his *Epistle to the Bishop of Verona*, Dec. 3, 1924, thus describes the gravity of deliberate blasphemy: "Blasphemy is an insolent contempt for the goodness of God, for it is in contradiction with the very faith we profess; not only does it involve the malice of apostasy, but aggravates it, since it adds heartfelt detestation combined with verbal execration. Consequently blasphemy, when knowingly and deliberately indulged in, owing to its own intrinsic perversity as being an insult aimed at God himself who is the author of law, as well as by its implied repudiation of the faith, is the gravest of sins, though it may not outwardly appear so if we judge only by evidently harmful results."

[230] Cf. Ex 20:8; 31:13; Dt 5:12-15

204. **What were the festival days in the old testament?**
In the old testament, there were many festival days, but the chief one was the sabbath, the very name of which signifies the rest needful for the worship of God, whence it is called "the day of rest."

205. **Why is the sabbath day not observed under the new testament?**
The sabbath day is not observed under the new testament, because in its place the Church keeps Sunday in honor of the resurrection of Jesus Christ, and the coming down of the Holy Spirit at Pentecost; the Church also adds other festival days.[231]

206. **To what, then, are we bound nowadays as regards keeping festival days holy?**
As regards keeping festival days holy, we are today bound to sanctify, in the manner prescribed by the Church, the Sundays and other feast days appointed by her.[232]

[231] The commandment about keeping the sabbath holy was not, if we consider only the day actually stated, a fixed and constant one, but a variable one; nor was it so much a moral as a ceremonial precept. If, however, we consider the commandment itself, it will be evident that it has its moral aspect and forms part of the natural law. Moreover, the date at which the keeping of the sabbath was removed was precisely that at which the rest of the Hebrew cult and ceremonial was to cease—namely, the day of Christ's death (see TCCI 7:422-423).

[232] The holy days of obligation appointed by the Church will be found explained under q. 243ff, below.

THE REMAINING SEVEN COMMANDMENTS OF THE DECALOGUE WHICH REFER TO OURSELVES AND OUR NEIGHBOR

The Fourth Commandment of the Decalogue

207. **What does God command in the fourth commandment, "Honor thy father and thy mother"?**
In the fourth commandment, "Honor thy father and thy mother," God bids us show due honor to our parents and those who hold their place; such honor involves love, attention, obedience, and service.[233]

208. **Is it merely honor that we owe to our parents?**
We ought not only to honor our parents but to afford them assistance, especially in their temporal or spiritual needs.

209. **What reward does God promise to children who show due honor to their parents?**
To children who show due honor to their parents, God promises a blessing and, if he judges it good for their soul's salvation, length of life.[234]

210. **Does this commandment insist solely on the duties of children toward their parents?**
This commandment lays down not only the duties of children toward their parents, but also indirectly the duties of husband and wife to one another and to their children, the mutual rights and duties of subjects and superiors, and of workpeople and their employers.[235]

[233] Cf. Ex 20:12; Dt 5:16; 27:16; Ecclus 7:29-30; Eph 6:1-3; Col 3:20. See the *Catechism of the Council of Trent*: "To honor is to have reverential thoughts of a person and to put a high value on all that concerns him; honor such as this comprises love, respect, obedience, and service" (see TCCI 7:430).

[234] Cf. Dt 5:16; Ecclus 3:2-18; Eph 6:1-3; TCCI 7:435-437

[235] Only the Church of Christ can secure peace and concord between the different classes of men. For men do not belong to different classes in order that they may attack one another, but rather that they may be united by a mutual love and assistance as

211. **What are the duties of married people toward one another?**

Married people owe one another mutual love, assistance, and fidelity, while wives owe obedience to their husbands.[236]

212. **What are the duties of parents toward their children?**

The duties of parents toward their children flow from the law of nature itself; they have to see to their proper education, especially their religious and moral education, while they have, according to their means, to provide for their temporal welfare.[237]

213. **Have any besides the parents the right and duty of seeing to the fitting education of young people?**

The right and duty of seeing to the fitting education of youth belongs—apart from the parents—to the state, which, for the good of the community, makes up for the deficiencies of parents; it belongs too in a more especial way to the Church, from the very fact that Christ commissioned her to teach all nations and lead them to a supernatural holiness and finally to eternal life.[238]

becomes those who are brethren in Christ, see this emphatically stated by Leo XIII in his encyclical, *Rerum novarum* of May 15, 1891.

[236] Cf. 1 Cor 11:3; Eph 5:22-23; Col 3:18-19; Ti 2:4-5; 1 Pt 3:1; *Codex Juris Canonici*, Can. 1033, 1128

[237] Cf. Ecclus 7:25-27; 30:1-3; Eph 6:4; Col 3:21; *Codex Juris Canonici*, Can. 1113; TCCI 7:437-439. Since formation in religion and the moral life depends very largely on catechetical instruction, parents are strictly bound in duty to see that their children are properly taught their catechism. This especially applies to mothers, who ought to instill into their children from their earliest years the elements of the catechism. If, however, they are compelled by circumstances to delegate this duty to others, parents should bear in mind that their position makes it incumbent on them to choose such schools and teachers as are really suited for the proper fulfillment of this duty. They must not neglect due supervision of the education, both religious and moral, given to their children; and if they find it insufficient, they must supplement it. Of course, if they find it is unsound, they must not hesitate to hand their children over to better teachers.

[238] Cf. Pius XI, Encyclical *Divini illius Magistri*, Dec. 31, 1929

214. **What are the duties of subjects toward their lawful superiors?**
Subjects owe to their lawful superiors, whether ecclesiastical or civil, reverence and obedience comparable to the filial piety that children should show to their parents.[239]

215. **Who are the ecclesiastical superiors to whom we ought to give not only reverence but obedience?**
The ecclesiastical superiors to whom we ought to give not only reverence but obedience according to canon law are the pope, our own bishop or any other prelate possessing ecclesiastical jurisdiction, and our own parish priest in the exercise of his ministerial duties.

216. **Why do we owe reverence and obedience to legitimate civil authority?**
We owe reverence and obedience to legitimate civil authority in whatever person it happens to reside, because, like civil society itself, it springs from nature and therefore from God the author of nature.[240]

217. **What are the duties of superiors toward their subjects?**
Superiors ought, each in his own sphere, to look after those subject to them and show them a good example in all things, as having to render an account for them not only to men but to God himself.[241]

218. **What are the duties of workers toward their masters?**
Workers owe to their masters complete and faithful fulfillment of any free and equitable agreement into which they have entered. They must not do damage to their masters' property or offer violence to their persons; in upholding their own rights, they must refrain from violence; they must

[239] Cf. Rom 13:1-7; 1 Tm 2:1-3; Heb 13:17; 1 Pt 2:13-18; Leo XIII, Encyclical *Immortale Dei*, Nov. 1, 1885

[240] Cf. Ws 6:4; Prv 8:15. "There is no power but from God, and those that are ordained of God. Therefore he that resisteth the power resisteth the ordinance of God; and they that resist purchase unto themselves damnation" (Rom 13:1-2). See Leo XIII, Encyclical *Immortale Dei*, n. 6-7, 11; Chrysostom, *Homily 33 on Romans*, Ch. 1.

[241] Cf. Heb 13:17; 1 Tm 4:12

not resort to sedition, and they must avoid mixing themselves up with evil-minded men.[242]

219. **What are the duties of masters toward their workpeople?**

Masters owe it to their workpeople to love them as brethren in Christ, to pay them the wages due to them, to see that they have time for the practice of their religion, not for any reason to lead them away from their domestic duties, or the exercise of thrift, or put upon them work dangerous to their health or beyond their strength or unbefitting their age or sex.[243]

220. **When ought we not to obey our parents or other superiors?**

We ought not to obey our parents or other superiors when their commands conflict with those of some higher authority—when, for instance, they command something contrary to the law of God or of the Church.[244]

221. **When are we allowed not to obey them?**

We are allowed not to obey them when they bid us do something that does not come under their jurisdiction—for example, when they give us a command about our choice of a state of life.[245]

[242] Cf. Eph 6:5-8; Col 3:22-25; Ti 2:9-10; 1 Pt 2:18; Leo XIII, Encyclical *Rerum novarum*, May 15, 1891; TCCI 7:431, 433-435

[243] Cf. Eph 6:9; Col 4:1; Jas 5:4; *Codex Juris Canonici*, Can. 1524. "In deciding what is a just wage, many questions have to be weighed; but, generally speaking, employers and wealthy people should bear in mind that to oppress the needy and poor for the sake of one's own profit, to strive for gain out of another person's needs, is permitted by no law, human or divine. Moreover, to deprive a person of his just wage by fraud is a grave sin calling for heaven's vengeance: 'Behold the hire of the laborers...which by fraud has been kept by you, crieth, and the cry of them hath entered into the ears of the Lord of Sabaoth' (Jas 5:4). Lastly, the rich should be especially careful not to dissipate the savings of the poor by violence, craft, or usury, and this all the more because the poor have no sufficient protection against wrongdoers and their own impotence; the more scant their property, the more sacred it ought to be" (Leo XIII, Encyclical *Rerum novarum*).

[244] Cf. Mt 10:37; Lk 14:26. "We have to obey God rather than men" (Acts 5:29). Cf. also Leo XIII, Encyclical *Quod Apostolici muneris*, Dec. 28, 1878; *Summa Theologiae*, II-II, q. 104, a. 5

[245] "There can be no doubt whatever that in choosing a state of life everyone is free to make deliberate choice either of following Christ's counsel of virginity or of entering the married state" (Leo XIII, Encyclical *Rerum novarum*).

The Fifth Commandment of the Decalogue

222. **What does God forbid in the fifth commandment, "Thou shalt not kill"?**
In the fifth commandment, "Thou shalt not kill," God forbids us to cause death either to our neighbor or to ourselves, or to inflict on him or ourselves any other harm to body or soul, or cooperate in so doing.[246]

223. **How can harm be done to the soul?**
Harm can be done to the soul by scandal, that is, by wrong words or deeds giving occasion of spiritual harm to our neighbor.[247]

224. **To what are we bound if we do harm to our neighbor?**
If we do harm to our neighbor's person, we are bound to make restitution, so far as we can, for the harm we have inflicted.

225. **Does God by this commandment forbid suicide?**
By this commandment, God forbids suicide, because, like murder, it is contrary to justice, since it infringes God's rights over the life of man; it is also contrary to the charity that we owe to ourselves and others, and, of its very nature, it deprives us of time for repentance.[248]

226. **Does this commandment also forbid dueling?**
This commandment also forbids dueling undertaken on private authority, no matter for what reason; for dueling incurs the malice both of murder and suicide.[249]

[246] Cf. Ex 20:13; Dt 5:17; Mt 5:21-22, 43-47; 18:6-9. Hence, by this commandment, it is forbidden to procure abortion. But to repel force by force against an unjust aggressor, while careful to preserve due moderation in a blameless self-defense, is permitted by every law and right.

[247] Cf. *Summa Theologiae*, II-II, q. 43, a. 1

[248] Cf. *Codex Juris Canonici*, Can. 1240, sect. 1, n. 3; Can. 2350, sect. 2; *Summa Theologiae*, II-II, q. 64, a. 5

[249] Cf. Alexander VII, Decree of Sept. 24, 1665, the second of certain condemned Propositions; Leo XIII, Epistle *Pastoralis officii*, Sept. 22, 1891; *Codex Juris Canonici*, Can. 1240, sect. 1, n. 4; Can. 2351

227. **Are the above the only acts forbidden by this commandment?**
This commandment forbids not only the abovementioned acts but private revenge, anger, hatred, envy, quarrels, and disputes, for these readily lead to the abovementioned acts.[250]

The Sixth Commandment of the Decalogue

228. **What does God forbid in the sixth commandment, "Thou shalt not commit adultery"?**
In the sixth commandment, "Thou shalt not commit adultery," God forbids not only infidelity to one another on the part of married people, but also any other external sin against chastity and anything that may lead to sins of impurity.[251]

229. **What are the principal things that lead to sins against chastity, and which should therefore be carefully avoided?**
Apart from the suggestions of the devil and the impulse of concupiscence, the principal things that lead to sins against chastity and are therefore to be carefully avoided are idleness, intemperance in food and drink, bad company, bad talk and reading, debasing plays, immodest dances and dress, dangerous familiarities and occasions.[252]

[250] Cf. Mt 5:21-22; 1 Jn 3:15

[251] Cf. Ex 20:14; Dt 5:18; Mt 5:27-28; Rom 1:26-27; 1 Cor 5:9ff; 6:9-10, 13ff; Eph 5:3-7; 1 Thes 4:4; 1 Tm 1:9-10; Heb 13:4. Sins against chastity result from incontinence or *luxuria*, which is defined as disorderly desire or use of venereal things; when willed directly, expressly intended, and admitted into the mind with full deliberation, it is always mortal sin. The sixth commandment of the decalogue forbids external sins of *luxuria*; the ninth forbids internal ones.

[252] Cf. Prv 7:5ff; Ecclus 9:1-13; 19:2; 42:12; 1 Cor 15:33; Eph 5:3-4, 18; Col 3:8; Pius XI, Encyclical *Divini illius Magistri*, Dec. 31, 1929. If you would preserve the fair virtue of chastity, you will need a far greater watchfulness than is called for in preserving the other virtues, for it is not simply a question of external assailants plotting to rob you of your treasure, but also of pleasurable desires and movements from within, which have their origin in our sinful flesh. Moreover, no matter how much care you take, it will all be in vain unless you have the support of God's grace, which, however, will never be refused when rightly asked for. It is a good practice, then, to say the prayer which a priest says when preparing for Mass: "Consume, O Lord, with the fire of thy Holy Spirit our reins and our heart that so we may serve thee with a chaste body and please thee with a clean heart."

230. **What are the usual consequences of sins of incontinence?**
Besides the harm often resulting to a person's health, the usual consequences of sins of incontinence are dullness of the mind, loss of the fear of God, distaste for divine things and the practice of virtue, hardness of heart, loss of the faith, and sometimes final impenitence.[253]

231. **What are the chief means for preserving chastity?**
The chief means for preserving chastity are guarding and mortifying the senses, the avoidance of dangerous occasions, temperance in food and drink, prayer, a real devotion to the Blessed Virgin, and especially frequent confession and Communion.

The Seventh Commandment of the Decalogue

232. **What does God forbid in the seventh commandment, "Thou shalt not steal"?**
In the seventh commandment, "Thou shalt not steal," God forbids all unjust taking of another person's property or damaging it, also cooperation in so doing.[254]

233. **To what are those bound who break this commandment?**
Those who break this commandment are bound in justice, so far as they can, to restore the other person's property and make good any damage done.

234. **When does the obligation of restitution and reparation become grave?**
The obligation of restitution and reparation becomes grave when, according to common estimation, the matter in question is serious, or when grave harm has been done to the owner.

[253] Cf. Jb 31:9-12; Prv 23:27; 29:3; Ecclus 19:3; Os 4:11-12; 5:4; Rom 1:24ff; 1 Cor 2:14; 5:1-5; Eph 5:3-4; Col 3:5-8; 1 Pt 4:3-4. Cf. also St. Thomas Aquinas (*Summa Theologiae*, II-II, q. 153, a. 5) where he enumerates among the daughters of *luxuria* blindness of heart, heedlessness, rashness, inconstancy, self-love, hatred of God, love of the present world, and horror of the next.

[254] Cf. Ex 20:15; Dt 5:19; 1 Cor 6:10; Apoc 9:21

THE EIGHTH COMMANDMENT OF THE DECALOGUE

235. **What does God forbid in the eighth commandment, "Thou shalt not bear false witness against thy neighbor"?**
In the eighth commandment, "Thou shalt not bear false witness against thy neighbor," God forbids lying, false swearing, and any harm we may do to our neighbor by our words.[255]

236. **How do we injure our neighbor by words?**
We injure our neighbor by words, especially by calumny, detraction, insults, and rash judgments, or by betraying secrets.[256]

237. **To what are they bound who have injured their neighbor's reputation by words?**
Those who have injured their neighbor's reputation by words are bound in justice to repair it so far as they can, and to make compensation for the damage done; if the damage done is great, the obligation to repair it becomes grave.

[255] Cf. Ex 20:16; Dt 5:20; Prv 6:19; 12:22; Ws 1:11; Ecclus 7:13; 20:26-28; Eph 4:25; Col 3:9

[256] A *lie* strictly so-called is a statement that is knowingly untrue, and of its very nature calculated to lead a person into error. *Calumny* means damage done to another person's reputation by circulating to his discredit a story which is untrue. *Detraction* means damaging our neighbor's reputation by circulating without any good reason stories about him which are true but not otherwise known. *Contumely* is, strictly-speaking, dishonor offered to another's reputation when he is actually or at least morally present; though, in a general sense, it applies also to dishonor thus offered in a person's absence, whether by word of mouth or in writing. *Rash judgment* is a positive judgment that a person has committed such and such a sin, yet without there being sufficient grounds to go upon. *Betrayal of secrets* means unjustly discovering for oneself, or making known to others, something that is hidden or should be kept hidden; it also includes making use of knowledge thus obtained. "The whisperer and the double-tongued is accursed, for he hath troubled many that were at peace" (Ecclus 28:15; Cf. Prv 8:13). St. Thomas says: "To take away another's reputation is a very grave thing, since a man's reputation seems to be the most precious of his temporal possessions; if he loses it, he is prevented from doing many good actions, as we read: 'Take heed of a good name; for this shall continue with thee more than a thousand treasures precious and great'" (Ecclus 41:15; *Summa Theologiae*, II-II, q. 73, a. 2).

The Last Two Commandments of the Decalogue

238. **What does God forbid in the ninth commandment, "Thou shalt not covet thy neighbor's wife"?**
In the ninth commandment, "Thou shalt not covet thy neighbor's wife," God forbids not only such unchaste desires but also every interior thought contrary to chastity, just as the sixth commandment expressly forbids external acts.[257]

239. **What does God forbid in the tenth commandment, "Thou shalt not covet thy neighbor's goods"?**
In the tenth commandment, "Thou shalt not covet thy neighbor's goods," God forbids all unjust and inordinate desire for another's property.[258]

240. **What is the sum of all the commandments of the decalogue?**
The sum of all the commandments of the decalogue is: "Thou shalt love the Lord thy God with thy whole heart, and with thy whole soul, and with all thy strength,...and thy neighbor as thyself."[259]

241. **Are all people bound to the observance of the duties proper to their state of life?**
All are bound to the careful observance of the duties proper to their state of life—that is, of those duties to which they are bound in virtue of their position or office.

[257] Cf. Ex 20:17; Dt 5:21

[258] Cf. Ex 20:17; Dt 5:21; 1 Tm 6:10

[259] Lk 10:27; Cf. Lv 19:18; Dt 6:5; Mt 22:37-40; Mk 12:30-31; Lk 10:27; Rom 13:10; Gal 5:14; Jas 2:8. Leo the Great: "Love of our neighbor is love of God, who declared that the fullness of the law and the prophets lay in this unity of a twofold love" (Sermon 9, *De Jejunio septimi mensis*). See *Summa Theologiae*, I-II, q. 100, a. 3, rep. 1; TCCI 7:429-430.

The Precepts of the Church

242. **How many precepts of the Church are there?**
There are many precepts of the Church, and a Catholic is bound to keep them all—for example, not to have in his possession or to read forbidden books; not to join Masonic or similar societies; to forego all solemnities in a marriage taking place within the forbidden times; not to cremate the bodies of the faithful; as well as other things. At the beginning of this catechism, only five precepts of the Church are enumerated, for these more particularly concern the ordinary spiritual life of the faithful in general.

THE FIRST PRECEPT OF THE CHURCH

243. **What does the Church lay down in the first precept, "On Sundays and other holy days of obligation, to hear Mass and refrain from servile works"?**
In this first precept, "On Sundays and other holy days of obligation, to hear Mass and to refrain from servile works," the Church lays down the way in which we are to sanctify Sundays and other holy days of obligation; this is done especially by hearing Mass and refraining from servile works.[260]

244. **Does not the very law of nature demand that a man should devote a certain amount of time to the service of God?**
The very law of nature demands that a man should devote a certain amount of time to the service of God, so that, freed from business and bodily toil, he may devoutly worship and venerate God his Creator, from whom too he has received innumerable benefits.[261]

[260] Cf. *Codex Juris Canonici*, Can. 1248
[261] Cf. TCCI 7:418

245. **Which are the holy days of obligation observed in the universal Church?**
The holy days of obligation observed in the universal Church, in addition to the Sundays, are Christmas day, the Circumcision, the Epiphany, the Ascension, Corpus Christi, the Immaculate Conception, the Assumption of Our Blessed Lady, St. Joseph, the Apostles Sts. Peter and Paul, and All Saints.[262]

246. **How, in addition to hearing Mass, ought a Christian to occupy himself on Sundays and other holy days of obligation?**
In addition to hearing Mass, it is only fitting that a Christian should on Sundays and other holy days of obligation devote himself to works of piety and religion, so far as he can, especially by assisting at the ceremonies of the Church, hearing sermons and instructions.

247. **What works are called "servile"?**
Those works are said to be "servile" which are performed by serfs or for wages; they are more particularly such as involve bodily labor and are concerned mainly with bodily gain.

248. **Are any servile works permitted on Sundays and other holy days of obligation?**
Those servile works are permitted on Sundays and other holy days of obligation which particularly concern the service of God or the ordinary necessities of domestic and public life; also such as are demanded by charity, or such as could not be omitted without grave inconvenience; such, too, as approved custom allows.

249. **Ought we on Sundays and other holy days of obligation to refrain only from servile works?**
On Sundays and other holy days of obligation, we ought to refrain not only from servile works, but also from public undertakings and—unless legitimate custom or some concession allows it—from commerce, marketing, and public buying and selling.

[262] Cf. *Codex Juris Canonici*, Can. 1247ff. In England, the feasts of the Immaculate Conception and St. Joseph are not holy days of obligation.

250. **Do those sin who do not keep the precept regarding Sundays and other holy days of obligation, or prevent others from doing so?**
Those who, without just cause, do not keep the precept regarding Sundays or other holy days of obligation, or prevent others from doing so, sin gravely.

THE SECOND PRECEPT OF THE CHURCH

251. **What does the Church lay down in the second precept, "On days appointed by the Church, to fast and abstain from flesh meat"?**
In the second precept, "On days appointed by the Church, to fast and abstain from flesh meat," the Church lays down that, on days appointed by her, we are either to fast, or to abstain from flesh meat, or both to fast and abstain from flesh meat as well.[263]

252. **What does the law of fasting command?**
The law of fasting commands that there should be only one full meal in the day, but it does not forbid us to take a small quantity of food in the morning and evening, if we keep to the local custom regarding its quantity and quality.

253. **What does the law of abstinence from flesh meat forbid?**
The law of abstinence from flesh meat forbids us to eat meat or soup made from meat, but it does not forbid the use of eggs, milk-foods, or any condiments made from animal fats.

254. **On what days do these laws bind?**
Unless there is a dispensation granted by lawful authority,
1. the law of abstinence binds on every Friday;
2. the law of fasting and abstinence binds on Ash Wednesday, the Fridays and Saturdays of Lent, the Ember days, the Vigils of Pentecost, of the Assumption of Our Blessed Lady, and of All Saints, and on Christmas Eve;
3. the law of fasting binds on every day of Lent, except the Sundays.

[263] Cf. *Codex Juris Canonici*, Can. 1250ff

255. **Are there certain days on which these laws do not bind?**
On Sundays, and other holy days of obligation, and on Holy Saturday after midday, the laws of abstinence only, or of fasting and abstinence combined, or of fasting only, do not bind except when the holy day of obligation falls during Lent. Vigils are not anticipated.[264]

256. **Who are bound to keep the laws of fasting and abstinence?**
Unless lawfully excused or dispensed, all who are of sane mind and have completed their seventh year are bound to abstain, while all who have completed their twenty-first year are bound to fast until they begin their sixtieth year.

257. **Why does the Church prescribe fasting and abstinence?**
The Church prescribes fasting and abstinence so that the faithful may do penance for the sins they have committed, may be shielded from future sins, and may give themselves more effectively to prayer.[265]

THE THIRD AND FOURTH PRECEPTS OF THE CHURCH

258. **What does the Church lay down in the third precept, "To confess our sins at least once a year"?**
In the third precept, "To confess our sins at least once a year," the Church lays down that, as soon as they have come to the age of discretion, the faithful must, at least once a year, confess all mortal sins not directly remitted in previous confessions.[266]

[264] Cf. *Codex Juris Canonici*, Can. 1252, par. 4

[265] Cf. Tb 12:8; Jl 2:12, 15; Mt 6:16; 9:15; 17:20; Mk 2:20; Lk 2:37; 5:35; Rom 13:13; 2 Cor 6:5; 11:27; Eph 5:18; 1 Thes 5:6; Ti 2:2

[266] Cf. Fourth Lateran Council, Const. 21; Council of Trent, Session 14, "Doctrine on the Sacrament of Penance," Ch. 5. If you desire to keep free from sin and lead a life such as befits a Christian, then go frequently to confession and be careful to prepare yourself well; try, too, always to go to confession as though this were your last and you were about to die. And when you have received absolution, thank God who has shown you such mercy; if possible, say your penance at once.

259. **What does the Church lay down in the fourth precept, "To receive the sacrament of the Holy Eucharist at least at Easter"?**
In the fourth precept, "To receive the sacrament of the Holy Eucharist at least at Easter," the Church lays down that all the faithful who have reached the age of discretion shall receive the Holy Eucharist at least at Easter or thereabouts.[267]

260. **Should the faithful fulfill this precept each according to his own rite and in his own parish church?**
Although the faithful are not strictly bound to do so, yet it is advisable that each should fulfill this precept according to his own rite and in his own parish church. Those, however, who fulfill it according to another rite or in another parish should take care to inform their parish priest that they have fulfilled their obligation.[268]

261. **Why does the Church add to the third and fourth precepts the words *at least*?**
The Church adds to these two precepts the words *at least* to teach us that it is most fitting and in accordance with her wishes that the faithful—even those conscious of only venial sin or of mortal sins already directly remitted—should often go to confession, and that they should frequently, even every day, devoutly receive Holy Communion.[269]

[267] Cf. Fourth Lateran Council, Const. 21; Council of Trent, Session 13, "On the Most Holy Sacrament of the Eucharist," Can. 9; *Codex Juris Canonici*, Can. 859, par. 1

[268] Cf. *Codex Juris Canonici*, Can. 859, par. 3; Can. 866, par. 2. In the Latin Church, Holy Communion is received under one kind only; in many of the Churches of the East, under both kinds.

[269] See the Decree of the Sacred Congregation of the Council, *Sacra Tridentina Synodus*, Dec. 20, 1905; also the Decree of the Sacred Congregation of the Discipline of the Sacraments, *Quam singulari*, Aug. 8, 1910, n. 6. Go frequently to Holy Communion with ardent desires and in purity of soul. There is no more precious moment than that in which you hold so closely and intimately united with yourself the Savior who loves you. Do not grudge spending some time with him in thanksgiving.

262. **What is the age of discretion at which the precepts of confession and Communion begin to bind?**

The age of discretion at which the precepts of confession and Communion begin to bind is the age at which a child begins to reason, that is, about his seventh year more or less.[270]

263. **Does this obligation which children incur also fall upon others?**

This obligation which children incur falls chiefly on those who have care of them, that is, on their parents, guardians, teachers, confessors, and parish priests.[271]

264. **What knowledge of Christian doctrine is requisite so that a child can and ought to be admitted to his first Communion?**

For a child's admission to his first Communion,

1. if he is in danger of death, it is enough for him to know how to distinguish between the body of Christ and ordinary bread, and so be able to adore it with reverence;
2. when there is no danger of death, a child must also know, according to his capacity, those mysteries of the faith which are necessary as means of salvation; he must also be able to distinguish the bread of the Holy Eucharist from common bread, so that he may be able to receive the Holy Eucharist with a devotion proportionate to his age.[272]

[270] See the Decree of the Sacred Congregation of the Discipline of the Sacraments, *Quam Singulari*, Aug. 8, 1910, n. 1.

[271] See the Decree of the Sacred Congregation of the Discipline of the Sacraments, *Quam Singulari*, Aug. 8, 1910, n. 4; *Codex Juris Canonici*, Can. 860 and 1340

[272] See the Decree of the Sacred Congregation of the Discipline of the Sacraments, *Quam Singulari*, Aug. 8, 1910, n. 2-3; *Codex Juris Canonici*, Can. 854; TCCI 7:276-277. The conditions requisite for fitting and devout reception of Holy Communion are set out under q. 399ff.

265. **To what are children bound after their first Communion?**
After their first Communion, children are bound to learn gradually and according to their capacity the entire catechism especially prepared for those who have made their first Communion.[273]

266. **What is the duty on this point of parents and of others who have care of children?**
On this point, it is the grave duty of parents and of others who have care of children to see that they go to the public catechism classes; if they cannot go, then those responsible must provide for their religious education in some other way.[274]

267. **How long does paschal time, or the time during which people must receive Holy Communion, last?**
The paschal time appointed for the reception of Holy Communion lasts from Palm Sunday to Low Sunday, unless some further concession is granted by lawful authority.[275]

268. **Does the obligation of receiving Holy Communion cease if it has not been fulfilled during paschal time?**
The obligation of receiving Holy Communion, if not fulfilled during paschal time, does not cease, and must be obeyed within the same year at the first opportunity.

269. **Is the obligation of yearly confession and Easter Communion fulfilled by a sacrilegious confession or Communion, or by a deliberate bad confession?**
The obligation of yearly confession and Easter Communion is fulfilled neither by a sacrilegious confession and Communion, nor by a deliberate

[273] See the Decree of the Sacred Congregation of the Discipline of the Sacraments, *Quam Singulari*, Aug. 8, 1910, n. 2.

[274] See the Decree of the Sacred Congregation of the Discipline of the Sacraments, *Quam Singulari*, Aug. 8, 1910, n. 6.

[275] Cf. *Codex Juris Canonici*, Can. 859, par. 2

bad confession; in fact, owing to the presence of a fresh sin, the obligation is only increased.[276]

THE FIFTH PRECEPT OF THE CHURCH

270. **What does the Church lay down in the fifth precept, "To relieve the necessities of the Church and her clergy"?**
In the fifth precept, "To relieve the necessities of the Church and her clergy," the Church urges on the faithful a divine command, namely, to relieve the temporal necessities of the Church and her clergy according to local regulations and accepted custom.[277]

271. **Why is this enjoined?**
This is enjoined because it is but just that the faithful should provide for the sacred ministers who work for their salvation, so that they may be able to meet the expenses of divine worship and support themselves decently.

The Evangelical Counsels

272. **In addition to the commandments of God and the precepts of the Church are there certain counsels?**
In addition to the commandments of God and the precepts of the Church, there are certain counsels first given by Christ in the gospel, whence their name of "evangelical counsels."

[276] Cf. *Codex Juris Canonici*, Can. 902; Decree of the Congregation of the Holy Office, Sept. 24, 1665

[277] Cf. Dt 18:1-8; Mt 10:10; Lk 10:7; 1 Cor 9:9-14; 1 Tm 5:18; *Codex Juris Canonici*, Can. 1502; *Summa Theologiae*, II-II, q. 87, a. 1

273. **What are evangelical counsels?**
Evangelical counsels are means set before us by Christ whereby people may more easily and completely attain to spiritual perfection.

274. **What are the chief evangelical counsels?**
The chief evangelical counsels are voluntary poverty, perfect chastity, and entire obedience, undertaken for the love of Jesus Christ.[278]

275. **How does the practice of these counsels secure the more easy and complete attainment of spiritual perfection?**
The practice of these counsels makes the attainment of spiritual perfection more easy and complete because by dedicating to God our wills by obedience, our bodies by chastity, external good things by poverty, we are led on to more perfect charity.[279]

276. **Who should practice the evangelical counsels?**
Those should practice the evangelical counsels who have freely bound themselves to do so—for example, religious who are bound by vow to the observance of the three evangelical counsels in accordance with the rule of their own particular institute.[280]

[278] For poverty, see Mt 19:21; Mk 10:21; Lk 18:22; for chastity, Mt 19:12; 1 Cor 7:25, 32, 34; for obedience, Lk 10:16; Jn 13:20; *Summa Theologiae*, II-II, q. 86, a. 9, rep. 1.

[279] Cf. Pius XI, Encyclical *Quas primas*, Dec. 11, 1925, toward the end; *Summa Theologiae*, I-II, q. 108, a. 4

[280] Those who, in following a divine vocation, embrace any religious institute approved by the Church, while they strive, each according to his capacity, to attain to Christian perfection in accordance with the evangelical counsels, also forward the salvation of their neighbors, and are exceedingly helpful to civil society as a whole by their assiduity in prayer, by the example afforded by their virtues, or by their care for the sick and indigent of all sorts, also by educating youth, or by their theological learning. It is only fitting, then, that not only individuals, but families and states as well, should treat such people with reverence and give proof of their admiration for them and their gratitude to them. (See Leo XIII, Epistle *Testem benevolentiae*, Jan. 22, 1899, to Cardinal Gibbons; Epistle *Au milieu des consolations*, Dec. 23, 1900, to Cardinal Richard; Pius XI, Epistle *Unigenitus Dei Filius*, March 19, 1924; *Codex Juris Canonici*, Can. 487.)

277. **Do we need any special help to believe as we ought the things taught by our faith, to keep God's commandments and the Church's precepts, and to practice the evangelical counsels?**
To believe as we ought the things taught by our faith, to keep God's commandments and the precepts of the Church, and to practice the evangelical counsels, we need the grace of God.[281]

Grace

278. **What is grace?**
Grace is a supernatural gift freely bestowed by God on rational creatures so that they may attain to eternal life.[282]

279. **How many kinds of grace are there?**
There are two kinds of grace—habitual (also called "sanctifying" or "justifying grace," or grace that makes us pleasing to God) and actual.

280. **What is habitual grace?**
Habitual grace is a supernatural quality dwelling in the soul, by which man is made a partaker in the divine nature, a temple of the Holy Ghost, a friend of God, his adopted son, and heir to the glory of heaven, and so capable of performing acts meriting eternal life.[283]

[281] Cf. Jn 15:5; 1 Cor 3:6; 4:7; 2 Cor 3:5; Eph 2:8-10

[282] The "supernatural" is that which exceeds nature. It is of two kinds: 1) when it transcends nature by the way in which it happens, though the fact itself belongs to the natural order, for example, when life is restored to a dead person; 2) when the fact itself in its essential character completely transcends the whole natural order, since it shares in the intimate life of God himself, as, for example, sanctifying grace, the infused virtues, and their corresponding acts, so, too, life eternal or the intuitional vision of God and beatific love of him.

[283] Cf. Ws 7:14; Jn 1:12-13; 3:5; 15:4, 14; Rom 5:5; 8:14-17; 1 Cor 4:7; 12:3; Eph 2:8ff;

281. **Is habitual grace necessary for obtaining eternal life?**
Habitual grace is absolutely necessary for all, even infants, if they would obtain eternal life.

282. **What do we merit by the good deeds we perform when justified by God's grace and the merits of Christ?**
By the good deeds we perform when justified by the grace of God and the merits of Christ, we merit an increase in grace, the attainment of eternal life—if, that is, we depart this life in the grace of God—and an increase in glory.[284]

283. **How is habitual grace lost?**
Habitual grace is lost by any mortal sin.[285]

284. **How is habitual grace regained?**
Habitual grace is regained by giving up mortal sin and, at the same time, making use of the means appointed by Christ for winning justification.

285. **Can any good works at all be performed when one is in a state of mortal sin?**
When one is in a state of mortal sin, some good works can be performed which, while they do not merit eternal life, yet do, with the help of actual grace, dispose a sinner for justification.[286]

286. **What is actual grace?**
Actual grace is a supernatural help from God by which he enlightens our minds and moves our wills to do good and shun evil for the sake of eternal life. Unlike habitual grace, actual grace is not a quality dwelling in the

2 Pt 1:4; 1 Jn 3:1; Council of Trent, Session 6, Can. 11; Cyril of Alexandria, *On John*, Ch. 1, n. 9

[284] Cf. Second Council of Orange, Can. 18; Council of Trent, Session 6, Can. 32

[285] Cf. Rom 6:23; 1 Cor 6:9ff; Jas 1:15; 1 Jn 3:8; Council of Trent, Session 6, Can. 27; Basil, *Sermo Asceticus*, n. 1. For these means, see above, q. 178.

[286] Cf. Ecclus 21:1; Ez 18:30; Dn 4:24; Rom 2:14; Council of Trent, Session 6, "Decree on Justification," Ch. 6; Augustine, *On the Spirit and the Letter*, Ch. 48

soul, but a divine impulse from without, moving a person to perform acts beyond his natural powers, such as an act of contrition.[287]

287. **Is actual grace necessary for us?**
Actual grace is absolutely necessary for us if we would do good and shun evil for the sake of eternal life. For since eternal life belongs to the supernatural sphere, we cannot by our merely natural powers think or desire or do anything, as we ought, to attain to it.[288]

288. **Does God grant to all the graces they need for eternal life?**
God, who wishes all men to be saved, grants to all the graces they need for obtaining eternal life. But people who are grown up must, if they would attain to eternal life, freely cooperate with his help, which, by inspiring good desires, anticipates our good deeds, and by actual help furthers them.[289]

289. **Which are the chief means for obtaining God's grace?**
The chief means for obtaining God's grace are prayer, whereby we ask for it, and the use of the sacraments, which contain it and apply it.

[287] See Ephraem, *De Epiphania*, x, 14; Cyril of Alexandria, *De Adoratione in spiritu et veritate*, n. 1. Only interior grace is divided into habitual and actual, but under the general term *grace* we can, and frequently do, understand any gift freely bestowed on men by God for the sake of their eternal salvation, for example, such external graces as a good upbringing, the sacraments, the teaching office of the Church, sermons, reading good books, advice given to us, or punishments; sicknesses too, and the various trials and discomforts of life, even death itself; all these can rightly be termed at times the 'actual graces of God' so far as they are ordained or directed by his all-seeing providence for our salvation. It is most important that a Christian should strive to see in this light all the events of his life.

[288] Cf. 2 Cor 3:5; Phil 2:13; Second Council of Orange, Can. 3-6; Council of Trent, Session 6, Can. 1-3; Gregory Nazianzen, *Oration 37*, n. 13; Chrysostom, *Homily 25 on Genesis*, n. 7

[289] Cf. Ez 33:11; Jn 1:9; 1 Tm 2:4; 4:10; 2 Pt 3:9; Council of Trent, Session 6, "Decree on Justification," Ch. 11; Innocent X, Constitution *Cum occasione*, against the errors of Jansensius, May 31, 1653, the first condemned Proposition; Chrysostom, *Homily 16 on Hebrews*, n. 4

Prayer

PRAYER IN GENERAL

290. **What is prayer?**

Prayer is the devout raising up of the soul to God, to adore him, to thank him for benefits received, to beg his pardon for our sins, and to ask him for other things necessary or useful for ourselves or for others.

291. **Is it necessary for us to pray?**

It is necessary for us to pray, because God so wills, and also because God does not, as a rule, give the aid we always need, except to those who ask him for it.[290]

292. **How many kinds of prayer are there?**

There are two kinds of prayer: mental prayer, wherein we speak to God with our minds and our hearts and meditate upon the truths of eternity; vocal prayer, which, while spoken with the lips, is accompanied by the attention of the mind and the heart's devotion.

293. **How many kinds of vocal prayer are there?**

Vocal prayer is of two kinds: private prayer, whether offered by individual people or by a family together, either for themselves or for others, but not through the Church's ministers; public prayer, offered by the Church's

[290] Cf. Ecclus 18:22; Mt 7:7-8; Lk 11:9-13; 18:1; Rom 12:12; Eph 6:18; Col 4:2; 1 Thes 5:17; Chrysostom, *Homily 30 on Genesis*, n. 5; TCCI 7:493ff. As breathing is needful for the life of the body, so prayer for the life of the soul: whoso is in the habit of praying works for his salvation, whoso has no habit of prayer works for his own damnation. Pray, then, often, constantly beseech God from your heart. Learn some practical form of morning and evening prayers, and, in times of temptation, humble yourself before God; grave deeply in your heart the words: "He knows how to live well who knows how to pray well."

ministers and in the name of the Church; when it is set forth by the Church in her liturgical books, this latter is also called "liturgical prayer."

294. **What should we chiefly ask for in prayer?**
In prayer, we should chiefly ask for the glory of God, for eternal salvation for ourselves and for others, and the necessary suitable means for obtaining it.[291]

295. **Are we allowed to pray for temporal good things?**
We are allowed to pray for temporal good things if they are in accordance with God's will—according, that is, as they make for the glory of God, or help our own eternal salvation or that of others, or at least do not hinder it.[292]

296. **To whom is prayer addressed?**
All prayer is addressed to God, who alone can give us what we ask; but, that they may intercede for us with God, we pray also to all the blessed in heaven, especially the Blessed Virgin, and even to the souls in purgatory.[293]

297. **How ought we to pray so that our prayers may be heard?**
That our prayers may be heard, they should be offered in the name of Jesus Christ, on whose merits they depend; they should be devout, full of faith, hope, and humility, also persevering.[294]

298. **How is it that we do not always obtain what we ask for in our prayers?**
Sometimes we do not obtain what we ask for in our prayers; this is either because we do not ask right, or because we ask for what is not expedient for us; but we are not therefore to suppose that God will not in his own good time give us other and even greater graces.[295]

[291] Cf. Mt 6:9-13; 21:22; 26:41

[292] Cf. Mt 8:2, 6, 25; 9:18; 15:22; 17:14; Mk 1:40-42; 7:32; *Summa Theologiae*, II-II, q. 83, a. 6; TCCI 7:502-503

[293] Cf. Tb 12:12; Jb 42:8; 2 Mc 15:14; Apoc 5:8; 8:3

[294] Cf. Tb 12:8; Ecclus 35:21; Mt 6:5-6; 7:7-11; 17:20; 21:22; Mk 11:24; Jn 16:23-24; Jas 1:5-6; 4:3; 5:16-18; Augustine, *Tractate 102 on John*, n. 1; *Summa Theologiae*, II-II, q. 83, a. 4

[295] Cf. TCCI 7:496

299. **Which is the most perfect of all prayers?**
The most perfect of all prayers is the Lord's Prayer or Our Father, to which is usually added the Angelic Salutation or Hail Mary.

THE OUR FATHER AND HAIL MARY

THE OUR FATHER

300. **Why is the Our Father called the "Lord's Prayer"?**
The Our Father is called the "Lord's Prayer," because our Lord Jesus Christ himself taught it to us.[296]

301. **Why is the Lord's Prayer the most perfect of all prayers?**
The Lord's Prayer is the most perfect of all prayers, because it contains all that we ought to ask for, whether concerning God, in the first three petitions, or as regards ourselves and our neighbor, in the remaining petitions.[297]

302. **Whom do we invoke by the words, "Our Father"?**
By the words, "Our Father," we invoke God as a most loving Father, to show our love and trust in him, and to incline his goodness and mercy toward us.

[296] Cf. Mt 6:9-13; Lk 11:2-4

[297] "As St. Augustine points out, the Lord's Prayer is the most perfect of prayers, because, 'if we pray aright, we can say naught else save what is set down in that prayer. For prayer is in some sort the expression before God of our desires; consequently, we can only rightly ask in our prayers for what we can rightly desire. Now, in the Lord's Prayer, we not only find all the petitions that we can rightly desire to make, but they are set down in the very order in which we ought to desire them, so that this prayer not only teaches us how to ask but serves as a guide to all our desires'" (*Epistle 130*, n. 12; *Summa Theologiae*, II-II, q. 83, a. 9). All, then, should say the Lord's Prayer with proper attention and devotion.

303. **Why do we call God "Our Father"?**
We call God "Our Father" not only because he created us, preserves us, and governs us, but specially because by his grace he makes us his adopted children.[298]

304. **Why do we say "Our Father" and not "My Father"?**
We say "Our Father" and not "My Father" because, owing to the gift of the divine adoption, all the faithful are brethren in Christ, and ought therefore to have feelings of brotherly love for one another, and should therefore pray not for themselves alone but for others as well.[299]

305. **What do we mean by the words, "who art in heaven"?**
The words, "who art in heaven," make us think of the infinite power and majesty of God, which shines out so clearly in the heavens which are his work; they remind us too that we have to ask him for the good things of heaven and all that they imply.[300]

306. **What do we ask in the first petition, "hallowed be thy name"?**
In the first petition, "hallowed be thy name," we ask that the holy name of God may become known to all men and be praised by all in thought, word, and deed.[301]

307. **What do we ask in the second petition, "thy kingdom come"?**
In the second petition, "thy kingdom come," we ask that God may reign on earth over us and all men by his grace, and over all society and every nation by his law, so that at last we may be made partakers of his eternal glory in heaven.[302]

[298] Cf. Dt 32:6; Jn 16:26-27; Rom 8:15-17, 29; 1 Cor 1:9; 1 Jn 3:1-3; TCCI 7:516-522
[299] Cf. TCCI 7:522-525
[300] Cf. TCCI 7:526-527
[301] Cf. Ps 112:1-3; Phil 2:9-11
[302] Cf. Rom 14:17; 1 Cor 6:9-10; 15:50; Gal 5:19-21; Eph 5:5; TCCI 7:533-542

308. **How can we cooperate in the advancement of God's kingdom on earth?**
We can cooperate in the advancement of God's kingdom on earth by keeping Christ's law and cultivating the supernatural life of grace in ourselves, and by helping forward the task of the Church by our prayers and our work; for the Church's task is to strive to secure that men's private lives, as also their domestic and public lives, should conform to God's laws, that those too, who have strayed away, may return to the unity of the Church, and that the light of the gospel may spread to those that "sit in darkness and the shadow of death."[303]

309. **What do we ask in the third petition, "thy will be done on earth as it is in heaven"?**
In the third petition, "thy will be done on earth as it is in heaven," we ask that, as all the blessed in heaven and the souls in purgatory always and in all things lovingly do the will of God, so men may do it on earth.

310. **What do we ask in the fourth petition, "Give us this day our daily bread"?**
In the fourth petition, "Give us this day our daily bread," we ask that God may give us both spiritual bread—that is, all things necessary for the spiritual life of the soul—especially the bread of the Holy Eucharist—and also the body's bread, that is, all things needful for the support of the body.

311. **What do we ask in the fifth petition, "and forgive us our trespasses as we forgive them that trespass against us"?**
In the fifth petition, "and forgive us our trespasses as we forgive them that trespass against us," we ask God to forgive us the sins we have committed against him and remit the punishments we have deserved for them, as we ourselves forgive men the offenses they commit against us.[304]

[303] Lk 1:79
[304] Cf. Mt 6:14-15; 18:35; Mk 11:25-26; Lk 11:4

312. **What do we ask in the sixth petition, "and lead us not into temptation"?**
In the sixth petition, "and lead us not into temptation," acknowledging our own weakness, we turn to God, praying him to deliver us from temptations, or at least to grant us the help of his grace to overcome them.

313. **Why does God permit us to be tempted?**
God permits us to be tempted that we may realize our own weakness, that our faith may be tested, and in order that, overcoming temptation by his grace, we may gain virtue by practice and obtain the reward of eternal life. Moreover, God will never permit us to be tempted beyond what, with the help of his grace, we are able to bear.[305]

314. **Which are the most effective remedies against temptations?**
The most effective remedies against temptations are: avoidance of dangerous occasions, thought on the last things, and frequent approach to the sacraments. At the actual time of temptation, make the sign of the cross, humbly call on your guardian angel and specially on the holy names of Jesus and Mary.[306]

315. **What do we ask in the seventh petition, "but deliver us from evil"?**
In the seventh petition, "but deliver us from evil," we ask especially that God may deliver us from spiritual evil, or sin, and therefore from the devil who induces us to sin, as also from other evils, at least those that can give us occasion to sin.

316. **What does the word *Amen* at the end of the last petition mean?**
The word *Amen* at the end of the last petition means "so be it," that is, "as we have prayed"; we show thereby our confidence in God's promises.

[305] Cf. Tb 12:13; Ws 3:5; 1 Cor 10:13; Jas 1:2, 14; 2 Pt 2:9; Council of Trent, Session 6, "Decree on Justification," Ch. 11

[306] Cf. Prv 18:10; Mt 17:20; 26:41

The Hail Mary

317. **Why do we add the Hail Mary to the Lord's Prayer?**
We add the Hail Mary to the Lord's Prayer in order that, through the intercession of the Blessed Virgin Mary, we may the more easily obtain from God the things we ask for in the Lord's Prayer.

318. **Who spoke the words, "Hail [Mary], full of grace, the Lord is with thee; blessed art thou among women"?**
The archangel Gabriel spoke the words, "Hail [Mary], full of grace, the Lord is with thee; blessed art thou among women," when he declared to the Blessed Virgin Mary the mystery of the incarnation;[307] hence this prayer is called the "Angelic Salutation."

319. **What do we do when we say Hail Mary?**
When we say the Hail Mary, we congratulate the Blessed Virgin Mary on the singular privileges and gifts which God bestowed on her beyond all other creatures, and we give glory to God on this account.

320. **Who spoke the words, "blessed is the fruit of thy womb," and what do they mean?**
St. Elizabeth spoke the words, "blessed is the fruit of thy womb," when she welcomed the Blessed Virgin Mary as her guest.[308] They mean that Christ the Lord, Son of the Blessed Virgin Mary, is blessed above all things forever.

321. **Whose are the words, "Holy Mary, Mother of God, pray for us sinners now and at the hour of our death," and what do we ask by them?**
The words, "Holy Mary, Mother of God, pray for us sinners now and at the hour of our death," were added by the Church; by them we ask for the

[307] Lk 1:28
[308] Lk 1:42

protection of the Blessed Virgin Mary in all our needs, but especially at the hour of our death.[309]

322. **Is the Blessed Virgin Mary, Mother of God, also our Mother?**
The Blessed Virgin Mary, Mother of God, is also our Mother by that adoption which makes us brothers of her Son; and this Jesus Christ himself confirmed at his death on the cross, when he gave all men in the person of St. John to the Blessed Virgin to be her children, saying, "Woman, behold thy son," and at the same time gave to all men his Mother to be their Mother: "Behold thy mother."[310]

323. **What reward do they receive who honor the Blessed Virgin Mary with loving devotion?**
Those who honor the Blessed Virgin Mary with loving devotion receive their great reward: that they are in their turn loved and protected by her with a special motherly love.[311]

324. **What devotion to the Blessed Virgin Mary does the Church particularly recommend?**
The devotion to the Blessed Virgin Mary which the Church particularly recommends is the recitation of the rosary.

[309] The Eastern Churches do not use this latter part of the Hail Mary, but add a different prayer to the angel's words.

[310] Jn 19:26-27; Cf. Rom 8:29; Leo XIII, Encyclical *Adjutricem populi*, Sept. 5, 1895; Pius X, Encyclical *Ad illum diem*, Feb. 2, 1904; Benedict XV, *Epistle to the Confraternity of Our Lady of a Happy Death*, March 22, 1918; Pius XI, Encyclical *Rerum Ecclesiae*, Feb. 28, 1926

[311] St. Bernard thus urges us to devotion to the Blessed Virgin: "In dangers, in troubles, in doubts, think of Mary, call upon Mary...If you follow her guidance, you will not go astray; if you ask her, you will not give up hope; if she upholds you, you will not stumble; if she protects you, you will not be afraid; if she leads you, you will not weary; if she is kindly to you, you will reach your goal" (*Homily 2 on the Gospels*, "Missus est"). These words of the saint are confirmed by many examples given in the *Lives of the Saints*.

The Sacraments

THE SACRAMENTS IN GENERAL

325. **What is meant by a "sacrament of the new law"?**

By a "sacrament of the new law" is meant some sign perceptible by the senses, instituted by Jesus Christ to signify grace and to confer it on those who worthily receive the sacrament.[312]

326. **What are the necessary constituents of a sacrament?**

Three elements go to the making of a sacrament:

1. Certain things as the matter.
2. Certain words as the form.
3. A minister conferring the sacrament with the intention at least of doing what the Church does.

Lack of any one of the above means that there is no sacrament.[313]

[312] Cf. Council of Florence, Session 8 (November 22, 1439), "Bull of Union with the Armenians"; Council of Trent, Session 7, "On the Sacraments in General," Can. 1 and 6; Pius X, Decree *Lamentabili sane*, July 3, 1907, the thirty-ninth, fortieth, and forty-first condemned Propositions; TCCI 7:171ff

[313] Cf. Council of Florence as in the previous note; Council of Trent, Session 7, "On the Sacraments in General," Can. 11. From the above, it follows that the constitutive elements of the sacraments are, like the sacraments themselves, of divine institution. Nor is this contradicted by the fact that, with the Church's approval, diversities of rites in the administration of the sacraments are to be found in various Churches, or at different periods in the history of the same Church. No variation which is purely a question of accidentals can be in opposition to the divine institution of the sacraments, for that is concerned solely with their substantial matter and the indications of their form. In cases where the variations are more profound, it is quite allowable to suppose that, in the case of certain sacraments, Christ did not, in instituting them, precisely define in what their matter and form consisted, but was content to give general indications which should suffice to express the meaning of the sacrament in question, while leaving it to the Church to choose proportionate matter and form.

327. **How many sacraments of the new law are there?**
There are seven sacraments of the new law: baptism, confirmation, the Holy Eucharist, penance, extreme unction, holy order, and matrimony.

328. **Why did Christ institute neither more nor less than seven sacraments?**
Christ instituted neither more nor less than seven sacraments, because these seven are necessary for the Church to do her work, and they suffice for that purpose.

329. **In what sense are these seven sacraments necessary and sufficient for the Church to do her work?**
These seven sacraments are necessary and sufficient for the Church to do her work in that the first five sacraments are intended to promote the spiritual perfection of the individual, while the last two are intended to promote the growth and the government of the whole Church.[314]

330. **What grace do the sacraments confer on us?**
The sacraments confer on us sanctifying grace or an increase of it, also sacramental grace or the right to special assistance whereby we may attain the effect intended by each sacrament.[315]

331. **How do the sacraments confer grace?**
The sacraments confer grace on those who put no hindrance to it, and this by the inherent power bestowed upon them by Christ who instituted them, or, as we say, *ex opere operato*.[316]

332. **Who put hindrances to the effect of the sacraments?**
Those put hindrances to the effect of the sacraments who receive them without the dispositions necessary for receiving grace.

[314] Cf. Council of Florence, Session 8 (November 22, 1439), "Bull of Union with the Armenians"; TCCI 7:182-184

[315] Cf. *Summa Theologiae*, III, q. 62, a. 2

[316] Cf. Council of Trent, Session 7, "On the Sacraments in General," Can. 7-8; Augustine, *Epistle* 98, n. 2; *Tractate 80 on John*, n. 3

333. **Can the personal wickedness of the minister hinder the effect of the sacraments he confers?**
The personal wickedness of the minister who confers the sacraments cannot hinder the effect of the sacraments, for in exercising his sacred functions, he is not acting in his own person but in the Person of Christ.[317]

334. **Which are the sacraments of the dead and which the sacraments of the living?**
The sacraments of the dead are baptism and penance; the rest are sacraments of the living.

335. **Why are baptism and penance called "sacraments of the dead" and the rest "sacraments of the living"?**
Baptism and penance are called "sacraments of the dead," because they were instituted primarily for those who, through sin actual or original, have no supernatural life, in other words, no sanctifying grace. The rest are called "sacraments of the living," because they are received lawfully only by those who already have supernatural life.

336. **What sin do they commit who approach the sacraments of the living in conscious mortal sin?**
Those who approach the sacraments of the living in conscious mortal sin not only receive no grace but also commit a grave sin of sacrilege.

337. **Can sanctifying grace or reconciliation with God be obtained even before receiving the sacraments of the dead?**
Even before receiving the sacraments of the dead, sanctifying grace or reconciliation with God can be obtained by making an act of perfect contrition; yet, even in this case, the reconciliation is to be ascribed to this contrition only so far as it includes a wish to be baptized or to go to confession.[318]

[317] Cf. TCCI 7:185

[318] Cf. Council of Trent, Session 14, "Doctrine on the Sacrament of Penance," Ch. 4

338. **What do you understand by this wish to receive the sacraments?**
This wish to receive the sacraments must be a genuine, serious, and solid determination to receive them.

339. **Which sacraments can be received only once?**
The sacraments that can be received only once are baptism, confirmation, and holy order, for these stamp an indelible character on the soul.[319]

340. **What do you mean by "sacramental character"?**
By "sacramental character," we mean an indelible spiritual sign stamped on the soul; even in the next life, it remains, to the glory of those who are saved, to the shame of the lost.[320]

341. **What effect has sacramental character?**
Sacramental character has a twofold effect: it serves to distinguish one person from another; and it fits us to receive or to exercise some sacred rite.[321]

342. **What character is imprinted by the three aforesaid sacraments?**

1. Baptism imprints a character whereby a person becomes a member of the mystical body of Christ—that is, of the Church—and is made fit to receive other sacraments.
2. Confirmation imprints a character whereby a person becomes a soldier of Christ, and so makes public profession of his faith.
3. Holy order imprints a character whereby a man becomes a minister of Christ with the power to make and administer the sacraments.[322]

319 Cf. Augustine, *Contra Epistolam Parmeniani*, Bk. 2, n. 28

320 Cf. *Codex Juris Canonici*, Can. 732

321 Cf. Council of Florence, Session 8 (November 22, 1439), "Bull of Union with the Armenians"; Council of Trent, Session 7, "On the Sacraments in General," Can. 9; Innocent III, Epistle *Majores Ecclesiae Causas*, A.D. 1201, to Humbert, the archbishop of Arles; TCCI 7:188-189

322 Cf. TCCI 7:189

343. **Why are godparents appointed in baptism and confirmation?**
Godparents are appointed in baptism and confirmation in order that they may always watch over those baptized or confirmed and may see to their Christian education, more especially if their parents are dead or neglect their duty.[323]

344. **Does any relationship arise from valid baptism and confirmation?**
From valid baptism, a spiritual relationship arises between the baptized person and the person baptizing him, also between the person baptized and his godparent; from valid confirmation, there arises a spiritual relationship between the person confirmed and his godparent.[324]

345. **Are all the sacraments equally necessary?**
All the sacraments are not equally necessary. Baptism is necessary for all; penance for those who, after being baptized, have fallen into mortal sin; holy order is necessary for the Church as a whole, but not for individuals; matrimony is necessary for the human race, for the establishment of the Christian family.[325]

346. **Which is the most excellent of all the sacraments?**
The most excellent of all the sacraments is the Holy Eucharist, in which is contained not only grace but the author of grace, Jesus Christ our Lord, who is really, truly, and substantially contained therein.[326]

347. **What do you understand by *sacramentals*?**
By *sacramentals*, we mean certain actions or things, after the pattern of the sacraments, which the Church is wont to make use of for obtaining by her

[323] Cf. *Codex Juris Canonici*, Can. 762ff. The Eastern Church does not have godfathers for baptism or confirmation.

[324] Cf. *Codex Juris Canonici*, Can. 768, 797, 1079

[325] Cf. TCCI 7:183

[326] Cf. *Summa Theologiae*, III, q. 65, a. 3

prayers certain effects, mainly spiritual ones—for example, exorcisms and devout consecrations and blessings of persons or things.[327]

INDIVIDUAL SACRAMENTS

BAPTISM

348. **What is the sacrament of baptism?**
The sacrament of baptism is a sacrament of cleansing instituted by Jesus Christ; by it, the person baptized is made a member of the true Church of Jesus Christ, obtains remission of original sin and of all actual sins if he has committed any, with all the punishment due to them, and becomes capable of receiving the other sacraments.[328]

349. **What is the matter and what the form of baptism?**
The remote matter of baptism is natural water; the proximate matter is the washing of the body by the water; the form consists in the words: "I baptize thee in the name of the Father and of the Son and of the Holy Ghost."[329]

350. **What, then, is meant when it is said in the new testament that the apostles baptized in the name of Christ?**
When it is said in the new testament that the apostles baptized in the name of Christ, the meaning is that the apostles conferred not the baptism

[327] Cf. *Codex Juris Canonici*, Can. 1144ff

[328] Cf. Mk 16:16; Acts 2:38; Rom 6:3-6; 1 Cor 6:11; Col 2:11-13; Ti 3:5; 1 Pt 3:21; Pius X, Decree *Lamentabili sane*, July 3, 1907, the forty-second condemned Proposition; Basil, *Homily 13*, n. 5

[329] To secure washing of the body, the water must touch the body, especially the head; it should flow in sufficient quantity to enable one to say that a person is really "washed" (cf. Mt 28:19; Jn 3:5; Acts 8:36; Eph 5:26; Heb 10:22; Council of Vienne, *Constitutio de Trinitate et Fide*, against the errors of Peter Oliva; Council of Florence, Session 8 [November 22, 1439], "Bull of Union with the Armenians"; Council of Trent, Session 7, "On the Sacraments in General," Can. 2; Innocent III, Epistle *Non ut apponeres*, March 1, 1206; *The Didache*, Ch. 7). In the Eastern Church, the form of words used is: "The servant of Christ is (or "let the servant of Christ be") baptized in the name of the Father and of the Son and of the Holy Ghost."

instituted by John the Baptist, but that instituted by Christ, with the form of words which our Lord and Savior had ordered.[330]

351. **Who is the minister of baptism?**

The ordinary minister of baptism is a priest, but its administration is reserved to the parish priest or to some priest delegated by him or by the bishop of the diocese; the extraordinary minister is a deacon with the permission of the bishop or the parish priest of the place, but this is not conceded save for very good reasons.

352. **Who can confer baptism in case of necessity?**

In case of necessity, anyone can confer baptism without the ceremonies. If, however, a priest is present, a deacon yields to him, a subdeacon to a deacon, a layman to a cleric, a woman to a man unless perhaps for modesty's sake it should prove more fitting for a woman to baptize than for a man, or if again it should prove that the woman knows the form and the method of baptizing better than the man.[331]

353. **How should the washing be done to secure the validity of the baptism?**

To secure the validity of the baptism, the washing should be done either by immersion in the water, or by pouring the water, or again by sprinkling it, according to the rites approved in that particular part of the Church.[332]

[330] Cf. TCCI 7:198

[331] Cf. Fourth Lateran Council, Const. 1; Council of Florence, Session 8 (November 22, 1439), "Bull of Union with the Armenians"; Augustine, *Contra Epistolam Parmeniani*, Bk. 2, n. 29; *Codex Juris Canonici*, Can. 738, 741, 742

[332] Cf. *Codex Juris Canonici*, Can. 758; TCCI 7:198-199. Baptism by aspersion, however, has fallen into disuse on the ground that it might well be difficult to say whether a person had received a bodily washing or not. Consequently, a person who has been baptized by aspersion should be rebaptized conditionally. Those who teach the catechism should explain how baptism is to be given in case of necessity.

354. **When should children be baptized?**
Children are to be baptized as soon as possible; parents and others who have care of children sin gravely if they allow the children to die without baptism, or if they put off their baptism without good reason.[333]

355. **With what dispositions should grown-up people come to be baptized?**
Grown-up people should come to be baptized knowing well what they are doing and after having been properly instructed. Moreover, if they have committed mortal sins, they must at least make an act of attrition for them.[334]

356. **What if a grown-up person is baptized in a state of conscious mortal sin and has not even attrition for it?**
A grown-up person who is baptized in a state of conscious mortal sin for which he has not even attrition is validly baptized and receives the baptismal character; but he commits a grave sin of sacrilege, nor does he obtain sanctifying grace until he has secured the remission of his sins by contrition or by attrition cooperating with his baptism.[335]

357. **What is the duty of a baptized person?**
The duty of a baptized person is to make profession of his faith in Christ in the Catholic Church, and to keep the commandments of Christ and of the Catholic Church.[336]

[333] Cf. Council of Florence, Session 11 (Feb. 4, 1442), "Decree for the Jacobites"; Pius X, Decree *Lamentabili sane*, July 3, 1907, the forty-third condemned Proposition; *Codex Juris Canonici*, Can. 770

[334] Cf. Acts 2:38; *Roman Ritual*, I, iii, 1; *Codex Juris Canonici*, Can. 752, n. 1; TCCI 7:210-212; Aquinas, *Sentences*, IV, d. 6, q. 1

[335] Cf. *Summa Theologiae*, III, q. 69, a. 10; Alphonsus Liguori, *Theologia Moralis*, Bk. 6, i, 3, n. 87

[336] Cf. Rom 6:3-13; Gal 3:27; Col 2:12; Council of Trent, Session 7, "On the Sacraments in General," Can. 7

358. **Is baptism necessary to all for salvation?**
Baptism is necessary to all for salvation, for Jesus Christ said: "Unless a man be born again of water and the Holy Ghost, he cannot enter into the kingdom of God."[337]

359. **What of the souls of those who die without baptism but in a state of original sin only?**
The souls of those who die without baptism but in a state of original sin only lack the beatific vision of God, but do not suffer other penalties such as are reserved for personal sins.[338]

360. **Can anything take the place of baptism?**
Both martyrdom and an act of love of God can take the place of baptism; but in such an act of love of God, there is necessarily implied perfect contrition for sin and a desire to be baptized; moreover, only baptism with water can confer the baptismal character and render a person capable of receiving the other sacraments.[339]

361. **What precisely is the martyrdom which can take the place of baptism?**
The martyrdom which can take the place of baptism consists in death unjustly inflicted, and—by a grown-up person—accepted for Christ's sake, in testimony to his faith and Christian virtue.[340]

[337] Jn 3:5; Cf. Second Council of Carthage (A.D. 418), Can. 2; Council of Florence, Session 11 (Feb. 4, 1442), "Decree for the Jacobites"; Council of Trent, Session 7, "On Baptism," Can. 5; Cyril of Jerusalem, *Catechetical Lecture 3*, n. 10

[338] Cf. Innocent III, Epistle *Majores Ecclesiae Causas*, A.D. 1201, to Humbert, the archbishop of Arles; Pius VI, Constitution *Auctorem Fidei*, against the errors of the Synod of Pistoia, Aug. 28, 1794, the twenty-sixth condemned Proposition; Pius IX, Epistle *Quanto conficiamur*, Aug. 10, 1863, to the bishops of Italy; Aquinas, *Sentences*, II, d. 33, q. 2, a. 1-2; *Disputed Questions, De Malo*, q. 5, a. 2-3. The state of these souls and the place where they dwell is spoken of as "limbo," but it is not to be confounded with the "limbo of the patriarchs," see above, q. 106.

[339] Cf. Mt 10:32; 16:25; Mk 8:35; Lk 9:24; 12:8; Jn 14:21, 23; Innocent II, Epistle *Apostolicam Sedem*, to the bishop of Cremona; Fulgentius, *De Fide*, n. 41; *Summa Theologiae*, III, q. 68, a. 2; q. 69, a. 4, rep. 2. Hence martyrdom is often called the "baptism of blood," and acts of love of God are called the "baptism of desire."

[340] Cf. *Summa Theologiae*, II-II, q. 124, a. 1

362. Why is the name of some saint given us at baptism?

The name of some saint is given to us at baptism in order that we may have a special patron and also may find in his life an example of virtue.[341]

Confirmation

363. What is the sacrament of confirmation?

The sacrament of confirmation is a sacrament instituted by Jesus Christ to confer special grace and the gifts of the Holy Ghost, that by them the person confirmed may be strengthened so as to enable him, as a perfect soldier of Christ, to make profession of his faith by word and deed.[342]

364. What is the matter of confirmation?

The remote matter of confirmation is chrism, or olive oil mixed with balsam and blessed by a bishop. The minister of this sacrament imposes his hands on the person to be confirmed and anoints him with chrism on the forehead in the form of a cross; this anointing is the proximate matter of confirmation.[343]

365. What is the form of confirmation?

The form of confirmation consists in the words used by the minister while applying the matter, namely, "I sign thee with the sign of the cross, and I

[341] Cf. *Codex Juris Canonici*, Can. 761. We must not forget that, in baptism, we made certain promises to God, and that when the priest handed to us the white garment, he said to us: "Receive this white garment, and be careful to bring it unspotted before the tribunal of our Lord Jesus Christ, so that you may have eternal life."

[342] Cf. Acts 8:14-17; 19:5-6; Second Council of Lyons, *Profession of Faith by Michael Palaeologus*; Council of Florence, Session 8 (November 22, 1439), "Bull of Union with the Armenians"; Council of Trent, Session 7, "On Confirmation," Can. 1-3; Innocent III, Epistle *Cum venisset*, Feb. 25, 1204, *ad Basilium Archiepiscopum Trinovitanum*; Pius X, Decree *Lamentabili sane*, July 3, 1907, the forty-fourth condemned Proposition; Cyril of Jerusalem, *Catechetical Lecture 21*, n. 3; Cyril of Alexandria, *Homily on Joel*, n. 32; *Summa Theologiae*, III, q. 72, a. 7; TCCI 7:226ff

[343] Cf. TCCI 7:230-232

confirm thee with the chrism of salvation, in the name of the Father and of the Son and of the Holy Ghost."[344]

366. **Who is the minister of confirmation?**

The ordinary minister of confirmation is a bishop, the extraordinary minister is a priest legitimately delegated for the purpose.[345]

367. **Besides being baptized and in a state of grace, what is required in those who receive confirmation?**

Besides being baptized and in a state of grace, those who receive confirmation must, if they have the use of reason, know the chief mysteries of faith and other truths regarding this sacrament.

368. **What if a person is confirmed in a state of conscious mortal sin?**

If a person is confirmed in a state of conscious mortal sin, he is guilty of the sin of sacrilege, but he is validly confirmed; at the same time, he will receive the grace of the sacrament only when he has obtained the remission of his sins, either by attrition combined with sacramental confession or by contrition combined with a desire to go to confession.[346]

369. **At what age is confirmation administered?**

Although in the Latin Church confirmation is quite fittingly deferred until children are about seven years of age, yet it can be conferred earlier if a child is in danger of death or it is thought to be expedient for just and grave reasons.[347]

[344] Cf. *Codex Juris Canonici*, Can. 780-781. In the Eastern Church, priests also bless the chrism and administer the sacrament without any imposition of hands and under the form: "The seal of the gift of the Holy Spirit."

[345] Cf. *Codex Juris Canonici*, Can. 782

[346] This reply is true also for the sacraments of extreme unction, holy order, and matrimony; for the sacrament of penance, see below, q. 445ff.

[347] Cf. *Codex Juris Canonici*, Can. 788. In the Eastern Churches, confirmation is generally given with baptism.

370. **Is confirmation absolutely necessary for salvation?**
Confirmation is not absolutely necessary for salvation, but it is wrong to neglect it, because it is a means for obtaining salvation more easily and fully.[348]

The Holy Eucharist

371. **What is the Holy Eucharist?**
The Holy Eucharist ("good grace" or "thanksgiving") is the most divine gift of our Redeemer, the mystery of faith; in it, under the appearances of bread and wine, Jesus Christ himself is contained, offered, and received; it is the sacrifice as well as the sacrament of the new law.[349]

The Real Presence of Jesus Christ in the Holy Eucharist

372. **When did Jesus Christ institute the Holy Eucharist?**
Jesus Christ instituted the Holy Eucharist at the last supper when, before he suffered, taking bread, he gave thanks, and gave to his disciples, saying: "Take ye and eat, this is my body"; and, taking the chalice, he gave it to them, saying: "Drink, this is my blood"; adding: "Do this in commemoration of me."[350]

373. **What took place when Jesus Christ pronounced the words of consecration over the bread and wine?**
When Jesus Christ pronounced the words of consecration over the bread and wine, there took place a wonderful and unique change of the whole

[348] Cf. TCCI 7:235. Remember that you are a soldier of Christ and that you have to fight his battles. Do not, then, give in to timidity, but boldly profess your faith by deeds as well as words; you should regard it as an honor when you have to put up with contempt or possibly persecution for it.

[349] Cf. Second Lateran Council, Can. 23; Council of Trent, Session 13, "Decree concerning the Most Holy Sacrament of the Eucharist," Ch. 1; Leo XIII, Encyclical *Mirae caritatis*, May 28, 1902; *Codex Juris Canonici*, Can. 801; TCCI 7:241-243

[350] Lk 22:19-20; Cf. Mt 26:26-28; Mk 14:22-24; 1 Cor 11:23-25; Council of Trent, Session 13, "Decree concerning the Most Holy Sacrament of the Eucharist," Ch. 1

substance of the bread into the body and of the whole substance of the wine into the blood of Jesus Christ, although the appearances of bread and wine remained.[351]

374. **What is this change called?**
This change is called "transubstantiation."[352]

375. **What do you mean by the "appearances" (species) of bread and wine?**
By the "appearances" of bread and wine, we mean the quantity, shape, smell, color, taste, and everything else in bread and wine that affects the senses.

376. **What did Jesus Christ intend by the added words, "Do this in commemoration of me"?**
By the added words, "Do this in commemoration of me," Jesus Christ made his apostles priests of the new covenant and commanded them and their successors in the priesthood in like manner to consecrate, offer, and administer his body and blood under the appearances of bread and wine.[353]

377. **When do priests exercise this power and carry out this command?**
Priests exercise this power and carry out this command when, acting in the Person of Jesus Christ, they offer the Sacrifice of the Mass.

[351] Cf. Council of Trent, Session 13, "Decree concerning the Most Holy Sacrament of the Eucharist," Ch. 4; Justin Martyr, *First Apology*, Ch. 66; Ephraem, *In Hebdomadam Sanctam*, iv, 4, 6; Athanasius, Fragment of a *Sermon to the Baptized*; Cyril of Jerusalem, *Catechetical Lecture 22*, n. 1-3, 6, 9 and *Catechetical Lecture 23*, n. 7; Chrysostom, *Homily 82 on Matthew*, Ch. 4; John Damascene, *An Exposition of the Orthodox Faith*, Bk. 4, Ch. 13

[352] Cf. Fourth Lateran Council, Const. 1; Second Council of Lyons, *Profession of Faith by Michael Palaeologus*; Council of Constance, Session 8, Prop. 1-3; Council of Trent, Session 13, "Decree concerning the Most Holy Sacrament of the Eucharist," Ch. 1; Can. 2; Benedict XII, *Ex libello, Jamdudum*; Pius VI, Constitution *Auctorem Fidei*, against the errors of the Synod of Pistoia, Aug. 28, 1794, the twenty-ninth condemned Proposition; TCCI 7:261-265

[353] Cf. Lk 22:19; 1 Cor 11:24-25; Council of Trent, Session 22, "Doctrine on the Sacrifice of the Mass," Ch. 1; Can. 2

378. **What happens, then, when at Mass the priest pronounces the words of consecration over the bread and wine?**
When the priest in the Mass pronounces the words of consecration over the bread and wine, the body and blood of our Lord Jesus Christ, together with his soul and his Godhead, become truly, really, and substantially present under the appearances of bread and wine.

379. **After the consecration, is there present under the appearances of bread only the body, and under the appearances of wine only the blood of Christ?**
After the consecration, there is present under the appearances of bread not only Christ's body, nor under the appearances of wine only his blood, but under the appearances of either, and in every single portion of them, the whole and entire Jesus Christ, God and man.[354]

380. **Does Christ, when under the sacramental species or appearances, cease to be in heaven?**
When existing under the sacramental species, Christ does not cease to be in heaven, but is at the same time in heaven and under the sacramental species.

381. **How long does Jesus Christ remain under the sacramental species?**
Jesus Christ remains under the sacramental species not only when he is received but so long as those species remain uncorrupted.

382. **What is the proper matter out of which the Holy Eucharist is made?**
The proper matter for the Holy Eucharist is wheaten bread and wine of the grape.[355]

[354] Cf. Jn 6:58; 1 Cor 11:26-27; Council of Trent, Session 13, "Decree concerning the Most Holy Sacrament of the Eucharist," Ch. 3; Can. 3; TCCI 7:260-261

[355] By the Church's decree, unleavened bread has to be used in the Western Churches, but in several Eastern Churches, leavened bread is used. Also, before the consecration, a small quantity of water has to be added to the wine (see Council of Florence, "Decree for the Greeks," and also "Bull of Union with the Armenians"; Council of Trent, Session 22, "Doctrine on the Sacrifice of the Mass," Ch. 7).

383. **What form of words must necessarily be used in consecrating the Holy Eucharist?**

The words that must necessarily be used in consecrating the Holy Eucharist are the very words that Christ the Lord pronounced over the bread and wine at the last supper, and these the priest, acting in the Person of Christ, repeats when saying Mass.[356]

The Sacrifice of the Mass

384. **What is a sacrifice?**

A sacrifice is the offering of something that comes within the sphere of the senses by producing some change in it—an offering made to God alone in testimony of the supreme honor and reverence which man owes to God as his Creator, Lord, and last end.[357]

385. **Is the Mass the true and especial sacrifice of the new law?**

The Mass is the true and especial sacrifice of the new law; in it, Jesus Christ, by the ministry of the priest, offers his body and blood to God the Father, under the appearances of bread and wine, by a mystical immolation in an unbloody manner.[358]

[356] Cf. Council of Florence, Session 8 (November 22, 1439), "Bull of Union with the Armenians"; TCCI 7:250-254. Our Lord Jesus Christ at the last supper, "having loved his own who were in the world, loved them unto the end" (Jn 13:1), and showed this infinite love for them by instituting the Holy Eucharist, or, as the Council of Trent expresses it: "He poured out the wealth of his divine love for us men, leaving us a memorial of his wondrous doings" (Session 13, "Decree concerning the Most Holy Sacrament of the Eucharist," Ch. 2), for, as a devout writer says: "Though omnipotent, he could do no more; though infinitely wise, he knew of nothing greater that he could give; though abounding in riches, he had no more to give." We should, then, devoutly recall this pledge of God's love, and so excite in ourselves ever-growing feelings of love for him who has pursued us with such love, nor ever ceases so to pursue us.

[357] Cf. *Summa Theologiae*, II-II, q. 85, a. 1-4

[358] Cf. Ps 109:4; Mal 1:2; Lk 22:19-20; 1 Cor 11:24-25; Heb 13:10; Fourth Lateran Council, Const. 1; Council of Trent, Session 22, "Doctrine on the Sacrifice of the Mass," Ch. 1; Irenaeus, *Against Heresies*, Bk. 4, Ch. 17, n. 5

386. **Why did Christ institute this wondrous sacrifice?**
Christ instituted this wondrous sacrifice in order to leave to his Church a visible sacrifice such as the nature of man requires, whereby the bloody sacrifice which has been offered once and for all on Calvary should be represented, and the memory of it abide to the end of time, and also that the saving power of that sacrifice might be applied for the remission of those sins into which we daily fall.[359]

387. **How does the Mass represent the sacrifice of the cross?**
The Mass represents the sacrifice of the cross in that the separate consecration of the bread and wine represents, by force of the words used, that real separation of his body and blood which Christ Jesus our Lord underwent in his bloody death on the cross.[360]

388. **Is the Mass merely a bare representation of the sacrifice of the cross?**
The Mass is not merely a bare representation of the sacrifice of the cross, but it is the actual sacrifice of the cross which is renewed; for the victim is one and the same, now offering himself through the ministry of his priests, as he then offered himself on the cross, only the manner of offering being different.[361]

[359] Cf. Lk 22:19; 1 Cor 11:24-26; Council of Trent, Session 22, "Doctrine on the Sacrifice of the Mass," Ch. 1; Gregory the Great, *Dialogues*, Bk. 4, Ch. 58

[360] Cf. Council of Trent, Session 13, "Decree concerning the Most Holy Sacrament of the Eucharist," Ch. 3; *Summa Theologiae*, III, q. 74, a. 1; TCCI 7:280-285

In other words, by the consecration of the bread the body of Christ is present by force of the very words used, *Hoc est corpus meum*, and in the consecration of the wine the blood is present by force of the words, *Hic est calix sanguinis mei*; but the precious blood, as well as the soul of Christ, are present at the consecration of the bread, as also Christ's body and his soul in the consecration of the wine, owing to the natural connection and concomitance whereby the various parts of Christ our Lord—who "rising from the dead dieth now no more" (Rom 6:9)—are intimately knit together. His Godhead, too, is rendered present by the consecration of either element, owing to the marvelous hypostatic union subsisting between his Godhead and his body and soul. Moreover, this mystical separation (by the twofold consecration of the separate elements) represents that real separation which took place in the sacrifice of the cross.

[361] Cf. Council of Trent, Session 22, "Doctrine on the Sacrifice of the Mass," Ch. 2; TCCI 7:280-285

389. **How are the fruits of the sacrifice of the cross applied to us in the Sacrifice of the Mass?**

The fruits of the sacrifice of the cross are applied to us in the Sacrifice of the Mass in that God, appeased by this immolation, bestows on us the graces that Jesus Christ merited for us at the price of his blood.[362]

390. **With what object is the Sacrifice of the Mass offered?**

The Sacrifice of the Mass is offered:

1. To adore God, whence the Mass is called the "sacrifice of praise."
2. To thank God for his great glory and for the benefit he has bestowed upon us, whence the Mass is called the "Eucharistic sacrifice."
3. To obtain other benefits, whence the Mass is called an "impetratory sacrifice."
4. To obtain God's mercy for the living, for their sins and the penalties incurred, and for the souls detained in purgatory, whence the Mass is called a "propitiatory sacrifice."[363]

391. **To whom is the Sacrifice of the Mass offered?**

The Sacrifice of the Mass is offered to God alone, since supreme dominion, such as is implied in *sacrifice*, belongs to God alone.

392. **Why does the Church also offer the Sacrifice of theMass in honor of our Blessed Lady and the saints?**

Although the Church has the custom of offering the Sacrifice of the Mass in honor of our Lady and the saints, yet she does not offer the sacrifice to them but to God alone, as a thanksgiving for the victory won by them and to implore their patronage with God.[364]

393. **To whose advantage is the Sacrifice of the Mass applied?**

Every Mass, since it is the sacrifice of the Catholic Church offered in the public ministrations of the Church, is applied not for the advantage of

[362] Cf. Ibid.

[363] Cf. Cyril of Jerusalem, *Catechetical Lecture 23*, n. 10

[364] Cf. Council of Trent, Session 22, Can. 5

the celebrant only, but for the common advantage of the faithful, whether living or dead, and more particularly for those whom the celebrant commemorates in the Mass.[365]

394. **Can the priest apply the Mass to some particular person or for some particular object?**
The priest can apply the Mass to some particular person, whether living or dead, also for some particular object; whence it follows that, other things being equal, that Mass avails in an especial manner for the particular person or object specified.[366]

395. **What is the best way of assisting at Mass?**
The best way of assisting at Mass is for the faithful who are present to join with the priest in offering the divine victim to God, calling to mind the sacrifice of the cross, and uniting themselves to Jesus Christ by sacramental or at least spiritual Communion.[367]

The Sacrament of the Holy Eucharist

396. **What is the sacrament of the Holy Eucharist?**
The sacrament of the Holy Eucharist is a sacrament instituted by Christ wherein Jesus Christ himself, the author of grace, is truly, really, and substantially contained under the appearances of bread and wine for the spiritual refreshment of our souls.[368]

[365] Cf. Council of Trent, Session 22, "Doctrine on the Sacrifice of the Mass," Ch. 6; TCCI 7:284-285

[366] Cf. Pius VI, Constitution *Auctorem Fidei*, against the errors of the Synod of Pistoia, Aug. 28, 1794, the thirtieth condemned Proposition

[367] There is no practice of the Christian religion which is more holy in itself, none which gives greater glory to God, none which more avails for the salvation of souls than the Holy Sacrifice of the Mass, for in it is enshrined the whole and entire fruit of that redemption which Christ effected on the cross. We should, then, be present frequently at this glorious sacrifice, and try to assist at it with the same devotion as we should have felt had we been present on Calvary.

[368] Cf. Jn 6:54-58; TCCI 7:243ff, 281-282

397. **Why did Christ institute the sacrament of the Holy Eucharist?**

Christ instituted the sacrament of the Holy Eucharist:

1. That out of his deep love for us he might ever remain present in our midst and thus induce us to love and worship him.
2. That he might be united to us in Holy Communion, might be the heavenly food of our souls, and thus enable us to safeguard and preserve our spiritual life, and finally be our viaticum for our journey to eternity at the close of our lives.[369]

398. **How is the sacrament of the Holy Eucharist distinguished from the sacrifice?**

The sacrament of the Eucharist is distinguished from the sacrifice:

1. Because the sacrament is completed by the consecration and remains, whereas the whole idea of *sacrifice* consists in its being offered up—hence the sacred host, when in the tabernacle or when taken to the sick, is to be regarded as a sacrament and not as a sacrifice.
2. Because the sacrament is the cause of merit in those who receive it and is for the profit of their souls, whereas the sacrifice is not only a source of merit but also has the power of making satisfaction.[370]

399. **In order to receive the Holy Eucharist worthily, what is required?**

In order to receive the Holy Eucharist worthily, in addition to being baptized (for baptism is requisite for the reception of any other sacrament) and in a state of grace (which is requisite for the reception of all sacraments of the living), we must also, under pain of grave sin, keep the natural fast.[371]

[369] Cf. Jn 6:50ff; 1 Cor 10:16-17; Council of Trent, Session 13, "Decree concerning the Most Holy Sacrament of the Eucharist," Ch. 2; Ignatius of Antioch, *Epistle to the Ephesians*, Ch. 20; Irenaeus, *Against Heresies*, Bk. 5, Ch. 2, n. 3; Chrysostom, *Homily 46 on John*, Ch. 3; *Homily 24 on First Corinthians*, Ch. 2; *Summa Theologiae*, III, q. 79, a. 4, 6; TCCI 7:281-282

[370] Cf. TCCI 7:281-282

[371] Cf. 1 Cor 11:27-29; Chrysostom, *Homily 82 on Matthew*, Ch. 5

400. **What should a person do who, when about to receive Holy Communion, discovers that he is in a state of mortal sin?**
A person who, when about to receive Holy Communion, discovers that he is in a state of mortal sin, should, even though he feels that he is truly contrite, go to confession first. But if there is some urgent necessity and there is no confessor at hand, he should try to make an act of perfect contrition before approaching Holy Communion.[372]

401. **What does the "natural fast" mean?**
The "natural fast" means that, from midnight until the time of receiving Holy Communion, we take nothing by way of food or drink, or even medicine.[373]

402. **What sin do we commit if we receive Holy Communion not fasting?**
If we receive Holy Communion not fasting, we commit a grave sin of sacrilege.

403. **When is Holy Communion allowed without fasting?**
Holy Communion is allowed without fasting when there is danger of death, or when it is necessary in order to prevent some irreverence to the Blessed Sacrament.[374]

404. **Are any invalids allowed to receive Holy Communion not fasting?**
Invalids who have been ill in bed for a month and have no certain hope of quick recovery are allowed, with the prudent advice of their confessor, to receive Holy Communion once or twice a week, even though they have taken medicine or something to drink beforehand.[375]

[372] Cf. Council of Trent, Session 13, "Decree concerning the Most Holy Sacrament of the Eucharist," Ch. 7; *Codex Juris Canonici*, Can. 856

[373] Cf. *Codex Juris Canonici*, Can. 858, par. 2; TCCI 7:274. See, too, *Codex Juris Canonici*, Can. 33: "For receiving Holy Communion…even when the local time differs, each one is at liberty to follow either the local time, whether it is the true time or the mean time, or the legal time, whether that of the district or based on some other computation."

[374] Cf. *Codex Juris Canonici*, Can. 33

[375] Cf. *Codex Juris Canonici*, Can. 33, par. 2

405. **What is necessary for receiving Holy Communion devoutly?**
For receiving Holy Communion devoutly, it is necessary to make careful preparation and also fit thanksgiving according to our capacity, condition, and duties.[376]

406. **In what does preparation for Holy Communion consist?**
Preparation for Holy Communion consists in meditating attentively and devoutly for a while on what we are about to receive and in making diligent acts of faith, hope, charity, and contrition.[377]

407. **In what does thanksgiving after Holy Communion consist?**
Thanksgiving after Holy Communion consists in meditating attentively and devoutly for a while on what we have received and in making acts of faith, hope, and charity, with good resolutions, acts of gratitude, and petitions.

408. **What ought we particularly to ask for after Holy Communion?**
After Holy Communion, we should particularly ask our Lord for the graces necessary for our own and our neighbor's salvation, more especially the grace of final perseverance, for the Church that she may prevail against her enemies, and for the souls of the faithful departed.

409. **What effects does Holy Communion produce in those who receive it worthily and devoutly?**
In those who receive it worthily and devoutly, Holy Communion produces the following effects:

1. It increases sanctifying grace and the fervor of charity.
2. It remits venial sins.

[376] See the Decree of the Sacred Congregation of the Council, *Sacra Tridentina Synodus*, Dec. 20, 1905.

[377] Cf. Basil, *The Shorter Rules*, q. 172; TCCI 7:270ff

3. It does much to secure final perseverance by lessening concupiscence, preserving them from mortal sin, and strengthening them in the practice of good works.[378]

410. **Besides the precept of Easter Communion, is there any obligation to receive it at any other time?**
Besides the precept of Easter Communion, there is an obligation to receive it when in danger of death from whatever cause it may arise.[379]

411. **When a person has already received Holy Communion, can he receive it again on the same day?**
When a person has already received Communion, he can receive it again on the same day as viaticum if he should prove to be in danger of death; also when it may be necessary in order to prevent some irreverence toward the Blessed Sacrament.[380]

412. **How should we worship Jesus Christ present in the Blessed Sacrament?**
We ought to worship Jesus Christ present in the Blessed Sacrament:
1. By adoring him with the most profound reverence.
2. By repaying him love for love.
3. By asking him with supreme confidence for the graces we need.[381]

[378] Cf. Jn 6:48ff; TCCI 7:267-270

[379] Cf. *Codex Juris Canonici*, Can. 864, par. 1-2. Those who have corporal or spiritual care of the sick should be careful not to delay in seeing that they receive the viaticum; they should also be careful to see that the sick receive Holy Communion while in full possession of their faculties.

[380] Cf. *Codex Juris Canonici*, Can. 857-858

[381] As often as you enter a church where the Blessed Sacrament is reserved, remind yourself that you are in the presence of Jesus Christ who is God himself and whom the angels adore. Beware, then, of any irreverence. For this is your truest friend, and he dwells there day and night out of love for you. Pay frequent visits to him there, and thank him for the immense love he has shown you. His hands are full of heavenly gifts, and his only desire is to give them to you if you will but ask him.

Penance

413. **What is the sacrament of penance?**

The sacrament of penance is a sacrament instituted by Jesus Christ for the faithful, so that, as often as they fall into sin after baptism, they may be reconciled to God.[382]

414. **When did Jesus Christ institute this sacrament?**

Jesus Christ instituted this sacrament more especially when, after his resurrection, he breathed on his assembled disciples and said, "Receive ye the Holy Ghost; whose sins ye shall forgive, they are forgiven, and whose sins ye shall retain, they are retained."[383]

415. **What special character did Christ attach to this sacrament?**

Christ instituted this sacrament in the form of a judicial tribunal in which the confessor is the judge and the penitent is both prosecutor and witness; the material with which the tribunal is concerned is sins committed subsequent to baptism and now confessed by the penitent.

416. **Who is the lawful minister of the sacrament of penance?**

The lawful minister of the sacrament of penance is a priest duly approved for hearing confessions; all the faithful have the right to confess their sins to any lawfully approved confessor they prefer, even though he may belong to some different rite.[384]

[382] Cf. Council of Trent, Session 14, "Doctrine on the Sacrament of Penance," Ch. 1; "On the Most Holy Sacrament of Penance," Can. 1

[383] Jn 20:22-23; Cf. Mt 16:19; 18:18; Council of Trent, Session 14, "Doctrine on the Sacrament of Penance," Ch. 1; Pius X, Decree *Lamentabili sane*, July 3, 1907, the forty-seventh condemned Proposition; Chrysostom, *On the Priesthood*, Bk. 3, n. 5

[384] Cf. *Codex Juris Canonici*, Can. 905

417. **What are the parts of this sacrament?**
The parts of this sacrament are the acts of the penitent, constituting its matter, namely: contrition, confession, and satisfaction; and the absolution given by a lawful minister, which is its form.[385]

418. **In what sense are examination of conscience and a firm purpose of amendment included in these three acts of the penitent?**
Examination of conscience and a firm purpose of amendment are included in the three acts of the penitent since an examination of one's conscience must necessarily precede the above acts, while contrition without a firm purpose of amendment is meaningless.

419. **What sins are the necessary material of this sacrament?**
The necessary material of this sacrament is all mortal sins committed after baptism, and not already directly forgiven by the power of the keys.

420. **Why are the above sins called the "necessary material" of this sacrament?**
The above sins are called the "necessary material" of this sacrament, because there is a strict obligation of confessing them.

421. **What sins constitute the free and sufficient material for the sacrament?**
All sins committed subsequent to baptism, whether venial sins or even mortal sins already confessed for which the penitent has received absolution, are the free and sufficient material for this sacrament.

422. **Why are the above sins called the "free and sufficient material" for this sacrament?**
The above sins are called the "free and sufficient material" for this sacrament, because they can be submitted to the tribunal of penance, and it is expedient that they should be, though it is not of obligation.[386]

[385] Cf. Council of Trent, Session 14, "Doctrine on the Sacrament of Penance," Ch. 3; "On the Most Holy Sacrament of Penance," Can. 4; *Roman Ritual, De Sacramento Poenitentiae*, III, i, 1; TCCI 7:292-294

[386] Cf. Mt 16:19; 18:18; Jn 20:22-23; Council of Trent, Session 14, "Doctrine on the

The Acts of the Penitent

Examination of Conscience

423. **What should a penitent do before approaching the tribunal of penance?**
Before approaching the tribunal of penance, the penitent should make a careful examination of his conscience.

424. **What is examination of conscience?**
Examination of conscience means recalling as carefully as possible the sins committed since the last good confession.

425. **How is this examination of conscience to be made?**
In examining his conscience, the penitent first asks for the help of God, and then carefully calls to mind any mortal sins committed by thought, word, deed, or omission against the commandments of God and the Church, and against the special duties of his state.

426. **What should we try to recall in examining our conscience?**
In examining our conscience, we should try to recall the number of our sins, and their character and any circumstances that may alter their character.

427. **What circumstances alter the character of our sins and should therefore necessarily be confessed?**
Circumstances that alter the character of our sins and should therefore necessarily be confessed are such as turn a venial sin into a mortal sin—when a lie, for example, does grave harm to our neighbor—or when a mortal sin is multiplied by circumstances—when, for example, a theft is committed in a sacred place or when the thing stolen is sacred.[387]

Sacrament of Penance," Ch. 3; "On the Most Holy Sacrament of Penance," Can. 7; *Codex Juris Canonici*, Can. 901-902

[387] Cf. TCCI 7:313

Contrition and Firm Purpose of Amendment

428. **What is contrition for sin?**

Contrition for sin is heartfelt sorrow for the sins we have committed, with hatred of them and a firm purpose of amendment.[388]

429. **What is a firm purpose of amendment?**

A firm purpose of amendment is a resolution not to commit sin again and to avoid as far as possible the proximate occasions of it.

430. **What kind of contrition for sin ought we to have?**

Contrition for sin ought to be inward, supernatural, profound, and universal.

431. **What do you mean by "inward contrition"?**

Inward contrition is that which is not merely on the lips but flows from the heart.

432. **What is supernatural contrition?**

Supernatural contrition is that which, under the influence of grace, springs not from natural, but from supernatural motives, that is, from motives realized supernaturally by our faith.

433. **What is profound contrition?**

Profound contrition is that whereby we hate sin above any other evil.[389]

[388] Cf. Ps 50:3ff; Jer 2:19-21; Ez 18:21-23, 27-28; 33:14-16; Jl 2:12-18; Jn 5:14; 8:11; Lk 15:17-24; Council of Trent, Session 14, "Doctrine on the Sacrament of Penance," Ch. 4; Gregory the Great, *On the Gospels*, Bk. 2, Homily 34, n. 15; Augustine, *Sermon 351*, n. 12

[389] "Profound contrition" may thus be briefly described in the words of St. Thomas: Contrition, or sorrow for the sins we have committed, ought to be profound "appreciatively," in that a penitent person ought to have such a detestation of his sins that for no consideration would he commit them and so offend God; but it is in no way requisite that his sorrow should be "profound" in an intensive sense, that is, that its vehemence should surpass all other grief he has ever experienced. Nor is it wise to try and institute a comparison between contrition or sorrow for sin, and other sorrows which a person may have sensibly experienced by reason of temporal evils which may have come to him (cf. *Summa Theologiae*, III-Sup., q. 3, a. 1).

434. **What is universal contrition?**

Universal contrition includes all mortal sins committed since baptism and not directly remitted by the power of the keys.

435. **What if the penitent has only venial sins of which to accuse himself, or mortal sins already directly remitted?**

If the penitent has only venial sins of which to accuse himself, or mortal sins already directly remitted, then he should make an act of sorrow for some, or at least one of them, and this suffices.

436. **How many kinds of contrition are there?**

Contrition can be either perfect—and this is usually called simply "contrition"—or imperfect—and this is called by the special name of "attrition."[390]

437. **What is perfect contrition?**

Perfect contrition is a sorrow and hatred for sin, springing from charity, inasmuch as sin is an offense against God, who is supremely good and worthy to be loved above all things.[391]

438. **What is the effect of perfect contrition?**

Perfect contrition immediately washes away sin and reconciles man to God, even apart from the sacrament of penance; yet such contrition implies the desire of receiving the sacrament of penance.[392]

[390] Cf. Council of Trent, Session 14, "Doctrine on the Sacrament of Penance," Ch. 4

[391] Cf. TCCI 7:300ff

[392] Cf. Prv 8:17; 10:12; Jn 14:21, 23; 1 Pt 4:8; 1 Jn 4:7; Council of Trent, Session 14, "Doctrine on the Sacrament of Penance," Ch. 4; Peter Chrysologus, *Sermon 94*. A Christian should acquire the habit of making the act of perfect contrition to be found at the beginning of this catechism (p. 211-213), and this more especially if he should happen to fall into mortal sin, for then he should at once try to blot it out by making such acts of perfect contrition, and going to confession as soon as he can. In this way, the good he may have done will not be rendered void to eternity, nor will he be afraid of sudden death. Many attain to eternal life because they have departed this life in a state of perfect contrition, though meeting death in circumstances which made it impossible for them to receive the sacraments.

439. **What is imperfect contrition?**
Imperfect contrition is that supernatural sorrow and hatred for sin which is aroused either by reflection on the baseness of sin or by fear of hell and its torments.[393]

440. **What kind of contrition is sufficient for the valid reception of the sacrament of penance?**
Imperfect contrition is sufficient for the valid reception of the sacrament of penance, though we should try to have perfect contrition.

441. **What kind of sin does a person commit who goes to confession knowing well that he has no contrition?**
A person who goes to confession knowing well that he has no contrition not only does not obtain forgiveness of his sins, but also commits a grave sin of sacrilege.

Confession

442. **What is confession of sins?**
Confession is to accuse oneself of one's sins to a priest lawfully approved, in order to obtain sacramental absolution.[394]

443. **Why did Christ will that we should confess our sins if we desire their forgiveness?**
Christ willed that we should confess our sins if we desire their forgiveness so that a sinner might humble himself by making known his sins to a priest

[393] Cf. Mt 10:28; Lk 3:7-9; 15:17; Council of Trent, Session 14, "Doctrine on the Sacrament of Penance," Ch. 4; Leo X, Bull *Exurge Domine*, against the errors of Luther, June 15, 1520, the sixth condemned Proposition; Pius VI, Constitution *Auctorem Fidei*, against the errors of the Synod of Pistoia, Aug. 28, 1794, the twenty-third, twenty-fifth, and thirty-sixth condemned Propositions; Gregory of Nyssa, *Homily 1 on the Canticle of Canticles*

[394] Cf. Chrysostom, *De Lazaro*, Discourse 4, n. 4; Homily *Quod frequenter sit conveniendum*, n. 2

as to a judge and physician, in order to make due satisfaction for them and learn what remedies to make use of.[395]

444. **What kind of confession is necessary for the valid reception of the sacrament of penance?**
For the valid reception of the sacrament of penance, confession must be vocal or at least the equivalent of vocal, and integral or complete.

445. **When is a confession integral or complete?**
A confession is integral or complete when the penitent confesses all mortal sins not already directly forgiven, of which, after careful examination, he is conscious, with their number and character, and the circumstances that alter their character.[396]

446. **What ought a person to do if he cannot remember the number of his mortal sins?**
If a person cannot remember the number of his mortal sins, he should state their probable number and add "about."

447. **What if a person omits a mortal sin in confession, through no fault of his own?**
If a person through no fault of his own omits a mortal sin in confession, the sacrament is validly received and the sin forgotten is indirectly forgiven;

[395] Cf. Jn 20:23; Mt 16:19; 18:18; TCCI 7:307

[396] Cf. Council of Trent, Session 14, "Doctrine on the Sacrament of Penance," Ch. 5; "On the Most Holy Sacrament of Penance," Can. 7; Gregory the Great, *On the Gospels*, Bk. 2, Homily 26, n. 4-6; Cyprian, *On the Lapsed*, n. 28-29; Jerome, *On Matthew*, Bk. 3, Ch. 16, n. 19. A general confession, wherein one confesses the sins of one's whole life, is necessary when there is a real ground for thinking that one's previous confessions have been invalid; it is advisable if there is really grave doubt about their validity; it is permissible if it seems probable that the penitent will derive profit from it, and this especially at certain more important moments in life, for example, after making a retreat or when in danger of death. In other cases, it should be forbidden to a penitent as being without utility and sometimes even harmful, for example, in the case of scrupulous persons.

but when he remembers it, the penitent is bound to accuse himself of it in his next confession.[397]

448. **What sin does a person commit who culpably keeps back a mortal sin in confession?**
A person who culpably keeps back a mortal sin in confession not only gains nothing by his confession but adds a grave sin of sacrilege.

449. **What should a person do if he has deliberately kept back a mortal sin in confession, or if he confesses without due contrition mortal sins that have not yet been remitted?**
A person who has deliberately kept back a mortal sin in confession or who confesses without due contrition mortal sins not yet remitted, should state how many confessions of this kind he has made, also how many sacrilegious Communions, and should now tell all the mortal sins, whether confessed or kept back, in those confessions, also any other mortal sins he may have committed since.

450. **Is anything else required for the lawful reception of the sacrament of penance?**
For the lawful reception of the sacrament of penance, the confession should also be humble and devout; that is, the penitent should briefly, clearly, and modestly, without useless words, humbly confess his sins, without excusing, minimizing, or exaggerating them, and accept the admonitions of the confessor.[398]

Satisfaction

451. **What is satisfaction?**
Satisfaction is the penance imposed on the penitent by the confessor for the sins made known to him in confession; this penance has, by the merits

[397] Cf. Alexander VII, Decree of Sept. 24, 1665, the eleventh of certain condemned Propositions; TCCI 7:314

[398] Cf. TCCI 7:314-315

of Jesus Christ which are applied through the sacrament, special virtue for the payment of the debt of temporal punishment due to sin.

452. **Why does the confessor impose a penance?**
The confessor imposes, as prudence suggests and in proportion to the character of the sins confessed and the dispositions of the penitent, a salutary and fitting penance—not only as a help to the penitent in leading a new life and as a remedy for his weakness, but also as a penalty and a correction for past sins now forgiven.[399]

453. **When should the penitent perform the penance given him by the confessor?**
The penitent should perform the penance given him by the confessor as soon as possible, unless the latter appoints some particular time for its fulfillment.

454. **What should a penitent do if he finds himself absolutely unable, or at least not able without grave inconvenience, to perform the penance imposed?**
A penitent who finds himself absolutely unable, or at least not able without grave inconvenience, to perform the penance given him should state this with becoming deference to his confessor and ask him to change it.

Sacramental Absolution

455. **What is sacramental absolution?**
Sacramental absolution is the act whereby the confessor in the name of Jesus Christ, by pronouncing the proper form of words, remits the sin duly and with true sorrow confessed by the penitent.

456. **Can the confessor refuse or defer sacramental absolution?**
The confessor can and ought to refuse absolution only when he arrives at the prudent decision that it is not certain that the penitent has the requisite dispositions. Sometimes, too, he can for good reason defer absolution

[399] Cf. Council of Trent, Session 14, "Doctrine on the Sacrament of Penance," Ch. 8-9

for a time, especially if the penitent agrees to this with a view to preparing himself better.[400]

457. **Is the confessor bound by the seal of confession?**
The confessor is bound by an inviolable sacramental seal; not only is he forbidden to reveal sins heard in confession, but he must take great care not to betray the sinner for any reason by word or sign or in any other way. Moreover, he is forbidden to make any such use of knowledge derived from the confession as shall prejudice the penitent, even when there is no danger of the secret being violated. Nor can superiors, or confessors who subsequently become superiors, make use of knowledge acquired through the confessional in their government of their house.[401]

458. **Does the above law bind others besides the confessor?**
All who in any way become aware of anything derived from a sacramental confession are bound by the same law as the confessor.[402]

The Effects of the Sacrament of Penance; Indulgences

459. **What effects does the sacrament of penance produce when a penitent confesses with due dispositions mortal sins not hitherto remitted?**
When a penitent confesses with due dispositions mortal sins not hitherto remitted, then, by the sacrament of penance:

[400] Cf. *Codex Juris Canonici*, Can. 886. The *Roman Ritual* says: "Those are incapable of receiving absolution who give no sign of sorrow for their sins, who refuse to lay aside some hatred or enmity, to restore when they can someone else's property, to avoid some proximate occasion of sin, or who are unwilling to give up their sinful lives and amend them; those again who have given public scandal but refuse to make public reparation and remove the scandal. Finally, a confessor should refuse to absolve sins reserved to a higher authority" (III, i, 23).

[401] Cf. Fourth Lateran Council, Const. 21; *Codex Juris Canonici*, Can. 889-890. In order to safeguard the sacred character of this sacrament, very severe penalties are enacted by canon law against confessors who break the seal of confession. The history of the Church has preserved for us the names of priests who, rather than break the seal, have submitted to all sorts of trial, even to death itself; in this respect, St. John Nepomucene is an example to all, since he died a martyr for this reason, A.D. 1383.

[402] Cf. *Codex Juris Canonici*, Can. 889; 890, par. 2

1. his sin and its eternal punishment, also—at least partially—the debt of temporal punishment due to sin, are remitted;
2. his merits, which were annulled by his mortal sins, revive—that is, they regain the efficacy which, before his falling into mortal sin, they had for winning him eternal life;[403]
3. a special grace is given for avoiding sin in the future.

460. **What effects does this sacrament produce when the penitent has to confess only venial sins, or mortal sins already remitted?**

If the penitent confesses with due dispositions only venial sins, or mortal sins already remitted, the sacrament of penance remits his venial sins, increases his sanctifying grace, helps him to avoid sin in the future, and pays still more completely the debts of temporal punishment due to his sins.

461. **When absolution has been given and the penance performed, is the whole debt of temporal punishment for sin always paid?**

When absolution has been given and the penance performed, the whole debt of temporal punishment for sin is not always paid; but it may be paid by other voluntary penances, especially by gaining indulgences.[404]

462. **What do we mean by an "indulgence"?**

By an "indulgence," we mean the remission by God of the temporal punishment due to sins whose guilt has already been forgiven; such remission the Church grants apart from the sacrament of penance.[405]

[403] Cf. *Summa Theologiae*, III, q. 89, a. 5

[404] Cf. Council of Trent, Session 6, "Decree on Justification," Ch. 14; Can. 30; Session 14, "Doctrine on the Sacrament of Penance," Ch. 8; "On the Most Holy Sacrament of Penance," Can. 12

[405] Cf. Mt 16:19; 18:18; 2 Cor 2:6, 10; Council of Trent, Session 25, "Decree concerning Indulgences"; Clement VI, Constitution *Unigenitus Dei Filius*, Jan. 25, 1343; Leo X, Bull *Exurge Domine*, against the errors of Luther, June 15, 1520, the seventeenth through the twenty-second condemned Propositions; Pius VI, Constitution *Auctorem Fidei*, against the errors of the Synod of Pistoia, Aug. 28, 1794, the fortieth condemned Proposition; Pius XI, Bull *Infinita Dei misericordia*, May 29, 1924, "The Indiction of the Universal Jubilee for the Holy Year, 1925"; *Codex Juris Canonici*, Can. 911-924

463. **How does the Church remit by means of indulgences the temporal punishment due to sin?**

The Church by means of indulgences remits the temporal punishment due to sin by applying to the living, by way of absolution, and to the dead, by way of suffrage, the infinite satisfaction paid by Jesus Christ as well as the superabundant satisfaction wrought by the Blessed Virgin Mary and the saints; these constitute the spiritual treasury of the Church.[406]

464. **Who have the power of granting indulgences?**

The Roman pontiff can grant indulgences, since to him was committed by Christ the administration of the entire spiritual treasury of the Church; others, too—for example, the bishops—have this power conceded to them either by the Roman pontiff or by canon law.[407]

465. **How many kinds of indulgences are there?**

There are two kinds of indulgences:

1. Plenary, whereby the entire debt of temporal punishment is remitted.
2. Partial, whereby a portion only of the debt is remitted.

466. **In what sense is a plenary indulgence said to be granted?**

A plenary indulgence is said to be granted in the sense that if a person cannot gain it in full or plenary fashion, he can yet gain it partially, according to his dispositions.[408]

467. **What are the conditions for gaining an indulgence?**

The conditions for gaining an indulgence are:

1. The person must be baptized and not excommunicated.[409]
2. He must have at least the general intention of gaining indulgences.
3. He must duly perform the good works demanded.

406 Cf. Rom 5:15-21
407 Cf. *Codex Juris Canonici*, Can. 912
408 Cf. *Codex Juris Canonici*, Can. 926
409 Cf. *Codex Juris Canonici*, Can. 925

4. He must be in a state of grace, at least when he finishes the works prescribed, and—if it is a question of gaining a plenary indulgence—he must not have his affections set on any venial sin.

468. **To whom can we apply any indulgences we may have gained?**
Unless the contrary is stated, we can apply the indulgences we gain to the souls detained in purgatory when such indulgences have been granted by the Roman pontiff; but no indulgences can be applied by us to other people still living.[410]

Extreme Unction

469. **What is the sacrament of extreme unction?**
The sacrament of extreme unction is a sacrament instituted by Jesus Christ whereby spiritual assistance is bestowed on people who have come to the age of reason, who are sick and in grave danger of death; this assistance is most profitable when death is imminent, and even sometimes affords relief from bodily ailments.[411]

470. **What is the effect of extreme unction?**
Extreme unction

1. brings an increase of grace;
2. relieves the mind of the sick person from anxiety, and is especially helpful in meeting the temptations of one's last agony;
3. removes the vestiges of sins, remits venial sins, even mortal sins when the sick person is not conscious of them and has at least attrition for them and is unable to make his confession;

[410] Cf. *Codex Juris Canonici*, Can. 930

[411] Cf. Second Council of Lyons, *Profession of Faith by Michael Palaeologus*; Council of Florence, Session 8 (November 22, 1439), "Bull of Union with the Armenians"; Council of Trent, Session 14, "On the Sacrament of Extreme Unction," Ch. 1; Innocent III, Epistle *Ejus exemplo*, Dec. 18, 1208, to the archbishop of Tarragona; Pius X, Decree *Lamentabili sane*, July 3, 1907, the forty-eighth condemned Proposition

4. sometimes cures sickness—when, that is, God sees that such a cure is for the good of a person's soul.[412]

471. **Who is the minister of this sacrament?**
The ordinary minister of this sacrament is the parish priest of the place where the sick man is living; but in case of necessity, or when leave to do so can be reasonably expected from the parish priest or the bishop of the diocese, any priest can administer the sacrament.[413]

472. **What is the matter of extreme unction?**
The remote matter of extreme unction is olive oil blessed by a bishop or by a priest who has leave from the Apostolic See to bless it; the actual anointing with this oil is the proximate matter of the sacrament.

473. **What is the form of extreme unction?**
The form of extreme unction is the prayer prescribed in the liturgical books of the particular rite to which the ministering priest belongs, and which he repeats while anointing the sick person.[414]

474. **On whom is this sacrament conferred?**
This sacrament is conferred on any member of the faithful who, after attaining the use of reason, is in danger of death through sickness or old age.

475. **How often can this sacrament be given?**
This sacrament can be given only once in the course of the same period of danger of death; but, if the danger passes away and then recurs, the sacrament can be repeated.[415]

[412] Cf. Jas 5:14-15; Council of Trent, Session 14, "On the Sacrament of Extreme Unction," Ch. 2; Caesarius of Arles, *Sermon 265*, n. 3, among the sermons attributed to St. Augustine. By the "vestiges of sin" are meant the weaknesses of the soul and bad habits resulting from sin.

[413] Cf. *Codex Juris Canonici*, Can. 938, par. 2

[414] Cf. Council of Trent, Session 14, "On the Sacrament of Extreme Unction," Ch. 2

[415] Cf. *Codex Juris Canonici*, Can. 940, par. 2

476. **Can this sacrament be given to a sick person who is not in possession of his senses?**

This sacrament can be given to a sick person who is not in possession of his senses if, when he was in possession of them, he asked for it, at least implicitly, or probably would have asked for it, even though he afterward loses the use of his senses or even of his reason.[416]

477. **What should a sick person do before receiving extreme unction?**

Before receiving extreme unction, a sick person should

1. confess his sins if he can—otherwise, he should make an act of contrition;
2. make acts of faith, hope, charity, and complete submission to the will of God.

478. **Is this sacrament necessary for salvation?**

This sacrament is not absolutely necessary for salvation, but it is wrong to neglect it; indeed we ought to be most careful, when a sick person begins to be in danger of death, to see that he receives this sacrament, as soon as possible, and while still in possession of his senses.[417]

Holy Order

479. **What is the sacrament of holy order or ordination?**

The sacrament of holy order or ordination is a sacrament instituted by Jesus Christ for providing the Church with bishops, priests, and other ministers, each receiving power and grace for the due fulfillment of the sacred duties belonging to the degree conferred on him.[418]

[416] Cf. *Codex Juris Canonici*, Can. 943

[417] Cf. *Codex Juris Canonici*, Can. 944. It is a hateful and a cruel thing under pretext of affection or prudence not to summon a priest in good time to administer the last sacraments to sick folk. It only means depriving your brethren of the last consolations of religion; it may even mean shutting them out from the kingdom of heaven. Those who do this will have a terrible account to render.

[418] Cf. Acts 6:6; 13:3; 1 Tm 4:14; 5:22; 2 Tm 1:6; Second Council of Lyons, *Profession of Faith by Michael Palaeologus*; Council of Florence, Session 8 (November 22, 1439), "Bull of Union with the Armenians"; Council of Trent, Session 23, Can. 3; Pius X, Decree *Lamentabili sane*, July 3, 1907, the forty-ninth and fiftieth condemned Propositions

480. **Are the said degrees all equal?**
These degrees are not all equal, but some are higher than others; and thus is formed the sacred hierarchy of holy order.[419]

481. **When precisely did Jesus Christ institute this sacrament?**
Jesus Christ instituted this sacrament precisely when he gave to the apostles and to their successors in the priesthood the power to offer the Sacrifice of the Mass and to remit or to retain sins.[420]

482. **Of what kind is the dignity of the priesthood?**
The dignity of the priesthood is very great, for the priest is the minister of Christ and the dispenser of the mysteries of God; he is a mediator between God and man, with power over the real as well as over the mystical body of Christ. Christ is the "one mediator of God and men";[421] that is, he alone is the mediator of redemption. But the priest, acting in the Person of Christ, applies to men the fruits of that redemption and is thus rightly called a "mediator."[422]

483. **What is the matter and what the form of the sacrament of holy order?**
The matter in ordination is the imposition of hands or the handing to the candidate of the instruments of the order to be received, as laid down in the Pontifical; the form consists in the appropriate words pronounced by the minister while imposing hands on the candidate or handing him the said instruments.

[419] Cf. Mt 16:18-19; 18:18; Jn 21:17; Acts 6:6; 1 Tm 3:1-13; Ti 1:5-9; Council of Trent, Session 23, Can. 2, 6, 7

[420] Cf. Mt 18:18; Lk 22:19; Jn 20:23; 1 Cor 11:23-25

[421] 1 Tm 2:5

[422] Cf. 1 Cor 4:1; 2 Cor 5:20; 6:4; 1 Tm 5:17; Heb 13:17; Pius XI, Epistle *Officiorum omnium*, Aug. 1, 1922. Those alone are to be admitted to the priestly dignity who are called by God, approved by their superiors, and who undertake the duties of their office for the glory of God and the salvation of souls; "Neither doth any man take the honor to himself but he that is called by God, as Aaron was" (Heb 5:4). See TCCI 7:340ff.

484. **How should the faithful regard their priests?**
The faithful should show all honor and reverence toward their priests, and they should ask God to bestow holy and worthy ministers on his Church.[423]

485. **Do parents sin if they compel their sons to become priests, or if they prevent them doing so?**
Parents sin if they compel their sons to become priests, for in so doing they are usurping God's rights, since he has reserved to himself the right of choosing his ministers through the bishops. They sin, too, if they prevent them from becoming priests, for in so doing they are resisting the will of God and refusing to their children the right to follow a divine vocation; moreover, they are depriving themselves and their children of many very special graces.[424]

486. **Who is the minister of holy order?**
The ordinary minister of holy order is the bishop of the candidate or a bishop delegated by him; the extraordinary minister is one who by canon law or by a special indult from the Holy See has received the power to confer certain orders.[425]

MATRIMONY[426]

487. **What is the sacrament of matrimony?**
The sacrament of matrimony is marriage between Christians—that is, all who are baptized—validly entered upon; it was raised by Jesus Christ to the dignity of a sacrament whereby grace is bestowed on husband and wife that they may rightly fulfill their duties to one another and to their children.[427]

[423] Cf. Mt 9:38; 10:40; Lk 10:2, 16; Jn 13:20
[424] Cf. Jn 15:16
[425] Cf. *Codex Juris Canonici*, Can. 951
[426] The canonical prescriptions given here concerning the nature of matrimony, impedient and diriment impediments, the consent required, the manner of celebrating a marriage, etc., will be found fully set forth in the *Codex Juris Canonici*, Can. 1012ff.
[427] Cf. Eph 5:22-23; Council of Florence, Session 8 (November 22, 1439), "Bull of Union with the Armenians"; Council of Trent, Session 7, "On the Sacraments in General," Can. 1; Session 24, Can. 1; Leo XIII, Encyclical *Arcanum Divinae Sapientiae*, Feb. 10, 1880; Cyril of Alexandria, *On John*, Ch. 2, n. 1

488. **Can there be a valid marriage between Christians without its being a sacrament?**
There cannot be a valid marriage between Christians without its being necessarily a sacrament, for Jesus Christ deigned to raise such marriage to the dignity of a sacrament.[428]

489. **Who are the ministers of this sacrament?**
The ministers of this sacrament are the contracting parties.

490. **What is the matter and what the form of the sacrament of matrimony?**
The matter of the sacrament of matrimony is the mutual giving on the part of both of a right over their bodies, with a view to the object of matrimony; the form is their mutual acceptance of this gift.

491. **What are the essential qualities of matrimony?**
The essential qualities of matrimony are unity and indissolubility, which in Christian marriage are rendered peculiarly stable owing to the sacrament.[429]

492. **In what does the unity of matrimony consist?**
The unity of matrimony consists in the fact that the husband cannot during the life of his wife have another wife, nor can the wife during her husband's life have another husband.[430]

493. **In what does the indissolubility of matrimony consist?**
The indissolubility of matrimony means that the bond of matrimony can be dissolved only by death.[431]

[428] Cf. Leo XIII, Encyclical *Arcanum Divinae Sapientiae*, Feb. 10, 1880; *Codex Juris Canonici*, Can. 1012

[429] Cf. Mt 5:32; 19:3-9; Mk 10:2-12; Lk 16:18; Rom 7:2-3; 1 Cor 6:16; 7:10-11, 39; Leo XIII, Encyclical *Arcanum Divinae Sapientiae*, Feb. 10, 1880; Augustine, *De Conjugiis Adulterinis*, Bk. 1, Ch. 9; *On Marriage and Concupiscence*, Bk. 1, Ch. 11

[430] Cf. Mt 19:4-6; Council of Trent, Session 7, "On the Sacraments in General," Can. 1; Session 24, Can. 2; Innocent III, Epistle *Gaudemus in Domino*, A.D. 1201, to the bishop of Tiberias

[431] Cf. Mt 19:6; Mk 10:11-12; Lk 16:18; Rom 7:3; 1 Cor 7:10-11, 39; Council of Trent,

494. **By what law is Christian marriage governed?**
Christian marriage is governed by the law of God and of the Church, saving the authority of the state as regards purely civil effects.

495. **What are the "purely civil effects" of matrimony?**
The "purely civil effects" of matrimony are effects that do not touch the essence of matrimony—for example, the amount of the dowry, rights of succession to property by the surviving partner, or of the children to their parents, etc.

Session 24, Can. 6-7; Pius IX, *The Syllabus of Errors*, the sixty-seventh condemned Proposition; Leo XIII, Encyclical *Arcanum Divinae Sapientiae*, Feb. 10, 1880. The indissoluble character of matrimony may be thus briefly set forth in view of cases that frequently occur:

A) A marriage between believers,

1. when ratified and consummated is indissoluble;

2. when only ratified is by the law itself dissolved by solemn religious profession, also by a dispensation granted by the Apostolic See, if at least one party asks for it.

B) A marriage between unbelievers,

1. if neither party has received baptism, is of its nature indissoluble;

2. if only one party has been baptized, is dissolved:

a) ipso jure in favor of the faith through the "Pauline privilege"—if, that is to say, the infidel party both refuses to believe and be baptized and at the same time declines to live peacefully with the other but insults his Creator, and the believing party has contracted a fresh marriage; also

b) by dispensation granted by the Apostolic See for such a dissolution, if the believing party seeks it.

3. if both parties are converted to the faith:

a) if the marriage was consummated subsequent to baptism, then it is indissoluble;

b) if the marriage was consummated neither before nor after baptism, then by actual law the marriage is dissolved through solemn religious profession, also by a dispensation granted by the Apostolic See at the request of at least one of the parties;

c) if the marriage was consummated before (but not if after) baptism, then it can be dissolved by the Apostolic See at the request of at least one of the parties.

C) In the case of a marriage contracted between a believer and an unbeliever with a dispensation from the impediment arising from "disparity of worship," (in other words, between a baptized and an unbaptized person) then:

1. such a marriage is not dissolved by the Pauline privilege; but

2. if not consummated, it can be dissolved by solemn religious profession and by a dispensation granted by the Apostolic See;

3. if consummated, it can be dissolved by a papal dispensation. It is evident that the exercise of this papal power demands just, grave, and urgent causes, and the absence of scandal.

496. **What do we mean by "impediments to matrimony"?**
By "impediments to matrimony," we mean anything that makes the celebration of a marriage either unlawful (termed an "impedient impediment") or invalid (termed a "diriment impediment").

497. **Who has the power to declare that, in the case of baptized people, certain things are impediments to matrimony?**
Only the supreme ecclesiastical authority has the right to make laws, whether in general or in particular cases, establishing certain impediments to matrimony on the part of people who are baptized; it alone has the right of declaring when the divine law is an impediment to or wholly precludes a marriage.[432]

498. **What are the impediments that simply impede a marriage—impedient impediments?[433]**
The impediments that simply impede a marriage are:
1. A simple vow either of virginity, or of perpetual chastity, or not to marry, or of receiving holy orders, or of embracing the religious life.
2. Difference in the religions of the parties concerned.
3. Legal kinship arising from adoption—in those countries, that is, where the civil law regards this as an impediment to marriage.

499. **Which are the impediments that render a marriage null—diriment impediments?[434]**
The impediments that render a marriage null are:
1. Age.
2. Impotence that is antecedent to the marriage and perpetual.
3. A bond arising from an already existing marriage.
4. Diversity of religion, that is, when one of the parties is not baptized.
5. Holy orders.
6. Solemn profession in a religious order.

[432] Cf. Council of Trent, Session 24, Can. 4
[433] Cf. *Codex Juris Canonici*, Can. 1058-1066
[434] Cf. *Codex Juris Canonici*, Can. 1067-1080

7. Abduction.
8. Crime.
9. Consanguinity.
10. Affinity.
11. Public decency.
12. Spiritual relationship arising from baptism.
13. Legal relationship due to adoption—in countries, that is, where the civil law regards this as a diriment impediment to marriage.

500. **What is required for a valid marriage?**

For a valid marriage, the contracting parties must:

1. be free from all diriment impediment;
2. freely consent to the marriage;
3. if baptized in the Catholic Church or converts to it, marry in the presence of the parish priest or the bishop of the diocese, or a priest delegated by either of the above, and before two witnesses.

501. **What is further required for a lawful marriage?**

In order to contract a lawful marriage, the contracting parties must:

1. be in a state of grace;
2. be sufficiently instructed in Christian doctrine;
3. be free from any impedient impediment;
4. observe any other precepts laid down by the Church for the due celebration of a marriage.

502. **Does the Church dispense at times from the impediments arising from diversity of religion—that is, when one of the parties is not baptized—or from a mixed marriage?**

Only for very grave reasons does the Church dispense from the impediments arising from diversity of religion or from a mixed marriage, and permit a marriage between a Catholic and one who is not a Catholic.

503. **When the Church grants such a dispensation and permits a marriage of this sort, on what does she insist?**
When the Church grants such a dispensation and permits such a marriage, she demands from the non-Catholic party a promise not to interfere with the religion of the Catholic party; from both parties she demands a promise that all the children of the marriage shall be baptized and brought up in the Catholic faith.

504. **What tribunal has competence in matrimonial cases?**
Matrimonial cases affecting the bond of marriage between baptized persons belong exclusively to the ecclesiastical courts, though the rights of the civil authorities remain—so far as purely civil effects are concerned—untouched.[435]

505. **Are the faithful bound to make known to the ecclesiastical authorities impediments of which they are aware?**
The faithful are bound to make known to the ecclesiastical authorities any impediments of which they are aware, more especially since the whole idea of publishing the banns of marriage is to ensure such manifestation.[436]

[435] Cf. Council of Trent, Session 24, Can. 12; *Codex Juris Canonici*, Can. 1960-1961

[436] When choosing a state of life, before all things, consider God and the salvation of your soul. If, after mature reflection, you decide that marriage is more suitable for you, you ought then to set the matter before your parents, for they have the right, indeed the duty, of advising you in so serious a matter. At the same time, they have no right to set their faces against any particular marriage for you, nor have they a right to make you marry someone whom you do not want to marry. Then pray much about it and devote yourself to good deeds. More particularly should you strive to lead a good life and thus prepare yourself well for marriage. Go to confession before the marriage, and when the time for celebrating this great sacrament of matrimony arrives, set God's seal upon it by receiving Holy Communion with your partner; by this means you will draw down on yourselves the blessings of God in your married life. Make a firm resolution to observe faithfully the laws which should govern married life, also determine that you will bring up the children God may give you in a good life and the true religion.

The Virtues

506. **What is a virtue?**

A virtue is a habit or permanent disposition leading a person to do good and avoid evil.

507. **How are virtues divided?**

Virtues fall into two classes, theological and moral, according to their subject matter.

THE THEOLOGICAL VIRTUES

The Theological Virtues in General

508. **What is a theological virtue?**

A theological virtue is one whose immediate object is man's supernatural end—namely, God, to whom it directly leads him.[437]

509. **How many theological virtues are there?**

There are three theological virtues—faith, hope, and charity.

510. **Can the theological virtues be acquired by our natural acts?**

The theological virtues cannot be acquired by our merely natural acts, for of their very nature they are supernatural; consequently, God alone infuses them together with his sanctifying grace.[438]

511. **When are theological virtues infused?**

Theological virtues are infused into a person at the moment when he acquires justification and the remission of his sins, whether by the sacrament

[437] Cf. *Summa Theologiae*, I-II, q. 62, a. 1-2

[438] Cf. Jn 6:44; 15:5; Rom 5:5; 2 Cor 3:5; Phil 1:29

of baptism or by an act of contrition accompanied by a desire to receive that sacrament.[439]

512. **Are the theological virtues necessary for salvation?**
The theological virtues are absolutely necessary for salvation, for without them the right direction of mind and will toward our supernatural end is impossible.[440]

513. **Which is the greatest of the theological virtues?**
The greatest of the theological virtues is charity, which is "the perfection of the law"[441] and will not cease even in heaven.[442]

514. **When are we bound to make acts of faith, hope, and charity?**
We are bound to make at least implicit acts of faith, hope, and charity often during life, especially when, after attaining the use of reason, we have sufficient knowledge of divine revelation; more particularly, too, when such acts are requisite in order to fulfill some obligation or to overcome temptation, also when in danger of death.[443]

439 Cf. Rom 5:2; 8:24; 1 Cor 13:13; 1 Thes 1:3; Heb 11:6; 1 Jn 4:15-19; Council of Trent, Session 6, "Decree on Justification," Ch. 7; Clement V, Constitution *De Summa Trinitate et fide Catholica*, at the Council of Vienne, A.D. 1311, against the errors of Peter John Oliva; Polycarp, *Epistle to the Philippians*, Ch. 3; Chrysostom, *Homily 40 on Acts*, Ch. 2; TCCI 7:218

440 Cf. Mk 16:16; Jn 4:15-20; Acts 8:37; 10:43; Rom 5:2; 8:24; Heb 11:6

441 Rom 13:10

442 Cf. Mt 22:35-40; Jn 13:14; 14:21, 23; 1 Cor 13:1-13; Col 3:14; Jas 2:8; Benedict XII, Constitution *Benedictus Deus*, January 29, 1336; Clement of Rome, *Epistle to the Corinthians*, Ch. 49; *Summa Theologiae*, II-II, q. 23, a. 6-7

443 Cf. Alexander VII, Decree of Sept. 24, 1665, the first of certain condemned Propositions; Innocent XI, Decree of the Sacred Congregation of the Inquisition, March 2, 1679, the sixth, seventh, sixteenth, and seventeenth condemned Propositions

Individual Theological Virtues

Faith

515. **What is faith?**

Faith is a supernatural virtue whereby, through the inspiration and help of God's grace, we believe that what God has revealed and has taught us through the Church is true, not because by the natural light of reason we perceive its intrinsic truth, but on the authority of God who reveals it, for he can neither deceive nor be deceived.[444]

516. **Must we believe all revealed truths?**

We must believe all revealed truths, at least implicitly; for example, "I believe whatever God has revealed and his Church proposes for my belief," or, more briefly, "I believe whatever holy mother Church believes." Explicitly we must believe that God exists and will reward us; also in the mysteries of the most Holy Trinity, the incarnation, and the redemption.[445]

517. **Can faith be contrary to reason?**

Although faith is above reason, it is in no sense contrary to it, nor can there ever be any real disagreement between faith and reason.[446]

[444] Cf. 1 Cor 2:5, 7-13; Heb 11:1; Rom 10:14-17; First Vatican Council, Constitution *Dei Filius*, Ch. 3; Leo the Great, *Sermon 27*, n. 1; Chrysostom, *Homily 82 on Matthew*, Ch. 4

[445] Cf. Mt 28:19; Jn 3:15, 18, 36; 17:3; 20:31; Heb 11:6; Innocent XI, Decree of the Sacred Congregation of the Inquisition, March 2, 1679, the twenty-second and sixty-fourth condemned Propositions; Decree of the Congregation of the Holy Office, Jan. 25, 1703. To believe the above truths is necessary for salvation (*necessitate medii*), belief in other truths is necessary (*necessitate praecepti*); for a thing is said to be necessary (*necessitate medii*) when, if it is omitted, even blamelessly, the goal cannot be obtained; whereas something is said to be necessary (*necessitate praecepti*) when inculpable omission of it does not preclude us from obtaining the goal proposed. It follows that whatsoever is necessary for salvation (*necessitate medii*) is also necessary (*necessitate praecepti*).

[446] Cf. First Vatican Council, Constitution *Dei Filius*, Ch. 4

518. **Why can there never be any real disagreement between faith and reason?**
There can never be any real disagreement between faith and reason, because the selfsame God who reveals mysteries and infuses into us faith bestowed on us the light of reason; God cannot contradict himself, nor can truth be opposed to truth.[447]

519. **Can faith and reason support one another?**
Faith and reason can support one another, since sound reason can demonstrate the foundations of faith, and, illumined by that same faith, can develop a knowledge of divine things; conversely, faith can safeguard reason and free it from many errors, while providing it with manifold knowledge.[448]

520. **When ought we to make external profession of our faith?**
We ought to make external profession of our faith as often as our silence, hesitation, or mode of acting would imply a denial of our faith, contempt for our religion, insult to God, or scandal to our neighbor.[449]

521. **How do we show our faith?**
We show our faith by professing it in word and deed, even, if necessary, giving our lives for it.[450]

522. **How is faith lost?**
Faith is lost by apostasy or heresy—when, that is, a baptized person repudiates all or some of the truths of faith, or deliberately calls them in question.

523. **Who, besides apostates and heretics, sin against the faith?**
Besides apostates and heretics, the following sin against the faith:

[447] Cf. Ibid.; Pius IX, Encyclical *Qui pluribus*, Nov. 9, 1846

[448] Cf. Fifth Lateran Council, Session 8; First Vatican Council, Constitution *Dei Filius*, Ch. 4

[449] Cf. Rom 10:10; 2 Tm 2:12; *Codex Juris Canonici*, Can. 1325

[450] Cf. Rom 10:9-10; Gal 5:6; Jas 2:18-21

1. Unbaptized people who repudiate the faith after it has been sufficiently clearly put before them—this is "positive infidelity."
2. People who neglect to secure sufficient religious instruction such as suits their age and condition in life.
3. People who embrace errors condemned by the Church and which approximate more or less to heresy.
4. People who deliberately expose themselves to the danger of losing their faith—those, for example, who without leave and due precautions read books prohibited by the Church, especially books written by apostates, heretics, or schismatics in defense of their apostasy, heresy, or schism.[451]

Hope

524. **What is hope?**

Hope is a supernatural virtue whereby, because of the merits of Jesus Christ, and relying on the goodness, omnipotence, and faithfulness of God, we look for eternal life and the graces necessary to obtain it, because God has promised it to those who do good works.[452]

525. **How do we show our hope?**

We show our hope not only in word but also in deed when, by putting wholehearted trust in the divine promises, we bear the hardships and afflictions and even the persecutions of this life with patience.[453]

526. **How is hope lost?**

Hope is lost by the sins of despair or presumption, also by sins that lead to loss of faith.[454]

[451] Cf. *Codex Juris Canonici*, Can. 2318, par. 1

[452] Cf. Jn 6:40; Rom 5:2; 8:24; 2 Cor 5:2; Col 1:23, 27; Ti 1:2; Heb 3:6; Benedict XII, Constitution *Benedictus Deus*, January 29, 1336; Chrysostom, *Homily 14 on Romans*, Ch. 6

[453] Cf. Rom 8:17-18, 23-25; 1 Cor 9:25; 2 Cor 1:7; 4:8-18; 7:1

[454] Cf. Gn 4:13; Mt 3:9; 19:25-26; 27:5; Acts 1:16-19, 26

527. **What is despair?**
Despair is deliberate failure to trust that we shall obtain from God eternal life and the means necessary thereto.

528. **What is presumption?**
Presumption is a rash confidence that we shall obtain eternal life without grace or without good works.

Charity

529. **What is charity?**
Charity is a supernatural virtue whereby we love God above all things for his own sake, and ourselves and our neighbor for the sake of God.[455]

530. **How should we set about proving our love of God?**
We should set about proving our love of God by keeping his commandments.[456]

[455] Cf. Mt 22:37-39; 1 Jn 3:17-18; 4:20-21. The above definition of charity can be stated more fully thus: charity is called a "supernatural" virtue, because by it we love God not simply as he is known to us by our natural powers, but as he is known by an infused gift from God. "Whereby we love God"—the primary object, then, on which charity falls is God himself; "above all things"—for while our wills tend to what is good yet God is the supreme good and therefore desirable above all things; "for his own sake"—that is, by reason of his own intrinsic goodness, so that the formal object or motive of charity is the infinite goodness of God. And since, further, love of another for his own sake is the love of benevolence, and God himself pursues us with a love of benevolence, and since again mutual benevolence is friendship, it follows that charity is a species of friendship between God and men (see *Summa Theologiae*, II-II, q. 23, a. 1). It continues: "and ourselves and our neighbor"—whence it follows that we ourselves and our neighbor are the secondary objects of charity; "for God's sake"—for whosoever loves another with the love of benevolence loves also those whom that other loves; whence it follows that we love ourselves and our neighbors because we love God and he loves both us and our neighbors; wherefore we too by charity desire for ourselves and for our neighbor what God himself desires for us and for them, namely, grace in this present life and eternal glory in the next.

[456] Cf. Jn 14:15, 21, 23; 1 Jn 5:3; Gregory the Great, *On the Gospels*, Bk. 2, Homily 30, n. 1-2

531. **What further proof can we give of our love of God?**
We can give a further proof of our love of God by doing other good works which, though not commanded by him, are acceptable to him—in other words, works of supererogation.

532. **How can we lose our love of God?**
We lose our love of God by any mortal sin; but, while grace is thus lost by mortal sin, it does not always follow that faith and hope are therefore lost.[457]

533. **How ought we to love ourselves?**
We ought to love ourselves by seeking in all things the glory of God and our own eternal salvation.

534. **How ought we to love our neighbor?**
We ought to love our neighbor by inward and outward acts—that is, we ought to pardon his offenses, avoid causing him loss, injury, or scandal, and help him in his needs so far as we can, especially by the corporal and spiritual works of mercy.[458]

535. **What are the spiritual works of mercy?**
The spiritual works of mercy are:

1. To counsel the doubtful.
2. To instruct the ignorant.
3. To convert the sinner.
4. To comfort the sorrowful.
5. To forgive injuries.
6. To bear wrongs patiently.
7. To pray for the living and the dead.[459]

[457] Cf. Jas 2:10-11; 1 Jn 3:6, 8-9; 1 Cor 13:1-3; Jas 2:14, 17, 24; 1 Jn 3:15-18; Council of Trent, Session 6, "Decree on Justification," Ch. 15; Can. 27-28; *Summa Theologiae*, II-II, q. 24, a. 12

[458] Cf. Innocent XI, Decree of the Sacred Congregation of the Inquisition, March 2, 1679, the tenth and eleventh condemned Propositions

[459] Cf. 2 Mc 12:46; Mt 10:10; Lk 10:26ff; Rom 12:12-17; Gal 6:1-2; Eph 4:1-2, 32; 6:18; Col 4:2; 1 Thes 5:14-17; 1 Tm 2:1-2; Jas 5:19-20

536. **What are the corporal works of mercy?**

The corporal works of mercy are:

1. To feed the hungry.
2. To give drink to the thirsty.
3. To clothe the naked.
4. To harbor the harborless.
5. To visit the sick.
6. To visit the imprisoned.
7. To bury the dead.[460]

537. **Does charity toward our neighbor also extend to our enemies?**

Charity toward our neighbor also extends to our enemies, for they too are our neighbors, and Christ himself has given us a commandment and an example on this subject.[461]

THE MORAL VIRTUES

538. **What is a moral virtue?**

A moral virtue is one whose immediate object is good actions done in accordance with right reason.

539. **Can acts of the moral virtues be divided according to the end toward which they are directed?**

Acts of the moral virtues, by reason of the end toward which they are directed, can be either natural—for example, if a person fasts lest food prove harmful to his health—or supernatural—for example, if a person fasts to obtain from God the pardon of his sins or to chastise his body and bring it into subjection.[462]

[460] Cf. Tb 4:1-12; 12:12; Ecclus 7:39; Is 58:7; Ez 18:7, 16; Mt 25:35-45; Heb 13:2, 16; Jas 1:27

[461] Cf. Mt 5:44; Lk 6:27, 35; 23:34; Acts 7:59; Rom 12:20; TCCI 7:445

[462] Cf. 1 Cor 9:27; *Summa Theologiae*, I-II, q. 63, a. 4

540. **Which are the principal moral virtues, and how many are there?**
The principal moral virtues are four—prudence, justice, fortitude, and temperance; these are also called "cardinal" virtues.[463]

541. **Why are these virtues called "cardinal"?**
These virtues are called "cardinal," because they are, as it were, the hinges (*cardines*) on which turns the whole structure of the moral life; to them the other moral virtues are reducible.[464]

542. **How do the cardinal virtues help us?**
1. Prudence helps us to form a right judgment in all circumstances as to what we should seek or avoid for the sake of eternal life.
2. Justice helps us to render to everyone his due.
3. Fortitude prevents us from being deterred in our pursuit of what is good by any difficulty or persecution, even death itself.
4. Temperance helps us to curb evil desires and to use the good things of the senses only in accordance with right reason.

THE GIFTS OF THE HOLY SPIRIT

543. **When a person is justified, does he receive anything else besides the remission of his sins and the infusion of the theological virtues?**
When a person is justified, he receives, in addition to the remission of his sins and the infusion of the theological virtues, the gifts of the Holy Spirit.

[463] Cf. Ws 8:7; Augustine, *Tractate 8 on First John*, to the Parthians; *Summa Theologiae*, I-II, q. 61

[464] Consequently, under justice we can group religion, piety, observance, obedience, gratitude, truthfulness, liberality, friendliness…; under fortitude we place magnanimity, patience, perseverance…; under temperance come abstinence, propriety, sobriety, chastity, virginity, continence, meekness, modesty, humility…Humility is the most fundamental virtue of all, since it cuts away that pride which is the beginning of all sin.

544. **How many gifts of the Holy Spirit are there?**

There are seven gifts of the Holy Spirit: wisdom, understanding, counsel, fortitude, knowledge, piety, and the fear of the Lord.[465]

545. **To what end are these gifts infused?**

These gifts are infused into a just man so that he may more easily and readily receive and correspond with the movements of the Holy Ghost, whereby he is in many and various ways urged to do good and avoid evil.[466]

546. **What help do the gifts of the Holy Spirit afford us?**

1. Wisdom helps us to find delight in the contemplation of divine things, also by divine principles to judge of things human as well as divine.
2. Understanding helps us to grasp, so far as we mortal men can, the credibility of the mysteries of faith.
3. Counsel puts us on our guard against the deceits of the devil and the world, and helps us in dubious cases to see what is more to the glory of God and more conducive to our own and our neighbor's salvation.
4. Fortitude affords us remarkable strength in resisting temptation and overcoming hindrances to our spiritual life.
5. Knowledge helps us to distinguish rightly between what we should and should not believe; by it, too, we are guided in those things which concern our spiritual life.
6. Piety shows us how to offer due worship and service to God, also to the saints and to those men who stand in the place of God in our regard; finally, it shows us how, for the love of God, to assist those who are in trouble.[467]
7. Fear of the Lord helps us to avoid sin through a fear of offending the Divine Majesty; this fear springs from a reverential and filial love of God.[468]

[465] Cf. Is 11:2-3; Ambrose, *On the Mysteries*, Ch. 7, n. 42; *On the Sacraments*, Bk. 3, Ch. 2, n. 8

[466] Cf. Leo XIII, Encyclical *Divinum illud munus*, May 9, 1897; *Summa Theologiae*, I-II, q. 68, a. 3; Canisius, *De Donis et Fructibus Spiritus Sancti*, iii, B

[467] Cf. *Summa Theologiae*, II-II, q. 101, a. 3

[468] Cf. *Summa Theologiae*, II-II, q. 7, a. 1

THE BEATITUDES AND THE FRUITS OF THE HOLY SPIRIT

547. **What are the effects of the theological virtues and of the gifts of the Holy Spirit?**

The effects of the theological virtues and of the gifts of the Holy Spirit are the beatitudes and the fruits of the Holy Spirit.

548. **What are the beatitudes?**

The beatitudes are those taught us by Christ himself in the Sermon on the Mount, namely:

1. Blessed are the poor in spirit, for theirs is the kingdom of heaven.
2. Blessed are the meek, for they shall possess the land.
3. Blessed are they that mourn, for they shall be comforted.
4. Blessed are they that hunger and thirst after justice, for they shall have their fill.
5. Blessed are the merciful, for they shall obtain mercy.
6. Blessed are the clean of heart, for they shall see God.
7. Blessed are the peacemakers, for they shall be called the children of God.
8. Blessed are they that suffer persecution for justice's sake, for theirs is the kingdom of heaven.[469]

549. **Why does Jesus Christ call those people "blessed" who have the above dispositions?**

Jesus Christ calls those who have such dispositions "blessed" because, owing to these dispositions, they have already in this present life a certain foretaste of the blessedness that is to come.[470]

550. **Who are the "poor in spirit" who are styled "blessed"?**

The "poor in spirit" who are styled "blessed" are those who are in spirit detached from external good things, especially from wealth and dignities;

[469] Cf. Mt 5:3-10; Lk 6:20-22

[470] Cf. Leo XIII, Encyclical *Divinum illud munus*, May 9, 1897; *Summa Theologiae*, I-II, q. 69, a. 1

so much so that, if circumstances permit, of their own accord they despise them; if they do possess them, they make a moderate and good use of them; if they have them not, they make no anxious search after them; if they happen to lose them, they bear the loss in obedience to God's will.

551. **Who are the "meek"?**
The "meek" or "gentle" are those who are gracious in their dealings with their neighbor and who bear, without complaint or desire of revenge, anything they may have to suffer at his hands.

552. **Who are "they that mourn" and are yet termed "blessed"?**
"They that mourn" and are yet termed "blessed" are they who have no desire for the pleasures of this world, who in obedience to God's will gladly bear the troubles of this present life, who do penance for their sins and grieve over the evils and scandals of the world and the danger in which so many are of losing their eternal salvation.

553. **Who are "they that hunger and thirst after justice"?**
"They that hunger and thirst after justice" are they who strive to make daily advance in good works and in charity.

554. **Who are the "merciful"?**
The "merciful" are they who, for the love of God, share what they have with their neighbors and try to help them in their bodily as well as in their spiritual difficulties.

555. **Who are the "clean of heart"?**
The "clean of heart" are they who not only avoid mortal sin, especially impurity, but who keep, so far as is possible, from even venial sin.

556. **Who are the "peacemakers"?**
The "peacemakers" are they who not only live in peace with their neighbors, but try to help them to live peaceably with one another.

557. **Who are "they that suffer persecution for justice's sake"?**
"They that suffer persecution for justice's sake" are they who patiently bear contempt, calumny, and persecution, out of love of Christ.

558. **How many fruits of the Holy Spirit are there, and in what do they consist?**
The apostle St. Paul enumerates twelve fruits of the Holy Spirit—charity, joy, peace, patience, benignity, goodness, longanimity, mildness, faith, modesty, continence, chastity.[471]

Actual or Personal Sins[472]

559. **What does a person do who breaks God's law, despite the grace which he always bestows for our salvation?**
A person who, despite the grace which God always bestows for our salvation, willfully breaks his law, commits an actual or personal sin.

560. **What then is actual sin?**
Actual sin is a conscious and deliberate breach of God's law.[473]

561. **In how many ways can actual sin be committed?**
Actual sin can be committed by thought, word, and deed, whether of commission or omission, against either God, or ourselves, or our neighbor, according as the law we break is directly concerned with God, or ourselves, or our neighbor.

[471] Cf. Gal 5:22-23; *Summa Theologiae*, I-II, q. 70, a. 1, 3

[472] For original sin, see above, q. 59ff.

[473] The above definition of sin is correct not only in the case of a sin against the divine law, but also of sin against human law, for it is God who gives to men the power to make laws; "all power is of God," and he bids us observe laws enacted by legitimate authorities: "Obey your prelates" (Heb 13:17).

562. **What results from the repetition of the same actual sin?**
From the repetition of the same actual sin there results a habit that gives us an inclination to do wrong; such a habit is called a "vice."

563. **How is actual sin divided?**
Actual sin is divided into mortal sin and venial sin.[474]

564. **What is mortal sin?**
Mortal sin is conscious and deliberate breach of God's law by one who is aware of the grave obligation involved.

565. **Why is this sin called "mortal"?**
This sin is called "mortal," because it turns away the soul from its final end, robs it of its supernatural life or sanctifying grace, makes it deserving of eternal death in hell, and destroys all merits acquired, so that they no longer avail for salvation until they revive by the recovery of grace; it also prevents us from performing works meriting eternal life.[475]

566. **What is venial sin?**
Venial sin is a conscious and deliberate breach of God's law by one who is aware of the lesser obligation involved.[476]

[474] Cf. Jerome, *Against Jovinianus*, Bk. 2, n. 30; Caesarius of Arles, *Sermon 104*, n. 2, among sermons attributed to St. Augustine.

[475] Cf. Ez 18:24; 33:13; 1 Cor 6:9-10; 13:1-3. We should be ready to suffer the loss of all earthly joys, even to welcome death itself, rather than be defiled by a single mortal sin; for a mortal sin is the one real evil a man can experience, it is an infinite offense against God, it means the depth of ingratitude, the height of presumption, and it involves the ruin of a man's soul. When tempted, think of the pit of hell into which you are casting yourself if you sin mortally; think of Christ crucified and of the way in which you would, by so doing, tread underfoot his wounds and his precious blood; remember the words: "Flee from sin as you would from the face of a serpent" (Ecclus 21:2).

[476] A mortal sin may also be defined as the deliberate transgression of a grave law, that is, of a law concerning some grave matter. A venial sin is the breaking of a lesser law, of one concerned with some minor matter. Whether, however, the law is grave or not has to be decided either from God's revelation in the scriptures, or from the teaching of the fathers of the Church, or from the Church's explicit declaration, or from general agreement on the point among the Church's doctors, and herein the faithful will have to be guided by

567. **Why is this sin called "venial"?**

This sin is called "venial," because, since it does not turn away the soul from its final end or cause its supernatural death, it can be more easily pardoned, even without sacramental confession; it is a weakness of the soul that can of its very nature be easily cured.[477]

568. **What are the chief effects of venial sin?**

The chief effects of venial sin are that it lessens the fervor of charity, and makes it easier to sin mortally; by it, too, a person incurs a debt of temporal punishment which has to be paid either in this world or in the next.

569. **Are all mortal sins equal, or all venial sins?**

Sins, whether mortal or venial, are not all equal; but just as some venial sins are less grave than others, so too some mortal sins are graver than others.[478]

570. **Which mortal sins are of their very nature most grave?**

Those mortal sins are of their very nature most grave which are committed directly against God.

571. **What are the sins against the Holy Ghost?**

The sins against the Holy Ghost are:

1. Despair of salvation.
2. Presumption of gaining salvation without merits.
3. Resisting the known truth.

the wise judgment of their confessors. But when, though the sin committed is mortal so far as the actual law thus broken is concerned, yet the person who breaks it is not aware of its gravity, his sin will be venial; and conversely, if he thought it grave when it was not really so, his sin will be mortal; hence the definitions given above in the text remain true.

[477] Cf. Pius V, Constitution *Ex omnibus afflictionibus*, against the errors of Baius, Oct. 1, 1567, the twentieth condemned Proposition. Hence the mere repetition or multiplication of venial sins can never of itself become a mortal sin; so much so that even when, by repeated venial sins, the material part becomes grave through accumulation (for example, as theft may become grave by repetition) it is the resulting gravity of the matter that makes it mortal, not the repetition of the venial sins.

[478] Cf. Jn 19:11; *Summa Theologiae*, I-II, q. 73, a. 2

4. Envy of another's spiritual good.
5. Obstinacy in sin.
6. Final impenitence.[479]

572. **Why are these sins said to be "sins against the Holy Ghost"?**
These sins are said to be "sins against the Holy Ghost," because he who thus sins spurns out of malice the very things that could keep him from sin; for he is despising grace, which is peculiarly attributed to the Holy Spirit as the source of all good things.[480]

573. **Which are the sins against our neighbor that cry to heaven for vengeance?**
The sins against our neighbor that cry to heaven for vengeance are:
1. Willful murder.
2. The sin of Sodom.
3. Oppression of the poor.
4. Defrauding laborers of their wages.[481]

574. **Why are these sins said to "cry to heaven for vengeance"?**
These sins are said to "cry to heaven for vengeance," because they, more than other sins, are peculiarly and patently wicked and call down on those who commit them the wrath and vengeance of God.[482]

575. **Which are the capital sins?**
The capital sins are:
1. Pride.
2. Avarice.

[479] Cf. Mt 12:31-32; Mk 3:28-29; Lk 12:10. For the first and second of these sins, see above, q. 527-528. He commits the third kind of sin who repudiates a known truth of faith so as to indulge more freely in his sin. The fourth sin does not mean mere envy of one's brethren's personal gifts, but disgust at the spread of God's grace in the world. The fifth sin involves a determination to persevere in sin, the sixth a determination not to repent (see *Summa Theologiae*, II-II, q. 14, a. 1-2).

[480] Cf. Canisius, *De Peccatis in Spiritum Sanctum*, i; *Summa Theologiae*, II-II, q. 14, a. 1-2

[481] Cf. Gn 4:10; 18:20; Ex 22:23, 27; Dt 24:15; Jas 5:4

[482] Cf. Rom 1:28-32; 12:1-6; 1 Cor 3:16-17; 5:11; 6:9-10; Gal 5:19-21; 1 Tm 6:9-10; 2 Tm 3:2-5; Canisius, *De Peccatis in caelum clamantibus*

3. Lust.
4. Anger.
5. Gluttony.
6. Envy.
7. Sloth.

576. **Why are these sins called "capital"?**

These sins are called "capital," because they are, as it were, the source and origin of all other sins and vices.[483]

577. **What are the virtues opposed to the capital sins?**

The virtues opposed to the capital sins are respectively:

1. Humility.
2. Liberality.
3. Chastity.
4. Meekness.
5. Temperance.
6. Joy in our neighbor's welfare.
7. Diligence.

[483] Cf. *Summa Theologiae*, I-II, q. 84, a. 2-3. Hence pride (the disorderly desire of one's own excellence) is the source and root of presumption, ambition, vainglory, and boasting...; avarice (the disorderly desire of temporal good things) is the source of hard-heartedness toward the poor, of theft, fraud, and deceit...; anger (the disorderly desire of revenge) is the source of indignation, contumely, blasphemy, imprecations, quarrels, murders...; gluttony (the disorderly desire of food and drink) is the source of dullness of mind, talkativeness, and scurrilous speech...; envy (or sadness because some other person possesses good things which we regard as detracting from our own excellence) is the source of hatred, detraction, calumny, joy in our neighbor's misfortunes, and distress at his prosperity...; sloth (*acedia*, sadness with regard to spiritual good things because of the bodily labor they involve) is the cause of disgust with spiritual things, of neglect to perform good works which are of grave obligation, of gloomy views of our friendship with God...As regards lust (*luxuria*) see q. 228, note 251, above, and q. 229, note 252, above.

578. **Ought we to avoid not only sin but also the occasions of sin?**
We ought to avoid not only sin but also, so far as we can, proximate occasions of it, namely, those in which a person exposes himself to grave danger of sin; for "he that loveth the danger shall perish in it."[484]

579. **Is it possible that we may have to give an account to God for the sins of other people?**
It is possible that we may have to give an account to God for the sins of other people, in proportion, that is, as we have been the cause of them by command, counsel, or consent, or by not preventing them when we could and ought to have done so.

The Last Things

580. **What very effective means for avoiding sin does God recommend to us in holy scripture?**
In holy scripture, God recommends to us a very effective means for avoiding sin, when he bids us reflect on the last things: "In all thy works remember thy last end, and thou shalt never sin."[485]

581. **What is meant by "the last things"?**
By "the last things," we mean the things that will befall men at the last—death, judgment, hell, heaven (though between judgment and heaven, purgatory may intervene).

582. **What should be our principal reflections on death?**
Our principal reflections on death should be that it is a punishment for sin; that it is the moment on which our eternity hangs, so that after death

[484] Ecclus 3:27
[485] Ecclus 7:40; Cf. Basil, *Sermon on Psalm 33*

there is no further room for repentance and merit; also that its time and circumstances are uncertain.[486]

583. **What happens to the soul immediately after death?**
Immediately after death, the soul stands before the tribunal of Christ, to face the particular judgment.[487]

584. **About what things will the soul be judged at the particular judgment?**
At the particular judgment, the soul will be judged about every single thing—its thoughts, words, deeds, and omissions. The sentence then passed on the soul will be ratified at the general judgment, when it will be made publicly manifest.[488]

585. **What will happen to the soul after the particular judgment?**
After the particular judgment, the soul, if, owing to mortal sin, it is not in the grace of God, will be at once consigned to the punishment of hell; if it is in a state of grace and free from all venial sin and all debt of temporal punishment, it will at once be taken up into the glory of heaven; if it is in a state of grace but with some venial sin or with some debt of temporal punishment still unpaid, it will be detained in purgatory until it shall have fully satisfied God's justice.[489]

586. **What will be the state of the damned in hell?**
In hell, also called "the pit" or "Gehenna" in holy scripture, the devils—and with them the damned (their souls only, before the general judgment, their bodies too thereafter)—are tormented with everlasting punishments.[490]

[486] Cf. Gn 2:17; 3:19; Ecclus 14:12-13; 41:1-3; Mt 24:42-44; Lk 12:39-40; Rom 5:12; 6:23; 1 Thes 5:22; Heb 9:27; Council of Trent, Session 6, "Decree concerning Original Sin," Can. 1

[487] Cf. Ecclus 11:28; Rom 14:10; Heb 9:27; Benedict XII, Constitution *Benedictus Deus*, January 29, 1336; Augustine, *On the Soul and Its Origin*, Bk. 2, Ch. 8. For the general judgment, see above, q. 112ff.

[488] Cf. Mt 10:26; 12:36; 1 Cor 4:5

[489] Cf. 2 Mc 12:46; Lk 16:22; 23:43; 2 Cor 5:1-3; Council of Florence, Session 6 (July 6, 1439), "Decree for the Greeks"; John Damascene, *An Exposition of the Orthodox Faith*, Bk. 4, Ch. 27

[490] Cf. Mt 8:12; 13:42; 24:51; 25:30, 31, 46; Lk 13:27-28; 16:22, 24, 28; 2 Thes 1:9; Apoc 14:9-11; Fourth Lateran Council, Const. 1; Council of Florence, Session 6 (July 6, 1439), "Decree for the Greeks"; Vigilius, *Adversus Origenem*, Can. 9; Benedict XII, Constitution *Benedictus Deus*, January 29, 1336; Pius IX, Epistle *Quanto conficiamur*, Aug. 10, 1863, to the bishops of Italy

587. **What are the punishments endured by the damned in hell?**

The punishments endured by the damned in hell are:

1. The pain of loss—the perpetual privation of the beatific vision of God.
2. The pain of sense—a real fire torturing yet never consuming; darkness and gloom, remorse and anguish of conscience, and the company of the demons and of the other lost souls.[491]

588. **Are the sufferings of the damned the same for all alike?**

The pain of loss is the same for all alike; not so the other sufferings, for they will vary according to the number and gravity of the sins committed.[492]

589. **What will be the state of the soul in purgatory?**

In purgatory, the soul pays any debt of temporal punishment due to sin not fully paid in this life, until it shall have fully satisfied God's justice, and so can be admitted to heaven.[493]

590. **What punishments are inflicted on the soul in purgatory?**

In purgatory, the soul is punished by the pain of loss and also by the pains of sense—in other words, by being deprived for a time of the beatific vision of God and by other grievous sufferings.

591. **Are the sufferings of the souls in purgatory the same for all alike?**

The sufferings of the souls in purgatory are not the same for all alike, but differ in length and intensity according to the venial sins and the debt of temporal punishment for which each is responsible; moreover, their

[491] Cf. Mt 3:12; 13:42; 18:8; 24:51; 25:30, 41, 46; Lk 13:28; 16:24, 28; Apoc 21:8; TCCI 7:117-118

[492] Cf. Council of Florence, Session 6 (July 6, 1439), "Decree for the Greeks"; Gregory the Great, *Dialogues*, Bk. 4, Ch. 43; Augustine, *Enchiridion*, Ch. 111

[493] Cf. 2 Mc 12:43-46; Mt 12:32; 1 Cor 3:12-15; Second Council of Lyons, *Profession of Faith by Michael Palaeologus*; Council of Florence, Session 6 (July 6, 1439), "Decree for the Greeks"; Council of Trent, Session 25, "Decree concerning Purgatory"; Benedict XII, Constitution *Benedictus Deus*, January 29, 1336; Leo X, Bull *Exurge Domine*, against the errors of Luther, June 15, 1520, the thirty-seventh through the fortieth condemned Propositions; Pius IV, Constitution *Injunctum nobis*, Nov. 13, 1564, *Professio Fidei Tridentina*; Gregory the Great, *Dialogues*, Bk. 4, Ch. 39

sufferings can be rendered shorter and less grievous by means of the prayers offered for them.

592. **Will purgatory cease with the general judgment?**
Purgatory will cease with the general judgment, and all the souls then in purgatory will, in God's appointed ways, have fully satisfied his justice and be received into paradise.[494]

593. **What will be the state of the souls of the just in heaven?**
In heaven, the souls of the just, separated from their bodies before the general judgment, but united with them after it, enjoy forever the beatific vision of God, and with it all good things, without the presence or fear of any evil, in the company of our Lord Jesus Christ, of the Blessed Virgin Mary and all the inhabitants of heaven.[495]

594. **Do all the blessed in heaven enjoy eternal happiness to the same degree?**
The blessed in heaven do not all enjoy eternal happiness equally, but some more perfectly than others.[496]

595. **What is the reason of this difference?**
The reason of this difference is that the blessed in heaven see God by the "light of glory" given to each by God—to the angels according to their dignity and the grace they have received, to men according to their merits, yet so that all, though possessing the light of glory in differing degrees, are perfectly happy and blessed.

[494] Cf. Mt 25:31-34; 41, 46; Jn 5:29; Augustine, *City of God*, Bk. 21, Ch. 13, n. 16

[495] Cf. Ws 3:7-8; 5:5, 16-17; Is 49:10; 60:18-22; Mt 13:43; 19:28-29; 25:34, 46; Lk 16:22; 22:29-30; Jn 17:24; 1 Cor 2:9; 15:41ff; 2 Cor 12:4; 1 Pt 1:4; 5:4; Apoc 7:9, 16-17; 21:1-4, 10-14; 22:1-5; Fourth Lateran Council, Const. 1; Council of Vienne, A.D. 1311-1312, against the errors of the Beguards and the Beguines, the fifth condemned Proposition; Benedict XII, Constitution *Benedictus Deus*, January 29, 1336; Council of Florence, Session 6 (July 6, 1439), "Decree for the Greeks"; TCCI 7:162ff

[496] Cf. Council of Florence, Session 6 (July 6, 1439), "Decree for the Greeks"; Council of Trent, Session 6, Can. 32; Gregory the Great, *Moralia in Job*, Bk. 4, Ch. 35, n. 70; Aphrahat, *Demonstration 22*, n. 19; Ephraem, *Hymni et Sermones*, 11; Jerome, *Against Jovinianus*, Bk. 2, n. 32-34; *Apology against Rufinus*, Bk. 1, n. 23; Augustine, *Sermon 87*, n. 4, 6; *Tractate 67 on John*, n. 2

Appendix VI

TESTIMONIES REFERRED TO IN THE CATECHISM: FROM THE ECUMENICAL COUNCILS, THE ROMAN PONTIFFS, THE FATHERS OF THE CHURCH, AND THE ROMAN CONGREGATIONS

QUESTION 2

For the Council of Florence, see below, q. 349; for the Council of Trent, see below, q. 532.

Benedict XV, Encyclical *Ad beatissimi*, Nov. 1, 1914:

> "The nature and character of the Catholic faith is such that nothing can be added to it or taken from it; either the whole is accepted or the whole repudiated. 'This,' says the Athanasian Creed, 'is the Catholic faith; unless a person faithfully and firmly believes this he cannot be saved.'[497] There is no need, then, for qualifying words wherewith to signify one's profession of the Catholic faith; it is quite sufficient for a person to say: 'Christian is my name, Catholic my surname';[498] a man has only to strive to be in reality what these names signify."[499]

QUESTION 4

St. Augustine, *Tractate 118 on John*, n. 5:

> "What but the cross of Christ is the sign of Christ which everybody knows? Unless this sign is set on the foreheads of believers, on the

[497] Editor's note: The Athanasian Creed, or *Quicumque Vult*, is included in Volume VI of this series, p. 3-5.

[498] Pacian, Ep. i, *P.L.*, xiii, 1055

[499] *Acta Apostolicae Sedis*, yr. 6, p. 577

water whereby they are regenerated, on the chrism wherewith they are anointed, on the sacrifice whence they are nourished, none of these things are rightly done."[500]

QUESTION 5

Innocent III, *De Sacro Altaris Mysterio*, Bk. 2, n. 45:

"The sign of the cross is made with three fingers because it is impressed upon us in the name of the Holy Trinity...from the forehead we pass to the breast, from the right hand to the left. Some make it from the left hand to the right, so as to sign themselves and others in the same way."[501]

QUESTION 7

First Vatican Council, Constitution *Dei Filius*, Ch. 4:

"In addition to those things to which man's natural reason can attain there are also set before us for our belief certain mysteries hidden in God which we could not know without divine revelation...Divine mysteries of their very nature so transcend the powers of the human understanding that, even when revealed and received in faith, they yet remain shrouded in the veil of faith, wrapped, as it were, in a certain obscurity so long as, in this mortal life, 'we are absent from the Lord.'"[502]

Pius IX, Epistle *Tuas libenter*, Dec. 21, 1863, to the archbishop of Munich and Freisingen:

"Hence we dare not question but that those who took part in these conferences were at the same time quite prepared—since they recognized and accepted the abovementioned truth—to reject and reprobate

[500] *P.L.*, xxxv, 1950
[501] *P.L.*, ccxvii, 825
[502] 2 Cor 5:6

whole-heartedly that novel and preposterous notion of philosophy which, while admitting revelation as a historical fact, would yet subordinate to the investigations of human reason the ineffable truths set before us by divine revelation, almost as though those truths were the object of reason, or as though reason could, by its own powers and using its own principles, attain to the understanding and knowledge of any of the supernatural truths and mysteries of our most holy faith; for these so transcend human reason that the latter can never be sufficiently equipped to grasp or demonstrate them by its own powers or the use of its natural principles."[503]

QUESTION 12

First Vatican Council, Constitution *Dei Filius*, Ch. 2:

"The same holy mother Church holds and teaches that God, the beginning and end of all things, can certainly be known from created things by the natural light of human reason, 'for the invisible things of him, from the creation of the world, are clearly seen, being understood by the things that are made.'[504] Yet she also teaches that it has seemed good to the wisdom and goodness of God to reveal himself and the eternal decrees of his will to the human race by another and a supernatural way, for the apostle says: 'God, who, at sundry times and in divers manners, spoke in times past to the fathers by the prophets, last of all, in these days hath spoken to us by his Son.'"[505]

First Vatican Council, Constitution *Dei Filius*, "On Revelation," Can. 1:

"If anyone shall say that the one true God, our Creator and Lord, cannot by the things that are made be known for certain by the natural light of the human reason, let him be anathema."

[503] *Acta* of Pius IX, I, iii, 641
[504] Rom 1:20
[505] Heb 1:1-2

Pope Pius X, Motu proprio *Sacrorum Antistitum*, Sept. 1, 1910, the *Oath against Modernism*:

"I firmly embrace and receive every single thing defined, set forth, and declared by the teaching office of the Church, which cannot err, especially those doctrinal points which are directly opposed to the errors of the present day. And first of all: I profess that God, the beginning and end of all things, can by the natural light of reason 'by those things that are made,'[506] that is, by the visible works of creation, be certainly known, as a cause is known by its effects, and can therefore be demonstrated."[507]

St. Irenaeus, *Against Heresies*, Bk. 2, Ch. 9, n. 1:

"The very fashioning of the world shows forth him who founded it; its formation hints at him who made it; the world declares him who so arranged it. And this tradition the Church throughout the world has received from the apostles."[508]

St. Augustine, *Sermon 141*, n. 2:

"Why do these impious people 'detain the truth'?[509] Is it because God has spoken to some one of them? Have they received a law, as the people of Israel did through Moses? How comes it, then, that they 'detain the truth' even in the midst of their iniquity? Listen to what follows and you will see: 'Because that which is known of God was manifest in them. For God hath manifested it unto them.'[510] What? God has made a revelation to people to whom he gave no law? See, then, how he has manifested it: 'For the invisible things of him...are clearly seen,

[506] Rom 1:20

[507] *Acta Apostolicae Sedis*, yr. 2, p. 669. [Editor's note: The *Oath against Modernism* is included in full in Volume VIII of this series, p. 337-339.]

[508] *P.G.*, vii, 734

[509] Rom 1:18

[510] Rom 1:19

being understood by the things that are made.'[511] Ask the world, ask the glory of the heavens, ask the glory and harmony of the stars...ask all these and see if they will not, almost with voices, reply: 'God made us!' True-minded philosophers have asked these questions and have recognized the artist in his art."[512]

QUESTION 13

For the First Vatican Council, see above, q. 12.

QUESTION 17

First Vatican Council, Constitution *Dei Filius*, Ch. 2:

"To this same divine revelation we have to attribute the fact that even those divine truths which are not of themselves beyond human reason can, in the present condition of the human race, be known by all with promptitude, certainty, and with no admixture of error."

QUESTION 18

First Vatican Council, Constitution *Dei Filius*, Ch. 3:

"Yet in order that the assent given by faith might also be in harmony with our reason, it has pleased God to add to the interior assistance of his Holy Spirit certain external arguments in favor of his revelation, namely, certain divine facts, especially miracles and prophecy, which, since they clearly show forth the omnipotence and infinite wisdom of God, constitute most certain signs of divine revelation; they are moreover adapted to all intelligences."

[511] Rom 1:20
[512] *P.L.*, xxxviii, 776

Origen, *Contra Celsum*, Bk. 6, Ch. 10:

"It is a property of the deity to foretell the future in a way that is beyond human power and that will, by the event, show that the Spirit of God was the author of such prediction."[513]

QUESTION 21

St. Theophilus of Antioch, *To Autolycus*, Bk. 3, Ch. 12:

"The sayings of the prophets and the evangelists agree, for they both spoke by the one Spirit of God."[514]

St. Epiphanius, *Adversus Haereses*, Heresy 61, Ch. 6:

"We have need, too, of tradition; for we cannot derive all these things from scripture. For that reason, the holy apostles have delivered some things to us in writing, others by traditions."[515]

QUESTION 23

Council of Trent, Session 4, "Decree concerning the Canonical Scriptures":

"The holy, Ecumenical and General Synod of Trent...having ever before its eyes the removal of error and the preservation of the gospel in its purity in the Church—the gospel which, promised beforehand by the prophets in holy scripture, our Lord Jesus Christ first promulgated by his own mouth and then ordered to be preached by his apostles 'to every creature,'[516] as being the source of all salutary truth and moral life; realizing, too, that this same truth and code of morals is contained in written books and in unwritten traditions which, received by the

[513] *P.G.*, xi, 1306
[514] *P.G.*, vi, 1138
[515] *P.G.*, xli, 1047
[516] Mk 16:15; Cf. Mt 28:19ff

apostles from Christ's own mouth or at the dictation of the Holy Spirit, have come to us, delivered to us as it were by hand; this same holy synod, following the example of the orthodox fathers, reverently receives with like devotion and veneration all the books of the old and the new testament alike, since the one God is the author of both; it also receives with a like devotion and reverence traditions concerning both faith and morals, as given us by Christ by word of mouth or dictated by the Holy Spirit and preserved in the Catholic Church by an unbroken succession. The synod has judged it well to append to this decree a list of these books, lest doubts should arise as to which are received by it.

"They are the following:

"In the old testament: the five books of Moses, that is, Genesis, Exodus, Leviticus, Numbers, Deuteronomy; Josue, Judges, Ruth, the four books of Kings, the two of Paralipomena, the first of Esdras and the second known as Nehemias, Tobias, Judith, Esther, Job, the Davidic Psalter of 150 Psalms, Parables,[517] Ecclesiastes, Canticle of Canticles, Wisdom, Ecclesiasticus, Isaias, Jeremias with Baruch, Ezechiel, Daniel, the twelve minor prophets, or Osee, Joel, Amos, Abdias, Jonas, Michaeas, Nahum, Habacuc, Sophonias, Aggeus, Zacharias, Malachias; two books of Maccabees, the first and second.

"In the new testament: the four gospels, according to Matthew, Mark, Luke, and John; the Acts of the Apostles written by Luke the evangelist; fourteen epistles of St. Paul, to the Romans, two to the Corinthians, to the Galatians, Ephesians, Philippians, Colossians, two to the Thessalonians, two to Timothy, to Titus, to Philemon, to the Hebrews; two of Peter the apostle, three of John the apostle, one of James the apostle, one of Jude the apostle, and the Apocalypse of John the apostle.

"If, however, anyone should not receive as sacred and canonical the entire books with all their parts, as they are wont to be read in the Catholic Church and are contained in the old Vulgate Latin edition, and if anyone should knowingly and of set purpose despise the aforesaid traditions, let him be anathema."

[517] Or Proverbs.

First Vatican Council, Constitution *Dei Filius*, Ch. 2:

"Moreover this supernatural revelation is, in accordance with the faith of the universal Church set forth by the holy Synod of Trent, contained 'in written books and in unwritten traditions which, received by the apostles from Christ's own mouth or at the Holy Spirit's dictation to them, have reached us, delivered as it were by hand...' And these entire books of the old and the new testaments, with all their parts, as enumerated in the decree of that synod and given in the old Vulgate Latin edition, have to be received as sacred and canonical. Now, the Church regards these books as sacred and canonical, not because they have been produced by human industry and she has afterward given them her authoritative approval, nor merely because they contain revelation without error; but because, being written by the inspiration of the Holy Spirit, they have God for their author and as such have been delivered to the Church herself."

Leo XIII, Encyclical *Providentissimus Deus*, Nov. 18, 1893:

"For all the books which in their integrity the Church receives as sacred and canonical, with all their parts, were written by the dictation of the Holy Spirit; and so far is it from being possible that any error can coexist with inspiration, that inspiration not only is essentially incompatible with error, but excludes and rejects it as absolutely and necessarily as it is impossible that God himself, the supreme truth, can utter that which is not true.

"This is the ancient and unchanging faith of the Church, solemnly defined in the Councils of Florence and Trent, and finally confirmed and more expressly formulated by the Council of the Vatican, which made the positive statement that 'the books of the old and the new testaments have God for their author.' Hence we cannot say that because the Holy Ghost employed men as his instruments, it was these inspired instruments who perchance have fallen into error, and not the primary author. For, by his supernatural power, he so moved and impelled them to write—he was so present to them as they wrote—that all the things which he ordered, and those only, they both rightly understood, then willed faithfully to write down, and finally expressed in apt words and with infallible truth. Otherwise it could not be said that God was the author of the entire scripture...And so emphatically were all the fathers and doctors agreed that the divine writings, as left by the sacred writers, are free from all error, that they labored earnestly, with no less skill than reverence, to reconcile with each other those numerous passages which seem at variance—indeed in great measure those very passages which have been exploited by the 'higher criticism'; for they were unanimous in laying it down that those writings in their entirety and all their parts were equally from the *afflatus* of Almighty God, and that God, speaking by the sacred writers, could not set down anything but what was true."[518]

QUESTION 25

For the Council of Trent and the First Vatican Council, see above, q. 23.

QUESTION 27

First Vatican Council, Constitution *Dei Filius*, Ch. 4:

"Nor are the teachings of the faith which God has revealed to be regarded as merely philosophical propositions to be worked out by human ingenuity, but rather as a divine deposit delivered to the spouse of Christ for her faithful safekeeping and infallible exposition. Consequently we have always to hold fast to that interpretation of these sacred dogmas which holy mother Church has once and for all laid down; nor can we ever depart from that interpretation on the plea of some explanation supposed to be more profound. By all means, let intelligence, knowledge, wisdom, grow and make strides on the part of one and all, of individuals and of the entire Church, of all men and in every age; but each only in his own order; that is, in the same doctrine, the same meaning and interpretation of it."

[518] *Acta* of Leo XIII, xiii, 357-359

First Vatican Council, Constitution *Pastor Aeternus*, Ch. 4:

"To meet the demands of their pastoral office, Our Predecessors have toiled unweariedly to secure that the saving teaching of Christ should be propagated amongst all the peoples of the earth, and with like zeal have ever been on the watch to see that, where it has once been planted, it should be preserved pure and untainted. For this reason, the bishops of the entire world, now individually, now gathered in synod, have, in accordance with the long-established practice of the Churches and the norm provided by ancient rules, brought to the notice of this Apostolic See dangers which they saw emerging touching the faith, so that losses accruing to the faith might there be made good 'where the faith can suffer no lapse.'[519] And the Roman pontiffs have, according as the times and the state of affairs urged them, at one time by convoking ecumenical councils or exploring the mind of the Church spread throughout the world, at other times by local synods, at others again by taking such measures as divine providence suggested, defined that that should be held which they, by God's assistance, recognized as in harmony with holy scripture and apostolic tradition. Not that the Holy Spirit was promised to St. Peter's successors in the sense that by his revelation they were to propound some new doctrine, but that by his assistance they might safeguard and faithfully expound the revelation given through the apostles, in other words, the deposit of faith. This doctrine of the apostles all the venerable fathers and orthodox doctors have embraced, venerated, and followed. For they well knew that the See of St. Peter was to remain free from all error in accordance with the divine promise made by our Savior to the prince of his apostles: 'I have prayed for thee, that thy faith fail not, and thou, being once converted, confirm thy brethren.'"[520]

St. Irenaeus, *Against Heresies*, Bk. 3, Ch. 3, n. 1ff:

"Hence it is easy for all who are willing to see the truth, to discover in all the Church the tradition of the apostles made manifest throughout the

[519] Bernard, *Epistle 190*
[520] Lk 22:32

world; and we can enumerate the bishops appointed by the apostles, also their successors down to our own time...But since it would be a lengthy affair in a volume like this to give the order of succession in all the Churches, by pointing out the tradition received from the apostles and the faith preached by the Church founded and established by the glorious apostles Peter and Paul at Rome, the oldest, the greatest Church and the one best known to all, the Church whose tradition has come down to us by the succession of its bishops, we can put to confusion all those who draw conclusions otherwise than is fitting.

"For to this Church [of Rome] it is necessary, owing to its dominating principality, that every Church should come—that is, the faithful who are everywhere—for in that Church is preserved by those who are spread abroad the tradition derived from the apostles."[521]

QUESTION 36

Fourth Lateran Council, A.D. 1215, Const. 1, against the Albigenses:

"We firmly believe and freely acknowledge that there is but one true God, eternal, immense, unchangeable, incomprehensible, omnipotent, ineffable, the Father, the Son, and the Holy Spirit; three Persons indeed but one wholly simple essence, substance or nature; the Father from no other, the Son from the Father alone, the Holy Spirit equally from both; without beginning, always, and without end; the Father begetting, the Son begotten, the Holy Spirit proceeding; consubstantial, coequal, coomnipotent, and coeternal; one principle of all things; Creator of all things visible and invisible, spiritual and corporeal; who by his almighty power, simultaneously, at the beginning of time, fashioned out of nothing the spiritual and corporeal creation, that is, the angels and this world; and afterward, the human race, commingled as it were of spirit and body. For the devil and the other demons were created by God good by nature, but through themselves they became bad, while man sinned at the suggestion of the devil.

[521] *P.G.*, vii, 849

> "This Holy Trinity, undivided according to its common nature, distinguished according to its personal attributes, gave to the race of men, first of all through Moses and the holy prophets and its other servants, teachings in accordance with the due disposition of times."[522]

First Vatican Council, Constitution *Dei Filius*, Ch. 1:

> "The holy, catholic, apostolic, Roman Church believes and confesses that there is one true living God, Creator and Lord of heaven and earth, omnipotent, eternal, immense, incomprehensible, infinite in understanding, will, and perfection; and since he is one, individual, wholly simple and unchangeable spiritual substance, he is to be pronounced distinct in nature and being from the world, in and of himself most happy, and ineffably exalted above all things which are or can be conceived of as being other than himself.
>
> "This one and only true God, of his goodness and almighty power, not to add to or acquire his happiness but to manifest his perfection through the good things he communicates to created things, of his own deliberate counsel, simultaneously, at the beginning of time, fashioned out of nothing the spiritual and corporeal creation, that is, the angels and this world, and afterward the human race, commingled as it were of spirit and body.
>
> "And the universe thus fashioned, God, by his providence, watches over and governs, 'reaching from end to end mightily and ordering all things sweetly,'[523] 'for all things are open and naked to his eyes,'[524] even such things as were afterward to happen by the free action of his creatures."

[522] Mansi, *Concilia*, xxii, 981ff
[523] Ws 8:1
[524] Heb 4:13

St. Cyril of Jerusalem, *Catechetical Lecture 4*, n. 5:

> "This Father of our Lord Jesus Christ is limited by no place, nor is he less than heaven; indeed the heavens are the works of his hands, the entire world is contained in his grasp, he is at the same time in all things and outside them...He foreknows the future and is more powerful than all things, he knows all things and does all things as he wills, he is subject to no chain of events, to no kind of thing, neither to fortune nor to any fateful necessity. In all things he is perfect, equally possessing every species of power. He is neither diminished nor increased but ever the same and in the same way; for the sinner he has prepared punishment, for the just their reward."[525]

QUESTION 37

For the First Vatican Council, see above, q. 36.

QUESTION 39

Fourth Lateran Council, A.D. 1215, Const. 2:

> "We, with the approbation of this holy and universal council, believe and confess with Peter [the Lombard] that there exists one supreme being, incomprehensible, ineffable, who is most truly Father, Son, and Holy Ghost, three Persons together, and each of them individually. Hence in God there is only a Trinity, not a Quaternity. For each of the three Persons is that—namely, the divine substance, essence or nature—which alone is the principle of the universe, beside which there is no other. It is neither generating, nor generated, nor proceeding, but it is the Father who begets, the Son who is begotten, the Holy Spirit who proceeds; the distinctions, then, are in the Persons, the unity in the nature. Although, then, one is the Father, one the Son, another the Holy Spirit, each a different Person, yet are they not each a different thing; for that which is the Father, that also wholly is the Son, and that

[525] *P.G.*, xxxiii, 459

likewise the Holy Spirit, so that—in accordance with the Catholic orthodox faith—they are to be believed consubstantial. For the Father by begetting the Son from eternity gave him his nature, as the Son himself testifies: 'That which my Father hath given me is greater than all.'[526] Nor can it be said that the Father gave to the Son part of his substance while retaining part for himself; for the substance of the Father is indivisible, being wholly simple. Neither can it be said that the Father transmitted his substance to the Son by begetting him, as though he so gave it to the Son as not to retain it for himself; for, in that case, the substance would cease to be. It is clear, then, that the Son, by being born, received the Father's substance without any diminution of it, and that thus Father and Son have one and the same substance; so, too, Father and Son are one thing, as also the Holy Spirit proceeding from both. When, then, the truth prays for them that believe in him, saying: 'I pray that they may be one in us, as we also are one,'[527] this word *one* in the case of the faithful is to be understood as signifying the union of charity by grace, but in the case of the divine Persons as signifying the union of identity in nature, as the truth himself says elsewhere: 'Be ye perfect as your heavenly Father is perfect,'[528] as though more explicitly he would say: 'Be ye perfect' with the perfection of grace, 'as your heavenly Father is perfect' by the perfection of nature—each, that is, in his own way."[529]

Second Council of Lyons, A.D. 1274, *De Processione Spiritus Sancti*:

"We faithfully and devoutly profess that the Holy Spirit proceeds eternally from the Father and the Son, not as from two principles, but from one, not by two breathings (spirations) but from a single breathing (spiration). This has always been the profession of the holy Roman Church, this she has preached and taught, this she, the mother and teacher of all the faithful, firmly holds, preaches, professes, and teaches; this is the unchangeable and true mind of the fathers and doctors,

[526] Jn 10:29
[527] Jn 17:21
[528] Mt 5:48
[529] Mansi, *Concilia*, xxii, 983ff

Greeks and Latins alike. Since, however, some, through ignorance of the aforesaid irrefragable truth, have fallen into various errors, we, in our desire to put a stop to such errors, do, with the approval of this sacred council, condemn and reprobate those who dare to deny that the Holy Spirit proceeds eternally from the Father and the Son; also those who rashly assert that the Holy Spirit proceeds from Father and Son as from two and not from one principle."[530]

Council of Florence, Session 6 (July 6, 1439), "Decree for the Greeks":

"In the name of the Holy Trinity, of the Father, Son, and Holy Ghost; with the approbation of this holy and universal Council of Florence, we define that the following truth of the faith is to be believed and received by all Christians: all are to make profession that the Holy Spirit is eternally from Father and Son and that he derives his subsistent being from Father and Son simultaneously, and proceeds from both eternally as from one principle and by one breathing (spiration). We declare moreover that when the holy fathers and doctors say that the Holy Spirit proceeds from the Father through the Son they mean thereby to signify that the Son also is the cause, according to the Greek fathers, or the principle according to the Latins, of the subsistence of the Holy Spirit, just as is the Father. And since all that belongs to the Father apart from his fatherhood the Father has given to his only-begotten Son by begetting him, the Son derives from the Father eternally the very fact that the Holy Spirit proceeds from the Son himself who is eternally begotten of the Father. We define moreover that the expression *Filioque* as an explanation of the preceding words was lawfully and reasonably added to the Creed for the purpose of stating a truth and through urgent necessity."[531]

[530] Mansi, *Concilia*, xxiv, 81
[531] Mansi, *Concilia*, xxxi, 1030

St. Augustine, *On the Trinity*, Bk. 1, Ch. 4, n. 7:

"All the Catholic commentators on the books of the old and new testaments who have written up to now and whom I have had an opportunity of reading have aimed at teaching, in accordance with the scriptures, that Father, Son, and Holy Spirit imply a divine unity in inseparable equality of one and the same substance and that consequently there are not three gods, but one God, although since the Father 'begot,' the Son is therefore not the one who is Father; similarly, since it is the Son who is 'begotten,' the Father is not the one who is Son; nor is the Holy Spirit either Father or Son but only the Spirit of Father and Son, though he is coequal with Father and Son and belongs to the same Unity of the Trinity."[532]

St. Epiphanius, *Ancoratus*, Ch. 8:

"Each of these appellations is individual, nor does one signify what the other signifies. For the Father is *Father*, nor has he anything that can be set over against him; nor is he joined with any other father, so as to make two gods. The only-begotten Son, true God of true God, does not arrogate to himself the title of *Father*, nor is he different from the Father but existing of one Father; he is termed *only-begotten* to show that he alone is to be called *Son*; he is called 'God of God' to show that it is one God who is called Father and Son. And the one and only Holy Spirit does not usurp to himself the title of *Father*, nor that of *Son*, but is called the *Holy Spirit*, nor is he different from the Father. For the only-begotten Son himself speaks of 'the Spirit of the Father,'[533] also of him who 'proceeds from the Father.'[534] He also says that 'he shall receive of mine,'[535] lest that Holy Spirit should be reputed different from either Father or Son, whereas he is of one and the same substance and divinity with them, the divine Spirit, the Spirit of truth, the Spirit of God...God, then, is in the Father, in the Son, in the Holy Spirit who

[532] *P.L.*, xlii, 824
[533] Cf. Jn 15:26
[534] Ibid.
[535] Ibid.; Jn 16:14ff

likewise is God and from God. For he is the Spirit of God, the Spirit of the Father, the Spirit of the Son, not by any mingling such as that whereby in ourselves body and soul are joined, but he is betwixt Father and Son, proceeding from Father and Son, third in name."[536]

St. John Damascene, *An Exposition of the Orthodox Faith*, Bk. 1, Ch. 12:

"The Father is source and author both of Son and Holy Spirit; of the Son alone is he Father, and of the Holy Spirit producer. But the Son is Son, the Word, Wisdom, power, image, splendor, the Father's figure and from the Father. The Holy Spirit is not the Son of the Father, but the Spirit of the Father, as the one who proceeds from the Father, for there is no impulse without the Spirit. At the same time, he is called the Spirit of the Son, not as proceeding from him but through him proceeding from the Father. The Father alone is author."[537]

QUESTION 41

Council of the Lateran under Martin I, A.D. 649, Can. 1, against the Monothelites:

"If anyone shall not, with the holy fathers, really and truly confess Father, Son, and Holy Spirit, the Trinity in Unity and Unity in Trinity, that is one God in three consubstantial subsistencies of equal glory, the identity in Godhead of the three in nature, substance, virtue, power, kingdom, empire, will, uncreated operation, without beginning, incomprehensible, unchangeable, creative and protective of all—let him be condemned."[538]

[536] *P.G.*, xliii, 29
[537] *P.G.*, xciv, 950
[538] Mansi, *Concilia*, x, 1151

St. Fulgentius, *De Fide*, Ch. 1, n. 4:

"Since in that Trinity which is the one true God it is naturally true that not only is God one but also that there is a Trinity, it is therefore true that God himself is in Persons threefold and in nature one. By this unity in nature the whole Father is in the Son and Holy Spirit, the whole Son in Father and Holy Spirit, the whole Holy Spirit in Father and Son. No one of these is outside the other, for none preceded the other in eternity, exceeded in magnitude, or surpassed in power."[539]

St. Ephraem the Syrian, *Hymnus de defunctis et Trinitate*, n. 11-12:

"The Father is the begetter, the Son begotten of his bosom; the Holy Spirit proceeding from Father and Son; the Father the Maker who made the world out of nothing; the Son the Creator who with his begetter made the universe.

"The Holy Spirit, the Paraclete and the compassionator by whom is perfected all that was, will be, and is; the Father, the Mind, the Son, the Word, the Spirit, the Voice, three names, one will, one power."[540]

St. Gregory Nazianzen, *Oration 33*, n. 16:

"The faithful adore Father, Son, and Holy Spirit, one Godhead; God the Father, God the Son, God the Holy Spirit, one nature in three properties, understanding, perfect, subsisting of themselves, distinct indeed in number, not distinct in Godhead."[541]

QUESTION 46

For the Fourth Lateran Council and the First Vatican Council, see above, q. 36.

[539] *P.L.*, lxv, 673-674
[540] *Ed.* Lamy, *Sti. Ephremi Hymni et Sermones*, iii, 242ff
[541] *P.G.*, xxxvi, 235

QUESTION 47

For the First Vatican Council, see above, q. 36.

QUESTION 48

St. John Chrysostom, *Contra Anomaeos*, Ch. 12, n. 4:

> "God not only produced created things but also watches over and cherishes them, whether you term them angels or archangels or superior powers, or all those things which do or do not come under our senses; all enjoy his providential care and, if destroyed by his effective act, are dissipated, vanish, and perish."[542]

QUESTION 49

St. Augustine, *On the Spirit and the Letter*, Ch. 58:

> "But 'God wills all men to be saved and to come to the knowledge of the truth';[543] not, however, so as to take away their free will, for the good or bad use of which they are most justly judged. When this happens, it is true that unbelievers act contrary to God's will when they do not believe in his gospel; but that does not mean that they conquer God, but that they deprive themselves of the great and supreme good and involve themselves in evils as their reward, afterward to experience in their punishment his power whose mercies they despised in his gifts."[544]

[542] *P.G.*, xlviii, 810
[543] 1 Tm 2:4
[544] *P.L.*, xliv, 238

QUESTION 50

St. Ephraem the Syrian, *Carmina Nisibena*, Hymn 3, n. 8-10:

"It is well-known that the good God did not desire the calamities which have at all times afflicted the human race, though he it was who sent them; but it was our sins that were the cause of our own afflictions. No one ought to complain of our Creator; it is of ourselves we ought to complain since by sinning we forced him, against his will, to be angry with us and, contrary to his good pleasure, to afflict us...Even a man inflicts chastisement so as himself to gain profit out of it. For everybody chastises his own servants so as to keep possession of them; whereas the good God chastises his servants that they may learn to possess themselves. Your afflictions should be like a book which admonishes you."[545]

QUESTION 52

St. John Damascene, *An Exposition of the Orthodox Faith*, Bk. 2, Ch. 3:

"An angel, then, is an intelligent substance, endowed with perpetual motion and free will, without a body, subservient to God, immortal in nature through the gift of God; his precise nature and definition his Creator alone knows. Only in comparison with us men is he incorporeal and immaterial, for everything, when compared with God—who alone can be compared to nothing—is crass and material. For the divine nature alone is truly immaterial and incorporeal."[546]

QUESTION 53

St. Athanasius, *De Virginitate*, n. 5:

"Humility of soul is a mighty remedy working for our salvation; it was not for harlotry, adultery, or theft that Satan was cast out of heaven,

[545] *Ed.* G. Bickell, p. 80

[546] *P.G.*, xciv, 866ff

but pride cast him thence into the abyss of hell, for he said: 'I will ascend above the height of the clouds and set my throne next to God, and I will be like the most High.'[547] For these words was he cast down and eternal fire became his portion and his inheritance."[548]

St. Gregory the Great, *On the Gospels*, Bk. 2, Homily 34, n. 7-9:

"We have mentioned nine choirs of angels because from holy scripture we learn of angels, archangels, virtues, powers, principalities, dominations, thrones, cherubim, and seraphim.

"But we have to realize that the name *angel* signifies an office rather than a nature. For those holy spirits of our heavenly fatherland are indeed always spirits, yet they cannot always be spoken of as 'angels,' for they are such only when things are declared by them...Those whose business it is to declare to us things of less importance are called 'angels,' those who declare the great things, 'archangels'...Hence it was not a simple 'angel' who was sent to the Virgin Mary, but Gabriel, the 'archangel'; for it was but fitting that one of the highest angels should be entrusted with this supreme message. And these higher angels are known by special names significative of their office: namely, Michael—'who is like to God?'; Gabriel—'the strength of God'; Raphael—'the medicine of God.'"[549]

QUESTION 54

St. Jerome, *On Matthew*, Ch. 18:

"Great is the dignity of the human soul, since each one of them has from the very outset of his life an angel deputed to safeguard him."[550]

[547] Cf. Is 14:13-14: St. Athanasius is quoting loosely, from memory.

[548] *P.G.*, xxviii, 258

[549] *P.L.*, lxxvi, 1249ff

[550] *P.L.*, xxvi, 130

QUESTION 58

St. Irenaeus, *Against Heresies*, Bk. 5, Ch. 24, n. 3-4:

"But all that the devil—the apostate angel—can do is to seduce and lead away men's minds and so make them transgress God's commands; thus, little by little, he blinds the hearts of those who would serve God, with the result that in time they come to forget the true God and to worship the devil as God...More and more does he set himself against man through envy of his life and because he wishes to ensnare him by his own apostate power."[551]

QUESTION 60

Fifth Lateran Council, A.D. 1512-1517, Session 8, *De anima humana*:

"Since, then, in these our days, as we acknowledge with grief, the sower of tares, the ancient enemy of the human race, has, with growing audacity, dared to oversow the Lord's field with pernicious errors such as the faithful have always rejected, especially with errors concerning the rational soul—for example, that it is mortal, or that the whole human race has but one soul in common—and since some, rashly philosophizing, have ventured to maintain that these views are true at least according to philosophy, We, in our anxiety to apply proper remedies for such pestilential teachings, do, with the approbation of this holy council, condemn and reprobate all who maintain that the rational human soul is mortal, or that men have but one soul in common, also those who question whether this may not be so. For the human soul is not only of itself truly and essentially the form of the human body, as is set forth in the canon published in the council held at Vienne under Our Predecessor Pope Clement V of blessed memory, but it is also immortal and, according to the multitude of bodies into which it is infused, is capable of multiplication, is and will be multiplied...And since truth cannot be opposed to truth, We define that every assertion

[551] *P.G.*, vii, 1188

opposed to this truth of illumined faith is wholly false, and We strictly forbid anyone to teach otherwise; We also declare that all who cling to such erroneous assertions are to be avoided and punished as disseminators of damnable heresies, as detestable and hateful heretics, as men who would destroy the Catholic faith."[552]

Pius IX, Epistle *Dolore haud mediocri*, April 30, 1860, to the bishop of Wratislavia:

"It should also be remarked that when Baltzer had in his book reduced the entire controversy to the question whether there is not in the body a principle of life really distinct from the rational soul; he rashly went so far as to term the contrary opinion heretical and he adduced many arguments in support of his view. Now this notion we are compelled to repudiate when we reflect that the opinion which maintains that there is only one vital principle in a man, namely, his rational soul, whence his body receives both motion and all life and sensation, has always been that most widely held in the Church of God, and that many of the most learned and approved theologians have regarded it as so intimately linked up with the Church's dogma as to afford the only true and lawful interpretation of it, and consequently that it is impossible to deny it without erring in the faith."[553]

St. John Damascene, *An Exposition of the Orthodox Faith*, Bk. 2, Ch. 12:

"Now the soul is a living, simple, incorporeal substance, of its very nature eluding the vision of the bodily eye, immortal, sharing in reason and intelligence, using a body furnished with organs, and affording to this body life, growth, sensation, and the power of reproduction; it has not a mind distinct from itself, for the mind is nothing else than the soul's more subtle part, for what the eye is to the body that the mind is to the soul; it is endowed with freedom of choice and the capacity to will and to act."[554]

[552] Mansi, *Concilia*, xxxii, 842
[553] *Acta* of Pius IX, from which the *Syllabus* was taken, Rome, 1865, p. 178
[554] *P.G.*, xciv, 923ff

QUESTION 62

Benedict XII, Constitution *Benedictus Deus*, January 29, 1336:

"By this constitution, which is to hold good forever, We by apostolic authority define that, in accordance with the general ordinance of God, the souls of all the saints who departed from this world before the passion of our Lord Jesus Christ, as also the souls of the holy apostles, martyrs, confessors, virgins, and of the rest of the faithful who have departed this life after receiving Christ's baptism, in whom there was found nothing calling for purification when they died, nor shall be found in those yet to die, or in case there was or shall be anything in them demanding purification, when they shall have been thus purified after death; as also the souls of children who have been baptized and regenerated by the said Christian baptism and who die before attaining the use of free will—these, straightway upon their death, or after purification in the case of those who need it, even before the resurrection of their bodies and the general judgment, have been, are, and will be, since the ascension of our Lord and Savior Jesus Christ gathered into heaven, into the kingdom of heaven and the heavenly paradise together with Christ and the company of his holy angels, and have, ever since the passion and death of our Lord Jesus Christ, seen and do see the divine essence with an intuitive vision, face-to-face without the intervention of any created medium as the object of their vision, but the divine essence, immediately and nakedly, clearly and evidently, exhibits itself to them: moreover, that through this vision they wholly enjoy the divine essence, and further that, owing to this vision and fruition, the souls of those who have already departed this life are truly happy and possess eternal life and rest: also that the souls of those who are yet to die shall see the same divine essence and enjoy it before the general judgment; also that the said vision and fruition of the divine essence render void acts of faith and hope insofar as faith and hope are properly speaking theological virtues: also that after this intuitional and face-to-face vision and fruition shall have begun in these souls, this same vision and fruition will remain permanent in them without interruption or cessation of the said vision and fruition and will be continued until the last judgment and from thence onward into eternity.

"We also define that according to God's general ordinance the souls of those who depart this life in actual mortal sin descend straightway after death into hell where they suffer its torments; yet nonetheless in the day of judgment all will appear before the tribunal of Christ there to render an account of their actions 'that every one may receive the proper things of the body according as he hath done.'"[555]

St. John Damascene, *An Exposition of the Orthodox Faith*, Bk. 4, Ch. 27:

"Those who have done good things will, in company with the angels, shine like the sun in eternal life with our Lord Jesus Christ, to see him and be seen by him always, and derive thence a happiness that can never fail, praising him with the Father and the Holy Spirit through infinite ages."[556]

QUESTION 63

St. Pius V, Constitution *Ex omnibus afflictionibus*, against the errors of Baius, Oct. 1, 1567, the first through the tenth condemned Propositions:

Prop. 1: "Neither the merits of an angel nor those of the first man before his fall are correctly called 'grace.'"

Prop. 2: "Just as a bad deed is of its very nature deserving of eternal death, so is a good deed of its very nature deserving of eternal life."

Prop. 3: "Both for the good angels and for the first man—had he persevered in his state of innocence to the close of his life—happiness would have been a reward, not a grace."

Prop. 4: "Eternal life was promised to unfallen man and to the angels on the ground of good works; and good works proceeding from the law of nature suffice of themselves for the attainment of that reward."

[555] 2 Cor 5:10; *Bullarium Romanum*, ed. Turin, iv, 346ff

[556] *P.G.*, xciv, 1227

Prop. 5: "In the promise made to the angels and to the first man, there is enshrined the basis of natural justice, whereby eternal life is promised for good works without any further qualification."

Prop. 6: "It is a decree of the natural law that, if a man perseveres in obedience, he will pass to that life in which he will never die."

Prop. 7: "The merits of unfallen man were gifts of his creation, but in accordance with biblical language they are not properly called 'grace'; whence it follows that they ought to be called simply 'merits,' not 'grace.'"

Prop. 8: "In those who are redeemed by the grace of Christ, no good merit can be discovered which is not gratuitously conferred as on one undeserving of it."

Prop. 9: "The gifts granted to unfallen man can perhaps reasonably be termed 'grace'; but since according to scriptural usage only those gifts are comprised under the term *grace* which are conferred by Jesus Christ on the wicked and undeserving, it follows that neither merits nor rewards bestowed on them can be styled 'grace.'"

Prop. 10: "That we should, after living holily and righteously in this mortal life to the end of our days, attain eternal life is not strictly due to the grace of God, but is to be referred to a natural ordinance due to God's just decision from the beginning of creation; nor does the reward due to good works depend on Christ's merits, but solely on the primal institution of the human race when it was, by the natural law, ordained that according to God's just judgment eternal life is the reward for obedience to his commands."[557]

[557] Du Plessis, *Collectio Judiciorum*, III, ii, 110ff

Clement XI, Constitution *Unigenitus*, against the errors of Quesnel, Sept. 8, 1713, the thirty-fifth condemned Proposition:

> "The grace of Adam was a consequence of creation and a debt due to unfallen nature."[558]

Pius VI, Constitution *Auctorem Fidei*, against the errors of the Synod of Pistoia, Aug. 28, 1794, the sixteenth condemned Proposition:

> "The teaching of that synod touching the state of original innocence and depicting the state of Adam previous to his sin as implying not only a nature unfallen but one endowed with an interior righteousness, urged toward God by an impulse of love which is charity, adding, too, a primitive holiness which was in some sort restored after he had sinned: all this, inasmuch as—taken as a whole—it suggests that that state was the natural consequence of creation and due to the natural exigencies and condition of human nature and therefore not due to a gratuitous gift of God, is false teaching, already condemned in the cases of Baius and Quesnel; it is erroneous, and savors of the Pelagian heresy."[559]

QUESTION 65

St. John Chrysostom, *Homily 13 on Genesis*, Ch. 1:

> "Have you noticed how all things were formed by a word? But note, too, what is said afterward, when man is created: 'And God formed man.'[560] Note the careful way in which, for our infirmity's sake, he uses words which serve to indicate both the mode and the diversity of creation; he shows—if we may speak in human fashion—that man was formed by the hands of God, as indeed another prophet expresses it: 'Thy hands have made me and fashioned me.'"[561]

[558] Du Plessis, *Collectio Judiciorum*, III, ii, 462
[559] *Bullarii Romani Continuatio*, ed. Prati, VI, iii, 2710
[560] Gn 2:7
[561] Jb 10:8; *P.G.*, liii, 106

QUESTION 66

St. Ephraem, *On Genesis*, Ch. 2:

"Now, that Adam was created to the image and likeness of God we understand from three things. Do not imagine, however, that Adam's external appearance is called 'the image of God'; rather it is his spirit, endowed with free choice and equipped with power and authority over the rest of creation, that is so called; precisely, then, as all things are in the hand and gift of God, so too was the world made subject to Adam. Further, man received a pure and sinless soul, consequently one capable of receiving divine virtues and gifts. He received, too, intelligence and reason whereby he could comprehend, analyze, and compare all things; by these powers man reaches out everywhere, and so forms images of everything that he seems in his single self to contain all things."[562]

St. Basil the Great, *Sermo asceticus*, Ch. 1:

"Man was made to the image and likeness of God;[563] but sin, through the soul's impulse toward the vices and concupiscences, defaced that fair image. But God, who made man, is true life. Since, then, man had lost the likeness of God, he had thereby destroyed the fellowship of life with God; and he who is away from God cannot lead a happy life. Let us return, then, to the grace accorded us at the outset but from which we have fallen by sin; let us once more deck ourselves out to the image of God."[564]

St. Augustine, *On Psalm 49*, n. 2:

"It is clear, then, that since he called men 'gods' they can have been deified only by his grace; they were not so because born of his substance. For he justifies who is of himself just, not deriving his justice from another; he makes men gods who is of his own nature God, not deriving his Godhead from another. And he who justifies is he who

[562] *Opera omnia, ed. Romana*, i [Syriac and Latin], 128

[563] Cf. Gn 1:26

[564] *P.G.*, xxxi, 870ff

deifies, for it is by justifying us that he makes us sons of God: 'He gave them power to become the sons of God.'[565] If we have been made the sons of God, then we have become gods; but this through the favor of him who adopts us, not of one who begets us by nature."[566]

QUESTION 74

Second Council of Carthage, A.D. 418, approved by Pope Zosimus, Can. 2 against the Pelagians:

"It was also agreed that whosoever should deny that newborn children ought to be baptized, or say that, though baptized 'unto the remission of sin,' yet they do not derive from Adam any original sin calling for expiation in the laver of regeneration—with the consequence that, in their case, the formula of baptism 'unto remission of sins' is not true but false—let him be anathema. For in no other way can we understand the words of the apostle: 'As by one man sin entered into this world, and by sin death, and so death passed upon all men in whom all have sinned,'[567] than that in which the universal Catholic Church has always understood them. For by reason of this rule of faith, even children who have not as yet been able to commit sin in themselves are truly baptized 'unto the remission of sins,' so that what they derived from their generation may be cleansed in their regeneration."[568]

Second Council of Orange, A.D. 529, confirmed by Pope Boniface II, Can. 1 and 2 against the Semipelagians:

"Can. 1: If anyone shall say that by the prevarication of Adam it was not the whole man—that is, his body and his soul—that was changed for the worse, but that, while his soul's free will remained untouched, his body alone became the victim of corruption, such a man is misled

[565] Jn 1:12
[566] *P.L.*, xxxvi, 565
[567] Rom 5:12
[568] Mansi, *Concilia*, iii, 811

by the errors of Pelagius and contradicts the scripture, which says: 'The soul that sinneth, the same shall die,'[569] and again: 'Know ye not that to whom ye yield yourselves servants to obey, his servants ye are whom ye obey?'[570] and again: 'By whom a man is overcome, of the same also is he the slave.'[571]

"Can. 2: If anyone shall assert that Adam's prevarication harmed only Adam himself and not his offspring, or at least that only the death of the body, which is the penalty of sin, and not sin itself, which is the death of the soul, passed from one man to the entire human race, such a man does an injustice to God and contradicts the apostle, who says: 'By one man sin entered into this world, and by sin death, and so death passed upon all men, in whom all have sinned.'"[572]

Council of Florence, Session 11 (Feb. 4, 1442), "Decree for the Jacobites":

"[This council] firmly believes, professes, and teaches that no one conceived of man and woman was ever freed from the domination of the devil save by the merits of the mediator of God and men, Jesus Christ our Lord; he was conceived without sin, was born and died, and alone by his death overcame the enemy of the human race, blotting out our sins; he reopened the entrance into the kingdom of heaven which the first man, with all who succeeded him, had lost by his own sin; and he is one day to come again, as all the sacred rites, sacrifices, sacraments, and ceremonies of the old testament signify."[573]

Council of Trent, Session 5, "Decree concerning Original Sin":

Can. 1: "If anyone shall refuse to acknowledge that the first man, Adam, when he transgressed God's command in paradise, straightway lost the holiness and righteousness in which he had been constituted,

[569] Ez 18:20
[570] Rom 6:16
[571] 2 Pt 2:19
[572] Rom 5:12; Mansi, *Concilia*, viii, 712
[573] Mansi, *Concilia*, xxxi, 1738

and through this sin and prevarication incurred the wrath and indignation of God, and consequently the death with which God had already previously threatened him, and with death captivity under the power of him who henceforth held the empire of death, namely, the devil, and that the whole Adam, body and soul, was by that sinful prevarication changed for the worse both in body and soul, let him be anathema."

Can. 2: "If anyone shall assert that Adam's prevarication harmed himself alone and not his offspring, and that the holiness and righteousness received from God which he thereby lost he lost for himself alone and not for us too, or that, stained by that sin of disobedience he transmitted to the entire human race death and bodily pains alone, but not also the sin which is the death of the soul, let him be anathema, since he is contradicting the apostle, who says: 'By one man sin entered into this world, and by sin death, and so death passed upon all men, in whom all have sinned.'"[574]

Can. 3: "If anyone shall say that this sin of Adam's which in its origin is one, and which is transmitted to all by propagation, not by imitation—which in other words is personal to every man—can be removed either by the powers of human nature or by any other remedy save the merits of the one mediator, Jesus Christ our Lord who reconciled us to God in his blood, being 'made unto us justice, sanctification, and redemption';[575] or shall deny that the actual merits of Jesus Christ, conferred on us by the sacrament of baptism rightly administered according to the form of the Church, are applied both to adults and to children, let him be anathema, for 'there is no other name under heaven given to men whereby we must be saved.'[576] Hence the words: 'Behold the Lamb of God, behold him who taketh away the sin of the world';[577] and again: 'As many of you as have been baptized in Christ have put on Christ.'"[578]

574 Rom 5:12
575 1 Cor 1:30
576 Acts 4:12
577 Jn 1:29
578 Gal 3:27

Can. 4: "If anyone shall deny that newborn children, even when born of baptized parents, ought at once to be baptized, or shall say that they are indeed baptized unto the remission of sin but that they do not derive from Adam any vestige of original sin demanding expiation in the laver of regeneration for the attaining of eternal life—with the consequence that in their case the formula of baptism 'unto remission of sins' is not true but false—let him be anathema, for in no other way can we understand what the apostle says, 'By one man sin entered into this world and by sin death, and so death passed upon all men, in whom all have sinned,'[579] save as the Catholic Church, spread throughout the world, has always understood it. For by reason of this rule of faith, by apostolic tradition, even children who have not as yet been able to commit any sin in themselves are truly baptized 'unto the remission of sins' so that what they contracted by generation may be cleansed in them by regeneration. 'Unless a man be born again of water and the Holy Ghost, he cannot enter into the kingdom of God.'"[580]

Can. 5: "If anyone shall deny that the guilt of original sin is remitted by the grace of our Lord Jesus Christ conferred in baptism, or shall assert that that which has the real and true character of sin is not taken away in its entirety, but that it is only scraped off or not imputed, let him be anathema. For in the regenerated, God hates nothing, for there is no condemnation in those who are truly 'buried together with Christ by baptism into death,'[581] who 'walk not according to the flesh,'[582] but who, having put off 'the old man' and put on 'the new man who according to God is created,'[583] are made innocent, spotless, pure, blameless, and beloved of God, 'heirs indeed of God, and joint heirs with Christ';[584] so that nothing whatever delays their entrance into heaven. But that the tinder of concupiscence remains in those who are baptized this holy synod realizes and confesses. But, since it is left for our combat, it can do no harm to those who do not consent to it but manfully strive against it by

[579] Rom 5:12
[580] Jn 3:5
[581] Rom 6:4
[582] Rom 8:1
[583] Eph 4:22-24
[584] Rom 8:17

the grace of Jesus Christ; nay, rather: 'He is not crowned except he strive lawfully.'[585] The apostle sometimes terms this concupiscence 'sin,'[586] but this holy synod declares that the Church has never understood it to be termed 'sin' in the sense that sin truly and rightly so-called is in those who are regenerated, but only in the sense that it springs from sin and leads to it. If anyone thinks the contrary, let him be anathema."

Can. 6: "At the same time, this holy synod declares that it is not its intention to comprise in this decree, which deals with original sin, the blessed and immaculate Virgin Mary, the Mother of God, but that the constitutions of Pope Sixtus IV of blessed memory are to be observed, together with the penalties therein enacted and here renewed."

Pius IX, Allocution *Singulari quadam*, Dec. 9, 1854:

"Now, those who adhere tenaciously to human reason, who even worship it, who regard it as a perfectly safe teacher, and persuade themselves that with its guidance they can be sure of everything, these assuredly forget how grave and sore a wound was inflicted on human nature by the sin of our first parents, namely, a darkness obscuring the mind and a will rendered prone to evil. This explains how it came to pass that the famous philosophers of old, although they wrote much that was brilliant, yet mingled so much grave error with their doctrines. This serves, too, to explain the conflict we experience within ourselves and of which the apostle wrote: 'I see another law in my members fighting against the law of my mind.'"[587]

St. Cyril of Alexandria, *On Romans*, Ch. 5, n. 18:

"Now, we were made sinners owing to Adam's disobedience, and in this wise: Adam himself had been created for incorruption and life, and his way of life was holy in the paradise of delights; his mind was ever set on the contemplation of divine things; his body, too, was immune and at peace, disturbed by no evil desire, by no unreasonable rebellious

[585] 2 Tm 2:5
[586] Rom 6:12
[587] Rom 7:23; *Acta* of Pius IX, I, i, 624

motions. But afterward, when he fell into sin and the door to corruption lay open, straightway impure delights found their way into his natural flesh, and at that moment was born in us the fierce law of our members. Our nature, then, contracted disease from the disobedience of one man, Adam, whence many were made sinners. Not that all sinned simultaneously with Adam—for they did not yet exist, but because all are of the same nature with Adam, and that nature fell under the law of sin."[588]

QUESTION 75

For the Council of Trent, see above, q. 74.

Sixtus IV, Constitution *Cum praeexcelsa*, Feb. 28, 1476:

"We deem it indeed only fitting that all the faithful in Christ should give thanks and praise to Almighty God for the marvelous conception of the immaculate Virgin, should celebrate and take part in the Masses and other offices appointed for that purpose, and also strive to gain indulgences and the remission of their sins..."[589]

Pius IX, Constitution *Ineffabilis Deus*, Dec. 8, 1854:

"In honor of the Holy and undivided Trinity, to give glory and due honor to the Virgin Mother of God, for the exaltation of the Catholic faith and the increase of Christian religion, by the authority of our Lord Jesus Christ, of the blessed apostles Peter and Paul, and by Our own, We pronounce and define that the doctrine which states that the most Blessed Virgin Mary was, in the first instant of her conception, by the singular grace and privilege of God, in view of the merits of Jesus Christ the Savior of the human race, preserved immune from all stain of original sin, has been revealed by God and is therefore to be firmly and unswervingly believed by all the faithful. Wherefore if any should presume—which God avert—to think otherwise in their hearts

[588] *P.G.*, lxxiv, 790
[589] *Extravag. communes*, III, xii, 1-2

than We have defined, let them know and understand that they stand condemned by their own judgment, that they have made shipwreck of the faith, have fallen away from the unity of the Church, and that in consequence they automatically fall under the canonical penalties if they venture to make known by word or writing or in any other outward way what they think in their hearts."[590]

St. Ephraem, *Carmina Nisibena*, Hymn 27, n. 8:

"Of a truth, [O Lord,] thou and thy Mother are they alone who are in every way wholly fair; for in thee, O Lord, there is no spot, in thy Mother no stain."[591]

St. Augustine, *On Nature and Grace*, Ch. 42:

"With the exception therefore of the holy Virgin Mary, with regard to whom, when sin is in question, I cannot, out of respect for our Lord, permit of any discussion—for how can we know of any greater grace that could have been bestowed on her for complete victory over sin, when she merited to conceive and bring forth him who, we all know, had no sin? With the sole exception, then, of the Blessed Virgin, could we here assemble all the saints, both men and women, and ask them whether when they lived here on earth they were without sin, what do you imagine they would answer? Would they say what he [Pelagius] says, or what John the apostle says? I ask you: No matter how overwhelming the holiness of those saints when in the body, would they not, if such a question had been put to them, have shouted with one accord: 'If we say that we have no sin we deceive ourselves and the truth is not in us?'"[592]

[590] *Acta* of Pius IX, i, 616
[591] *Ed.* G. Bickell, p. 122-123
[592] 1 Jn 1:8; *P.L.*, xliv, 267

QUESTION 85

Piux XI, Encyclical *Quas primas*, Dec. 11, 1925:

"Cyril of Alexandria sets out clearly the basis on which rests this dignity and power of our Lord: 'He possessed, to put it briefly, dominion over all creation; a dominion not wrung from it by violence, nor acquired from some other source, but of his very essence and nature; that is to say, his principality rests on that marvelous union which we term *hypostatic*. Whence it follows not only that Christ is to be adored as God by men and angels, but also that, to his empire as man, men and angels must yield obedience and subjection. In other words: Christ has power over the whole of creation simply by the fact of the hypostatic union.' In truth, what more agreeable and pleasant subject for our contemplation could we have than the fact that Christ is our ruler not solely by an inborn right, but by a right acquired by his redemption of us? Oh, that heedless men would recall the price at which our preserver priced us: 'Ye were not redeemed with corruptible things as gold and silver... but with the precious blood of Christ, as of a lamb unspotted and undefiled.'[593] We are no longer our own since Christ bought us 'with a great price';[594] our very bodies are 'members of Christ.'"[595]

QUESTION 89

St. Ephraem, *In Hebdomadam Sanctam*, vi, 9:

"In the body he had assumed, Christ the only Word of God came to birth and growth, received a visible form and nourishment, became by his generation subject to times and numbers. In the Godhead and humanity thus hypostatically united, in the human nature which he used divinely and humanly, in his Lordship and subjection, in word and deed, the Son of God, he who was made man, is himself one and indivisible."[596]

[593] 1 Pt 1:18-19

[594] 1 Cor 6:20

[595] 1 Cor 6:15; *Acta Apostolicae Sedis*, yr. 17, p. 598

[596] *Ed.* Lamy, *Sti. Ephremi Hymni et Sermones*, l, c, i, 476-478

QUESTION 90

Council of Chalcedon, A.D. 451, "Definition on the two natures of Christ," against the Monophysites:

> "Following, then, in the footsteps of the holy fathers, we all teach in harmony that the Son and our Lord Jesus Christ are one and the same, one and the same perfect in Godhead, the same perfect in human nature, true God and true man, the same (made) of a rational soul and a body, consubstantial with the Father according to his Godhead, consubstantial with us according to his human nature, 'made in all things like to us, save without sin';[597] according to his Godhead begotten of the Father before all ages; the same, in these last days, for us and for our salvation born according to human nature of the Virgin Mary, the Mother of God; one and the same to be acknowledged as Christ the Son, the Lord, the Only-begotten, in two natures uncommingled, unchangeable, indivisible, inseparable; the differences between the two natures not removed by reason of their union but rather the characteristics of each preserved united together in one Person and subsistence, not divided nor shared among two persons, but one and the same: Son, Only-begotten, God, Word, Lord, Jesus, Christ, as the prophets before had said of him, as he himself taught us, and as the Creed of the fathers has handed down to us."[598]

Third Council of Constantinople, A.D. 680-681, "Definition of the two wills in Christ," against the Monothelites:

> "In harmony with the teaching of the holy fathers, we, like them, declare that there are in him two natural wills and two natural operations, indivisibly, inconvertibly, inseparably, not commingled; and two natural wills, not—of course—contrary to one another as the heretics say; his human will following, not resisting nor fighting against but rather subject to his divine and omnipotent will. For, as the truly wise Athanasius says: The will of his flesh had indeed to be moved, but in

597 Heb 4:15
598 Mansi, *Concilia*, vii, 115

subjection to his divine will. For just as his flesh is called and is the flesh of the Son of God, so too the natural will of his flesh is called and is the will of God the Word, as he himself said: 'I came down from heaven not to do my own will but the will of the Father who sent me';[599] where he calls his own will that which was the will of his flesh. For his flesh too was made. And precisely as his holy, immaculate, and animated flesh was not destroyed by being deified but remained in its own proper state and character, so neither was his human will destroyed by being deified; on the contrary, it is the more preserved, as Gregory, 'the Theologian,' says: 'When we speak of the Savior "willing" we do not mean something in opposition to God, for the whole is deified.'"[600]

Fourth Lateran Council, A.D. 1215, Const. 1, against the Albigenses:

"And finally, the only-begotten Son of God, Jesus Christ, made incarnate by the whole Trinity acting in unison, conceived of Mary ever Virgin by the cooperation of the Holy Spirit, made true man, of rational soul and human flesh combined, one Person in two natures, showed the way to life more manifestly. For though according to his Godhead immortal and impassible, yet was he himself according to his human nature made passible and mortal; moreover, for the salvation of the human race, he suffered and died on the tree of the cross, descended into hell, rose again from the dead and ascended into heaven…To come at the end of the world to judge the living and the dead, and to render to every one according to his works; both to the reprobate and the elect, all of whom shall, in their proper bodies which they now bear, rise again to receive in accordance with their works, as they have done good or ill, the latter an eternal punishment with the devil, the former everlasting glory with Christ."[601]

[599] Jn 6:38
[600] Mansi, *Concilia*, xi, 638
[601] Mansi, *Concilia*, xxii, 982

St. Leo IX, A.D. 1049-1054, *Symbolum Fidei*:

> "I also believe in the very Son of God, the Word of God born of the Father in eternity before all time, consubstantial, coomnipotent, coequal with the Father in all things in Godhead, born in time of the Holy Spirit of Mary ever Virgin, with a rational soul; having two nativities, one eternal of the Father, the other in time, of his Mother; having two wills and two operations, true God and true man; having in its perfection all that is peculiar to either nature; admitting no commingling nor division, not by adoption, not a mere appearance; the one and only God, the Son of God in two natures but in singleness of Person; impassible and immortal according to his Godhead, but in his human nature, for us men and our salvation, suffering a true suffering of the flesh, and buried; he rose again from the dead the third day by a true resurrection of the flesh; and, as a confirmation of this, ate with his disciples, not through need of food but of his own will and power; on the fortieth day after his resurrection, with the flesh with which he rose, and with his soul, he ascended into heaven and sitteth at the right hand of the Father; thence on the tenth day he sent the Holy Spirit; thence, too, just as he ascended so is he to come to judge the living and the dead and render to every one according to their works."[602]

QUESTION 91

For the Council of Trent, see above, q. 74.

St. Epiphanius, *Ancoratus*, n. 93:

> "For not in man does our hope of our salvation lie. For in truth, of all born of Adam none could bring us salvation; that was for God alone, the Word made man...Hence of our flesh the Lord took flesh, and, a man like unto us—God and the Word—willed to destroy suffering by suffering, by death to extinguish death."[603]

[602] Mansi, *Concilia*, xix, 662
[603] *P.G.*, xliii, 186ff

QUESTION 94

Leo XIII, Encyclical *Divinum illud munus*, May 9, 1897:

"Most fittingly has the Church been wont to attribute to the Father those works of the Godhead in which power predominates, to the Son those in which wisdom predominates, to the Holy Spirit those in which love predominates...Primarily, of course, we ought to look to Christ the founder of the Church, the Redeemer of our race. For assuredly, of all the exterior works of God, the mystery of the incarnate Word stands out preeminent; in it the light of the divine perfections so shines that nothing surpassing it can even enter our thoughts, than it nothing could be of greater saving power for human nature. This mighty work, although it belongs to the whole Trinity, is yet ascribed to the Holy Spirit as peculiarly his. Hence, of the Blessed Virgin, the gospel says: 'She was found with child of the Holy Ghost,' and, 'that which is conceived in her is of the Holy Ghost.'[604] Fittingly indeed is this ascribed to him who is the charity of Father and Son; for this 'great mystery of godliness'[605] proceeded from the supreme love of God for men, as St. John tells us: 'God so loved the world as to give his only begotten Son.'"[606]

QUESTION 95

Council of Ephesus, the "Anathemas of Cyril," Can. 1:

"If anyone should not confess that Emmanuel is truly God and that in consequence the Blessed Virgin is the Mother of God—for she brought forth according to the flesh the Word of God made flesh—let him be anathema."[607]

[604] Mt 1:18, 20
[605] 1 Tm 3:16
[606] Jn 3:16; *Acta* of Leo XIII, xvii, 130-132
[607] Mansi, *Concilia*, ix, 327

Second Council of Constantinople, A.D. 553, "The Three Chapters," Can. 6:

> "If any one shall say that the holy, glorious, and ever Virgin Mary was only in a certain sense and not most truly the Mother of God, or that she was so in some merely relative way as though it were simply a man that was born and not the Word of God that became incarnate and was born of her, or shall refer, as some do, the birth of the man to God the Word only in the sense that the Word was with the man when he was born; or if they calumniate the holy Synod of Chalcedon, which calls the Virgin the 'Mother of God,' by putting on those words the interpretation foisted on them by the detestable Theodore, calling her, for example, the 'mother of the man' or the 'Christotokos,' that is 'the mother of Christ,' as though Christ were not God, and thus refuse to acknowledge her to be—as she is—really and truly the very Mother of God since he who before the ages was God, the Word born of the Father, did in these last days take flesh of her and of her was born, as the holy Synod of Chalcedon has devoutly acknowledged, let such a man be anathema."[608]

Third Council of Constantinople, A.D. 680-681, "Definition of the two wills in Christ," against the Monothelites:

> "Further, in adherence to the synodical letters written by the blessed Cyril against the impious Nestorius and to those written to the bishops of the East, following, too, in the footsteps of the five holy and universal synods and of the holy and approved fathers, we unanimously define that our Lord Jesus Christ is to be acknowledged as our true God, one from the Holy and consubstantial Trinity which is the origin of life, perfect in Godhead, the same, too, perfect in human nature, truly God and truly man, the same made of a rational soul and a body; consubstantial with the Father according to Godhead, consubstantial with us according to human nature, 'in all things like unto us, save without sin';[609] according to Godhead begotten of the Father before the ages, but also in these last days the same conceived, for us men and for our salvation, of the Holy

608 Mansi, *Concilia*, ix, 379

609 Heb 4:15

Spirit and the Virgin Mary who was really and truly the Mother of God according to his human nature, one and the same to be acknowledged as Christ, only-begotten Son of God, in two natures, not commingled, not changed into one another, inseparable one from the other yet indivisible; the differences between these two natures in no sense removed by reason of their union, but rather the peculiar properties of each preserved, though concurring to form one Person and one subsistence; one and the same only-begotten Son of God, the Word, the Lord Jesus Christ, not divided nor shared between two persons, according as the prophets of old and our Lord Jesus Christ himself taught us and the Creed of the holy fathers has handed down to us."[610]

St. Gregory Nazianzen, *Epistle 101*:

"If anyone does not believe that holy Mary is the Mother of God, such a one is a stranger to the Godhead. If anyone shall say that (Christ) passed through the Virgin as through a channel and was not formed in her both in divine and human fashion—'divine' because without a husband's cooperation—'human' because conceived in accordance with human law, such a one too is an atheist. If anyone shall say that a man was made, and that afterward God entered into him—he renders himself liable to damnation."[611]

St. John Damascene, *Oratio prima de Virginis Mariae Nativitate*, n. 4:

"Let Nestorius be filled with shame and lay his hand on his lips. This child is God. How then shall she who bore him not be God's Mother? But if anyone refuses to acknowledge her as Mother of God such a one is far removed from the Godhead. These are not my words, though it is I who use them, for I inherited these glorious teachings from Gregory the Theologian."[612]

610 Mansi, *Concilia*, xi, 635
611 *P.G.*, xxxvii, 178ff
612 *P.G.*, xcvi, 667

QUESTION 96

Leo XIII, Encyclical *Quamquam pluries*, Aug. 15, 1889:

"That Saint Joseph should be named the 'Patron of the Church' and that the Church in her turn should trust to receive many advantages from his protection and patronage is based on the remarkable fact that he was the husband of Mary, and the father — as men thought — of Jesus Christ. This was the source of all his dignity, grace, holiness, and glory. The dignity, of course, of the Mother of God is such as nothing could surpass; yet, since between Joseph and the Blessed Virgin there was the bond of matrimony, it seems evident that for that very reason he approached more nearly than anybody else to that overwhelming dignity which makes the Mother of God so far superior to all other created things...If, then, God gave Joseph to Mary as her husband, he assuredly made him not simply the companion of her life, the witness to her virginity, the guardian of her reputation, but also, by reason of the bond of matrimony, a sharer in her lofty dignity. Hence he outdistances all others in that, by the counsel of God, he was the guardian of the Son of God, in men's opinion his father."[613]

QUESTION 97

St. Leo the Great, *Epistle to Flavian, Archbishop of Constantinople*:

"The same eternal only-begotten Son of the eternal Father was born of the Holy Spirit and the Virgin Mary...That is to say, he was conceived of the Holy Spirit in the womb of his Virgin Mother who brought him forth without detriment to her virginity, as, too, she had, without detriment to her virginity, conceived him."[614]

[613] *Acta* of Leo XIII, ix, 177-178
[614] *P.L.*, liv, 759

St. Ephraem, *Oratio ad Sanctissimam Dei Matrem*:

"But O Virgin Lady, immaculate Mother of God, my glorious Lady, my benefactress, higher than the heavens, far more pure than the sun in its rays of shining splendor,...the rod of Aaron that budded, truly hast thou appeared as a stem whose flower is thy true Son, our Christ, my God and my Maker; thou didst bear according to the flesh God and the Word, didst preserve thy virginity before his birth, didst remain a Virgin after his birth, and we have been reconciled to God by Christ thy Son."[615]

Didymus of Alexandria, *De Trinitate*, Bk. 3, Ch. 4:

"When we discuss such terms as *firstborn* and *only-begotten* the evangelist comes to our aid by telling us that Mary remained a Virgin 'until she brought forth her firstborn Son';[616] for neither did that most glorious Virgin, who is to be honored above all others, wed another and so become the mother of another; but, after bringing forth her Son, she always and through all time remained the immaculate Virgin."[617]

St. Epiphanius, *Adversus Haereses*, Heresy 78, Ch. 6:

"Was there ever a person who in speaking of Mary would, when questioned, refuse to add at once the epithet *Virgin*? For the proofs of her virtue shine out in the conjunction of those very terms...She is termed 'Holy Mary,' a title that will never be changed, for she ever remained inviolate."[618]

[615] *Opera omnia, ed Romana*, Graece et Latine, iii, 545
[616] Mt 1:25
[617] *P.G.*, xxxix, 831
[618] *P.G.*, xlii, 706ff

St. Jerome, *The Perpetual Virginity of Blessed Mary*, against Helvidius, n. 21:

"We believe that God was born of a Virgin because we read it; because we do not read it, we do not believe that Mary wedded again after the birth of her child. Nor do we say this because we would condemn marriage; for surely virginity itself is the fruit of marriage... You say Mary did not remain a Virgin: I go much further, and I say that Joseph too was a virgin for Mary's sake, that of a virginal marriage a Virgin Son might be born."[619]

QUESTION 100

St. Athanasius, *Epistle 59, to Epictetus*, n. 6:

"She who carried the human body of the Word presented to herself the Word which was joined to that body, that we too might be able to become sharers in the Godhead of the Word. How truly wonderful that here one and the same being should be suffering and not suffering: suffering indeed inasmuch as his own body suffered and he was himself in that body which suffered; not suffering, since the Word, by nature God, is incapable of suffering. Moreover, the Word incorporeal was in a body capable of suffering, while that body held within itself the Word that was incapable of suffering and which swallowed up the infirmities of that same body."[620]

QUESTION 102

Innocent X, Constitution *Cum occasione*, against the errors of Jansensius, May 31, 1653, the fifth condemned Proposition:

"It is Semipelagian to say that Christ died or shed his blood for absolutely all men."[621]

619 *P.L.*, xxiii, 213
620 *P.G.*, xxvi, 1059ff
621 *Bullarium Romanum*, ed. Turin, xv, 721

St. Ambrose, *Epistle 41*, n. 7:

"The devil had reduced the human race to a perpetual captivity, a cruel usury laid on a guilty inheritance whose debt-burdened progenitor had transmitted it to his posterity by a succession drained by usury. The Lord Jesus came; he offered his own death as a ransom for the death of all; he shed his own blood for the blood of all."[622]

QUESTION 103

Council of Trent, Session 6, "Decree of Justification," Ch. 3:

"Although it is true that he died for us all, yet not all benefit by his death, but those only to whom the merits of his passion are communicated."

QUESTION 104

Council of Trent, Session 6, "Decree on Justification," Ch. 7:

"The meritorious (cause of justification) is God's only-begotten and most beloved Son, our Lord Jesus Christ who, when we were enemies, merited, owing to the great love he bore us, justification for us by his most holy death on the tree of the cross, and made satisfaction for us to the Father."

Leo XIII, Encyclical *Tanetsi futura*, Nov. 1, 1900:

"Indeed when the fullness of the council of God had come, the only-begotten Son of God, made man, most completely and fruitfully made satisfaction for us men to the offended Majesty of his Father by his own blood, and claimed for his own the human race redeemed at such a price; 'You were not redeemed with corruptible things as gold or silver...but with the precious blood of Christ, as of a lamb

[622] *P.L.*, xvi, 1162

unspotted and undefiled.'[623] In this way he again brought under his dominion the entire race of men—already subject to his power and empire, owing to the fact that he is their Creator and preserver—by a true and real redemption: 'You are not your own, for you are bought with a great price.'"[624]

St. Ignatius of Antioch, *Epistle to the Smyrnaeans*, Ch. 2:

"And all these things he suffered for our sakes that we might attain salvation; for he really suffered, just as he really raised himself from the dead; not, as some unbelievers say, that he merely seemed to suffer, just as they themselves only seem to exist, and, in harmony with this empty wisdom of theirs, this will actually be their fate, for they are but phantasms and devilish."[625]

St. John Chrysostom, *Homily 17 on Hebrews*, Ch. 2:

"So too 'Christ was offered up once and for all.' By whom was he offered? By himself. Here St. Paul not only calls him a priest, but the victim and the sacrifice; and he proceeds to assign the cause of this offering: 'He was offered once and for all to exhaust the sins of many.'[626] Why 'of many' and not 'of all'? Because not all have believed. He indeed died for all, to save all—so far as himself was concerned; for his death was the full equivalent of the destruction under which all lay. Yet he did not exhaust nor take away the sins of all, because all would not have it so...He took away from men their sins and offered them to the Father, not for the Father to exact a penalty for them, but to remit them."[627]

[623] 1 Pt 1:18-19
[624] 1 Cor 6:19-20; *Acta* of Leo XIII, xx, 298
[625] *P.G.*, v, 710
[626] Heb 9:28
[627] *P.G.*, lxiii, 129

QUESTION 106

St. Cyril of Jerusalem, *Catechetical Lecture 4*, n. 11:

"In a tomb in the rock he was really laid, as a man,[628] but through fear of him were the rocks split.[629] He went down into the bowels of the earth to redeem the just who were there. Would you like, I ask you, the living to profit by his grace—though many of them were not holy—and, those who had, from the days of Adam, been so long shut up should not win their freedom? Read the prophet Isaias who lifted up his voice and foretold so many things of him—do you want the King not to go down and liberate his herald? There too were David and Samuel and all the prophets; John, too, who through his messengers had said: 'Art thou he who is to come, or look we for another?'[630] Would you rather he should not go down and free such men as these?"[631]

QUESTION 110

For the Fourth Lateran Council and St. Leo XI, see above, q. 90.

St. Leo the Great, *Sermon 73, de Ascensione Domini*, n. 4:

"Of a truth, great and unspeakable cause was there for rejoicing, when in the sight of that holy concourse our human nature ascended beyond the dignity of all the heavenly creation, to pass beyond the choirs of angels, to be raised above the highest archangels, to find no limit placed to his ascent till he came to the bosom of the eternal Father, to be associated with him in the glory of his throne with whom he was coequal in nature as his Son."[632]

[628] Cf. Mt 27:60
[629] Cf. Mt 27:51
[630] Mt 11:3
[631] *P.G.*, xxxiii, 470
[632] *P.L.*, liv, 396

St. Leo the Great, *Sermon 73, de Ascensione Domini*, n. 3-4:

"For the apostles had, in rapt contemplation, fixed their gaze on the Godhead of him who sat at the Father's right hand; theirs was no merely corporeal vision which should prevent them from so fixing their minds' gaze on that which, though coming down from heaven had not therefore left the Father, nor though ascending, had left the disciples. Then, therefore, dearly beloved, was the Son of Man, the Son of God, known more perfectly and in more hallowed fashion when he entered into the glory of the Majesty of his Father, and began in ineffable fashion to be more present by his Godhead, than he had been remote by his human nature."[633]

St. Irenaeus, *Against Heresies*, Bk. 1, Ch. 10, n. 1:

"The Church sown throughout the world, spread even to the bounds of the earth, received both from the apostles and from their disciples that faith which believes in....the passion, resurrection from the dead, and ascension into heaven—in his flesh—of Jesus Christ our Lord."[634]

QUESTION 111

St. Gregory Nazianzen, *Oration 45*:

"Believe...that he is to return, glorious and illustrious, to exercise judgment on the living and the dead, not indeed in his former fleshly form, nor yet without a body, but with a body more august and more divine such as he alone knew."[635]

633 *P.L.*, liv, 398
634 *P.G.*, vii, 550
635 *P.G.*, xxxvi, 423

QUESTION 112

For the Fourth Lateran Council and Leo IX, see above, q. 90; for Benedict XII, see above, q. 62.

St. John Chrysostom, *Homily 42 on First Corinthians*, n. 3:

> "Consequently, we beg and beseech you, and embracing your knees implore you, that so long as we are traveling on life's short path we may learn compunction from what we have just read, may be converted and made better; lest, like Dives in the parable, we should with him lament and weep, and our tears should then prove of no avail. For even though you should have father or son or anyone else whose trust is in God, yet none of these will be able to deliver you if your own deeds betray you. For that is what that judgment is; he judges solely by what you have done; and it is only by your deeds that you can be saved. In saying this I have no wish to drive you to despair, but simply to show you that we cannot afford to neglect the practice of virtue on the ground of some baseless hope, or through reliance on this man or that. If we shall be found to have been idle and negligent, then no saint, no prophet, not even one of the apostles, will be able to save us."[636]

QUESTION 116

Pius XI, Encyclical *Quas primas*, Dec. 11, 1925:

> "Jesus himself made clear to the Jews the judicial power wherewith the Father had endowed him, for when they grumbled at his violation of the sabbath rest by his wonderful cure of the sick man, he said: 'For neither doth the Father judge any man, but hath given all judgment to the Son.'[637] And herein is comprised—for you cannot disassociate it from his judicial power—his right to bestow rewards and punishments on people, even when still alive. Moreover, we must needs attribute to

[636] *P.G.*, lxi, 367ff
[637] Jn 5:22

Christ what is termed 'executive power,' for all have to obey his commands; this includes, too, the punishments threatened against such as prove contumacious, for none can escape them."[638]

QUESTION 119

For the Second Council of Lyons, see above, q. 39; for Leo XIII, see above, q. 94.

St. Augustine, *City of God*, Bk. 11, Ch. 24:

"Although the Father is spirit and the Son spirit, the Father holy and the Son holy, yet rightly is he termed 'the Holy Spirit,' as being holy in substance and consubstantial with both."[639]

QUESTION 121

St. Basil the Great, *Epistle 38*, n. 4:

"From the Holy Spirit flows all bestowal of good things on creation."[640]

QUESTION 122

Leo XIII, Encyclical *Divinum illud munus*, May 9, 1897:

"Here let it suffice to say that since Christ is the head of the Church, then is the Holy Spirit its soul: 'What the soul is to the body that the Holy Spirit is to Christ's body, which is the Church.'"[641]

[638] *Acta Apostolicae Sedis*, yr. 17, p. 599
[639] *P.L.*, xli, 338
[640] *P.G.*, xxxii, 330
[641] Augustine, *Sermon 187, De Temp.*; *Acta* of Leo XIII, xvii, 135

QUESTION 125

First Vatican Council, Constitution *Pastor aeternus*, at the beginning:

"The eternal shepherd and bishop of our souls, in order to perpetuate the saving work of our redemption, decreed to found holy Church, in which, as in the house of the living God, all the faithful should be held together by the bonds of the one faith and of charity. Wherefore, previous to his glorification, he prayed to his Father not for them (the apostles) only, but for them also 'who through their word shall believe in me, that they all may be one, as thou, Father, in me, and I in thee.'[642] Precisely, therefore, as he 'sent' the apostles, whom he had chosen out of the world, 'as he was sent by the Father,'[643] so in his Church he willed that there should be shepherds and teachers 'unto the consummation of the world.'"[644]

QUESTION 126

Council of Ephesus, A.D. 431, Act 3:

"No one questions, nay rather has it always been well known, that the holy and blessed Peter, the prince and head of the apostles, the pillar of the faith and the foundation of the Catholic Church, received from our Lord Jesus Christ, the Savior and Redeemer of the human race, the keys of the kingdom, and that the power to bind and loose sins was given to him; he, down to this present time and always, lives and exercises judgment in his successors."[645]

[642] Jn 17:20-21
[643] Jn 20:21
[644] Mt 28:20
[645] Mansi, *Concilia*, iv, 1295

First Vatican Council, Constitution *Pastor aeternus*, Ch. 1, *De apostolici primatus in Beato Petro institutione*:

"Hence we teach and declare, in accordance with the witness of the gospels, that the primacy of jurisdiction over the whole Church of God was immediately and directly promised to and conferred upon Peter the apostle by Christ the Lord. For to Simon alone—to whom he had already said, 'Thou shalt be called Cephas'[646]—did Christ, after Peter's confession, 'Thou art the Christ, the Son of the living God,' address the solemn words: 'Blessed art thou, Simon, Bar Jona, because flesh and blood hath not revealed it to thee, but my Father who is in heaven. And I say to thee, thou art Peter, and upon this rock I will build my church, and the gates of hell shall not prevail against it. And I will give to thee the keys of the kingdom of heaven. And whatsoever thou shalt bind upon earth shall be bound also in heaven, and whatsoever thou shalt loose upon earth shall be loosed also in heaven.'[647] So, too, on Simon Peter alone did Christ, after his resurrection, confer the jurisdiction of supreme pastor and ruler over the whole flock, when he said: 'Feed my lambs…Feed my sheep.'[648]

"If then anyone should say that St. Peter the apostle was not appointed by Christ to be the chief of all the apostles and the visible head of the Church militant, or that he received from our Lord Jesus Christ a primacy of honor only and not, immediately and directly, a primacy of real and true jurisdiction: let him be anathema."

Innocent X, Decree of the Congregation of the Holy Office, *De Primatu Romani Pontificis*, Jan. 24, 1647:

"Our most holy lord the pope has pronounced and declared heretical the following propositions: 'Sts. Peter and Paul are two heads of the Church who together make one,' or 'They are two leaders and supreme heads joined together in the most perfect unity,' or 'They constitute

[646] Jn 1:42
[647] Mt 16:16-19
[648] Jn 21:15-17

the twin heads of the universal Church, and by the power of God they have so coalesced as to form but one,' or 'They are the two supreme pastors and presidents of the Church who form but one head'—if, that is, these statements mean that there exists complete equality between St. Peter and St. Paul without any subordination of St. Paul to St. Peter in the supreme power over and government of the Church."[649]

St. Ephraem, *In Hebdomadam Sanctam*, iv, 1:

"Simon, my disciple, I placed thee as the foundation of holy Church. I had already called thee a 'rock' for thou art to bear up the entire edifice; thou art to be the inspector of all those who shall build up my Church on earth; if they try to build into it spurious material, it will be for you, the foundation, to repress them; thou art the source and the fount from which my teaching is drawn; thou art the head of my disciples; through thee will I give drink to all the nations; thine is that life-giving sweetness which I will dispense; thee have I chosen that, by my appointment, thou mayest be as it were the firstborn and mayest be made heir to my treasure; to thee have I given the keys of my kingdom. Behold I have made thee ruler over all my treasures."[650]

QUESTION 127

For the Council of Ephesus, see above, q. 126.

First Vatican Council, Constitution *Pastor aeternus*, Ch. 2, *De perpetuitate primatus Beati Petri in Romanis Pontificibus*:

"And that which the prince of pastors, the great shepherd of the sheep, Christ our Lord, established in the blessed apostle Peter for the perpetual salvation and the enduring profit of his Church, that same must—by the action of the same founder of the Church—last forever in the Church, which, being founded on a rock, will stand

[649] Du Plessis, *Collectio Judiciorum*, III, ii, 248
[650] *Ed.* Lamy, *Sti. Ephremi Hymni et Sermones*, i, 412

firm to the end of the ages. 'For no one questions, nay rather has it always been well known, that the holy and blessed Peter, the prince and head of the apostles, the pillar of the faith and the foundation of the Catholic Church, received from our Lord Jesus Christ, the Savior and Redeemer of the human race, the keys of the kingdom,' and that he, down to this present time and always, in his successors, the bishops of the holy Roman See founded by him and consecrated by the blood he there shed, 'lives,' presides, 'and exercises judgment.'[651] Consequently, whosoever succeeds Peter in this See, he, in accordance with the appointment of Christ himself, holds Peter's primacy over the universal Church. 'The appointment made, then, by the truth, stands firm, and blessed Peter, preserving in the rock-like strength he has received, does not relinquish the Church's helm put into his hands.'[652] It is for this reason that to the Roman Church, 'owing to its dominating principality, it is necessary'—as has always been the case—'that every Church should come—that is, the faithful who are everywhere,'[653] so that in that See whence there flow out to all 'the rights of religious fellowship,'[654] all, like members welded together through their head, grow into one compact body.

"If, then, anyone shall say that it is not by Christ's institution, nor by any divine right, that the blessed Peter has perpetual successors in his primacy over the universal Church, or that the Roman pontiff is not the successor of blessed Peter in the same primacy, let him be anathema."

[651] Council of Ephesus, A.D. 431, see above, q. 126.

[652] Leo the Great, *Sermon 3*

[653] Irenaeus, *Against Heresies*, Bk. 3, Ch. 3, n. 2

[654] Council of Aquileia, A.D. 381

QUESTION 131

Second Council of Lyons, A.D. 1274, *Profession of Faith by Michael Palaeologus*:

"The holy Roman Church, too, has full and complete primacy and principality over the universal Catholic Church; and he (Michael) truly and humbly acknowledges that she received this primacy from the Lord himself in the person of the blessed Peter, the prince or head of the apostles, whose successor in the fullness of power is the Roman pontiff. And, since the said Roman Church is bound beyond all others to defend the truth of the faith, if and when questions arise touching the faith, they ought to be decided by her judgment. To her anyone troubled about matters which come under the ecclesiastical courts can appeal; and in all causes which call for ecclesiastical investigation recourse can be had to her; to her, too, all Churches are subject, and their prelates render to her reverential obedience. Further, her plenitude of power consists in this: that she admits other Churches to a share in her burdens; many of the said Churches, more especially the patriarchates, she honored with divers privileges, while always safeguarding her own prerogatives both in general councils as well as in others."[655]

Council of Florence, Session 6 (July 6, 1439), "Decree for the Greeks":

"We also define that the holy Apostolic See and the Roman pontiff hold the primacy over all the world, and that the Roman pontiff himself is the successor of blessed Peter, the prince of the apostles, the true vicar of Christ, the head of the entire Church, the father and teacher of all Christians; also that to him, in the person of the blessed Peter, was given by our Lord Jesus Christ full power for feeding, ruling, and governing the Church, as is also set down in the Acts of the ecumenical councils and in the sacred canons."[656]

[655] Mansi, *Concilia*, xxiv, 71

[656] Mansi, *Concilia*, xxxi, 1031

First Vatican Council, Constitution *Pastor aeternus*, Ch. 3, *De vi et ratione Primatus Romani Pontificis*:

> "Wherefore, basing ourselves on the patent testimonies of holy scripture, in adherence to the explicit and clear pronouncements of Our Predecessors the Roman pontiffs, and of general councils, We renew the definition of the Council of Florence as given above...
>
> "We also teach and declare that the Roman Church has, by the Lord's appointment, the primacy of ordinary jurisdiction over all the rest of the Churches, and that this jurisdictional power of the Roman pontiff, which is truly episcopal, is immediate, and that to it the pastors and the faithful of whatsoever rite or dignity, are, both individually and collectively, bound by ties of hierarchical subordination and true obedience; and this not only in things that concern faith and morals but also in those that pertain to the discipline and government of the Church spread throughout the world; so that, union with the Roman pontiff in profession of the same faith and fellowship being safeguarded, the Church of Christ may be one flock under one supreme pastor. This is the teaching of Catholic truth, and from it no one can deviate without making shipwreck of his faith and his salvation.
>
> "So far, however, is it from being the case that this power of the supreme pontiff is derogatory to the ordinary and immediate jurisdictional power of the bishops, whereby the bishops, 'placed by the Holy Spirit,'[657] have succeeded to the apostles, and each of them, as true pastors, feed and govern their individual flocks, that these rights of theirs are asserted, corroborated, and vindicated by the supreme and universal pastor, or in the words of St. Gregory the Great, 'My honor is the honor of the universal Church. My honor is the compact vigor of my brethren. Then only am I truly honored when the honor due to every individual among them is not withheld.'[658]
>
> "Further, from this supreme power of the Roman pontiff in governing the universal Church, there follows his right—in the exercise of this

[657] Acts 20:28

[658] Gregory the Great, *Ep ad. Eulogium*, *P.L.*, lxxvii, 933

duty—of free communication with the pastors and the flocks of the whole Church, in order that they may be taught and directed by him in the way of salvation. Wherefore We condemn and reprobate the notion that this communication with pastors and flocks can lawfully be hindered, or that it is subordinate to secular authorities and that consequently decrees emanating from the Apostolic See, or published by its authority, for the government of the Church, have no value or force unless ratified by the secular authorities.

"And since the Roman pontiff presides over the whole Church by the divine right of an apostolic primacy, We also teach and declare that he is the supreme judge of the faithful, and that in all causes which call for ecclesiastical investigation, recourse can be had to his judgment; nor can the decision of the Apostolic See—than which there is no greater authority—be reversed by anyone, nor is it lawful for anyone to call it in question. Those, then, stray from the right path of truth who maintain that it is lawful to appeal from the decisions of the Roman pontiffs to an ecumenical council as to an authority superior to that of the Roman pontiff.

"If, then, anyone shall say that the Roman pontiff has only the duty of inspection or direction, and not full and supreme jurisdictional authority over the whole Church, not only in matters concerning faith and morals but also in things pertaining to the discipline and government of the Church spread throughout the world, or that he has indeed a preponderating authority, but not the full plenitude of supreme power; or that this power of his is not ordinary and immediate over all and every Church and all and every pastor or member of the faithful, let him be anathema."

St. Leo IX, Epistle *In terra pax hominibus*, Sept. 2, 1053, *ad Michaelem Caerularium et Leonem Acridanum, de primatu Romani Pontificis*:

Ch. 7: "Holy Church was built upon a rock, that is Christ, and upon Peter or Cephas, the son of John, who was before called Simon, because it was never to be overcome by the gates of hell, that is, by heretical speculations which lead weak folk to destruction. For the truth himself, by whom are true whatsoever things are true, made this promise: 'The gates of hell shall not prevail against it.'[659] Moreover, the same Son of God declared that he had won from his Father the fulfillment of this promise when he said to Peter, 'Simon, behold Satan...'[660] Will anyone be so foolish as to dare imagine that this prayer of him with whom 'to will' is 'to be able' could fail in any point? Is it not a fact that by the See of the prince of the apostles, namely, the Roman Church, both by the said Peter and by his successors, all the figments of heretics have been reprobated, convicted of error and exploded, also that the hearts of his brethren have been confirmed by the faith of Peter, a faith which so far has never failed, nor will fail to the end?"

Ch. 11: "By passing judgment on the supreme See—on which it is lawful for no man to pass judgment—you have incurred an anathema from all the fathers of all the venerable councils."

Ch. 31: "As the hinge, while remaining itself immovable, swings the door to and fro, so do Peter and his successors pass free judgment on every Church, since no one ought to try to undermine their position, for the supreme See can be judged by none."[661]

Boniface VIII, Bull *Unam sanctam*, Nov. 18, 1302:

"Our faith urges us to believe and to hold fast to the one, holy, catholic, and apostolic Church; and We, too, firmly believe and unreservedly confess that outside this Church there is no salvation nor remission of sin...Hence in this one and only Church there is but one body and one head; it is not a monstrosity, two-headed, but Christ and Christ's vicar Peter, and Peter's successor, as the Lord himself said to Peter himself: 'Feed my sheep.'[662] 'My' sheep he calls them, and that in general, not simply these or those; which shows that he has entrusted him with them all. If, then, the Greeks or others say that they were not entrusted to Peter and his successors, they must logically say that they do not

[659] Mt 16:18
[660] Lk 22:31
[661] *P.L.*, cxlii, 748, 751, 765
[662] Jn 21:17

belong to Christ's flock, since the Lord spoke in John's gospel of 'one sheepfold and one shepherd.'[663]

"That in this power of his there are two swords, the spiritual and the temporal, we learn from the gospel records...Both of these, then, that is, the spiritual and the temporal swords, are in the power of the Church. One wielded by the Church, the other for the Church; the one wielded by the priest, the other by kings and soldiers; yet by the latter at the beck and by the permission of the priest. For sword must be subordinate to sword; the temporal authority subordinate to the spiritual...That the spiritual power transcends in dignity and nobility any earthly authority whatsoever, we must as unreservedly acknowledge as we acknowledge that the things of the spirit transcend those of time...For, as the truth testifies, the spiritual power can both institute temporal powers and judge them if they do not prove good...If, then, any temporal power go astray, it will be judged by the spiritual power; if some lesser spiritual power go astray, it will be judged by a higher; if, however, the supreme spiritual power go astray, it can be judged by no man, but by God alone, as the apostle testifies: 'The spiritual man judgeth all things; and he himself is judged by no man.'[664] Moreover, this authority, although given to man and exercised by man, is not human, but divine, given by the divine voice to Peter and confirmed to him and his successors by him whom he confessed to be 'the rock,' for to Peter himself the Lord said: 'Whatsoever thou shalt bind...'[665] Whosoever, then, shall resist this power thus 'ordained' of God, he 'resisteth the ordinance of God...'[666] Furthermore, We declare, say, define, and pronounce, that it is wholly necessary for the salvation of every human creature to be subject to the Roman pontiff."[667]

[663] Jn 10:16
[664] 1 Cor 2:15
[665] Mt 16:19
[666] Rom 13:2
[667] *Extravag. communes*, I, viii, 1

QUESTION 132

St. Ignatius of Antioch, *Epistle to the Smyrnaeans*, Ch. 8:

"Let us all obey the bishop, as Jesus Christ obeyed his Father...Let none do apart from the bishop any of those things which concern the Church. That is to be regarded as a valid Eucharist which is celebrated under the bishop, or some one whom he has appointed. When the bishop is present, let the populace be there too, just as where Jesus Christ is there is the Catholic Church. It is not lawful either to baptize or celebrate the *agape* without the bishop, but whatsoever he shall approve that same is well-pleasing to God, so that all that is done may be sound and valid."

St. Irenaeus, *Against Heresies*, Bk. 3, Ch. 3, n. 1:

"In every Church then, there is opportunity for all those who wish to see the truth to learn the apostolic tradition made known throughout the world; we can enumerate those who were instituted by the apostles as bishops, as also their successors down to our times; and these never taught or even knew such absurdities as these people put forward."[668]

QUESTION 133

Pius XI, Encyclical *Mortalium animos*, Jan. 6, 1928:

"Now Christ the Lord instituted his Church as a perfect society, a thing of its nature external and the object of our senses; for it was to the end of time to be occupied with the task of the reparation of the human race under the leadership of one head,[669] by the teaching office of the living voice,[670] by the administration of the sacraments as sources of heaven's

[668] *P.G.*, vii, 848
[669] Cf. Mt 16:18ff; Lk 22:32; Jn 21:15-17
[670] Cf. Mk 16:15

grace;[671] hence it was that Christ compared this society to a kingdom,[672] to a house,[673] to a sheepfold,[674] and to a flock.[675] Now, this Church, thus marvelously founded, assuredly could not cease with the death of its founder or of the apostles who led the way in its propagation, for to it the commission was given of bringing to eternal salvation all men — all without distinction of time or place: 'Going therefore, teach all nation's.'[676] Now no one is in this one Church, no one perseveres, unless he acknowledges and obediently accepts the power and authority of Peter and his legitimate successors."[677]

QUESTION 136

Fourth Lateran Council, A.D. 1215, Const. 1, against the Albigenses:

"But there is only one universal Church of the faithful and outside it none at all can be saved."[678]

Council of Florence, Session 11 (Feb. 4, 1442), "Decree for the Jacobites":

"[The holy Roman Church] firmly believes, professes, and teaches that none of those who are not within the Catholic Church, not only pagans, but Jews, heretics, and schismatics, can ever be partakers of eternal life, but are to go into the eternal fire 'prepared for the devil and his angels,'[679] unless, before the close of their lives, they shall have entered into that Church; also that the unity of the ecclesiastical body is such that the Church's sacraments avail only those abiding in that Church, and that fasts, almsdeeds, and other works of piety which

671 Cf. Jn 3:5; 6:48-59; 20:22ff; Cf. also Mt 18:18; etc.
672 Cf. Mt 13
673 Cf. Mt 16:18
674 Cf. Jn 10:16
675 Cf. Jn 21:15-17
676 Mt 28:19
677 *Acta Apostolicae Sedis*, yr. 20, p. 15
678 Mansi, *Concilia*, xxii, 982
679 Mt 25:41

> play their part in the Christian combat are in her alone productive of eternal rewards; moreover, that no one, no matter what alms he may have given, not even if he were to shed his blood for Christ's sake, can be saved unless he abide in the bosom and unity of the Catholic Church."[680]

Innocent III, Epistle *Ejus exemplo*, Dec. 18, 1208, to the archbishop of Tarragona, "Profession of faith prescribed for the Waldensians Durandus de Osca and his companions":

> "With our hearts we believe and with our lips we confess but one Church, not that of the heretics, but the holy, Roman, catholic, and apostolic, outside which we believe that none can be saved."[681]

For Boniface VIII, see above, q. 131.

Pius IX, Allocution *Singulari quadam*, Dec. 9, 1854:

> "Not without grief have we learned of another no less fatal error which has crept into some parts of the Catholic world; for there has grown up in the minds of not a few Catholics the notion that there can be good hope for the eternal salvation of all those who are by no means members of the true Church of Christ. In consequence of this attitude, they frequently discuss the future fate and condition after death of people who are in no sense adherents of the Catholic faith, and, basing themselves on the flimsiest of arguments, they suggest answers which favor their false notions. Far be it from Us, venerable brethren, to dare to set limits to the divine mercy, for it is boundless; far be it from us to try and peer into the secret counsels and those 'judgments of God' which are 'a mighty abyss,'[682] and which no human thought can fathom. But, in accordance with the duty of our apostolic office, we would stir up your episcopal solicitude and viligance and beg you to strive by all means in

680 Mansi, *Concilia*, xxxi, 1739
681 *P.L.*, ccxv, 1511
682 Ps 35:7

your power to drive out of men's minds the impious and fatal notion that the way of eternal salvation may lie in any form of religion men please. Use all the knowledge and skill you have to make the flocks entrusted to your care realize that the dogmas of the Catholic faith can never be in opposition to the mercy and justice of God.

"For we have to hold as of faith that no one can be saved outside the apostolic Roman Church, that she is the one ark of salvation, that whoso does not enter her will perish in the flood. But at the same time it is to be held equally certain that those who labor under ignorance of the true religion will never—provided their ignorance is invincible—be held guilty in the eyes of God of this fault. Who would dare claim to be able to assign limits to such ignorance when he reflects on the diversity he sees among peoples, localities, characters, and a host of other points? Assuredly when, released from the fetters of the body, we shall see God as he is, we shall then clearly see the intimate and exquisite way in which the mercy and justice of God are combined; but let us, so long as here on earth we are weighed down by this mortal body which dulls the soul, hold firmly to our Catholic doctrine: 'One God, one faith, one baptism';[683] to try and probe deeper is criminal..."[684]

Leo XIII, Encyclical *Satis cognitum*, June 29, 1896:

"As a matter of fact, if we reflect on what actually was done, Jesus Christ did not fashion and form a Church which was to comprise many generically similar yet distinct communities, nor did he form communities which should, when bound together by bonds such as these, constitute one individual and only Church such as that in which we declare our belief when we say in the Creed, 'I believe in one...Church.' No, when Jesus Christ spoke of this mystical building, he only made mention of 'one' Church, and this he calls his own: 'I will build my church.'[685] Any other church, then, which we can picture apart from this, cannot, since not founded by Jesus Christ, be the true Church of Christ...

683 Eph 4:5
684 *Acta* of Pius IX, I, i, 625
685 Mt 16:18

Consequently, the Church is bound to spread abroad amongst all men and to propagate in all ages the salvation brought by Jesus Christ and the benefits which flow from it. For this reason, the Church must, by the will of its founder, be of necessity one in all lands and throughout all time...The Church of Christ is, then, the only one and the perpetual one; whosoever are outside it depart from the will and the commands of Christ the Lord; they have left the way of salvation and gone aside to destruction."[686]

St. Cyprian, *On the Unity of the Church*, n. 6:

"The bride of Christ cannot be falsified: she is chaste and incorrupt. She knows but one home; she with scrupulous chastity keeps inviolate her one bridechamber. She it is who preserves us for God; she finds places in the kingdom for the children she has begotten. Whoso separates himself from the Church is joined to an adulterer and has cut himself off from the promises made to the Church; no one who quits the Church of Christ will attain to the rewards of Christ. He is a stranger, profane, an enemy. He cannot have God for his Father who has not the Church for his mother. If anyone was able to escape who was outside the ark of Noe, then whosoever is outside the Church escapes."[687]

St. Jerome, *Epistle 15 to Damasus*, n. 2:

"I, following no leader save Christ, am associated in fellowship with your blessedness, that is, with the See of Peter. On that rock I know the Church was built. Whoso eats the Lamb outside that house is profane. If anyone shall be outside the ark of Noe he shall perish when the flood prevails."[688]

686 *Acta* of Leo XIII, xvi, 163-165, 168
687 *P.L.*, iv, 518ff
688 *P.L.*, xxii, 355

St. Augustine, *Sermo ad Caesariensis Ecclesiae plebem*, n. 6:

"No man can find salvation save in the Catholic Church. Outside the Catholic Church he can find everything save salvation. He can have dignities, he can have the sacraments, can sing 'Alleluia,' answer 'Amen,' accept the gospels, have faith in the name of the Father, the Son, and the Holy Ghost, and preach it too, but never save in the Catholic Church can he find salvation."[689]

QUESTION 137

Pius XI, Encyclical *Rerum Ecclesiae*, Feb. 28, 1926:

"Careful students of the history of the Church cannot fail to notice how, from the very first days of the redemption wrought by Christ, the Roman pontiffs have bestowed especial care and thought on the task of bringing to the knowledge of 'the people that sit in darkness and the shadow of death'[690] the light of the gospel-teaching and the benefits accruing from Christian civilization; from this task they have allowed no dangers or difficulties to deter them. For the Church was founded for no other purpose than, by spreading the kingdom of Christ throughout the world, to make all men sharers in that redemption which leads to salvation. Whosoever, then, is the divinely constituted vicar on earth of Jesus, the prince of pastors, fails in his primary duty if he is content merely to safeguard and watch over the flock committed to his government; nay, rather has he to strive with all diligence to gain over to Christ the strangers that are without."[691]

St. Augustine, *Against the Fundamental Epistle of Manichaeus*, Ch. 4, n. 5:

"There are many things which with good reason keep me in the Catholic Church. The agreement of all nations and peoples keeps me there; its authority, first established by miracles, fed by hope, increased

689 *P.L.*, xliii, 695
690 Lk 1:79
691 *Acta Apostolicae Sedis*, yr. 18, p. 65

by charity, confirmed by its antiquity—these all keep me there; the succession in the priesthood down to the present episcopate and starting from the very See of Peter—the apostle to whom the Lord entrusted the feeding of his sheep after his resurrection—this keeps me there. Finally, the very name *Catholic* keeps me there; for not without reason has this Church, alone among so many heresies, so made this title her own, that though all heretics would like to be called 'Catholics,' yet were a stranger to ask them where was the meeting place of the Catholics, no heretic would dare show him his own church or house."[692]

St. Augustine, *A Sermon to Catechumens on the Creed*, Ch. 14:

"She is the holy Church, the one Church, the true Church, the Catholic Church, the Church which strives against all heresies; she can fight; she can never be out-fought. All heresies have departed from her—like useless twigs lopped from the vine; but she herself abides in her root, in her vine, in her charity."[693]

QUESTION 138

St. Ambrose, *On Psalm 40*, n. 30:

"He is Peter to whom Christ said: 'Thou art Peter and upon this rock I will build my church.'[694] Where, then, Peter is, there is the Church, and where the Church is, there is no death, but life eternal."[695]

St. Cyprian, *Epistle 39*, n. 5:

"God is one and Christ is one, his Church is one, his See is one, founded by the voice of the Lord on Peter. No other altar can be set

[692] *P.L.*, xlii, 175
[693] *P.L.*, xl, 635
[694] Mt 16:18
[695] *P.L.*, xiv, 1134

up, no other priesthood instituted apart from that one altar and that one priesthood. Whoso gathers elsewhere, scatters."[696]

QUESTION 144

Adamantius, *Dialogus de recta in Deum Fide*, Pt. 5, n. 28:

"She...the Catholic Church, by the truth alone, lives righteously, devoutly, and in holiness; those who have turned aside from her and gone astray are far from the truth; they proclaim indeed that to them the truth is known, but in reality they are far removed from it."[697]

St. Cyprian, *Epistle 54*, n. 14, *Inter Sti. Cornelii Epistolas*:

"Heretics have the audacity to take ship and present letters from profane and schismatical folk to the See of Peter and to the principal Church whence sprang the unity of the priesthood. They never seem to realize that these latter are Romans whose faith the apostle proclaimed and praised; to them unfaith can have no access."[698]

St. Peter Chrysologus, *Ep. ad Eutychen*, Ch. 2:

"We exhort you, honorable brother, to pay in all things obedient attention to what is written by the most blessed pope of the city of Rome; for the blessed Peter, who lives and presides in his own See, always helps those who seek the true faith. We ourselves, for the sake of peace and of the faith, cannot, without the consent of the bishop of the city of Rome, hear causes which concern the faith."[699]

[696] *P.L.*, iv, 345
[697] *P.G.*, xi, 1883
[698] *P.L.*, iii, 844ff
[699] *P.L.*, liv, 741ff

QUESTION 147

First Vatican Council, Constitution *Pastor aeternus*, Ch. 4, *De Romani Pontificis infallibili magisterio*:

"We therefore, adhering faithfully to the tradition received from the beginnings of the Christian faith, for the glory of God our Savior, the exaltation of the Catholic religion, and the salvation of the Christian peoples, do, with the approbation of this holy council, teach and define that it is a divinely revealed dogma that the Roman pontiff, when he speaks *ex cathedra*—that is, when, acting as shepherd and teacher of all Christians, he, by his supreme apostolic authority, defines a doctrine touching faith or morals which is to be held by the whole Church—enjoys, by the divine assistance promised to him in blessed Peter, that infallibility with which the divine Redeemer willed that his Church should be endowed when defining a doctrine touching faith or morals; consequently such definitions by the Roman pontiff are of themselves—not by the consent of the Church—irreformable.

"If anyone shall presume—which God avert—to contradict this Our definition, let him be anathema."

QUESTION 148

First Vatican Council, Constitution *Dei Filius*, Ch. 3:

"Furthermore, all those things are to be believed with divine and Catholic faith which are contained in the word of God, whether in writing or in tradition, and which are set forth by the Church either in her solemn decisions or in the exercise of her ordinary and universal teaching office, to be believed as being divinely revealed."

QUESTION 150

First Vatican Council, Constitution *Dei Filius*, Ch. 4, *De fide et ratione*:

"Furthermore, the Church, which, together with the apostolic duty of teaching, received a command to safeguard the deposit of faith, has also divinely bestowed upon it the right and the duty of proscribing science falsely so called: 'Beware lest any man cheat you by philosophy and vain deceit.'[700] All the Christian faithful, then, are not only forbidden to defend, as though they were legitimate conclusions of science, such opinions as are recognized as opposed to the teachings of the faith—more especially if they have been repudiated by the Church—but on the contrary are absolutely bound to regard them as errors which have only a specious appearance of truth."

QUESTION 151

For the First Vatican Council, see above, q. 150.

Alexander VII, Constitution *Regiminis Apostolici*, Feb. 15, 1664:

"I, N., submit myself to the Apostolic Constitution of Innocent X, May 31, 1653, also to the Constitution of Alexander VII, Oct. 16, 1656, the supreme pontiffs; I also sincerely reject and condemn the Five Propositions drawn from the book of Cornelius Jansenius, entitled Augustinus, and this I do in the sense intended by the said author, and according as the Apostolic See has condemned them in the aforesaid constitutions; and so I swear: so help me God and these holy gospels."[701]

Clement XI, Constitution *Vineam Domini Sabaoth*, July 16, 1705:

"In order that all future occasions of error may be wholly precluded, and that all the children of the Catholic Church may learn to hear the

[700] Col 2:8

[701] Du Plessis, *Collectio Judiciorum*, III, ii, 315

Church herself, not simply by keeping silence—for the wicked keep silence in the dark—but also by an interior compliance which is the true obedience of an orthodox person, We hereby, by apostolic authority, decree, declare, enact, and ordain by this present constitution of Ours which is to hold in perpetuity, that the obedience due to the aforementioned apostolic constitutions is in no sense met by simply obsequious silence, but that the meaning condemned in the said Five Propositions from Jansenius' book, the meaning plainly attaching, as already said, to those Propositions, is to be condemned and repudiated by all the faithful in Christ as heretical, and this not merely by word of mouth but with the heart as well; nor can the abovementioned formulas be lawfully subscribed to in any other sense, intention, or belief, so that those who may understand, hold, preach, teach, or assert, in writing or speaking, any or all of these Propositions in any other way, are to be regarded as transgressors of the said apostolic constitutions, and fall under all the censures and penalties attaching to them."[702]

Pius X, Decree *Lamentabili sane*, July 3, 1907, the seventh condemned Proposition:

"When the Church proscribes errors, she cannot demand of the faithful any internal assent in their acceptance of her decisions."[703]

QUESTION 152

Pius IX, Epistle *Tuas libenter*, Dec. 21, 1863, to the archbishop of Munich and Freisingen:

"Since it is a question of that submission which binds in conscience all Catholics who are devoted to speculative science with a view to aiding the Church by their writings, those who have taken part in these Congresses ought to recognize that it is not enough for wise Catholics to receive with reverence the aforesaid dogmas of the Church, but

[702] Du Plessis, *Collectio Judiciorum*, III, ii, 448
[703] *Acta Apostolicae Sedis*, yr. 40, p. 471

that it is also necessary to submit themselves both to those decisions concerning doctrine which emanate from the Pontifical Congregations and to those points of doctrine which, by the general and consistent consent of Catholics, are regarded as theological truths and conclusions so certain that, though opinions which conflict with them cannot be termed 'heretical,' they yet deserve some form of theological censure."[704]

Pius X, Decree *Lamentabili sane*, July 3, 1907, the eighth condemned Proposition:

"Those who regard as of no importance condemnations emanating from the Sacred Congregation of the Index, or other Roman Congregations, are to be held blameless."[705]

QUESTION 158

St. Augustine, *Of Faith and the Creed*, Ch. 10, n. 21:

"We believe, too, in holy Church, assuredly the Catholic Church. For heretics and schismatics call their assemblies 'churches.' But heretics, since they hold false ideas of God, violate the faith itself, while schismatics, although believing what we do, have by their wicked divisions broken away from fraternal charity. Heretics, then, do not belong to the Catholic Church—for it loves God; nor do schismatics—for the Church loves its neighbor."[706]

[704] *Acta* of Pius IX, I, iii, 642-643
[705] *Acta Sanctae Sedis*, vol. 40, p. 471
[706] *P.L.*, xl, 193

QUESTION 162

Innocent II, Epistle *Apostolicam Sedem*, A.D. 1130-1143, to the bishops of Cremona:

> "To your question We reply as follows: We unhesitatingly assert that the priest who, as you tell Us, died without being baptized, was, since he persevered in the faith of holy mother Church and in the confession of the name of Christ, freed from original sin, and has won the joy of the kingdom of heaven; this We base on the authority of Sts. Ambrose and Augustine; read St. Augustine, *City of God*, Bk. 8, where you will find amongst other things the statement that 'baptism is administered invisibly when necessity and not contempt for religion precludes its being given'; see, too, St. Ambrose, *De Obitu Valentiniani*, where he makes the same assertion. On questions thus already settled, hold fast to the opinions of the learned fathers; but remember to have frequent prayers and sacrifices offered to God in your Church for the said priest."[707]

Pius IX, Encyclical *Quanto conficiamur*, Aug. 10, 1863, to the bishops of Italy:

> "And here, beloved sons and venerable brethren, We must once more draw attention to and reprobate a very grave error with which some Catholics are unfortunately infected; for some fancy that people who have lived in error, and are strangers to Catholic unity, can attain eternal life. But this is absolutely opposed to Catholic teaching. We, and you too, know well that those who labor under invincible ignorance of our holy religion, yet keep the precepts of the law of nature graven by God in all men's hearts, who are prepared to obey God, and who lead an honorable and upright life, are able, by the powerful workings of God's light and grace, to attain eternal life. For God, who sees distinctly, who searches into and knows the mind, spirit, habits, and thoughts of all men, would never of his supreme goodness and mercy permit anyone to be punished eternally unless he had incurred the guilt of voluntary sin. But it is also a perfectly well-known Catholic

[707] *P.L.*, clxxix, 624

doctrine that no one can be saved outside the Catholic Church, and that those who contumaciously resist her authority and definitions and who obstinately remain separated from the unity of that Church and from Peter's successor the Roman pontiff—to whom the custody of the vine was entrusted by our Savior—cannot obtain eternal salvation."[708]

QUESTION 163

For Pius IX, see above, q. 162.

QUESTION 166

Leo XIII, Encyclical *Immortale Dei*, Nov. 1, 1885:

16. "The only-begotten Son of God founded a society on earth which is called 'the Church'; to it he entrusted the perpetuation down the ages of the divine and lofty task which he had himself received from his Father..."

18. "This society, though composed, like any civil society, of men, is by reason of its appointed goal and the means it employs for its attainment, supernatural and spiritual; consequently, it is distinguished from and differs from the civil society. And, what is of more importance, that society is, of its very nature and by right, perfect, since by the will and favor of its founder it possesses in itself and of itself all the means necessary for its unimpaired action. And as the goal toward which the Church tends is the noblest of all, so too its power transcends all others; nor can it be regarded as inferior to the civil state or in any sense subordinate to it..."

24. "Thus God has divided the charge of the human race between two powers, the ecclesiastical and the civil, setting one over the things of God, the other over human affairs. Each is chief in its own department; each has its own limits which it cannot overstep and which are precisely defined by the nature of the task committed to it, so that a

[708] *Acta* of Pius IX, I, iii, 613

certain sphere is, as it were, marked out within which lie the actions proper to each..."

25. "But since each of these bears sway over the same subjects, and since it may come to pass that one and the same thing may—while remaining the same thing though under different aspects—fall under the jurisdiction and judgment of either, God in his supreme providence must—since both are founded by him—have correctly and harmoniously arranged the paths along which either should walk, 'for the powers that are, are ordained of God.'[709]..."

26. "There must, then, be some appointed means for harmonizing these two powers, something not unreasonably likened to the link whereby soul and body are bound together in man. But what this link is and how real it is, we can, as we have said, only discover by considering the nature of each of them and weighing the relative excellences of their respective goals. Such reflection will show us that whereas the chief and immediate care of one of them is to provide for the needs of this mortal life, the business of the other is to secure heavenly and everlasting good things. Whatsoever in human affairs, then, is reputed sacred in anyway, whatsoever pertains to the salvation of souls and the worship of God, whether it be so of its own nature or be regarded as such by reason of some question involved, all that must fall under the authority and judgment of the Church; but other things, such as civil or political affairs, are rightly the subject matter of the civil authorities, since Jesus Christ himself said: 'Render to Caesar the things that are Caesar's, but to God the things that are God's.'[710]..."

54. "As a matter of fact, if the Church decides that different kinds of divine worship ought not to have the same legal standing as the true religion has, she does not therefore condemn ministers of public affairs who, 'for the sake of obtaining some great good, or the warding off some great evil,' tolerate diverse habits and practices and allow each to find a place in the state."[711]

[709] Rom 13:1
[710] Mt 22:21
[711] *Acta* of Leo XIII, v, 124-125, 127-128

Leo XIII, Encyclical *Au milieu*, Feb. 16, 1892:

"This [see previous extract] is the state of affairs in certain countries. It is a *modus vivendi* which, despite many incongruities, yet offers various advantages, more especially when the authorities, with a naive disregard for logic, really act from Christian principles. For the ensuing advantages, while they do not justify the false principle of schism nor allow us to defend it, yet do make tolerable a state of things which, in practice, might be much worse."[712]

Leo XIII, Epistle *Longinqua Oceani*, Jan. 6, 1895:

"In your part of the world, the Church enjoys, without any interference by the civil authorities, perfect and unhampered liberty of life and action; it is hindered by no laws, it is defended against violence by common law and justice. But while this is true, it would be wrong for anyone to conclude that we have to look to America for an example of the Church in its ideal state, or that it is lawful and expedient that religious and civil affairs should be everywhere totally dissociated after the American fashion."[713]

QUESTION 167

Leo XIII, Encyclical *Diuturnum illud*, June 29, 1881:

"Assuredly the Church of Christ ought not to be regarded with suspicion by secular rulers, nor ought she to be disliked by the populace. For though she does, it is true, teach rulers to pursue justice and in no way to depart from their duties, yet at the same time she fortifies and supports their authority in many ways. She recognizes and insists that matters concerning civil government come under their supreme authority and rule, while in matters that, under different aspects, concern both the religious and the civil authorities, she is anxious that harmony should prevail between these two, for only thus can dissensions which might prove fatal to either be avoided."[714]

[712] *Acta* of Leo XIII, xii, 39
[713] *Acta* of Leo XIII, xv, 7
[714] *Acta* of Leo XIII, ii, 285

For the Encyclical *Immortale Dei*, see above, q. 166.

Pius X, Encyclical *Vehementer*, Feb. 11, 1906:

> "That the affairs of Church and state should be kept rigidly apart is certainly a false, even a dangerous notion. First of all, because, based on the idea that the state ought to have nothing to do with religion, it is an insult to God, who is as much the founder and preserver of human society as he is of individual men; whence it follows that God has to be worshipped not only privately but publicly. Moreover, this notion really amounts to a denial that there is anything supernatural. For it regards state action solely from the point of view of prosperity in this mortal life. And though this is in fact the immediate aim of civil society, yet the abovementioned view ignores the ultimate goal of all the citizens of the state—namely, the eternal happiness offered to men after this brief span of life—on the plea that this is no concern of the state. Whereas, precisely as the whole series of fluctuating events here on earth is arranged for men's attainment of that supreme and absolute good, so is it true that it is the duty of the state not only not to hinder its attainment but to further it. Moreover, this notion tends to the subversion of the arrangement of human affairs so wisely planned by God, inasmuch as that arrangement clearly demands that there should be harmony between these two societies, the civil and the religious. For since each of these societies—though of course each in its own order—exercises sway over the same people, it must necessarily often happen that cases arise which fall under the jurisdiction of both. If, then, the state and the Church do not work in harmony, the seeds of very acute discord are readily sown when such things happen, and these, in addition to the distress of mind they cause, make it difficult to discover where the truth lies. Finally, the aforesaid notion does great harm to the state itself; for no state can flourish or last long while religion—always man's best guide and teacher when it is question of how to safeguard the exercise of his rights and duties—is neglected."

QUESTION 169

Pius IX, Epistle *Gravissimas inter acerbitates*, Dec. 11, 1862, to the archbishop of Munich and Freisingen:

"Consequently the Church has, by the power committed to her by her divine author, not only the right but also the special duty of not merely tolerating but of proscribing all errors when the integrity of the faith and the salvation of souls demand it. Hence it is the duty of every philosopher who wishes to be a son of the Church—as indeed it is the duty of philosophy itself—never to say anything contrary to what the Church teaches, also to withdraw opinions about which the Church may have admonished him. We pronounce therefore and declare that opinions teaching the opposite of this are wholly erroneous and most injurious to the faith, to the Church, and to her authority."[715]

Leo XIII, Encyclical *Immortale Dei*, Nov. 1, 1885:

"Of course, if it is a question of simply political problems, for example, of the best kind of government, whether to conduct the affairs of state in this way or that, it is plain that discussion of such matters can be quite right and fitting. When, then, men's filial devotion is known from other sources, and when it is clear that they are ready to accept obediently the decrees of the Apostolic See, justice cannot allow that their disagreement with Us on questions on which We have pronounced should be labeled criminal; and a far greater injury is done when such men are accused, or at least suspected, of sinning against the faith, though We grieve to say that this has been done more than once.

"This admonition of Ours has especially to be borne in mind by those who commit their thoughts to writing, especially the editors of reviews. In discussing these grave matters, there is no room for contention, for intestinal quarrels or factions, but all should, by harmoniously working together, strive to preserve religion and the state; for this is really what all alike have in view. If, then, there have been dissensions in the past,

[715] *Acta* of Pius IX, I, iii, 554-555

they should be deliberately buried; if rash or injurious things have been said or done, then the guilty parties should atone for it by mutual good feeling and should make amends by showing peculiar devotion to the Apostolic See.

"In this way Catholics will secure two very excellent results: they will be coming forward as collaborators with the Church in the task of propagating and preserving Christian wisdom, and they will be conferring an immense benefit on civil society, whose welfare is especially endangered by wicked teachings and cravings."[716]

QUESTION 174

Council of Trent, Session 25, "On the Invocation, Veneration, and Relics of Saints, and on Sacred Images":

"The holy synod bids all bishops and others whose duty it is to teach, diligently to instruct the faithful in accordance with the practice dating from the earliest ages of the Christian faith, and in harmony with the consentient teaching of the holy fathers and the decrees of councils, concerning the intercession and invocation of the saints, the honor due to relics, and the legitimate use of images. They are to teach that the saints reigning with Christ offer to God prayers for us men; that it is a good and profitable thing humbly to invoke them and, in order to obtain benefits from God through his Son, Jesus Christ our Lord, our only Redeemer and Savior, to appeal to them for their prayers, help, and assistance…Also that the bodies of the holy martyrs and others now living with Christ, bodies which were members of Christ and temples of the Holy Spirit and which are one day to be raised up by him and glorified in eternal life, are to be venerated by the faithful, and that through them many benefits are bestowed by God upon men."

[716] *Acta* of Leo XIII, v, 149-150

St. Jerome, *Against Vigilantius*, Ch. 6:

"You say in your book that, whilst we are alive, we can pray for one another, but that after we are dead no man's prayer for another is heard; and you base this on the fact that the martyrs could not by their prayers obtain the avenging of their blood. But if the apostles and martyrs could, while still in the flesh, pray for other people—when they still had reason to be anxious for themselves—how much more can they do so when they have won their victory, their crown, and their triumph?"[717]

QUESTION 175

St. Cyril of Jerusalem, *Catechetical Lecture 23*, n. 9:

"Then we remember those who have fallen asleep: first the patriarchs, prophets, apostles, and martyrs, that God may receive our petitions through their prayers and intercessions; then we pray for the dead, for our holy fathers and bishops and for all in general among us who have departed this life; for we believe that this will prove of great assistance to those souls for whom such prayer is offered whilst the holy and tremendous victim lies here (on the altar)."[718]

St. Augustine, *City of God*, Bk. 20, Ch. 9:

"The souls of the faithful departed are not cut off from the Church, which even now is the kingdom of Christ. Were it so, we should not make commemoration of them at God's altar when receiving the Communion of the body of Christ."[719]

[717] *P.L.*, xxiii, 344
[718] *P.G.*, xxxiii, 1115
[719] *P.L.*, xli, 674

QUESTION 177

Fourth Lateran Council, A.D. 1215, Const. 1, against the Albigenses:

> "And if after receiving baptism anyone should fall into sin, his fault can always be repaired by true penitence."[720]

For the Council of Trent, see below, q. 413.

St. Leo IX, Epistle *Congratulamur vehementer*, April 16, 1053, *Symbolum fidei*:

> "I believe the holy, catholic, and apostolic Church to be the one true Church in which is conferred one baptism and true remission of all sins."[721]

QUESTION 179

Fourth Lateran Council, A.D. 1215, Const. 1, against the Albigenses:

> "And finally the only-begotten Son of God Jesus Christ...is to come at the end of the world, to judge the living and the dead, to render to every one according to his works, both the reprobate and the elect; they will all rise again in their very own bodies such as they now have, to receive according to their works, insofar, that is, as they have been good or bad, the latter everlasting punishment with the devil, the former everlasting glory with Christ."[722]

St. Leo IX, Epistle *Congratulamur vehementer*, April 16, 1053, *Symbolum fidei*:

> "I also believe in the true resurrection of this very flesh which I now have, and in life everlasting."[723]

720 Mansi, *Concilia*, xxii, 982
721 *P.L.*, cxliii, 772
722 Mansi, *Concilia*, xxii, 982
723 *P.L.*, cxliii, 772

Innocent III, Epistle *Ejus exemplo*, Dec. 18, 1208, to the archbishop of Tarragona, "Profession of faith prescribed for the Waldensians Durandus de Osca and his companions":

> "We believe with our hearts and confess with our lips the resurrection of this very flesh we now have, and no other."[724]

St. Cyril of Alexandria, *On John*, Ch. 8, n. 51:

> "All will rise and return to life, both believers and unbelievers. Nor is this resurrection for some only, but the same for all, in that all must return to life."[725]

St. John Chrysostom, *Sermones panegyrici, De resurrectione mortuorum*, n. 8:

> "Since, then, the resurrection is common to all, to the pious and the impious, to good and bad alike, you are not to imagine that there will be something unjust about the judgment, nor are you to say to yourself: 'What! the wicked, idolaters, men who have never known Christ—are they to rise again and enjoy the same honor as I?'...The bodies of sinners do rise again immortal and incorruptible, but the honor thus accorded to them will but serve to provide kindling wood and food for their punishment and retribution; they rise incorruptible so as to burn forever."[726]

QUESTION 180

St. John Chrysostom, *Sermones panegyrici, De resurrectione mortuorum*, n. 7:

> "Nor put this difficulty: How can the body rise again and be made free from incorruption? For when it is God's power that works, that *how* has no place...How, pray, did he make those mighty powers, the

[724] *P.L.*, ccxv, 1512
[725] *P.G.*, lxxiii, 918
[726] *P.G.*, l, 430

heavenly cohorts of angels and archangels, and the hosts even greater than they? Tell me how he made them. My only answer must be that his simple will sufficed. Cannot he, then, who formed these incorporeal hosts, renew once more man's corrupt body and advance it to a still greater dignity?"[727]

QUESTION 182

St. Cyril of Jerusalem, *Catechetical Lecture 18*, n. 18-19:

"This very body will rise again, not indeed in its present weakness, yet it will be the same body that rises. Endowed with incorruptibility, it will be transformed, just as iron when put in the fire becomes fire, or rather as the Lord who raises it up knows how. The body, then, will rise again; but it will not remain as it now is, but will be eternal; no longer will it need for life's support the food we now make use of. For it will be something wonderful, spiritual, and in dignity something beyond what words can depict…We shall, then, rise again, and we shall all have eternal, though not all of us similar bodies. For if any man is just, he will receive a heavenly body so as to live fittingly with the angels; if any is a sinner, he will receive an eternal body capable of enduring the penalties of his sins, so that, burning forever in the fire, he may never be consumed."[728]

QUESTION 189

Council of Trent, Session 6, "Decree on Justification," Ch. 11:

"No one, howsoever much he may be justified, ought to deem himself free not to keep the commandments; no one ought to give voice to the notion that God's commandments are impossible for a man to keep when justified—a rash statement condemned by the fathers under anathema. For God does not bid impossible things; but in bidding he

[727] P.G., I, 430ff

[728] P.G., xxxiii, 1039

admonishes us both to do what we can and to ask for what we cannot do; and he helps us to be able to do them, for 'his commandments are not heavy,'[729] and his yoke is sweet and his burden light.[730] For they who are the sons of God, love Christ, and they who love him, as he himself bears witness, keep his word;[731] and this they assuredly can do with his divine assistance."

QUESTION 196

St. John Damascene, *De Imaginibus*, Oration 2, n. 5:

"We should fall into error were we to fashion an image of the invisible God; for what is not corporeal, nor visible, nor circumscribed, nor endowed with a figure cannot possibly be depicted. Again, we should be acting wickedly were we to fancy that the images of men that we make are gods, and were to offer them divine honor as to deities. None of these things can we ever permit."[732]

St. John Damascene, *De Imaginibus*, Oration 3, n. 41:

"Let us adore God alone, the Creator and Maker of all things. To him let us offer the worship of *latria* as to God who is of his very nature adorable. Let us adore, too, the holy Mother of God, not indeed as God, but as God's Mother according to the flesh. The saints, too, let us adore, as the chosen friends of God, for by them is afforded us easy access to him."[733]

[729] 1 Jn 5:3
[730] Cf. Mt 11:30
[731] Cf. Jn 14:23
[732] *P.G.*, xciv, 1287
[733] *P.G.*, xciv, 1358

QUESTION 197

Second Council of Nicea, A.D. 787, *De Sacris Imaginibus*, Act 7:

> "Keeping to the royal track, following the divinely inspired teaching of our fathers and the traditions of the Catholic Church—for this tradition is, we know, the work of the Holy Spirit who dwells in her—we define with all care and diligence that there may be set up, in the same way as the figure of the precious and life-giving cross, venerable and holy images, whether painted or in mosaic, or in any other material suitable to the churches of God; these may be depicted on vessels, vestments, walls, or tablets, on houses or by the wayside; that is to say, images of our Lord God and Savior Jesus Christ, also of our Lady the holy and unspotted Mother of God, of the glorious angels, of all the saints, and of good men. For so often as such imaginative representations are looked on, men who contemplate them feel their minds uplifted by such reminders of those who have preceded them, they feel a desire to imitate them, they are moved to kiss them and exhibit toward them due reverence; not of course real *latria*, for that concerns only the faith, and pertains solely to the divine nature. Hence the practice of offering incense and candles before the image of the precious and life-giving cross, before the holy gospels, and other sacred relics, in order to do them honor; and such practices are consecrated by ancient custom. For the honor paid to an image passes on to what it represents, so that he who adores an image adores the thing therein depicted...We therefore command that if any have the audacity to hold or teach contrary opinions, devise novelties and go so far as to throw out things which have been destined for the churches, whether it be the gospels, or images of the cross, or pictures, or the relics of the holy martyrs; if, in their crafty wickedness, they plot the subversion of practices based on the legitimate traditions of the Catholic Church; if they convert to secular uses the sacred vessels or famous monasteries, then we command that such, if they be bishops or clerics, be deposed, if monks or laymen, be excommunicated."[734]

For the Council of Trent on the foregoing, see above, q. 174.

[734] Mansi, *Concilia*, xiii, 378

QUESTION 198

For the Second Council of Nicea, see above, q. 197; for the Council of Trent, see above, q. 174.

St. Cyril of Alexandria, *On Psalm 113*, n. 16:

> "Although we make images of good men, we must not adore them as gods; but when we look at them, we should feel roused to imitate them. And we make images of Christ so that our minds may be stirred up to the love of him."[735]

QUESTION 213

Pius XI, Encyclical *Divini illius Magistri*, Dec. 31, 1929:

> "The task of education is not one for individuals but belongs of necessity to society. Now there are three forms of society which are necessary and which, while differing from one another, are in God's purpose knit together; in these, man is enrolled from birth. Two of them, the family and the state, are in the natural order; the third, the Church, belongs to the supernatural order. The family holds the first place, since, founded and instituted by God himself in order that it may devote itself to the upbringing of its offspring, it consequently, of its very nature and by its own intrinsic rights, antedates civil society. Nonetheless, the family is an imperfect society in this sense: that it does not possess all the means requisite for the perfect attainment of the exalted aim set before it. The state, on the other hand, since it has at its disposition everything requisite for attaining its appointed goal, namely, the general well-being of our lives here on earth, is a society which is in all respects perfect and complete.
>
> "Whence it follows that the state has to provide the family with what it requires; for it is only as forming part of the state that the family can duly and safely fulfill its task. Lastly, the third society is the Church:

[735] *P.G.*, lxix, 1268

through it, men enter, by baptism, on the path of divine grace; this is a supernatural society which comprises the entire human race; it is perfect in itself since it itself provides all that is requisite for the attainment of its goal, namely, eternal life; consequently, it is, in its own order, supreme.

"The consequence of this is that education—which concerns the whole man and whereby men, both individually and as members of human society, whether in the order of nature or in that of divine grace—belongs to these three necessary societies in due proportion to the proper end of each in accordance with the present divinely constituted order.

"And in the first place, education belongs more particularly to the Church, by the double title of the supernatural rank which God conferred on it alone and which therefore constitutes a far greater and more effective title than any arising from the natural order.

"The primary basis of this title is the supreme teaching office and function conferred on the Church by her divine founder when he said: 'All power is given to me in heaven and on earth. Going therefore teach ye all nations, baptizing them in the name of the Father and of the Son and of the Holy Ghost; teaching them to observe all things whatsoever I have commanded you. And behold I am with you all days even to the consummation of the world.'[736] To this teaching office Christ the Lord attached immunity from error when bidding them teach all men his doctrine. Consequently, 'the Church was established by her divine author as "the column and ground of truth,"[737] so that she might teach all men divine faith, might keep inviolate and entire the deposit of faith entrusted to her, and might guide men and form in them, in their associations and their actions, sound morals and blameless lives in accordance with the standards of revealed teaching.'[738]

"The second basis on which this right rests is the supernatural maternal character of the Church. By it she, as the most pure spouse of Christ,

736 Mt 28:18-20
737 1 Tm 3:15
738 Pius IX, Encyclical *Cum non sine*, July 14, 1864

bestows on men life in accordance with divine grace, and nourishes it and furthers it in them by her sacraments and her teachings. Rightly does St. Augustine say: 'He will not have God for his Father who refuses to have the Church for his mother.'[739]

"Now in all those things which concern the Church's function of educating, that is, 'in teaching people faith and morals, God has made his Church a sharer in his own divine position as the divine teacher, and by the same beneficent action has made her incapable of being deceived. Hence the Church is the chiefest and safest guide for us mortal men, and in her there resides an unassailable right to liberty in teaching.'[740] Whence it necessarily follows that neither as regards her duty of educating, nor in her exercise of that duty can the Church be subordinate to any earthly authority, whether in matters which directly concern her duty in this respect, or in matters which necessarily concern her if she is to carry it out. Hence, as in the case in other departments of learning and in human concerns which are of their very nature the common concern of all—that is, of every individual citizen as well as of the whole state—the Church has, independently of any other authority, the right to make use of such studies and especially of arriving at decisions about them according as they seem in her judgment to be helpful or not as regards Christian education. And this the Church can do both because, being a perfect society, she is her own mistress in choosing and making use of such means and helps as will secure the attainment of her goal, and because all teaching and all institutions—as indeed all human actions—are necessarily dependent on the final goal and hence cannot be independent of the precepts of the law of God of which the Church is the guardian, interpreter, and mistress, immune from all danger of error."[741]

[739] Cyprian, *On the Unity of the Church*, n. 6; Cf. Augustine, *A Sermon to Catechumens on the Creed*, Ch. 1

[740] Leo XIII, Encyclical *Libertas*, of June 20, 1888

[741] *Acta Apostolicae Sedis*, yr. 22, p. 52ff

QUESTION 214

Leo XIII, Encyclical *Immortale Dei*, Nov. 1, 1885:

"Fitting reverence will of course be gladly shown by the citizens to the majesty of the law. For when once men realize that rulers are endowed with authority from God, they will feel that they in justice owe them due service, that they have to obey the commands of their rulers and exhibit in their regard an allegiance and loyalty comparable to that shown by children to their parents: 'Let every soul be subject to higher powers.'[742] For to despise lawful authority—no matter in whom it may reside—is no more lawful than it would be to resist the divine will, and to resist the latter means incurring voluntary destruction. 'He that resisteth the power resisteth the ordinance of God.'[743] To refuse obedience, then, and to start sedition by mob violence is treason, not only to man but to God."[744]

QUESTION 216

Leo XIII, Encyclical *Immortale Dei*, Nov. 1, 1885:

"Whence it follows that public authority can, of its very nature, only be from God. For God alone is the supreme and mighty Lord of things; him, all things, whatsoever they may be, must serve, and to him be subject; so that all who have the right to command can only owe that right to God, the supreme principle of all things: 'For there is no power but from God.'"[745]

St. John Chrysostom, *Homily 33 on Romans*, Ch. 1:

"In order to show that this command extends to all alike, to priests and monks as well as to laity, he says at the very outset: 'Let every

[742] Rom 13:1
[743] Rom 13:2
[744] *Acta* of Leo XIII, v, 121-122
[745] Rom 13:1; *Acta* of Leo XIII, v, 120

soul be subject to higher powers'[746] whether, that is, he be an apostle, an evangelist, a prophet, or anybody else; for such subjection is not subversive of piety. Nor was he content to say 'let him obey' but 'let him be subject to.' And a fundamental argument in support of such a declaration, one, too, which is in harmony with sound reasoning, is the fact that these precepts were given by God: 'There is no power but from God.'[747] 'What?' you will ask, 'is every prince set up by God?' 'I do not mean that,' the apostle answers, 'for I am not talking of individual rulers but of the principle itself. That there are such things as principalities, that some rule while others obey, that all does not happen by mere chance, that the populace is not driven about hither and thither like the waves, that, I say, is due to the divine Wisdom.' Hence he does not say, 'there is no prince but from God,' but, speaking of the principle itself, he says, 'for there is no power but from God': but the powers that are are ordained of God."[748]

QUESTION 218

Leo XIII, Encyclical *Rerum novarum*, May 15, 1891:

"And first of all, full religious training, of which the Church is the exponent and guardian, can be of very great value in the task of bringing into harmony and combining the wealthy classes and the lower, namely, by reminding each class of its duty to the other, more particularly on questions of justice. Among these duties some concern the lower classes and the workers: for example, that they must faithfully and honestly keep to work-contracts freely and fairly entered into; that they must do no damage to property nor offer violence to their masters; that, while safeguarding their own interests, they must refrain from violence and must not start seditious movements; that they must avoid being mixed up with criminal-minded people who hold out to them unreasonable expectations and preposterous promises which, as a rule,

[746] Rom 13:1
[747] Ibid.
[748] *P.G.*, lx, 615

merely result in vain regrets and great pecuniary loss. Then there are the duties incumbent on those who are rich and masters: they must not regard their workpeople as slaves; they must respect in them that equality in personality which springs from what we term the 'Christian character.' Further, that productive arts are—if we consult nature and Christian philosophy—no disgrace to a man but to his honor, since they provide him with fitting means for supporting himself. It is assuredly inhuman and disgraceful to make an ill use of men for the sake of things or for the sake of gain, or to act as though men's only value lay in what their sinews and muscles can supply. Similarly, it is a precept that in the case of the poorer classes, religion and the good of their souls has to be taken into account; consequently, that it is the business of masters to secure for their workpeople sufficient leisure for the practice of their religion; nor should they expose a man to the allurements of vice and the attractions of sin; nor, again, hinder him in any way from exercising due care for his family and the cultivation of thrifty habits. Nor, once more, should they impose on people more work than they are capable of, nor work disproportionate to their sex or age. Of all the duties which fall on masters, the primary one must be to do justice to all."[749]

QUESTION 220

Leo XIII, Encyclical *Quod Apostolici muneris*, Dec. 28, 1878:

"If, however, it should happen that rulers exercise their power over the people without consideration or restraint, the teaching of the Catholic Church does not permit their subjects to rebel against them on their own initiative, lest peace and tranquility should thereby be only the more disturbed and society thence suffer even greater loss. When, however, things do come to such a pitch, the Church teaches that some seasonable remedy has to be sought by meritorious patience and earnest prayer to God...And if legislators and rulers have permitted or commanded things contrary to the divine or to the natural law, then

[749] *Acta* of Leo XIII, xi, 110-111

Christian dignity and duty, as well as the declaration of the apostles, tell us that 'we must obey God rather than men.'"[750]

QUESTION 226

Alexander VII, Decree of Sept. 24, 1665, the second of certain condemned Propositions:

> "A knight can, when challenged to a duel, accept the challenge, lest he should be reproached by others with cowardliness."[751]

Leo XIII, Epistle *Pastoralis officii*, Sept. 12, 1891, to the bishops of Germany and Austria:

> "Both the divine laws alike, namely, that promulgated by the light of natural reason as well as that promulgated in the scriptures written by divine inspiration, strictly prohibit any man from slaying or wounding another, apart from cases falling under the public administration of justice, unless he be compelled of necessity to do so to save his own life. But those who challenge others to private combat or accept such a challenge do so with the deliberate intent of either killing or at least wounding their adversary, and this without any necessity. Furthermore, both divine laws forbid any person heedlessly to throw away his life by putting himself in grave and evident danger when no argument from duty or charity urges it; yet such blind foolhardiness leading to contempt for life is clearly inherent in the very nature of dueling. Hence no one can have the least doubt that those who engage in duels fall into the two crimes of attempting the death of another, and of deliberately courting their own destruction. Lastly, there is hardly anything more baneful to orderly social life, more destructive of due harmony in the state, than the notion that citizens should be free by force or violence to assert for themselves their individual rights, and that a man should be allowed personally to avenge his honor when he fancies it has been sullied."[752]

[750] Acts 5:29; *Acta* of Leo XIII, i, 177
[751] Du Plessis, *Collectio Judiciorum*, III, ii, 321
[752] *Acta* of Leo XIII, xi, 284

QUESTION 229

For Pius XI, see above, q. 213.

QUESTION 258

Fourth Lateran Council, A.D. 1215, Const. 21, *De confessione facienda et non revelanda a sacerdote, et saltem in Pascha communicando*:

> "Let every member of the faithful of either sex, after he has come to the age of discretion, faithfully confess all his sins at least once a year, alone, to his own priest, and let him endeavor according to his capacity to perform the penance imposed on him; let him also receive the sacrament of the Holy Eucharist at least at Easter, save in the case where, on the advice of his own priest, he for some reasonable cause refrains for a time from doing so. If he fails in these points, then, during his lifetime, let him be forbidden to enter the Church, and at death let him be deprived of Christian burial. Let, then, this salutary statute be frequently published in the churches, lest any should plead the excuse of ignorance of it. If, however, anyone wishes, for some reasonable cause, to confess to some other priest he must first ask and obtain leave from his own priest, for otherwise, the former could not either absolve him or bind him. Let the priest, too, be discreet and prudent, let him like a skilled physician 'pour oil and wine'[753] into the sinner's wound, let him carefully inquire into the circumstances of the sinner as well as of his sin so that he may thence know what advice and appropriate remedies to give him, making use of varying methods for saving the sick man."[754]

Council of Trent, Session 14, "Doctrine on the Sacrament of Penance," Ch. 5:

> "The Church, through the Council of the Lateran, laid down that... the precept of going to confession at least once a year bound all and

[753] Lk 10:34
[754] Mansi, *Concilia*, xxii, 1007

each when once they had arrived at years of discretion. Hence has resulted in the universal Church, with immense gain to souls, the salutary practice of going to confession during 'the holy and acceptable time' of Lent; this custom the holy synod especially commends and regards it as one that is rightly to be preserved."

QUESTION 259

For the Fourth Lateran Council, see above, q. 258.

Council of Trent, Session 13, "On the Most Holy Sacrament of the Eucharist," Can. 9:

> "If anyone shall deny that all and singular of the faithful of either sex are bound, after arriving at years of discretion, to communicate once a year, at least at Easter, according to the commandment of the Church, let him be anathema."

QUESTION 261

Decree of the Sacred Congregation of the Council, *Sacra Tridentina Synodus*, Dec. 20, 1905, "On daily reception of the Holy Eucharist":

> "Frequent, even daily, Communion, as being in accord with the desires of Christ our Lord and the wishes of holy Church, is open to all the faithful of whatever rank or condition, so that no one who is in a state of grace and wishes to approach the holy table with a devout and upright intention can be precluded from so doing."[755]

[755] *Acta Apostolicae Sedis*, yr. 2, p. 896

Decree of the Sacred Congregation of the Discipline of the Sacraments, *Quam singulari*, Aug. 8, 1910, n. 6:

> "Those who have the care of children should take all possible pains to see that, after their first Communion, children approach frequently to the holy table, and, if possible, daily, in accordance with the desires of Jesus Christ and of holy Church, also that they do so with a devotion in harmony with their years."[756]

QUESTION 262

Decree of the Sacred Congregation of the Discipline of the Sacraments, *Quam singulari*, Aug. 8, 1910, n. 1:

> "The age of discretion both for confession and Communion is that at which children begin to reason, that is, about their seventh year, whether earlier or later. From that time begins their obligation of fulfilling both precepts, those namely of confession and Communion."[757]

QUESTION 263

Decree of the Sacred Congregation of the Discipline of the Sacraments, *Quam singulari*, Aug. 8, 1910, n. 4:

> "The obligation of the precept of confession and Communion which affects children especially concerns those who have charge of them, that is, their parents, confessors, teachers, and their parish priest. It is the duty of their father or whosoever takes his place, and—according to the *Catechism of the Council of Trent*—of their confessor, to admit them to their first Communion."[758]

[756] *Acta Apostolicae Sedis*, yr. 2, p. 582
[757] Ibid.
[758] Ibid. See TCCI 7:277.

QUESTION 264

Decree of the Sacred Congregation of the Discipline of the Sacraments, *Quam singulari*, Aug. 8, 1910, n. 2-3:

> 2. "For first confession and first Communion, a full and complete knowledge of Christian doctrine is not necessary. But a child ought to learn the entire catechism by degrees according to his mental capacity."
>
> 3. "The knowledge of his religion required in a child so that he may fittingly prepare himself for his first Communion is that whereby he may grasp, according to his capacity, those mysteries of the faith which are necessary as being the means required for salvation, and may be able to appreciate the difference between ordinary bread and the bread of the Holy Eucharist, and so approach to the Holy Eucharist with a devotion compatible with his age."[759]

QUESTION 265

For the Decree of the Sacred Congregation of the Discipline of the Sacraments, see above, q. 263.

QUESTION 266

Decree of the Sacred Congregation of the Discipline of the Sacraments, *Quam singulari*, Aug. 8, 1910, n. 6:

> "...Moreover, those who have the care of children should bear in mind the very grave obligation under which they lie of seeing that children come to the public catechism classes; if children cannot come, then their religious instruction must be provided for in some other way."[760]

[759] *Acta Apostolicae Sedis*, yr. 2, p. 582

[760] Ibid.

QUESTION 269

Decree of the Sacred Congregation of the Holy Office, Sept. 24, 1665, the fourteenth condemned Proposition:

> "A person who makes a confession which is deliberately null and void thereby satisfies the precept of the Church."[761]

QUESTION 275

Pius XI, Encyclical *Quam Primas*, Dec. 11, 1925:

> "The civil government ought of course to afford a similar freedom to such religious orders and sodalities of either sex. For they are most valuable helpers to the pastors of the Church and labor strenuously in promoting and strengthening the kingdom of Christ. Both by opposing to the threefold 'concupiscences of the world' their religious vows as also by their profession of a more perfect form of life, they secure that that sanctity which its divine founder demanded should be an especial mark of his Church, always and with ever-increasing splendor shines and coruscates in the sight of all men."[762]

QUESTION 276

Leo XIII, Epistle *Testem benevolentiae*, Jan. 22, 1899, to His Eminence Cardinal Gibbons:

> "From this species of contempt for the gospel virtues which some perversely regard as 'passive,' it is but a natural consequence that men should come by degrees to a contempt for the religious life itself. In fact, that this is a commonplace with certain champions of modern views can be gathered from the ideas they ventilate about the vows taken by religious orders. For they maintain that such vows are quite out of

[761] Du Plessis, *Collectio Judiciorum*, III, ii, 321

[762] *Acta Apostolicae Sedis*, yr. 17, p. 609

keeping with the age in which we live on the ground that they fetter human liberty; also, that they are more suited to weak characters than to strong; and again, that they do not really further Christian perfection nor the good of human society, in fact are really more of an obstacle and a hindrance to both of these. How false are such notions will be evident from the practice and the teaching of the Church, which has always warmly approved of the religious life...And when such people maintain further that religious life is of little or no assistance to the Church, they are saying things with which no one at all familiar with the history of the Church would agree, quite apart from the invidious character of their remarks about the religious orders."[763]

Leo XIII, Epistle *Au milieu des consolations*, Dec. 23, 1900, to His Eminence Cardinal Richard:

"Religious orders derive their ideals and origin, as everybody knows, from the sublime evangelical counsels addressed by our divine Redeemer to all such as throughout the ages should aim at Christian perfection, to those strong generous souls who by prayer and contemplation, by the practice of austerity and definite rules, ever strive to ascend to the heights of the spiritual life. Produced under the influence of the Church, whose authority sanctions their rule and discipline, religious orders constitute the chosen portion of the flock of Christ. They are, in the words of St. Cyprian, 'the honor and the glory of spiritual grace,'[764] while at the same time they witness to the fecundity of the Church. Their vows, made freely and spontaneously after a period of mature reflection during their novitiate, have in every age been regarded and respected as sacred things, as productive of remarkable virtue. The object of such vows is twofold: first of all, to raise those who make such vows to a higher degree of perfection; secondly, to fit them by the purification and strengthening of their souls for an external ministry in which they labor for the eternal salvation of their neighbors and for relieving the many miseries which befall mankind. Thus, work-

[763] *Acta* of Leo XIII, xix, 15-16

[764] Cyprian, *De Disciplina et habitu virginum*, ii

ing under the supreme direction of the Apostolic See for the realization of the ideal perfection traced out for them by our Lord, and living under rules which are in no sense whatever opposed to any form of civil government, these religious institutions are powerful cooperators with the Church's mission, for this latter essentially consists in the task of sanctifying souls and working for the good of the human race. Hence it is that wherever the natural right of every citizen to choose that kind of life which he deems most in conformity with his inclinations and most conducive to his moral perfection is respected, there too religious orders have sprung up as the spontaneous product of Catholic soil, and the bishops have rightly regarded them as valuable helpers in the work of the ministry and of Christian charity."[765]

Pius XI, Epistle *Unigenitus Dei Filius*, March 19, 1924:

"When the only-begotten Son of God came into this world to redeem the human race, he gave to men certain precepts touching the spiritual life which were to govern all who aimed at the goal set before them; but he also taught those who would follow more closely in his footsteps that they must embrace and carry out the evangelical counsels. Whosoever, then, pledging his faith to God, promises to keep these counsels, is not only freed thereby from those hindrances which keep back us mortal men from holiness—for instance, from problems arising from property, from the anxieties and cares of the married life, and from unchecked liberty in every department of life—but he has thereby set out on so straight and unimpeded path to perfection that he might almost seem to have already cast anchor in the harbor of salvation."[766]

[765] *Acta* of Leo XIII, xx, 340-341

[766] *Acta Apostolicae Sedis*, yr. 16, p. 133

QUESTION 280

Council of Trent, Session 6, Can. 11:

"If anyone shall say that a man is justified either solely by the imputation to him of the righteousness of Christ, or solely by the remission of his sins, excluding grace and charity which are poured into men's hearts by the Holy Spirit and inhere in them, or that the grace whereby we are justified is only God's favor, let him be anathema."

St. Cyril of Alexandria, *On John*, Ch. 1, n. 9:

"Being made participators in God by the Spirit, we are stamped with the seal of likeness to him, and we attain to the pattern-type of his image to which holy scripture says we are made. For thus—the aforetime beauty of our nature at length recovered and refashioned on the model of that divine nature—we shall overcome the evils accruing to us from Adam's prevarication. We ascend, then, to a supernatural dignity through Christ. Yet not as he, not without an immense difference between ourselves and him, do we become the sons of God, but 'to his image,' that is, through grace whereby we represent him by imitation. For he is the true Son of God, existing of the Father, we his adopted sons through his kindness, by force of grace that says: 'I have said, ye are gods and all of ye sons of the most High.'[767]

"For our created and servile nature is called to things that are supernatural solely by the Father's will and condescension. But the Son—God and Lord—does not derive his title to Godhead from the Father's condescension nor from his will alone, but since he shone forth from the very substance of the Father, he by his very nature lays claim to its proper good as his own."[768]

[767] Ps 81:6
[768] *P.G.*, lxxiii, 154

QUESTION 282

Second Council of Orange, A.D. 529, Can. 18:

> "Without any merits antecedent to grace, a reward is due to good works if they are performed; but grace, which is not a debt, precedes in order that they may be performed."[769]

Council of Trent, Session 6, Can. 32:

> "If anyone shall say that the good works of a man who is justified are in this sense the gift of God, that the merits of a man so justified are not themselves good works, or that a man by the good works whereby he is justified, and which he performs by the grace of God and the merits of Jesus Christ whose living member he is, does not truly merit an increase of grace, eternal life, and the attainment of that eternal life always provided he departs this life in a state of grace, and also an increase of glory, let him be anathema."

QUESTION 283

Council of Trent, Session 6, Can. 27:

> "If anyone shall say that the only mortal sin is unbelief, or that grace once given can be lost by no sin—however grave or heinous—save that of unbelief, let him be anathema."

For St. Basil the Great, see above, q. 66.

[769] Mansi, *Concilia*, viii, 715

QUESTION 285

Council of Trent, Session 6, "Decree on Justification," Ch. 6:

> "Men, however, are disposed for the reception of righteousness when, stirred up and helped by divine grace, they move freely toward God, believing those things to be true which have been divinely revealed and promised, and primarily, that a sinner is justified by God by his grace, by the redemption which is in Christ Jesus; and further, when realizing that they are sinners, they, through fear of the divine justice which terrified them for their profit, turn and dwell on the mercy of God and are uplifted by hope, trusting that God will be merciful to them for Christ's sake, and begin to love him as the source of all righteousness, and are in consequence stirred up to a hatred and detestation of sin, that is, to a repentance which ought to precede baptism; and finally, when they begin a new life and keep God's commandments. Of dispositions such as these is it written: 'He that would come to God must believe that he is, and is a rewarder to them that seek him';[770] and again: 'Be of good heart, son, thy sins are forgiven thee';[771] and again: 'The fear of God casteth out sin';[772] and again: 'Do penance and be baptized every one of you in the name of Jesus Christ, for the remission of your sins, and you shall receive the gift of the Holy Spirit';[773] and again: 'Going therefore teach ye all nations, baptizing them in the name of the Father and of the Son and of the Holy Ghost, teaching them to observe all things whatsoever I have commanded you';[774] and lastly: 'Prepare your hearts unto the Lord.'"[775]

[770] Heb 11:6
[771] Mt 9:2; Cf. Mk 2:5
[772] Ecclus 1:27
[773] Acts 2:38
[774] Mt 28:19-20
[775] 1 Kgs 7:3

St. Augustine, *On the Spirit and the Letter*, Ch. 48:

"But if those who 'do by nature those things that are of the law'[776] are yet not to be reckoned in the number of those whom the grace of Christ justifies, but rather amongst those of whom we read or know or hear that, though impious and not rightly worshipping the true God, they yet do certain things which we can not only not blame by any standard of righteousness, but must rightly and deservedly praise—yet when we come to examine their reason for doing such things we shall hardly find anything deserving the praise and support due to righteousness. Nonetheless, since the image of God in the human soul is not so completely destroyed by the stain of earthly affections that no slightest vestige of it remains, it can justly be said that, even in the midst of their wicked lives, such men do and show an appreciation for some things according to the law, if that is, this is what is meant by the words: 'The Gentiles that have not the law'—that is, the law of God—'do by nature those things that are of the law.'... Yet, even so, this will not remove the gulf that lies between the old testament and the new...For, precisely as venial sins do not preclude a just man from eternal life—for we cannot live here without such sins—so too, the fact that a wicked man does perform some good works—for it would be exceedingly difficult even for the worst of men to perform none—does not mean that such works avail for his eternal salvation."[777]

QUESTION 286

St. Ephraem, *De Epiphania*, x, 14:

"The good God toils, painfully as it were: for while he does not wish to coerce our liberty, yet neither does he permit us to be negligent. For, were he to use coercion, he would be taking away our power of choice; were he to leave us to our negligence, he would be depriving our souls of his help. The Lord, then, knowing that if he coerces us, he robs us, if

[776] Rom 2:14
[777] *P.L.*, xliv, 229ff

he withdraws his help, he loses us, but that if he teaches us, he gains us, neither coerces nor withdraws his help as does the evil one, but teaches, instructs, and so gains us, since he is the good one."[778]

St. Cyril of Alexandria, *De Adoratione in spiritu et veritate*, n. 1:

"Since man's nature is not very stable and he has not sufficient strength to escape from his vices, God helps him in this matter. Whence we realize that he gives us a twofold grace: for he persuades us by his admonitions and he also finds means to help us, and he renders those means more potent than the ever-present evil which does violence to us."[779]

QUESTION 287

Second Council of Orange, A.D. 529, against the Semipelagians, Can. 3-6:

Can. 3: "If anyone says that the grace of God can be conferred simply on men's asking for it, and that it is not grace which makes us ask for it, such a one contradicts Isaias the prophet, also the apostle, who says the same: 'I was found by them that did not seek me; I appeared openly to them that asked not after me.'"[780]

Can. 4: "If anyone argues that, in order that we may be purified from sin, God awaits our will, and does not acknowledge that our very desire to be purified is produced in us by the inpouring of the Holy Spirit and by his operation in us, such a one resists the Holy Spirit himself who says by the mouth of Solomon: 'The will is prepared by the Lord';[781] and by the apostle: 'It is God who worketh in you both to will and to accomplish, according to his good will.'"[782]

[778] *Ed.* Lamy, *Sti. Ephremi Hymni et Sermones*, I, 102
[779] P.G., lxviii, 174
[780] Rom 10:20; Cf. Is 65:1
[781] Cf. Prv 8:36
[782] Phil 2:13

Can. 5: "If anyone shall say that, just as the increase so also the beginning of faith and the inclination to believe—whereby we believe in him who justified the wicked, and so come to the regeneration of baptism—is not due to a gift of grace, that is, to the inspiration of the Holy Spirit correcting our will and leading it from unbelief, from impiety to piety, but is in us by nature, such a one is clearly contradicting the teachings of the apostles, for the blessed Paul says: 'Being confident of this very thing, that he who hath begun a good work in you will perfect it unto the day of Christ Jesus';[783] and again: 'For unto you it is given for Christ not only to believe in him, but also to suffer for him';[784] and again: 'By grace you are saved, through faith, and that not of yourselves, for it is the gift of God.'[785] For those who say that the faith whereby we believe in God is natural, in some sort make all those who are strangers to the Church of Christ believers."

Can. 6: "If anyone shall say that the mercy of God is divinely bestowed upon us, when, without the grace of God, we believe, will, desire, strive, labor, watch, study, ask, seek, knock, and shall refuse to acknowledge that our believing, willing, and doing all these things as we ought is by the inpouring and inspiration of the Holy Spirit in us, and shall hold that God adds the assistance of his grace to human obedience or humility, and shall not admit that to be obedient and humble is due to the gift of grace itself, such a one resists the apostle, who says: 'What hast thou that thou hast not received?'[786] and again: 'By the grace of God I am what I am.'"[787]

Council of Trent, Session 6, Can. 1-3:

Can. 1: "If anyone shall say that a man can be justified before God by good works done either by the natural power of human nature or

[783] Phil 1:6
[784] Phil 1:29
[785] Eph 2:8
[786] 1 Cor 4:7
[787] 1 Cor 15:10; Mansi, *Concilia*, viii, 713ff

through the teaching of the law, and without divine grace through Jesus Christ, let him be anathema."

Can. 2: "If anyone shall say that divine grace through Jesus Christ is given solely in order that a man may more easily live a just life and merit eternal life, as though a man can by free will and without grace do so, though only with difficulty and effort, let him be anathema."

Can. 3: "If anyone shall say that without the anticipatory inspiration and help of the Holy Spirit a man can believe, hope, love, or repent in such a way as is necessary for justifying grace to be bestowed upon him, let him be anathema."

St. Gregory Nazianzen, *Oration 37*, n. 13:

"For since there are some who by reason of certain things they have done rightly are so uplifted in mind that they ascribe the whole to themselves, nor attribute anything to their Creator, the author of their wisdom and the bestower of all good gifts, the words: 'It is not of him that willeth nor of him that runneth, but of God that showeth mercy,'[788] teach them that even rightly to will demands the help of God: nay—to speak more accurately—the will itself and choice of what is right and in accordance with our duty is a certain divine benefit. For even that we are saved must needs be both from ourselves and from God. Hence he says: 'It is not of him that willeth,' that is, not only of him that willeth, 'nor of him that runneth' only, 'but' also 'of God that showeth mercy.' Since, then, even to will is itself from God, most rightly does he attribute the whole to God. However much you run, however much you strive, you need him who bestows the crown."[789]

[788] Rom 9:16
[789] *P.G.*, xxxvi, 298ff

St. John Chrysostom, *Homily 25 on Genesis*, n. 7:

> "For it is impossible for us rightly to do any good work unless we are helped by grace from above."[790]

QUESTION 288

For the Council of Trent, see above, q. 189.

Innocent X, Constitution *Cum occasione*, against the errors of Jansensius, May 31, 1653, the first condemned Proposition:

> "Some of God's commands are, in view of the powers men now have, impossible for just men to fulfill, even though they wish and strive to do so; and the grace which would make such fulfillment possible for them is lacking."[791]

St. John Chrysostom, *Homily 16 on Hebrews*, n. 4:

> "It is not lawful to say 'I cannot,' for that means accusing the Creator. For if he made us incapable and yet gives us commands, the fault lies with him. Whence comes it, then, you will say, that so many 'cannot'? Because they will not. How, then, is it that they will not? Through sloth; for if they would but will they would be quite capable...For we have God to help and assist us; let us only choose: only approach it as a task, only be anxious, only apply our minds to it, and all things follow."[792]

[790] P.G., liii, 228
[791] Du Plessis, *Collectio Judiciorum*, III, ii, 261
[792] P.G., lxiii, 127ff

QUESTION 291

St. John Chrysostom, *Homily 30 on Genesis*, n. 5:

"Petition is a very good thing. For if from speaking with a person endowed with great power one derives no small profit, what great profit will one not derive from holding converse with God?...Is he not able to grant our petitions even before we ask him? Yet he defers and waits, to find an occasion for justly making us deserving of his providence."[793]

QUESTION 297

St. Augustine, *Tractate 102 on John*, n. 1:

"We must now examine the Lord's words: 'Amen, amen, I say to you: If you shall ask anything of the Father in my name he will give it you.'[794] Now in the earlier portion of this sermon of the Lord, it was, because of those who, though asking certain things of the Father in Christ's name yet do not obtain them, said that whatever is asked for and yet is opposed to our salvation is not really asked for 'in the name of our Savior.' For the words, 'in my name,' must not be considered simply according to the sound of the letters and syllables, but we must understand them according to what those sounds really and truly mean.

"Consequently, a person who has ideas of Christ which do not harmonize with his being the only Son of God does not ask 'in his name,' even when he rightly frames the letters and syllables that make up the name *Christ*. Whereas he whose ideas of Christ are correct really does ask 'in his name,' and he gets what he asks, provided always that he does not ask for something opposed to his salvation. He gets it, however, only when he ought to receive it. For some things are not refused us, though their bestowal is deferred to a fitting time. We must, then, understand the words 'he will give it you' as meaning such benefits as properly belong to those who ask. The saints of course are always heard for their

[793] P.G., liii, 280
[794] Jn 16:23

own sakes; but they are not heard when asking for all people, whether friends or enemies or any others you please; for he did not say, 'he will give it,' but, 'he will give it you.'"[795]

QUESTION 313

For the Council of Trent, see above, q. 189.

QUESTION 322

Leo XIII, Encyclical *Adjutricem populi*, Sept. 5, 1895:

"The mystery of Christ's wondrous love toward us shines out more especially in the fact that when dying he bequeathed his Mother to John the disciple as his Mother, in his thoughtful testament: 'Behold thy son.'[796] But, as the Church has always felt, in John Christ would signify the person of the human race, more especially those who would cling to him by faith. Thus St. Anselm of Canterbury: 'What more fitting, then, that thou, O Virgin, shouldst be the Mother of those whose father and brother Christ deigned to be?'[797] She, then, undertook her share in this exclusive and toilsome task and died great of soul amidst the consecrated tokens in the upper room."[798]

Pius X, Encyclical *Ad illum diem*, Feb. 2, 1904:

"Was not Mary Christ's Mother? Then she is our Mother too. For all must needs agree that Jesus, the Word made flesh, is the Savior of the human race. For as God-man he, like other men, received a material body; but as the restorer of our race he received a certain spiritual body, the 'mystical body' as we term it, namely, the company of those

[795] *P.L.*, xxxv, 1896
[796] Jn 19:26
[797] Anselm, *Oration* 47
[798] *Acta* of Leo XIII, xv, 302

who believe in Christ: 'We being many are one body in Christ.'[799] But the Blessed Virgin did not conceive the eternal Son of God only that he might be a man by taking human nature from her, but also that, through the nature derived from her, he might become the deliverer of the human race. Wherefore the angels said to the shepherds: 'This day is born to you a Savior who is Christ the Lord.'[800] Thus in one and the same womb of the most pure Mary did Christ both take to himself human flesh and at the same time add a spiritual body, fashioned and growing together out of those who were to believe in him. Hence, bearing in her womb the Savior, Mary can also be said to have borne all those whose life the Savior's life enshrined. All of us, then, as many as are knit to Christ, and who, as the apostle says, 'are members of his body, of his flesh, and of his bones,'[801] have come forth from Mary's womb, one body, as it were, knit together with its head. Hence, in spiritual and mystic fashion we are called 'Mary's children,' and she is the Mother of us all. 'Mother spiritually, it is true, yet clearly Mother of the members of Christ, which we are.'[802] If then, the Blessed Virgin is Mother both of God and of men, who can question that she strives with all her power that Christ, 'the head of the body, the Church,'[803] may pour out his gifts upon us his members, and especially that we may know him and 'that we may live by him'?"[804]

Benedict XV, *Epistle to the Confraternity of Our Lady of a Happy Death*, March 22, 1918:

"It is clear, too, that this most sorrowful Virgin, since appointed by Jesus Christ as the Mother of all men, received them as a testament of infinite charity left to her, and fulfills with motherly kindness the task of forwarding their spiritual life; nor can she fail more especially

[799] Rom 12:5
[800] Lk 2:11
[801] Eph 5:30
[802] Augustine, *Of Holy Virginity*, Ch. 6
[803] Col 1:18
[804] 1 Jn 4:9; *Acta* of Pius X, i, 152

to assist these most dear adopted children in that hour when it is a question of confirming unto eternity their salvation and sanctity."[805]

Pius XI, Encyclical *Rerum Ecclesiae*, Feb. 28, 1926:

"May Mary, the most holy Queen of apostles, kindly smile on all and prosper the work undertaken; for since on Calvary all men were entrusted to her motherly care, she does not less cherish and love those who are ignorant of the fact that they are redeemed by Jesus Christ, than she does those who happily enjoy the benefits of that redemption."[806]

QUESTION 325

Council of Florence, Session 8 (November 22, 1439), "Bull of Union with the Armenians":

"There are seven sacraments of the new law: baptism, confirmation, Holy Eucharist, penance, extreme unction, order, and matrimony, and these differ much from the sacraments of the old law. For these latter did not cause grace but only prefigured its future bestowal through the passion of Christ; whereas our sacraments both contain grace and confer it upon them that receive them worthily. The first five of these are intended for the spiritual perfection of each individual man; the two last for the government and multiplication of the whole Church. For, by baptism, we are spiritually born again; by confirmation, we grow in grace and are strengthened in the faith; thus, reborn and strengthened, we are fed with the divine food of the Holy Eucharist. And if through sin we incur sickness of the soul, then by penance are we spiritually healed; spiritually and corporally also, if it avails for our soul's good, by extreme unction; by holy order, the Church is governed and multiplied spiritually; by matrimony, it gains corporal increase. All these sacraments are perfected by three things: by things as their material part, by words as their formal part, and by the person of the minister

[805] *Acta Apostolicae Sedis*, yr. 10, p. 182
[806] *Acta Apostolicae Sedis*, yr. 18, p. 83

conferring the sacrament with the intention of doing what the Church does: if anyone of these be wanting, the sacrament is not completed."[807]

Council of Trent, Session 7, "On the Sacraments in General," Can. 1 and 6:

Can. 1: "If anyone shall say that the sacraments of the new law were not instituted by Jesus Christ our Lord, or that they are fewer or more than seven in number, namely: baptism, confirmation, Holy Eucharist, penance, extreme unction, holy order, and matrimony, or that any one of these seven is not truly and properly a sacrament, let him be anathema."

Can. 6: "If anyone shall say that the sacraments of the new law do not contain the grace which they signify, or that they do not confer grace on those who offer no hindrance, as though they were merely external signs of a grace or righteousness received through faith, certain marks of a man's profession of Christianity whereby people may be able to distinguish between believers and unbelievers, let him be anathema."

Pius X, Decree *Lamentabili sane*, July 3, 1907, the thirty-ninth, fortieth, and forty-first condemned Propositions:

Prop. 39: "The opinions held by the fathers of Trent, and unquestionably reflected in their dogmatic canons, are very different from those rightly held now by those who have made a historical study of Christianity."

Prop. 40: "Sacraments came into being owing to the fact that the apostles and their successors, moved by circumstances and events, interpreted some idea and intention of Christ's."

Prop. 41: "The only object of sacraments is to stir up in men's minds a sense of the ever-beneficent presence of the Creator."[808]

[807] Mansi, *Concilia*, xxxi, 1054
[808] *Acta Sanctae Sedis*, vol. 40, p. 475

QUESTION 326

For the Council of Florence, see above, q. 325.

Council of Trent, Session 7, "On the Sacraments in General," Can. 11:

> "If anyone shall say that it is not requisite that ministers, when making or conferring sacraments, should at least intend to do what the Church does, let him be anathema."

QUESTION 329

For the Council of Florence, see above, q. 325.

QUESTION 331

Council of Trent, Session 7, "On the Sacraments in General," Can. 7-8:

> Can. 7: "If anyone shall say that grace is not conferred by these sacraments always and to all, so far as God is concerned, even when people receive them rightly, or is only sometimes conferred, or to some only, let him be anathema."
>
> Can. 8: "If anyone shall say that by the sacraments of the new law grace is not conferred *ex opere operato*, but that faith in God's promises is alone sufficient for obtaining grace, let him be anathema."

St. Augustine, *Epistle* 98, n. 2:

> "That a man should be able to be regenerated through the action of another's will when he is offered for consecration is due to the action of the one Spirit by whom the person thus offered is regenerated. For it is not written: 'Unless a man be born again by the will of his parents or the faith of those who offer him or of the ministers,' but, 'Unless a man

be born again of water and the Holy Spirit.'[809] Hence water, exhibiting externally the sacrament of grace, and the Holy Spirit working internally the benefit of grace…regenerate in the one Christ a man born of the one Adam."[810]

St. Augustine, *Tractate 80 on John*, n. 3:

"'Now you are clean by reason of the word which I have spoken to you.'[811] Why does he not say: 'Ye are clean by reason of the baptism wherewith you are cleansed,' but, 'by reason of the word which I have spoken to you,' unless because even in water it is the word that cleanses? Take away the word and what is water but water? The word comes to the element and the sacrament is made, it too as it were some visible word."[812]

QUESTION 337

Council of Trent, Session 14, "Doctrine on the Sacrament of Penance," Ch. 4:

"The same holy synod also teaches that though such contrition may sometimes happen to be perfect charity, and a person may be reconciled to God before actually receiving the sacrament, yet nevertheless such reconciliation is not to be attributed to contrition without the desire of the sacrament, for such desire is included in such contrition."

[809] Jn 3:5
[810] *P.L.*, xxxiii, 360
[811] Jn 15:3
[812] *P.L.*, xxxv, 1840

QUESTION 339

St. Augustine, *Contra Epistolam Parmeniani*, Bk. 2, n. 28:

"Both of these (baptism and order) are sacraments, and both are conferred on men with a certain consecration, one when he is baptized, the other when ordained; consequently, in the Catholic Church neither can be repeated. For if at any time even bishops coming over from that schism (the Donatist) have been received for the sake of peace when they have set right their schismatic error, if it seemed necessary for them to continue to exercise the offices they had been wont to exercise, they were not reordained, but just as their baptism, so too their orders remained unimpaired in them; for while there was a defect in them owing to their state of separation, yet, in their sacraments, there was none, for sacraments wherever they are remain sacraments."[813]

QUESTION 341

Council of Florence, Session 8 (November 22, 1439), "Bull of Union with the Armenians":

"Among these sacraments, there are three, baptism, confirmation, and order, which imprint on the soul an indelible character or a certain spiritual distinctive stamp. Hence these sacraments are not repeated in one and the same person. The other four imprint no character and so admit of repetition."[814]

Council of Trent, Session 7, "On the Sacraments in General," Can. 9:

"If anyone shall say that in three sacraments, namely, baptism, confirmation, and order, no character is imprinted on the soul, that is a spiritual and indelible stamp, so that they cannot be repeated, let him be anathema."

[813] *P.L.*, xliii, 70
[814] Mansi, *Concilia*, xxxi, 1054

Innocent III, Epistle *Majores Ecclesiae Causas*, A.D. 1201, to Humbert, the archbishop of Arles:

> "Between one unwilling person and another, between one acting under compulsion and another, some make the reasonable distinction that a person who is driven by threats of punishment and receives baptism lest he should suffer through refusal, does—like a man who receives baptism in pretense only—receive the impressed character of a Christian, and that though he did not absolutely will it, yet he did so conditionally, and can therefore be compelled to observe the laws of the Christian faith...Whereas a person who never consented at all but absolutely refused receives neither the essence of the sacrament nor the character: for it is a greater thing expressly to refuse than not to give full consent...As for those who were baptized in their sleep or when mad: if before they became mad or fell asleep they had persisted in refusing, then—since their determination to refuse must be presumed to have continued—such people, even though subject to baptism, do not receive the sacramental character. But the contrary is the case with those who had up till that time been catechumens and had intended receiving baptism, for it is the practice of the Church to baptize such people on their deathbeds. Baptism in such cases imprints the sacramental character, since there exists no impediment arising from the person's will being opposed to it."[815]

QUESTION 348

Pius X, Decree *Lamentabili sane*, July 3, 1907, the forty-second condemned Proposition:

> "It was the Christian community that made baptism necessary by adopting it as a necessary rite, and attaching to it the obligation of the profession of the Christian faith."[816]

[815] Gregory IX, *Liber Extra*, Bk. 3, tit. 42, Ch. 3

[816] *Acta Sanctae Sedis*, vol. 40, p. 475

St. Basil the Great, *Homily 13*, n. 5:

> "Baptism is the captives' ransom, the condonation of their debts, the death of sin, the regeneration of the soul, the shining garment, the seal that nothing can break, the pathway to heaven, the foundation of the kingdom, the gift of adoption."[817]

QUESTION 349

Council of Vienne, A.D. 1311-1312, *Constitutio de Trinitate et Fide*, against the errors of Peter Oliva:

> "All the faithful must confess one only baptism which regenerates in Christ all the baptized, just as there is 'one God and one faith.'[818] We believe that this sacrament, celebrated in water and in the name of Father, Son, and Holy Spirit, is necessary for children and grown-up people alike, as the perfect remedy for salvation."[819]

Council of Florence, Session 8 (November 22, 1439), "Bull of Union with the Armenians":

> "Holy baptism holds the first place among the sacraments, for it is the door into the spiritual life, since by it we are made members of Christ and of his body the Church. And, since by the first man death came upon all, unless we are born again of water and the Holy Spirit we cannot, as the truth says, 'enter into the kingdom of heaven.'[820] The material part of this sacrament is true natural water, it matters not whether it is hot or cold. The formal part is: 'I baptize thee in the name of the Father, and of the Son, and of the Holy Spirit.' At the same time, we do not deny that true baptism may be conferred by the words: 'This servant of Christ is baptized in the name of the Father and of the Son

[817] *P.G.*, xxxi, 434

[818] Eph 4:5

[819] Mansi, *Concilia*, xxv, 411

[820] Jn 3:5

and of the Holy Spirit,' or, 'Such a one is baptized by my hands in the name of the Father and of the Son and of the Holy Spirit.' For since the principal cause whence baptism derives its efficacy is the Holy Trinity, and the instrumental cause the minister who performs the exterior rite, then, if the action performed by the minister is accompanied by the invocation of the Holy Trinity, the sacrament is perfected. The minister of this sacrament is a priest, for it belongs to his office. But, in case of necessity, not only a priest or a deacon but lay people, men and women, even pagans and heretics, can baptize provided they observe the form laid down by the Church and intend to do what the Church does. The effect of this sacrament is the remission of all sin, both original and actual, also of all penalties due to the guilt of such sin. Consequently, no penance or satisfaction for their sins is to be imposed on people at their baptism; and if they die before committing any sin, they straightway pass to the kingdom of heaven and the vision of God."[821]

Council of Trent, Session 7, "On the Sacraments in General," Can. 2:

"If anyone shall say that true and natural water is not necessary for this sacrament of baptism, and thus turn the words of our Lord Jesus Christ, 'Unless a man be born again of water and the Holy Spirit,'[822] into a species of metaphor, let him be anathema."

Innocent III, Epistle *Non ut apponeres*, March 1, 1206, *ad Thoriam Archiepiscopum Nidrosiensem*:

"You ask whether those children are to be regarded as Christians whom, when at the point of death, some simple-minded folk have, in the absence of a priest, and having no water at hand, anointed with saliva on the head and breast and between the shoulders. We reply that since in baptism two things are always and necessarily required, namely, the words and the element, just as the truth said of the words,

[821] Mansi, *Concilia*, xxxi, 1059

[822] Jn 3:5

'Go ye into the whole world...,'[823] so he said the same of the element: 'Unless a man...';[824] you therefore ought not to doubt but that such children have received no true baptism, since in their case not merely one of the aforesaid requisites has been omitted, but both."[825]

The Didache, Ch. 7:

"As concerns baptism, baptize thus: after you shall have already said all these things, baptize in the name of the Father and of the Son and of the Holy Spirit in living water."[826]

QUESTION 352

Fourth Lateran Council, A.D. 1215, Const. 1, against the Albigenses:

"But the sacrament of baptism (which is consecrated in water accompanied by the invocation of God and of the undivided Trinity, namely, Father, Son, and Holy Spirit) avails for the salvation both of children and grown-up people no matter by whom it is correctly conferred according to the form of the Church."[827]

For the Council of Florence, see above, q. 349.

St. Augustine, *Contra Epistolam Parmeniani*, Bk. 2, n. 29:

"Although even supposing a layman were compelled by a dying person's need to baptize him, and had, since he himself had received it, learned how to administer it, I question whether anyone would say it ought to be repeated. For if this were done without necessity, then it would mean that he had usurped someone else's function; if it were done through

[823] Mk 16:15; Cf. Mt 28:19
[824] Jn 3:5
[825] Gregory IX, *Liber Extra*, Bk. 2, tit. 42, Ch. 5
[826] *Patres Apostolici*, ed. Funk. I, xviiff
[827] Mansi, *Concilia*, xxii, 982

necessity, then it was no fault at all, or at most a venial one. And if without any necessity he thus usurped someone else's function and the sacrament was conferred by somebody or other on somebody or other, still what was 'given' cannot be said not to have been 'given,' though one could rightly say that it was not rightly given."[828]

QUESTION 354

Council of Florence, Session 11 (Feb. 4, 1442), "Decree for the Jacobites":

"This synod absolutely commands everybody who glories in the name of Christian to cease from the practice of circumcision at any time, whether before or after baptism; for whether a man place any reliance on it or not he cannot observe that rite without the loss of his eternal salvation. As regards children, this holy synod admonishes people that, owing to the danger of death, as may often happen, then, since children can be helped by no other remedy than baptism whereby they are delivered from the power of the devil, and made the adopted children of God, their baptism is not to be deferred for forty or eighty days as is done by some, but ought to be conferred as soon as can conveniently be done; and when there is imminent danger of death, they should be baptized at once without any delay and, in the absence of a priest, even by lay people, by men or by women, in the form of the Church, as is more fully set forth in the Decree for the Armenians."[829]

Pius X, Decree *Lamentabili sane*, July 3, 1907, the forty-third condemned Proposition:

"The practice of conferring baptism on children is due to a disciplinary evolution and was one of the causes leading to the division of the sacrament into two, namely, baptism and penance."[830]

[828] *P.L.*, xliii, 71
[829] Mansi, *Concilia*, xxxi, 1738ff
[830] *Acta Sanctae Sedis*, vol. 40, p. 475

QUESTION 357

Council of Trent, Session 7, "On the Sacraments in General," Can. 7:

"If anyone shall say that the baptized become by their baptism debtors only to the faith but not to the observance of the entire law of Christ, let him be anathema."

QUESTION 358

For the Second Council of Carthage, see above, q. 74; for the Council of Florence, see above, q. 349.

Council of Trent, Session 7, "On Baptism," Can. 5:

"If any shall say that baptism is free, that is, that it is not necessary for salvation, let him be anathema."

St. Cyril of Jerusalem, *Catechetical Lecture 3*, n. 10:

"If a person refuses baptism, he does not gain salvation, excepting only the holy martyrs who gain the kingdom without water."[831]

QUESTION 359

Innocent III, Epistle *Majores Ecclesiae Causas*, A.D. 1201, to Humbert, the archbishop of Arles:

"The penalty of original sin is the loss of the vision of God; the penalty of actual sin is the torment of everlasting hell."[832]

[831] *P.G.*, xxxiii, 439

[832] Gregory IX, *Liber Extra*, Bk. 3, tit. 42, Ch. 3

Pius VI, Constitution *Auctorem Fidei*, against the errors of the Synod of Pistoia, Aug. 28, 1794, the twenty-sixth condemned Proposition:

> "The teaching which regards as an exploded fable devised by the Pelagians that portion of the lower regions generally known to the faithful as the 'limbo of children,' in which the souls of those who have departed this life with only original sin are punished by the pain of loss but not by the pain of fire—as though, by removing the pain of fire, they have therefore secured a place and state free from sin and punishment, and intermediate between the kingdom of God and eternal damnation, such as the Pelagians dreamed of—is false, rash, and defamatory of the teaching of the schools of Catholic thought."[833]

For Pius IX, see above, q. 162.

QUESTION 360

For Innocent II, see above, q. 162.

St. Fulgentius, *De Fide*, n. 41:

> "From the time when our Savior said, 'Unless a man be born again of water and the Holy Ghost he cannot enter into the kingdom of God,'[834] no one, save those who have shed their blood without baptism but in the Catholic Church, can without baptism enter the kingdom of heaven, or obtain eternal life. For whosoever, whether in the Catholic Church or in any heretical or schismatical body, receives the sacrament of baptism in the name of the Father and of the Son and of the Holy Spirit, receives indeed the entire sacrament, but he will not have that salvation which is the virtue of the sacrament if he receives the sacrament itself outside the Catholic Church. He ought therefore to return to the Church, not there to receive baptism afresh—for no one ought to repeat that sacrament in the case of a person once baptized—but

[833] *Continuation of the Roman Bullarium*, p. 2711ff

[834] Jn 3:5

so that in the Catholic society he may receive eternal life, for the attainment of which no man is fit who, while having the sacrament of baptism, remains a stranger to the Catholic Church."[835]

QUESTION 363

Second Council of Lyons, A.D. 1274, *Profession of Faith by Michael Palaeologus*:

"The same holy Roman Church also holds and teaches seven ecclesiastical sacraments: one is baptism, of which we have spoken above; another is confirmation, which bishops confer by imposing hands on and anointing with chrism those regenerated; another is penance; another the Holy Eucharist; another the sacrament of order; another matrimony; another extreme unction, which, according to the teaching of St. James, is applied to the sick. The same Roman Church uses for the Holy Eucharist unleavened bread, holding and teaching that in this sacrament the bread is truly transubstantiated into the body, and the wine into the blood of our Lord Jesus Christ. As regards matrimony, she holds that neither can one man have many wives at the same time, nor one woman many husbands. But when the marriage is dissolved by the death of one partner, she declares that second or third successive marriages are lawful, provided no other canonical impediment arises from some other source."[836]

Council of Florence, Session 8 (November 22, 1439), "Bull of Union with the Armenians":

"The second sacrament is confirmation; its matter is chrism made from oil and signifying the shining beauty of the conscience, and from balsam signifying the odor of a good reputation; these are blessed by the bishop. The form is: 'I sign thee with the sign of the cross, and I confirm thee with the chrism of salvation, in the name of the Father and of the Son and of the Holy Ghost.' The ordinary minister is a bishop. And though

[835] *P.L.*, lxv, 692

[836] Mansi, *Concilia*, xxiv, 71

a simple priest can administer other anointings, this one the bishop alone ought to confer; for only of the apostles—whose place bishops hold—is it said that they conferred the Holy Spirit by the imposition of hands, as is clear from what we read in the Acts of the Apostles: 'Now when the apostles who were at Jerusalem had heard that Samaria had received the word of God, they sent unto them Peter and John, who, when they were come, prayed for them that they might receive the Holy Ghost, for he was not as yet come upon any of them; but they were only baptized in the name of the Lord Jesus. Then they laid their hands upon them, and they received the Holy Ghost.'[837] In place of that imposition of hands, confirmation is given in the Church. We read, however, that sometimes, by dispensation of the Holy See, and for reasonable and very urgent causes, a priest has administered the sacrament of confirmation with chrism prepared by a bishop. Now, the effect of this sacrament is—since in it the Holy Spirit is given for strength, as it was given to the apostles on the day of Pentecost—to enable a Christian boldly to confess Christ's name. The person to be confirmed is therefore anointed on the forehead, the seat of modesty, lest he should blush to confess Christ's name, and more especially his cross, which according to the apostle is 'to the Jews indeed a stumbling block and to the Gentiles foolishness';[838] for this reason is he signed with the sign of the cross."[839]

Council of Trent, Session 7, "On Confirmation," Can. 1-3:

Can. 1: "If anyone shall say that confirmation of those already baptized is an idle ceremony and not a true and real sacrament, or that originally it was only a species of catechism wherein those on the threshold of adolescence made profession of their faith in the presence of the Church, let him be anathema."

Can. 2: "If anyone shall say that they do an injury to the Holy Spirit who attribute any efficacy to the sacred chrism of confirmation, let him be anathema."

[837] Acts 8:14-17
[838] 1 Cor 1:23
[839] Mansi, *Concilia*, xxxi, 1055ff

Can. 3: "If anyone shall say that the ordinary minister of confirmation is not only a bishop but any simple priest, let him be anathema."

Innocent III, Epistle *Cum venisset*, Feb. 25, 1204, *ad Basilium Archiepiscopum Trinovitanum*:

"By the anointing with chrism on the forehead is meant the imposition of hands, also called 'confirmation,' since by it the Holy Spirit is conferred for growth and strength. Hence while a simple priest can apply other anointings, only a high priest, that is, a bishop, ought to confer this one, since it is only of the apostles—whose vicars the bishops are—that we read that they conferred the Holy Spirit by imposition of hands."[840]

Pius X, Decree *Lamentabili sane*, July 3, 1907, the forty-fourth condemned Proposition:

"There is nothing to show that the rite of confirmation was used by the apostles; moreover, the formal distinction between the two sacraments of baptism and confirmation finds no support in the history of primitive Christianity."[841]

St. Cyril of Jerusalem, *Catechetical Lecture 21*, n. 3:

"Take care not to regard this ointment as something empty and meaningless. For just as the Eucharistic bread is, after the invocation of the Holy Spirit, no longer ordinary bread but the body of Christ, so too is this ointment no longer, after the invocation, a bare—or as some would prefer to say—an ordinary ointment; it is the treasure chamber of Christ and of the Holy Spirit, made efficacious by the presence of his Godhead. And this is symbolically signified by the anointing of your forehead and other senses. While the body is thus visibly anointed with the ointment, the soul is sanctified by the holy and life-giving Spirit."[842]

[840] *P.L.*, ccxv, 285; Cf. Acts 8:14ff

[841] *Acta Sanctae Sedis*, vol. 40, p. 475

[842] *P.G.*, xxxiii, 1090ff

St. Cyril of Alexandria, *Homily on Joel*, n. 32:

"The living water of baptism is bestowed on us like rain; the living bread, as it were, in wheat, and the blood, as it were, in wine. There is, too, the use of oil to bring to perfection those already justified by holy baptism in Christ."[843]

QUESTION 371

Second Lateran Council, A.D. 1139, Can. 23:

"Those who, under a specious pretext of religion, repudiate the sacrament of the body and blood of the Lord, the baptism of children, the priesthood and other ecclesiastical orders, as well as legitimate matrimonial contracts, We condemn and expel from the Church of God as heretical, and We bid the civil authorities restrain them. Moreover, those who defend such men fall under the same condemnation."[844]

Council of Trent, Session 13, "Decree concerning the Most Holy Sacrament of the Eucharist," Ch. 1:

"To begin with, this holy synod teaches and openly and plainly professes that, in the bountiful sacrament of the Holy Eucharist, our Lord Jesus Christ, true God and true man, is, after the consecration of the bread and wine, truly, really, and substantially contained under the appearance of those sensible things. Nor is there any contradiction involved in the fact that our Savior, while always seated at the right hand of the Father according to his natural mode of existence, should nonetheless be sacramentally present with us in his own substance in many other places by that mode of existence which, though it can hardly be expressed in words, is yet possible with God, and which we can realize in thought illumined by faith, and are bound to believe most firmly. For our fathers before us, all who have been in the true

843 *P.G.*, lxxi, 374

844 Mansi, *Concilia*, xxi, 532

Church of Christ and who have treated of this most holy sacrament, have with the greatest clearness declared that our Redeemer instituted this wondrous sacrament at the last supper, when, after blessing the bread and wine, he declared in the plainest and most express terms that he gave to them his own body and blood. It would, then, be a most unworthy and criminal thing to distort these words, given by the holy evangelists and repeated afterward by St. Paul, since on the face of them they bear this strict and most evident interpretation in accordance with which they have been understood by the fathers; yet contentious and ill-disposed people do so, and—contrary to the universal teaching of the Church—regard them as mere images and figures of speech, with the result that the truth of the flesh and blood of Christ is denied. But the Church, 'the pillar and ground of truth,'[845] hates and detests as satanical these fabrications of wicked people, ever acknowledging with grateful and thankful spirit this superexcellent gift of Christ."

Leo XIII, Encyclical *Mirae caritatis*, May 28, 1902:

"And now We are moved, nay impelled, by that same apostolic charity which keeps watch over the needs of the Church, to add somewhat more by way of completion to what We have hitherto said. For We would, in the most especial way, commend to Christian people the most Holy Eucharist as being the most divine gift emanating from the depths of the heart of the Redeemer 'with desire desiring'[846] this wonderful union with men, which was especially designed to spread everywhere the life-giving fruits of his redemptive work...

"Truly nothing is more calculated to restore fervent and vigorous faith in our souls than the mystery of the Eucharist, rightly called the 'mystery of faith.'[847] For in this alone, by the wealth and variety of the miracles it enshrines, are contained all things that are supernatural: 'He hath made a remembrance of his wondrous works, being a merciful and

[845] 1 Tm 3:15
[846] Lk 22:15
[847] 1 Tm 3:9

gracious Lord; he hath given food to them that feared him.'[848] For whatever supernatural thing God has done he has done it with reference to the incarnation of his Word; for by that act of mercy, he would, as the apostle says, restore to salvation the human race: 'He hath purposed... to reestablish all things in Christ, that are in heaven and on earth, in him';[849] and the Eucharist—as the fathers bear testimony—must be regarded as a certain continuation and amplification of the incarnation. Hence, through the substance of the incarnate Word, God is knit to individual men and the supreme sacrifice of Calvary wondrously renewed, as Malachi has foretold: 'In every place there is sacrifice and there is offered to my name a clean oblation.'"[850]

QUESTION 372

For the Council of Trent, see above, q. 371.

QUESTION 373

Council of Trent, Session 13, "Decree concerning the Most Holy Sacrament of the Eucharist," Ch. 4:

> "But since Christ our Redeemer said that that was truly his body which he was offering up under the appearance of bread, it has always been the conviction of the Church of God—and this holy synod declares it anew—that by the consecration of the bread and wine the entire substance of bread is converted into the substance of the body of Christ our Lord, and the entire substance of wine into the substance of his blood, which conversion is by the Catholic Church fittingly and rightly termed 'transubstantiation.'"

[848] Ps 110:4-5
[849] Eph 1:9-10
[850] Mal 1:11; *Acta* of Leo XIII, xxii, 116, 122

St. Justin Martyr, *First Apology*, Ch. 66:

"And this food is amongst us called 'Eucharist'; of it none can partake save those who believe that what we teach is true, and who for the remission of sins and for regeneration have been cleansed in the laver (of baptism) and who so live as Christ taught. Nor do we receive this as ordinary bread or ordinary drink but, just as Jesus Christ our Savior, made flesh by the word of God, had both flesh and blood for our salvation's sake, so, too, we are taught that that food in which thanksgivings are offered through prayers enshrining his very words, and by which our flesh and blood are nourished through change, is the flesh and blood of the incarnate Jesus. For the apostles, in those commentaries of theirs which are known as 'gospels,' have handed it down to us that Jesus so commanded: namely, that he took bread and, after giving thanks, said: 'Do this in memory of me; this is my body,' and taking the chalice in like manner, he gave thanks and said: 'This is my blood,' and he delivered it to them alone."[851]

St. Ephraem, *In Hebdomadam Sanctam*, iv, 4, 6:

"Our Lord Jesus Christ first took into his hands simple bread, blessed it, sealed it, sanctified it in the name of the Father and of the Holy Spirit; he broke it and distributed it piece by piece to his disciples in his merciful bounty; he called that bread his 'living body' and he filled it with himself and the Spirit; and, stretching out his hand, he gave them the bread which with his right hand he had sanctified: 'Take, eat, all of this which my word hath sanctified. What I have now given you do not regard as bread; take, eat this bread, nor break up its particles; what I have called "my body" that it truly is. One shred of its fragments can sanctify a million men and suffices to give life to all who eat it. Take, eat in faith, hesitating in nothing, for it is my body, and those who eat it in faith eat in it fire and the Spirit. But if any eat it doubtingly, to him it becomes mere bread; to him, however, who eats in faith, this bread sanctified in my name, if he be pure, he is kept pure, if in sin, it is

[851] *P.G.*, vi, 427ff; Cf. Mt 26:26-28; Mk 14:22-24; Lk 22:19-20; 1 Cor 11:23-25

pardoned him. If any despise it or condemn it or treat it with contempt, let him be well assured that he is treating with contempt the Son who called it and really made it his body.'

"When the disciples had eaten this new and holy bread, and had understood by faith that they had eaten the body of Christ, then he went on to explain and teach them the whole sacrament. He took and mixed the chalice of wine; he then blessed it, sealed it, sanctified it, declaring that it was his blood which was to be poured out...Christ bade them drink, and he explained to them that the chalice of which they were drinking was his blood: 'This is my true blood which is shed for you all; take it, drink of it all of ye, for it is the new testament in my blood. As ye have seen me do, so do ye in memory of me. When ye are gathered together in my name in the church in any place do ye in memory of me what I have done; eat my body and drink my blood, the new testament and the old.'"[852]

St. Athanasius, Fragment of a *Sermon to the Baptized*:

"You see the deacons carrying bread and a chalice of wine and placing them on the table. Until the prayers and invocations are finished, it is nothing but bread and a chalice (of wine). But as soon as those great and wondrous prayers are finished, then the bread becomes the body and the chalice the blood of our Lord Jesus Christ.

"Come now to the perfecting of these mysteries. This bread and wine have, previous to the prayers and supplications, naught save their own nature; but when once those great and holy prayers and supplications have been pronounced, the Word descends on the bread and on the chalice and is made his body."[853]

[852] *Ed.* Lamy, *Sti. Ephremi Hymni et Sermones*, I, 416, 422
[853] *P.G.*, xxvi, 1326

St. Cyril of Jerusalem, *Catechetical Lecture 22*, n. 1-3, 6, 9 and *Catechetical Lecture 23*, n. 7:

> "This account of the institution would, if given by St. Paul alone,[854] suffice to afford you certain faith in these divine mysteries, whereby those who are worthy are made one with Christ's body and blood. For St. Paul now exclaims: 'In that night in which he was betrayed...' Since then Christ declared and pronounced of this bread, 'This is my body,' who would dare to question it after that? And when he went on to say, 'This is my blood,' who would dare call it in question and say that it is not his blood?
>
> "Of old, at Cana of Galilee, he had changed water into wine, which is akin to blood; shall we then think it unworthy of our belief that he changed wine into blood? If, when invited to material nuptials, he worked this stupendous miracle, shall we not even more readily believe that he gave to the children of the bridechamber his own body and blood to enjoy?
>
> "Let us therefore with fullest conviction receive it as the body and blood of Christ. For under the figure of bread is his body given you, under the figure of wine his blood, so that when ye receive the body and blood of Christ ye are made one with Christ's body, one with his blood. Then are we called 'Christ-bearers,' for his body and blood are distributed among our members: then, according to St. Peter, are we made 'partakers of the divine nature.'[855]...
>
> "Do not, then, look on it as mere bread and wine, for it is the body and blood of Christ according to the Lord's own declaration; your senses may suggest to you the former, but your faith renders you firm and secure. Judge not by the taste but by faith, put away hesitation and be certain that ye have been honored with the gift of the body and blood of Christ...

854 Cf. 1 Cor 11:23
855 2 Pt 1:4

"Taught thus; imbued with this most sure faith, that what seems bread is not bread—though to the sense of taste it may be so—but is the body of Christ; that what seems wine is not wine—though to the taste it may seem so—but is the blood of Christ; believing that of this did David of old sing in the psalms, 'And bread may strengthen man's heart and make the face cheerful with oil,'[856] in this faith strengthen thy heart, receive that bread as a spiritual thing, and make glad the face of thy soul.

"Finally, when we have sanctified ourselves by these spiritual praises, we pray our merciful God to send forth his Spirit on what we have set before him and so make this bread indeed the body of Christ and this wine the blood of Christ. For assuredly whatsoever the Holy Spirit shall touch that will be sanctified and changed."[857]

St. John Chrysostom, *Homily 82 on Matthew*, Ch. 4:

"Let us everywhere obey God, nor let us contradict him even when what he says seems contrary to reason and intelligence; rather, let his works prevail over our reason and intelligence. For that is what we do in the sacraments where we look not merely at what comes under our senses but hold fast to his words; his words cannot deceive, though our senses are easily deceived; his word can never fail, our senses are often misled. Now since he himself has said: 'This is my body,' let us obey, believe, and look upon it with the eyes of the spirit. For it was no merely sensible thing that Christ gave us, but even the things that come under the senses have all a spiritual significance. Thus even in baptism by something that comes under the senses is the gift of water granted us; but what is done is spiritual, namely, generation and renovation. Had you been incorporeal, he would have given you those gifts in naked and incorporeal fashion; but because the soul is joined to the body, he gives you spiritual gifts through the medium of the things of sense. How many say nowadays: 'I would like to see his form, his figure, his clothing, his footwear.' But, lo, you do see him, touch him, eat him."[858]

[856] Ps 103:15
[857] *P.G.*, xxxiii, 1098ff, 1114
[858] *P.G.*, lviii, 743

St. John Damascene, *An Exposition of the Orthodox Faith*, Bk. 4, Ch. 13:

"The body derived from the Blessed Virgin is truly united to the Godhead; not in the sense that the body taken up into heaven descends thence again, but that the bread and the wine are transformed into the body and blood of God. If you ask how this can be, it is enough for you to understand that this is done by the power of the Holy Spirit, precisely as the Lord took to himself of the holy Mother of God flesh which should subsist in himself, nor is there anything for us further to explore or discover save that the word of God is true, efficacious, and able to do all things; but the way in which it is done is beyond our investigation. This, however, it is not amiss to say: just as bread by being eaten, wine and water by being drunk, are naturally changed into the body and the blood of him who eats and drinks them, so that they do not make the body now to be some other body than it was before, so, too, the bread, the wine, and the water which were prepared by being offered, are, by the invocation and the coming of the Holy Spirit, in a fashion transcending the powers and efficacy of nature, converted into the body and the blood of Christ, so that they are no longer two things, but one and the same. Nor are the bread and wine figures of the body and blood of Christ—far be such a thought from us! No, they are the very body of the Lord endowed with the Godhead, for the Lord himself said: 'This is'—not 'a figure of my body'—but 'my body,'—not 'a figure of my blood'—but 'my blood.'...And if some have spoken of the bread and wine as the antitypes of the body and blood of the Lord, as did the divine Basil, they did not mean after the consecration, but they used this expression of the oblation previous to its consecration. Furthermore, the term *antitype* is used of things that are future, not indeed in the sense that they are not truly the body and blood of Christ, but that whereas now we are by it made sharers in the Godhead of Christ, then we shall be understanding him by actual vision."[859]

[859] *P.G.*, xciv, 1143ff

QUESTION 374

Fourth Lateran Council, A.D. 1215, Const. 1, against the Albigenses:

> "There is one universal Church of the faithful outside which absolutely no one is saved, in which Jesus Christ himself is both priest and victim, whose body and blood are truly contained in the Sacrament of the Altar under the appearances of bread and wine, the bread and the wine being by the divine power transubstantiated into his body and blood, so that for the perfecting of the mystery of unity we may receive of him what he took from us."[860]

Second Council of Lyons, A.D. 1274, *Profession of Faith by Michael Palaeologus*:

> "The same Roman Church makes the sacrament of the Eucharist out of unleavened bread, and holds and teaches that in this sacrament the bread is truly transubstantiated into the body and the wine into the blood of our Lord Jesus Christ."[861]

Council of Constance, A.D. 1414-1418, Session 8, Propositions 1-3, some of the errors of John Wyclif:

> Prop. 1: "The material substance of bread, and similarly the material substance of wine, remain in the Sacrament of the Altar."
>
> Prop. 2: "The accidents of bread do not remain without a subject in the said sacrament."
>
> Prop. 3: "Christ is not in the said sacrament identically and really in his own corporal presence."[862]

[860] Mansi, *Concilia*, xxii, 982
[861] Mansi, *Concilia*, xxiv, 71
[862] Mansi, *Concilia*, xxvii, 1207

For the Council of Trent, Session 13, "Decree concerning the Most Holy Sacrament of the Eucharist," Ch. 1, see above, q. 371.

Council of Trent, Session 13, Can. 2:

> "If anyone shall say that in the most Holy Sacrament of the Eucharist there remains the substance of bread and wine together with the body and blood of our Lord Jesus Christ, and shall deny that marvelous and unique conversion of the entire substance of the bread into his body and of the entire substance of wine into his blood, while the species of bread and wine alone remain, a conversion which the Catholic Church most fittingly terms 'transubstantiation,' let him be anathema."

Benedict XII, *Ex libello, Jamdudum*, A.D. 1341:

> "Also that the Armenians do not say that after the words of consecration have been pronounced there is made a transubstantiation of the bread and wine into that true body and blood of Christ which was born of the Virgin Mary, suffered and rose again; but hold that this sacrament is but a model or likeness or figure of the true body and blood of the Lord...and consequently do not speak of the Sacrament of the Altar as the body and blood of Christ, but as the 'victim' or 'sacrifice' or 'Communion.'"[863]

Pius VI, Constitution *Auctorem Fidei*, against the errors of the Synod of Pistoia, Aug. 28, 1794, the twenty-ninth condemned Proposition:

> "The teaching of this synod—wherein it undertakes to set forth the teachings of the faith touching the rite of consecration, and sets on one side scholastic questions concerning the way in which Christ is in the Eucharist—questions which the said synod exhorts priests to avoid when exercising their functions as teachers—is set forth in the two following propositions only: 1) that after the consecration, Christ is truly, really, and substantially present under the species; 2) that then the

[863] Mansi, *Concilia*, xxv, 1189

entire substance of bread and wine ceases to be, while the species alone remain; and it wholly omits any mention of the transubstantiation or conversion of the entire substance of the bread into the body and of the entire substance of the wine into the blood, which conversion the Council of Trent defined as an article of faith and which is contained in the profession of faith. By such an ill-advised and suspicious omission, attention is withdrawn both from an article touching the faith and from an expression consecrated by the Church for the preservation of the said article of faith against the attacks of heretics; moreover, it tends to make people oblivious of the doctrine itself, as though it were question of some merely scholastic dispute. (We therefore condemn it) as dangerous, as detracting from sound exposition of the Catholic truth touching the dogma of transubstantiation, and as encouraging heresy."[864]

QUESTION 376

Council of Trent, Session 22, "Doctrine on the Sacrifice of the Mass," Ch. 1:

"Since, according to the testimony of St. Paul, things were not, under the old dispensation, brought to perfection owing to the insufficiency of the Levitical priesthood, it was necessary that, in accordance with the disposition of God, the Father of mercies, another priest should arise according to the order of Melchisedec, our Lord Jesus Christ, who should be able to complete and bring to perfection all, as many as were to be sanctified. He, then, our Lord and God, although he was to offer himself once and for all to God the Father on the altar of the cross by his death, there to work out our eternal redemption, yet since his priesthood was not to be extinguished by his death, he, at the last supper, on the night in which he was betrayed, in order to leave to his beloved spouse, the Church, a visible sacrifice such as the exigencies of our human nature demanded, wherein that sacrifice of blood once and for all to be wrought upon the cross should be represented and its memory abide to the end of the world, and its saving power applied for the remission of those sins into which we all fall day by day,

864 *Bullarii Romani Continuatio*, ed. Prati, VII, iii, 2712

declaring himself to be the priest appointed forever according to the order of Melchisedec, offered his body and blood to God the Father under the appearances of bread and wine, and gave it, under the same appearances, to his apostles whom he then appointed priests of the new testament; to them, too, as to his successors in the priesthood, he, by the words, 'Do this in memory of me,' gave the command to offer it, as the Catholic Church has always understood and taught. For, after celebrating the old Passover, which in memory of their coming out of Egypt the multitude of the children of Israel used to offer, he instituted a new Passover, namely, himself, to be offered by the Church, through her priests, under visible signs, in memory of his passing over from this world to the Father, when, that is, by the shedding of his blood, he redeemed us, snatched us from the powers of darkness, and transferred us into his kingdom.

"This is indeed that clean oblation which can never be polluted by any unworthiness or wickedness of those that offer it, which, as the Lord foretold by Malachias, was to be offered, pure in every place, to his name, which was to be great among the Gentiles. To it, too, the apostle St. Paul makes no obscure allusion when he says, writing to the Corinthians, that those who are defiled by sharing in the table of demons cannot be sharers in the table of the Lord,[865] where by *table* he in both places means *altar*. Finally, this is that oblation which was prefigured by various kinds of sacrifices both under the law of nature and that of Moses, inasmuch as, being their consummation and perfection, it embraces all the good things signified by them."

Council of Trent, Session 22, Can. 2:

"If anyone shall say that by the words, 'Do this in memory of me,' Christ did not make his apostles priests or did not ordain them so that they and other priests might offer his body and blood, let him be anathema."

[865] Cf. 1 Cor 10:21

QUESTION 379

Council of Trent, Session 13, "Decree concerning the Most Holy Sacrament of the Eucharist," Ch. 3:

"The Holy Eucharist has this in common with the other sacraments: that it is a symbol of a sacred thing, a visible form of an invisible grace. But it excels them and is unique in this: that whereas the other sacraments exercise their power of sanctifying only when someone makes use of them, in the Eucharist, the author of salvation is himself there independently of its use. For the apostles had not yet received the Eucharist from the Lord's hands when he himself affirmed that it was his own body which he was offering them; and it has always been the belief of the Church that, immediately after the consecration, the true body of our Lord as well as his true blood, under the appearances of bread and wine, his soul also and his Godhead, are there; the body under the appearance of bread, the blood under the appearance of wine by force of the very words used, but the body too under the appearance of wine, and the blood under the appearance of bread, and the soul as well under either, by force of that natural connection and concomitance whereby the parts of Christ our Lord, who has now risen from the dead to die no more, are knit together; his Godhead also, by reason of his wonderful hypostatic union with his soul and body. Whence it is most true that as much is contained under either species as under both; for the whole and entire Christ is under the appearance of bread and under every particle of those species, the same, too, under the species of wine and of its every drop."

Council of Trent, Session 13, Can. 3:

"If anyone shall deny that in the venerable sacrament of the Eucharist the entire Christ is contained under either species and under every particle of either when separated, let him be anathema."

QUESTION 382

Council of Florence, Session 6 (July 6, 1439), "Decree for the Greeks":

"Also, that, whether in unleavened or leavened wheaten bread, Christ is truly made; and that priests should make the very body of Christ in either, that is each according to the practice of his own Church, whether Western or Eastern."[866]

Council of Florence, Session 8 (November 22, 1439), "Bull of Union with the Armenians":

"The third sacrament is that of the Eucharist, the material of which is wheaten bread and wine from the vine: to the latter a small quantity of water should be added previous to consecration. The water is added because, according to the testimonies of the fathers and doctors of the Church already alleged in this discussion, our Lord is believed to have instituted this sacrament in wine mingled with water. Also, because this practice harmonizes with the representation of the Lord's passion. For Pope Alexander, the fifth in succession to St. Peter, says: 'In the oblations of the sacraments offered to the Lord in the solemnity of the Mass, only bread, and wine mixed with water, are offered for the sacrifice. For in the Lord's chalice, we ought not to offer wine alone or water alone, but the two mixed together, for we read that both, that is blood and water, flowed from Christ's side.' This (the mixed chalice) fittingly signifies the effect of this sacrament, namely, the union of the Christian people with Christ. For the water signifies the people: 'The waters which thou seest…are many peoples.'[867] Similarly, Pope Julius, successor to Pope Silvester, says: 'The chalice of the Lord ought, according to the canons, to be offered of wine and water mingled, for in the water we see signified the people, in the wine the blood of Christ is shown forth. When, then, the wine and the water are mingled in the chalice, his people are knit to Christ and the faithful are united and joined to him in whom they believe.' Since, then, the holy Roman

[866] Mansi, *Concilia*, xxxi, 1031

[867] Apoc 17:15

Church, taught by the blessed apostles Peter and Paul, as also the other Churches of the Latins and the Greeks in which have shone forth luminaries of all holiness and doctrine, have always from the Church's very birth adhered to and do still adhere to this practice, it seems most unfitting that any country should fail to conform to this universal and most reasonable practice. We therefore decree that the Armenians too should conform to the universal Christian world and that their priests should add, as has been said, a little water in offering the chalice."[868]

Council of Trent, Session 22, "Doctrine on the Sacrifice of the Mass," Ch. 7:

"Finally, this holy synod points out that the Church bids her priests mix water with the wine in offering the chalice, both because Christ is believed to have done so, also because from his side there flowed water and blood, which mystery is recalled in this mingling (of water with the wine); also because, since in the Apocalypse of St. John, the people are termed 'water,' the union of the faithful with Christ their head is represented."

QUESTION 383

Council of Florence, Session 8 (November 22, 1439), "Bull of Union with the Armenians":

"The form of this sacrament is the Savior's words wherewith he made it; for the priest makes this sacrament when speaking in the Person of Christ. For by the power of those words, the substance of bread is converted into the body of Christ and the substance of wine into his blood; yet so that the entire Christ is contained under the appearance of bread and the entire Christ under the appearance of wine. The entire Christ is contained in every particle of the consecrated host or of the consecrated wine when these are separated. The effect which this sacrament produces in the souls of those that receive it worthily is the union of men with Christ. And since by grace man is incorporated in Christ

[868] Mansi, *Concilia*, xxxi, 1056

and united to his members, it follows that in those who receive this sacrament worthily grace is increased; and whatsoever effect is produced by material food and drink in our bodily life, sustaining, increasing, repairing, affording pleasure, that, too, this sacrament produces in our spiritual life; in it, as Pope Urban remarks, we recall with gratitude the memory of our Savior, we are kept from evil, we are strengthened in good, and we make increase in virtue and grace."[869]

QUESTION 385

Fourth Lateran Council, A.D. 1215, Const. 1, against the Albigenses:

"There is one universal Church of the faithful, in it, Jesus Christ is himself priest and sacrifice; his body and blood are truly contained in the Sacrament of the Altar under the appearances of bread and wine, the bread and the wine being transubstantiated into his body and blood by the power of God."[870]

For the Council of Trent, see above, q. 376.

St. Irenaeus, *Against Heresies*, Bk. 4, Ch. 17, n. 5:

"Moreover, counseling his disciples to offer firstfruits to God from his creatures — not as though he needed them but that they might not be either fruitless or ungrateful — he took one of the things he had created, bread, and gave thanks, saying: 'This is my body.'[871] Likewise the chalice which is of the same creation as we ourselves are, and he declared it to be his blood, and taught that it was the oblation of the new testament. The Church, receiving this oblation from the apostles, offers it to God throughout the world, to God, who provides us with food, it offers the firstfruits of his own gifts in the new testament. This Malachias, one of the twelve prophets, thus spoke of in anticipation:

[869] Mansi, *Concilia*, xxxi
[870] Mansi, *Concilia*, xxii, 982
[871] Mt 26:26

'I have no pleasure in you, saith the Lord of hosts, and I will not receive a gift of your hand. For from the rising of the sun even to the going down, my name is great among the Gentiles, and in every place there is sacrifice, and there is offered to my name a clean oblation; for my name is great among the Gentiles, saith the Lord of hosts.'[872] Wherein he most clearly showed that the former people would cease to make oblations to God, but that in every place oblation will be made to him, and a pure one, for his name is glorified among the Gentiles."[873]

QUESTION 386

For the Council of Trent, see above, q. 376.

St. Gregory the Great, *Dialogues*, Bk. 4, Ch. 58:

"This victim in unique fashion saves the soul from eternal destruction, for it repairs by the mystery of the Only-begotten that death which is in store for us; for the Only-begotten, though 'rising again from the dead he dieth now no more, death shall no more have dominion over him,'[874] and though in himself living immortally and incorruptibly, is yet again offered for us in this mystery of the sacred oblation. For there is his body received, his flesh divided for the salvation of the people, his blood shed, not now by the hands of unbelievers but on the lips of believers. Let us, then, weigh well the immensity of this sacrifice for us: it is always for our absolving, imitating the passion of the only-begotten Son."[875]

[872] Mal 1:10-11
[873] *P.G.*, vii, 1023
[874] Rom 6:9
[875] *P.L.*, lxxvii, 425

QUESTION 387

For the Council of Trent, see above, q. 379.

QUESTION 388

Council of Trent, Session 22, "Doctrine on the Sacrifice of the Mass," Ch. 2:

> "And since in this divine sacrifice enacted in the Mass, the very same Christ is contained and is offered in an unbloody manner who offered himself once and for all, in his blood, on the altar of the cross, this holy synod teaches that this sacrifice is truly propitiatory, and that by it, we, if we draw nigh to God with a true heart and right faith, with fear and reverence, contrite and penitent, obtain mercy and grace in seasonable aid. By the offering of this sacrifice God is appeased and bestows grace and the gift of repentance, forgiving us our heinous crimes and sins. For it is one and the same victim who now offers himself through the ministry of his priests as then offered himself upon the cross; it is the mode of the oblation alone that differs. Of that sacrifice in his blood the fruits are most fully received in this unbloody sacrifice, so true is it that this latter in no sense derogates from the former. Wherefore it is offered not alone for the sins of the faithful who are yet living, for their penalties, satisfactions, and other needs, but rightly, and in accord with apostolic tradition, for the dead also who are in Christ and who are not yet wholly purified."

QUESTION 389

For the Council of Trent, see above, q. 388.

QUESTION 390

St. Cyril of Jerusalem, *Catechetical Lecture 23*, n. 10:

> "Now, supposing that a king had sent into exile certain people by whom he had been offended, and supposing that later on some who were interested in them were to make a crown and offer it to the king for

the sake of those whom he had thus punished, would not that king graciously grant a remission of the punishment? In the same fashion, then, we too offer prayers to God for our dead even though they are sinners; we weave no crown, but we offer Christ slain for our sins, striving to win merit and propitiate the merciful God for them as well as for ourselves."[876]

QUESTION 392

Council of Trent, Session 22, Can. 5:

"If anyone shall say that to celebrate Mass in honor of the saints and to obtain their intercession with God, as the Church intends, is an imposture, let him be anathema."

QUESTION 393

Council of Trent, Session 22, "Doctrine on the Sacrifice of the Mass," Ch. 6:

"This holy synod could wish that at every Mass the faithful who are present should not only communicate spiritually, but should actually receive the Holy Eucharist so as to obtain the fullest fruit from this most holy sacrifice. Not that, when this cannot be done, this synod therefore means to condemn as 'private' and unlawful Masses in which the priest alone communicates sacramentally: for this synod approves and commends such Masses. The faithful, then, ought to look upon such Masses as 'public,' partly because at such Masses they can communicate spiritually; partly, too, because they are celebrated by the public minister of the Church, not for himself alone, but for all the faithful who belong to the body of Christ."

[876] *P.G.*, xxxiii, 1118

QUESTION 394

Pius VI, Constitution *Auctorem Fidei*, against the errors of the Synod of Pistoia, Aug. 28, 1794, the thirtieth condemned Proposition:

> "The teaching of that synod wherein, while professing 'to believe that the offering of the sacrifice (of the Mass) extends to all, yet at the same time there is place in the liturgy for special commemorations of certain people, whether living or dead, prayer being offered to God particularly for them,' with the subjoined statement, 'not of course that we believe it to be in the priest's power to apply the fruits of the sacrifice to whom he will, for that notion we condemn as most derogatory to God's rights, who alone distributes the fruits of the sacrifice to whom he wills and in the measure that pleases him,' a statement which enables the said synod to label as 'false the view commonly held among the people that those who give alms to a priest, and ask him to say a Mass, derive special fruit from that Mass'—this teaching, since by it the said synod means that, apart from the special prayers and commemorations, this particular offering or application of the sacrifice which the priest makes does not—other things being equal—avail more for those to whom it is applied than for any others; as though, that is, no special fruit was derived from the special application to definite persons or classes of people which the Church recommends us and bids us make, more particularly by the pastors for their flocks, as was expressly laid down by the Council of Trent as due to a divine command;[877] this doctrine, then, we condemn as false, rash, dangerous, an injury to the Church, and leading to the error elsewhere condemned in the case of Wyclif."[878]

[877] Cf. Council of Trent, Session 23, "Decree on Reformation," Ch. 1; Benedict XIV, Constitution *Cum semper oblatas*, Ch. 2

[878] *Bullarii Romani Continuatio*, ed. Prati, 2712ff

QUESTION 397

Council of Trent, Session 13, "Decree concerning the Most Holy Sacrament of the Eucharist," Ch. 2:

> "Therefore our Savior, when about to depart from this world to the Father, instituted this sacrament in which he would, as it were, pour out the riches of his love for men: 'He hath made a remembrance of his wonderful works';[879] in its reception he has bidden us cherish 'his memory' and 'show forth his death' until he shall come to judge this world.[880] He wished this sacrament to be received as the spiritual food of souls, whereby the living might be fed and strengthened by the life of him who said, 'He that eateth me, the same also shall live by me';[881] as an antidote, too, whereby we might be freed from daily faults and preserved from mortal sin. He also wished it to be a pledge of our future glory and everlasting happiness; also a symbol of that one body of which he is the head, and to which he wished us as members to be bound by the closely-knit bonds of faith, hope, and charity: 'That ye all speak the same thing, and that there be no schisms among you.'"[882]

St. Ignatius of Antioch, *Epistle to the Ephesians*, Ch. 20:

> "...You have all of you met, called by name, together, in one body, through grace, in one faith and in one Jesus Christ—who, according to the flesh, of the stock of David, is Son of Man, and also Son of God—that ye may obey the bishop and the clergy with united minds, together, breaking the one bread which is the medicine of immortality, the antidote to death, that so we may live forever in Jesus Christ."[883]

[879] Ps 110:4
[880] Cf. 1 Cor 11:26
[881] Jn 6:58
[882] 1 Cor 1:10
[883] *P.G.*, v, 662

St. Irenaeus, *Against Heresies*, Bk. 5, Ch. 2, n. 3:

"And just as the vine-stem planted in the earth brings forth its fruit in due time, and the grain of wheat, falling into the ground and there decaying, rises again manifold through the Spirit of God that containeth all things, and, receiving the Word of God, becomes the Eucharist; so, too, our bodies, fed on it, laid in the earth, resolved there into their elements, will rise in their due time, the Word of God bestowing on them a resurrection in the glory of God the Father."[884]

St. John Chrysostom, *Homily 46 on John*, Ch. 3:

"Therefore, so that not solely by charity but in very fact, we may be commingled with that flesh—a thing which is brought about by the food which he himself did give to show us how ardent was his love for us—he therefore commingled himself with us and formed us all into one body so that we might be, as it were, a body joined to its head."[885]

St. John Chrysostom, *Homily 24 on First Corinthians*, Ch. 2:

"'We being many are one bread, one body.' What do I mean, he says, by *partaking*?[886] We are that very body. For what is that bread? The body of Christ. And what happens when people 'partake'? They become the body of Christ; not many bodies, but one. For just as a loaf, though made up of many grains, is yet so united that those grains never appear, and, though they are there, their individual character does not show because they are so closely joined together; so, too, are we joined to one another and to Christ. For one is not fed with one body, another with another, but all with one and the same."[887]

[884] P.G., vii, 1127
[885] P.G., lix, 260
[886] 1 Cor 10:17
[887] P.G., lxi, 200

QUESTION 399

St. John Chrysostom, *Homily 82 on Matthew*, Ch. 5:

"Reflect how indignant you have felt against the betrayer, against those who crucified Christ; take care, then, lest you yourself be guilty of the body and blood of Christ. They slew that sacred body; you, after so many benefits, receive it with a sin-stained soul. He thought it not enough to become a man, to be scourged, to be slain, but he commingles himself with us; not by faith alone but in very deed he made us his own body. How pure, then, ought not he to be who enjoys this sacrifice?"[888]

QUESTION 400

Council of Trent, Session 13, "Decree concerning the Most Holy Sacrament of the Eucharist," Ch. 7:

"If it is unfitting that people should come to any sacred functions save with a sense of awe, then, assuredly, the more the holiness and divinity of this heavenly sacrament is appreciated by a Christian, the more diligent should he be lest he should come to receive it without great reverence and holiness; more especially when we read those awe-inspiring words of the apostle: 'He that eateth and drinketh unworthily eateth and drinketh judgment to himself, not discerning the body of the Lord.'[889] He, then, who would receive Communion should bear in mind the precept of the same apostle: 'Let a man prove himself.'[890] Now, the practice of the Church teaches us that the 'proving' necessary is that a man conscious to himself of mortal sin, no matter how contrite he may be, should not approach to Holy Communion without previous sacramental confession. The holy synod has decreed that this should always be observed by all, even by priests who have to celebrate, provided they have a sufficiency of confessors at hand; if, however, a priest has, in a case of urgent necessity, to celebrate, then let him go to confession as soon as possible."

[888] *P.G.*, lviii, 743
[889] 1 Cor 11:29
[890] 1 Cor 11:28

QUESTION 405

Decree of the Sacred Congregation of the Council, *Sacra Tridentina Synodus*, Dec. 20, 1905, "On daily reception of the Holy Eucharist":

> "Care should be taken that due preparation should precede Holy Communion and a fitting thanksgiving follow it, according to each person's capacity, state of life, and duties."[891]

QUESTION 406

St. Basil the Great, *The Shorter Rules*, q. 172:

> "Question 172: With what awe, feelings, and devotion ought we to receive the body and blood of Christ?
>
> "Answer: The apostle teaches us to fear when he says: 'He that eateth and drinketh unworthily eateth and drinketh judgment to himself';[892] as for the feelings we ought to have, we can gather them from the Lord's words: 'This is my body which is given for you. Do this for a commemoration of me.'"[893]

QUESTION 413

Council of Trent, Session 14, "Doctrine on the Sacrament of Penance," Ch. 1:

> "If in all the regenerated there existed such gratitude to God that they constantly preserved that justice which by his kindliness and grace they had received in baptism, there would be no need for the institution of any other sacrament than baptism for the remission of sins.

[891] *Acta Apostolicae Sedis*, yr. 2, p. 896
[892] 1 Cor 11:29
[893] Lk 22:19; *P.G.*, xxxi, 1195

But since God, 'rich in mercy,'[894] 'knoweth our frame,'[895] he hath furnished a life-giving remedy for such as have, after baptism, delivered themselves to the slavery of sin and the power of the demon, namely, the sacrament of penance whereby the benefits of the death of Christ may be applied to those who have fallen again after being baptized. Repentance was of course at all times necessary for people guilty of mortal sin, if they would gain grace and justification—even for those who sought to be cleansed by the sacrament of baptism—so that they might put aside their perversity, amend their lives, detest their great offenses against God, hate sin, and experience real grief of soul. Hence the prophet says: 'Be converted and do penance for all your iniquities, and iniquity shall not be your ruin.'[896] The Lord, too, said: 'Unless ye shall do penance, ye shall all likewise perish.'[897] And the prince of the apostles, St. Peter, when recommending repentance to sinners about to receive baptism, said: 'Do penance and be baptized, every one of you.'[898] On the other hand, previous to the coming of Christ, penance was not a sacrament, nor after his coming is it a sacrament for those as yet unbaptized. The Lord instituted this sacrament more particularly when, after his resurrection from the dead, he breathed on his disciples and said: 'Receive ye the Holy Ghost; whose sins ye shall forgive they are forgiven; and whose sins ye shall retain they are retained.'[899] By this striking act and these very express words the fathers have always and unanimously understood that the power of remitting and retaining sins for the reconciliation of the faithful, who have fallen away after baptism, was communicated to the apostles and their legitimate successors. With good reason, then, did the Catholic Church repudiate and condemn as heretics the Novatians who of old obstinately denied this power of remitting sin. Wherefore, the present holy synod, receiving and approving the above interpretation of the Lord's words, condemns all lying interpretations by men who falsely explain these words by

[894] Eph 2:4
[895] Ps 102:14
[896] Ez 18:30
[897] Lk 13:3
[898] Acts 2:38
[899] Jn 20:22-23

making them refer not to the institution of this sacrament, but to the power of preaching the word of God and the gospel of Christ.

Council of Trent, Session 14, "On the Most Holy Sacrament of Penance," Can. 1:

"If any one shall say that in the Catholic Church penance is not truly and really a sacrament instituted by Christ for the reconciliation of the faithful with God so often as they fall into sin after baptism, let him be anathema."

QUESTION 414

For the Council of Trent, see above, q. 413.

Pius X, Decree *Lamentabili sane*, July 3, 1907, the forty-seventh condemned Proposition:

"The words of the Lord, 'Receive ye the Holy Ghost; whose sins ye shall forgive they are forgiven, and whose sins ye shall retain they are retained,'[900] have no reference to the sacrament of penance, whatever the fathers of Trent may have thought fit to assert."[901]

St. John Chrysostom, *On the Priesthood*, Bk. 3, n. 5:

"For men living on earth and dwelling in it have received a commission for dispensing things that are in heaven, and have had entrusted to them a power which God gave neither to angels nor to archangels. For to these latter it was never said: 'Whatsoever you shall bind upon earth it shall be bound also in heaven, and whatsoever you shall loose upon earth it shall be loosed also in heaven.'[902] Those, indeed, who rule on earth have a power of binding, but it affects only our bodies; but the

[900] Ibid.
[901] *Acta Apostolicae Sedis*, yr. 14, p. 473
[902] Mt 18:18

bond here spoken of affects our very souls and transcends the heavens; whatsoever the priests do here below, that God confirms on high, and the Lord himself ratifies his servants' sentence. What else did he confer on them but a heavenly power? For he said: 'Whose sins ye shall forgive they are forgiven them, and whose sins ye shall retain they are retained.'[903] What greater power than this could there be? 'The Father... hath given all judgment to the Son,'[904] and all that I see conferred by the Son on these men."[905]

QUESTION 417

Council of Trent, Session 14, "Doctrine on the Sacrament of Penance," Ch. 3:

"Further, this holy synod teaches that the form of the sacrament of penance—wherein particularly its efficacy lies—is in those words of the minister: 'I absolve thee,' etc. To this, according to the custom of holy Church, certain prayers are laudably attached, though they neither affect the essence of that form nor are they necessary for the administration of the sacrament. But the acts of the penitent himself, namely, contrition, confession, and satisfaction are, as it were, the material part of this sacrament. And these, inasmuch as by God's institution they are, on the part of the penitent, requisite for the integrity of the sacrament and for the full and perfect remission of sin, are therefore called 'parts' of the sacrament of penance. Of course the thing, the effect, of this sacrament, considering, that is, its power and efficacy, is reconciliation with God; and this, in the case of holy people who devoutly receive this sacrament, is wont to be accompanied by peace and tranquility of conscience as well as immense spiritual consolation. This holy synod, while dealing thus with the parts of this sacrament and its effects, condemns at the same time the opinions of those who maintain that faith and a terror-stricken conscience are parts of penance."

[903] Jn 20:23
[904] Jn 5:22
[905] *P.G.*, xlviii, 643

Council of Trent, Session 14, "On the Most Holy Sacrament of Penance," Can. 4:

> "If any one shall deny that for the entire and perfect remission of sin there are required on the part of the penitent three acts, namely, contrition, confession, and satisfaction, which are termed the 'three parts of penance'; or if any one shall say that there are only two parts of penance, a conscience terror-stricken by the sense of sin, and faith drawn from the gospel, or absolution only in the sense that a person believes that his sins have been forgiven him by Christ, let him be anathema."

QUESTION 422

For Council of Trent, Session 14, "Doctrine on the Sacrament of Penance," Ch. 3, see above, q. 417.

Council of Trent, Session 14, "On the Most Holy Sacrament of Penance," Can. 7:

> "If any one shall say that for the remission of sin in the sacrament of penance it is not necessary by divine law to confess all and every mortal sin which we can call to mind after due and careful thought, even hidden ones and such as are contrary to the two last precepts of the decalogue, also the circumstances which alter the species of the sin, but that confession of that kind is useful only for the instruction and consolation of the penitent and was originally only used for the purpose of imposing canonical penances; or if any shall say that those who try to confess all their sins mean thereby to leave nothing for the divine mercy to forgive; or finally, that we ought not to confess venial sins, let him be anathema."

QUESTION 428

Council of Trent, Session 14, "Doctrine on the Sacrament of Penance," Ch. 4:

"Contrition, which holds the first place among the aforesaid acts of the penitent, is grief of spirit for and detestation of sins we have committed, with a firm purpose of not sinning in the future. Such movements of contrition were at all times necessary for obtaining pardon for sin, and, in the case of persons who have fallen into sin after baptism, they prepare the way for the remission of sins if accompanied by trust in the mercy of God, and a determination to fulfill whatsoever is requisite for the due reception of the sacrament. Consequently, this holy synod declares that this contrition is not simply cessation from sin and a proposal to lead a new life, nor actually beginning a new life, but that it includes a hatred of one's past life, in accordance with the words: 'Cast away from you all your transgressions by which you have transgressed, and make to yourselves a new heart and a new spirit.'[906] No one can reflect on such exclamations of the holy men of old as: 'To thee only have I sinned, and have done evil before thee';[907] 'I have labored in my groanings, every night I will wash my bed, I will water my couch with tears';[908] 'I will recount to thee all my years in the bitterness of my soul';[909] and many similar passages, without realizing that such expressions flowed from a vehement detestation of their former life and a great hatred of their sins.

"This holy synod further teaches that although this contrition of which we are speaking may at times approach to perfect charity, and that a person may be reconciled to God before actually receiving this sacrament, yet nonetheless such reconciliation is not to be attributed to contrition apart from desire to receive the sacrament, for such desire is included in the contrition. At the same time, the synod declares that that imperfect contrition which is called 'attrition'—since it generally

[906] Ez 18:31
[907] Ps 50:6
[908] Ps 6:7
[909] Is 38:15

arises either from consideration of the vileness of sin or from the fear of hell and punishment—not only does not make a person a hypocrite and a still greater sinner, if it excludes the will to sin and is accompanied by a hope for pardon, but is a gift of God and an impulse from the Holy Spirit—not indeed as yet indwelling in him, but only moving him; and that by the help of the same Holy Spirit a penitent prepares himself for the reception of justification. And while it is true that this attrition cannot of itself, without the sacrament of penance, bring a sinner to justification, yet nonetheless it does dispose him for the obtaining of God's grace in the sacrament of penance. It was by such fear that the Ninivites were, to their profit, overwhelmed when they heard the preaching of Jonas, did penance, and so won mercy from the Lord.[910] Those, then, calumniate Catholic writers who say that the latter maintain that the sacrament of penance confers grace independently of good dispositions on the part of those who receive it. This the Church of God has never taught nor thought. Those also teach falsely who say that contrition is something extorted and compulsory, and not free and voluntary."

St. Gregory the Great, *On the Gospels*, Bk. 2, Homily 34, n. 15:

"We cannot rightly do penance unless we understand the meaning of repentance. Now *to repent* means to lament over the evil we have done and not to do the evil we lament. For a person who deplores some of his sins, and yet commits others, is only pretending to do penance, or he does not understand."[911]

St. Augustine, *Sermon 351*, n. 12:

"It is not enough to change our ways for the better and quit the evil we have done, unless we make satisfaction to God for the evil we have done by the sorrow of repentance, the groans of humility, the sacrifice of a contrite heart, and accompanying alms."[912]

910 Cf. Jon 3
911 *P.L.*, lxxvi, 1256
912 *P.L.*, xxxix, 1549

QUESTION 436

For the Council of Trent, see above, q. 428.

QUESTION 438

For the Council of Trent, see above, q. 428.

St. Peter Chrysologus, *Sermon 94*:

> "See, O man, that you do not despair. For you have the means of making satisfaction to your kindly creditor. Would you be absolved? Then love. 'Charity covereth a multitude of sins.'[913] What could be worse than the crime of denying Christ? Yet by charity alone Peter was able to wash out this very crime, as the Lord bore testimony when he said: 'Peter, lovest thou me?'[914] Charity holds the first place among all the commandments of God."[915]

QUESTION 439

For the Council of Trent, see above, q. 428.

Leo X, Bull *Exurge Domine*, against the errors of Luther, June 15, 1520, the sixth condemned Proposition:

> "Contrition begotten of examining, comparing, and detesting one's sins, whereby a person recalls his years in the bitterness of his soul, and weighs the gravity, number, and hideousness of his sins, the loss of eternal happiness and the eternal damnation he has earned—such contrition makes a person a hypocrite, nay a greater sinner."[916]

913 1 Pt 4:8
914 Jn 21:15
915 *P.L.*, lii, 466
916 *Bullarium Romanum*, ed. Turin, v, 750

Pius VI, Constitution *Auctorem Fidei*, against the errors of the Synod of Pistoia, Aug. 28, 1794, the twenty-third, twenty-fifth, and thirty-sixth condemned Propositions:

> Prop. 23: "The teaching of that synod on a twofold love: viz., that of a dominating cupidity and that of a dominating charity, wherein it declares that a person without grace is under the power of sin, and that in that state, owing to the general influx of a dominating cupidity, all his actions are stained and corrupted—this teaching, inasmuch as it insinuates that cupidity so dominates a person who is under servitude to or in the state of sin, and deprived of that grace whereby he is freed from the servitude of sin and made a son of God, that—owing to its general influx—all his actions are in themselves stained and corrupted, or that all works done by him previous to justification, on whatever ground they were performed, are sins—as though, in all his actions, a sinner were the slave of a dominating cupidity—this teaching is false, dangerous, and leads to the error condemned by the Council of Trent as heretical, and condemned again in the case of Baius, Art. 40."
>
> Prop. 25: "The doctrine which—broadly speaking—declares that fear of punishment can only not be called 'evil' when it at least induces us to restrain our hands, as though actual fear of that hell—which our faith teaches us will be the punishment inflicted on sin—was not in itself good and profitable as being a supernatural gift of God and a movement inspired by him and preparing the way for a love of justice—is false, rash, dangerous, derogatory to God's gifts, elsewhere condemned, contrary to the teaching of the Council of Trent and the general opinion of the fathers that, in harmony with the usual preparation for justification, fear must first enter in, and through it must come charity; fear being the medicine, charity health..."
>
> Prop. 36: "The teaching of that synod wherein, after premising that 'when unequivocal signs are shown of a dominating love of God in a man's heart, he can rightly be adjudged worthy to be admitted to partake of the blood of Jesus Christ, as is done in the sacraments,' it goes on to speak of 'supposed conversions, due to attrition, as not generally efficacious nor lasting,' and concludes that 'a shepherd of souls ought

to insist on the presence of unequivocal signs of a dominating charity before he admits his penitents to the sacraments'; adds that the pastor can deduce the presence of these signs from the fact of a lasting cessation from sin and fervor in good works; wherein, moreover, the same synod regards the said 'fervor of charity' as a disposition which 'ought to precede absolution'; such teaching, then, understood as meaning that not only that imperfect contrition which is commonly known as attrition, but also contrition joined with charity, whereby a person begins to love God as the fount of all justice, nor only contrition informed by charity but 'the fervor of a dominating charity,' a contrition, too, that has been tested during a considerable period by a man's fervor in good works, is generally and absolutely required before a person can be admitted to the sacraments, more especially penitents admitted to the benefit of absolution—this teaching is false, rash, calculated to disturb the peace of men's souls, contrary to the safe and approved practice of the Church, minimizes and is derogatory to the efficacy of the sacraments."[917]

St. Gregory of Nyssa, *Homily 1 on the Canticle of Canticles*:

"For he who 'will have all men to be saved and to come to the knowledge of the truth,'[918] shows us the most perfect and blessed way of salvation. I mean that which is by charity. For to some of us, salvation comes through fear, when, that is, we look at the threatened punishments of hell and therefore keep ourselves from evil. For there are some who, for the sake of the reward laid up for those who live devoutly, lead right and virtuous lives, not laying hold of that good thing by charity but by expectation of the reward."[919]

917 *Bullarii Romani Continuatio*, ed. Prati, 2711, 2714
918 1 Tm 2:4
919 *P.G.*, xliv, 766

QUESTION 442

St. John Chrysostom, *De Lazaro*, Discourse 4, n. 4:

"If up to now we have been negligent, then let us by confession, by tears, and by accusing ourselves of our own faults, slay any iniquity we have performed. For nothing is more destructive of sin than to accuse ourselves of our sins and condemn them. Have you condemned your sin? Then you have cast away your burden. Who is it who says this? God our judge: 'Do you first tell your sins that you may be justified.'[920] Why then, I ask, are you ashamed and blush to tell your sins? Are you telling them to a man, to one who will overwhelm you with shame? Are you confessing them to your fellow-servant who will go and publish them? No, you are showing your wounds to him who is the Lord, who has a care for you, who is human, who is a physician...Unless you express the magnitude of your debt, you will not experience the immensity of his grace. I do not, he says, ask you to stand in the middle of the theater and summon a number of witnesses; tell your sins to me in private that I may heal your wounds and free you from your sorrow."[921]

St. John Chrysostom, Homily *Quod frequenter sit conveniendum*, n. 2:

"Do not, then, because you have sinned, be ashamed to come; nay, that is the very reason for coming. For no one says: 'As I have a wound, I will not go to the doctor, nor will I take remedies'; no, precisely for that very reason do we consult the doctor and have need of remedies. We too know how to pardon since we ourselves are liable to other sins."[922]

920 Is 43:26 (LXX version)
921 *P.G.*, xlviii, 1012
922 *P.G.*, lxiii, 463

QUESTION 445

Council of Trent, Session 14, "Doctrine on the Sacrament of Penance," Ch. 5:

"From the institution of this sacrament, as already explained, the universal Church has always understood that the Lord also instituted entire confession of sin, and that such was by divine law necessary for all those who after being baptized have fallen into sin. For our Lord Jesus Christ, when about to ascend from earth to heaven,[923] left his priests as his vicars, as presidents and judges before whom should be brought all mortal sins into which Christ's faithful might fall, so that they might, by the power of the keys, pronounce sentence of remission or retention of sins. For it is plain that priests cannot exercise such judgment unless they know the case; neither can they in equity impose penalties for sins if these are only set before them in general fashion and not specifically and individually. Whence it follows that all mortal sins of which penitents are conscious after due examination must be told in confession, even if they are most secret sins and only contrary to the last two precepts of the decalogue; for these sometimes inflict more grievous wounds on the soul and prove even more dangerous than those which are openly admitted. And though venial sins, which do not deprive us of the grace of God and into which we more frequently fall, may rightly, profitably, and without any presumption—as the practice of devout people shows—be told in confession—yet we commit no fault if we do not mention them; they can be met by many other remedies.

"But since all mortal sins, of whatever kind they be—even those of thought—render men children of wrath and enemies of God, pardon for them must be sought from God by open and humble-minded confession. When the faithful of Christ strive thus to confess all the sins which occur to their minds, they unquestionably exhibit them to the divine mercy for pardon. While those who do the contrary, and knowingly keep back some sins, offer nothing to the divine mercy for forgiveness through his priest. Were a sick man ashamed to exhibit his wounds

[923] Cf. Jn 20; Mt 28

to the doctor, the latter could not cure what he did not know. It follows, too, that those circumstances which alter the species of sin have to be stated in confession; for if these are not stated, then neither is the penitent making an entire confession, nor are his sins really known to the judges, nor can these latter really decide on the gravity of the sin, nor, again, can they impose a proportionate penalty for them. Hence it is unreasonable to maintain that these circumstances have been devised by men with nothing else to do; similarly, it is unreasonable to say that only one circumstance need be confessed, for example, that one has sinned against one's brother. It is criminal to say that confession of the kind we have indicated is impossible or to call it 'the slaughter-house of consciences.' For it is clear that the Church demands from penitents nothing further than that, after diligent examination and due exploration of the lurking places of conscience, a man should confess those sins whereby he remembers that he has mortally offended his Lord and his God. But all other sins—those which do not occur to the mind after careful thought—are understood to be generally included in a person's confession. For these we confidently say with the prophet: 'From my secret ones cleanse me, O Lord!'[924] The difficulty of such confession and the shame experienced in thus exhibiting one's sins would seem to be great, were it not made easy by the great advantages and consolation unquestionably conferred by absolution on all who worthily approach this sacrament. Further, as regards the practice of confessing in secret to a priest only, while Christ did not forbid people—in reparation for their crimes, for their own humiliation, and to afford an example to others, as well as for the edification of the Church—to make public confession of their offenses, yet this latter practice falls under no divine command, nor could any human law prudently demand that crimes, more especially secret ones, should be openly declared by public confession of them. Since, then, secret sacramental confession such as the Church has always practiced and still practices has always been commended by the striking unanimity of the holiest and most ancient fathers of the Church, we have therein a patent refutation of the empty calumny which is not ashamed to maintain that this practice is not in

[924] Ps 18:13

accordance with God's commands, but a human figment started by the fathers of the Lateran Council. For the Lateran Council did not enact that the faithful in Christ should confess their sins—that the Council understood to be necessary and instituted by divine law—but that the precept of confession had to be fulfilled at least once a year by all and singular on arriving at the age of discretion; whence it has come to pass that throughout the entire Church is observed, with immense fruit to souls, the salutary practice of going to confession at the most 'acceptable season' of Lent, a practice which this holy synod approves and welcomes as a devout one which deserves to be retained.

Council of Trent, Session 14, "On the Most Holy Sacrament of Penance," Can. 7:

"If any one shall say that for the remission of sin in the sacrament of penance it is not necessary by divine law to confess every individual mortal sin that we can call to mind after due and careful thought, even secret ones and those contrary to the last two precepts of the decalogue, as also circumstances which alter the species of the sin; and shall maintain that such confession is only useful for the instruction and consolation of the penitent, and that originally it was only observed with a view to imposing canonical satisfactions; or that people who try to confess all their sins wish to leave nothing to be forgiven by the divine mercy, or finally that it is not right to confess venial sins, let him be anathema."

St. Gregory the Great, *On the Gospels*, Bk. 2, Homily 26, n. 4-6:

"The disciples received the chief headship in the task of supreme judgment, that namely of retaining or remitting people's sins, as being vicegerents of God. It was fitting that they who had consented to be so humiliated for God's sake should be thus exalted by him. Lo, they who themselves dread God's stern judgment become judges of souls, they who fear lest they should be condemned condemn or free others! Their place the bishops assuredly now hold in the Church. They receive the power of binding or loosing who occupy the supreme place in the government. A great honor, but great the burden attaching to that honor!...The cases presented have to be weighed, and the power of binding and loosing has then to be exercised. They have to see what sin preceded, then what punishment followed on the fault, so that the pastor's sentence may absolve those whom Almighty God has visited with the grace of compunction."[925]

St. Cyprian, *On the Lapsed*, n. 28-29:

"Finally, how much greater in faith, how much better through their fear are they who, though they have not committed the crime of sacrificing (to idols) nor of having a *libellus*, yet who because they have merely thought of doing so, by sorrowful and simple confession cleanse their consciences on this point before God's priests, show him the load on their mind, ask for salutary remedies for these small and even trifling wounds; they realize that it is written: 'God is not mocked.'[926] Indeed God cannot be mocked, nor circumvented, nor deluded by any man's astute deceit...Let each of you, then, I beg you, brethren, confess his fault while the sinner is yet in this world, while confession is still possible, while the satisfaction and remission granted by the priests is still acceptable to God."[927]

St. Jerome, *On Matthew*, Bk. 3, Ch. 16, n. 19:

"We read in Leviticus (13:2ff) that the lepers are bidden to show themselves to the priests, and then, if they have the leprosy, they are declared by the priests to be unclean. Not that the priests make them lepers or unclean, but that they may know who are lepers and who not, and may be able to discern who is clean and who unclean. Precisely then as the priest there makes a man clean or unclean, so now does priest or bishop bind or loose, not, that is, bind the innocent or loose the guilty, but when, in accordance with his office, he has heard the circumstances of the sins, he knows who is to be bound and who to be loosed."[928]

[925] *P.L.*, lxxvi, 1199ff
[926] Gal 6:7
[927] *P.L.*, iv, 503
[928] *P.L.*, xxvi, 122

QUESTION 447

Alexander VII, Decree of Sept. 24, 1665, the eleventh of certain condemned Propositions:

> "We are not bound in a subsequent confession to mention sins omitted in a previous confession or forgotten owing to imminent danger of death, or for some other reason."[929]

QUESTION 452

Council of Trent, Session 14, "Doctrine on the Sacrament of Penance," Ch. 8-9:

> "Finally, as regards satisfaction: just in proportion as this 'part' of penance has always been most warmly commended by our fathers to the flock of Christ, so is it now in our time more particularly attacked than any other 'part' of this sacrament, and that, under the pretext of piety by men who have the outward appearance of piety but who refuse to recognize its real power. On this point, then, this holy synod declares that it is wholly false and contrary to the word of God to say that faults are never remitted by God without his, at the same time, remitting the entire penalty due to them. For patent and notable examples can be discovered in holy scripture—quite apart from divine tradition—which most clearly show how erroneous is this view. As a matter of fact, the very notion of the divine justice seems to demand that those who, previous to baptism, have sinned through ignorance should be admitted to God's grace in a very different fashion from those who have once already been delivered from the servitude of sin and the devil, and who, after having received the gift of the Holy Spirit, have not been afraid knowingly to 'violate the temple of God,'[930] and 'grieve the Holy Spirit.'[931] It is but in accord with the divine mercy that our sins should not be remitted without any satisfaction being made for

929 Du Plessis, *Collectio Judiciorum*, III, ii, 321

930 1 Cor 3:17

931 Eph 4:30

them, lest, taking occasion from this, we should fancy sins are not so very grave, and lest, as it were, regardless of God's rights, and 'offering affront to the Holy Spirit,'[932] we should fall into still graver sins and so 'treasure up to ourselves wrath against the day of wrath.'[933] Without any question these penal satisfactions greatly avail to keep us from sin, and they serve as a kind of bridle; for they make penitent people more watchful for the future; they heal us from the remains of sin, and, by inducing acts of the contrary virtues, they remove vicious habits due to a bad life. No more secure way has ever been devised in the Church of God for warding off the punishments threatened by the Lord than that men should, with true sorrow of heart, make abundant use of penitential works.

"Add to this that, when we suffer for our sins by making satisfaction for them, we are made conformable to Jesus Christ who made satisfaction for our sins and 'from whom' is all 'our sufficiency';[934] thence, too, we derive a most solid pledge, because 'if we suffer with him, then we shall be glorified with him.'[935] At the same time, this satisfaction which we offer for our sins is not ours in the sense that it is not through Jesus Christ; for we, who of ourselves can do nothing as by ourselves, can, with the cooperation of him 'who strengtheneth' us, 'do all things.'[936] Hence a man has not wherewith to glory, but all our glorying is in Christ, in whom we live, in whom we merit, in whom we make satisfaction, bringing forth fruits worthy of penance, fruits which derive their force from him, by him are offered to the Father, and through him are accepted by the Father. The Lord's priests, then, ought, so far as their prudence suggests, to impose salutary satisfactions proportionate to the sins and to the capacity of their penitents, lest perchance they may be conniving at sin and may, through dealing too indulgently with their penitents by imposing very trifling penances for very grave faults, become participators in the sins of others. Priests should be careful that the satisfactions they impose should not only serve as a protec-

[932] Heb 10:29
[933] Rom 2:5
[934] 2 Cor 3:5
[935] Rom 8:17
[936] Phil 4:13

tion to the new life the penitent is going to lead and a remedy for his weaknesses, but also as a punishment and a castigation for past sins. For the keys are committed to the priest not solely for loosing but also for binding, as the fathers of old believe and teach. Nor did they thereby mean that the sacrament of penance was to be a tribunal of wrath and penalties, nor again—though this is a thing no Catholic ever dreamed of—did they mean that by these satisfactions of ours the merits and satisfactions of our Lord Jesus Christ were obscured or in any sort diminished. In their anxiety to counteract ideas of this kind, some modern theorists urge that the best kind of penance is a new life, with the result that they do away altogether with the value and use of satisfaction.

"This holy synod also teaches that so immense is the divine munificence that not alone by the penalties we inflict on ourselves as reparation for our sins, nor only by those imposed on us by the priest in proportion to our faults, but also—and this is the greatest proof of his love—by the temporal sufferings wherewith God afflicts us and which we patiently bear, we can make satisfaction to God the Father through Jesus Christ."

QUESTION 457

Fourth Lateran Council, A.D. 1215, Const. 21, *De confessione facienda et non revelanda a sacerdote, et saltem in Pascha communicando*:

"Let the priest be most careful lest by word or sign or in any way whatsoever he betray the sinner. If, however, he feels the need of more prudent counsel, then let him seek it cautiously and without any reference to the person in question. For a priest who should presume to reveal a sin brought to his knowledge in the judicial tribunal is, we decree, not only to be deposed from his priestly office but to be relegated to some monastery of strict life, there to do penance for the rest of his life."[937]

[937] Mansi, *Concilia*, xxii, 1007

QUESTION 461

Council of Trent, Session 6, "Decree on Justification," Ch. 14:

> "But those who by sin have fallen away from the justifying grace they have received can be justified anew when, by the stirrings of God's grace, they have taken steps to recover through the sacrament of penance the grace of Christ which they have deservedly lost. This manner of justification provides reparation for those who have fallen away, and the fathers have fittingly termed it 'the second list,' that is of grace lost through shipwreck. For, for the sake of those who fall into sin after baptism, Christ Jesus instituted the sacrament of penance when he said: 'Receive ye the Holy Ghost; whose sins ye shall forgive they are forgiven them, and whose sins ye shall retain they are retained.'[938] We must, then, teach that the repentance of a Christian after falling into sin is very different from his repentance at baptism; for in the former is contained not only cessation from sin and detestation of it, not only a contrite and humble heart, but sacramental confession of sin, at least in intention, and to be made in due season, also priestly absolution and satisfaction for sin by fastings, almsdeeds, prayers, and other devout practices of the spiritual life. These are not meant to secure escape from eternal punishment, for that—together with the sin—is remitted by the sacrament or the desire of it. But they are meant to secure escape from temporal punishment, which, as holy scripture teaches, is not always wholly remitted—as it is in baptism—in the case of those who, unmindful of the grace of God which they have received, 'have grieved the Spirit of God,'[939] and have not been ashamed 'to violate the temple of God.'[940] Of this penance it is written: 'Be mindful whence thou art fallen, and do penance, and do the first works';[941] and again: 'For the sorrow that is according to God worketh penance, steadfast unto salvation';[942] and again: 'Do penance... and bring forth fruit worthy of penance.'"[943]

[938] Jn 20:22-23
[939] Eph 4:30
[940] 1 Cor 3:17
[941] Apoc 2:5
[942] 2 Cor 7:10
[943] Mt 3:2, 8

Council of Trent, Session 6, Can. 30

> "If any one shall say that, after the reception of justifying grace, the sins of any penitent sinner are so remitted, and the guilt of eternal punishment so blotted out, that there remains no debt of temporal punishment to be paid in this world nor in purgatory in the next, before entrance into the kingdom of heaven can be open to him, let him be anathema."

For the Council of Trent, Session 14, "Doctrine on the Sacrament of Penance," Ch. 8, see above, q. 452.

Council of Trent, Session 14, "On the Most Holy Sacrament of Penance," Can. 12:

> "If any one shall say that together with the sin the whole punishment due is always remitted by God, and that the penitents' satisfaction is nothing else than that faith whereby they believe that Christ has made satisfaction for them, let him be anathema."

QUESTION 462

Council of Trent, Session 25, "Decree concerning Indulgences":

> "Since the power of conferring indulgences has been granted by Christ to his Church, and the Church has from the very earliest times made use of this power divinely bestowed upon her, this holy synod teaches and orders that the use of indulgences, which are most salutary for Christians, and approved by the authority of sacred councils, is to be retained in the Church. It also condemns under anathema those who say that they are useless or who deny that the Church has the power to confer them. At the same time, the synod desires that moderation in granting indulgences should, according to ancient and approved custom in the Church, be used, lest through undue facility in granting them, ecclesiastical discipline should become enervated. With the aim, then, of amending and correcting abuses which have crept in on this point and which have led

to the glorious term *indulgence* being blasphemed by heretics, this present decree lays down as a general principle that all unbecoming questings for obtaining indulgences be wholly abolished, for those have proved a peculiar source of abuses among Christians.

"As for other abuses arising from superstition, ignorance, irreverence, or any other source, these, owing to manifold corruptions in various places and provinces where these abuses have occurred, cannot conveniently be grouped under a special prohibition. This synod therefore bids all bishops diligently make a list of all such abuses in their respective churches and place it before their next provincial synod, so that when the decisions of the other bishops are known they may straightway be sent to the supreme Roman pontiff, by whose authority and prudence it shall be decided what is expedient for the universal Church, in order that the benefit of holy indulgences may be devoutly, scrupulously, and without corruption, administered to all the faithful."

Clement VI, Constitution *Unigenitus Dei Filius*, Jan. 25, 1343:

"The only begotten Son of God…'made unto us wisdom and justice and sanctification and redemption,'[944] 'neither by the blood of goats or of calves, but by his own blood, entered once into the holies, having obtained eternal redemption.'[945] 'You were not redeemed with corruptible things as gold or silver…but with the precious blood of Christ as of a lamb unspotted and undefiled.'[946] This blood, then, we know that he shed when slain in his innocence on the altar of the cross—not merely a tiny drop of it, though, by reason of his union with the Word, that would have sufficed for the redemption of the entire human race—but as a full-flowing stream, so that 'from the sole of the foot, to the top of the head, no soundness'[947] should be found in him. What an immense treasure, then, he thereby stored up for his Church here warring on earth, lest his merciful shedding of his blood should be rendered idle,

[944] 1 Cor 1:30
[945] Heb 9:12
[946] 1 Pt 1:18-19
[947] Is 1:6

unprofitable, or superfluous. Our merciful Father desired to lay up treasure for his children, so that thence there might be 'an infinite treasure to men, which they that use become the friends of God.'[948]

"This treasure he entrusted to the blessed Peter, the key-bearer of heaven, and to his successors, his vicars on earth, to be by them administered for the profit of the faithful, and, for good and reasonable causes, to be mercifully applied to such as are truly penitent and have confessed their sins, now for the total, now for the partial remission of the debt of temporal punishment due for sin, whether that of all men or that of individuals.

"To this accumulated treasure the merits of the holy Mother of God as well as of all the elect, from the first just man down to the last, add their meed. Nor need we fear the exhaustion or diminution of this treasury: firstly, because Christ's merits are, as has been said, infinite; secondly, because the greater the number of those who are thereby brought to righteousness, the more does this treasure increase."[949]

Leo X, Bull *Exurge Domine*, against the errors of Luther, June 15, 1520, the seventeenth through the twenty-second condemned Propositions:

Prop. 17: "The treasury of the Church, whence the pope grants indulgences, is not the merits of Christ and his saints."

Prop. 18: "Indulgences are pious frauds on the faithful; an abatement of good works; they are to be numbered among those things which are lawful, but not among those that are expedient."

Prop. 19: "Indulgences do not, for those who actually win them, avail for the remission of the penalties due by divine justice to actual sins."

Prop. 20: "Those who believe that indulgences are salutary and useful and productive of the fruits of the Spirit are seduced."

948 Ws 7:14

949 *Extravag. communes*, V, ix, 2

> Prop. 21: "Indulgences are only necessary for public criminals, and are, properly speaking, granted only to obdurate and ungovernable people."
>
> Prop. 22: "There are six classes of people for whom indulgences are neither necessary nor useful: the dead or the dying, the sick, those legitimately hindered, those who have not committed crimes, those who have committed crimes—though not public ones, those who do the better things."[950]

Pius VI, Constitution *Auctorem Fidei*, against the errors of the Synod of Pistoia, Aug. 28, 1794, the fortieth condemned Proposition:

> "The Proposition which asserts that an indulgence is in its strict sense nothing more than a remission of a portion of the penance imposed on a sinner by the canons—as though an indulgence did not, in addition to the remission of such canonical penance, also avail for the remission of the temporal punishment due, according to the divine justice, to actual sins—is false, rash, derogatory to Christ's merits, and already condemned in the nineteenth Proposition against the errors of Luther."[951]

Pius XI, Bull *Infinita Dei misericordia*, May 29, 1924, "The Indiction of the Universal Jubilee for the Holy Year, 1925":

> "For whosoever repent and fulfill the salutary commands of the Apostolic See in the course of this great jubilee year both wholly recover and receive those merits and gifts which they had lost by sin; they are also delivered from the cruel dominion of Satan and can thus regain the freedom wherewith Christ has made us free; finally, they are, by the accumulated merits of Christ Jesus, of the Blessed Virgin Mary, and of all the saints, fully delivered from all those penalties which they ought to pay for their sins and vices."[952]

950 *Bullarium Romanum*, ed. Turin, 751
951 *Bullarium Romanum*, ed. Turin, 2715
952 *Acta Apostolicae Sedis*, yr. 16, p. 210

QUESTION 469

Second Council of Lyons, A.D. 1274, *Profession of Faith by Michael Palaeologus*:

> "The holy Roman Church also holds and teaches that there are seven sacraments of the Church...; another is extreme unction which, according to the teaching of St. James, is applied to the sick."[953]

Council of Florence, Session 8 (November 22, 1439), "Bull of Union with the Armenians":

> "The fifth sacrament is extreme unction; its material part is olive oil blessed by a bishop. This sacrament should not be given except to a sick person whose death is expected. He is to be anointed in the following places: on the eyes because of seeing; on the ears because of hearing; on the nostrils because of smelling; on the lips because of tasting and speaking; on the hands because of touching; on the feet because of walking; on the reins because of the pleasure therein residing. The form of this sacrament is as follows: 'By this holy anointing and his most kindly mercy may the Lord pardon you whatsoever by sight, etc....' and similarly for the other members. The minister of this sacrament is a priest. Its effect is the healing of the mind, and, insofar as it is expedient, of the body as well. Of this sacrament, St. James the apostle says: 'Is any man sick among you? Let him bring in the priests of the church, and let them pray over him, anointing him with oil in the name of the Lord. And the prayer of faith shall save the sick man, and the Lord shall raise him up; and if he be in sins, they shall be forgiven him.'"[954]

[953] Mansi, *Concilia*, xxiv, 70
[954] Jas 5:14-15; Mansi, *Concilia*, xxxi, 1058

Council of Trent, Session 14, "On the Sacrament of Extreme Unction," Ch. 1:

> "This anointing of the sick was instituted by Christ our Lord as truly and properly a sacrament of the new testament; it is referred to by St. Mark and commended to the faithful and promulgated by James the apostle and brother of the Lord: 'Is any man sick among you? Let him bring in the priests of the church, and let them pray over him, anointing him with oil in the name of the Lord. And the prayer of faith shall save the sick man; and the Lord shall raise him up; and if he be in sins, they shall be forgiven him.'[955] Basing herself on these words, the Church teaches, as she has learned from apostolic tradition received (as it were) by hand, the matter, the form, the proper minister, and the effect of this salutary sacrament. For the Church has understood that the material part is oil blessed by a bishop, for oil most fittingly represents the grace of the Holy Spirit wherewith the soul of the sick person is invisibly anointed; also that the form consists in the words: 'By this anointing, and,' etc."

Innocent III, Epistle *Ejus exemplo*, Dec. 18, 1208, to the archbishop of Tarragona, "Profession of faith prescribed for the Waldensians Durandus de Osca and his companions":

> "We venerate the anointing of the sick with consecrated oil."[956]

Pius X, Decree *Lamentabili sane*, July 3, 1907, the forty-eighth condemned Proposition:

> "James did not in his epistle (5:14-15) intend to promulgate any sacrament of Christ, but only to recommend a pious practice; and if he did recognize in this practice some means of grace, he did not take it in the rigorous sense in which the theologians who have formulated the idea and the number of the sacraments have taken it."[957]

[955] Jas 5:14-15
[956] *P.L.*, ccxv, 1512
[957] *Acta Sanctae Sedis*, vol. 40, p. 476

QUESTION 470

Council of Trent, Session 14, "On the Sacrament of Extreme Unction," Ch. 2:

> "Further, the thing and the effect of this sacrament is set forth in the words: 'And the prayer of faith shall save the sick man, and the Lord shall raise him up; and if he be in sins, they shall be forgiven him.'[958] For this *thing* is the grace of the Holy Spirit, whose unction blots out any sins if any yet remain to be expiated, as also the remains of sin; it also relieves and confirms the soul of the sick man by arousing in him a great confidence in the divine mercy, so that the sick person is consoled and thus bears more readily the inconveniences and discomforts of his sickness; he also resists more easily the assaults of the devil 'lying in wait for his heel,'[959] and sometimes, when it is expedient for the salvation of his soul, he recovers his bodily health."

St. Caesarius of Arles, *Sermon 265*, n. 3, among the sermons attributed to St. Augustine:

> "So often as any sickness comes upon a person, let him receive the body and blood of Christ: then let him anoint his body so that that may be fulfilled in him which is written: 'Is any man sick among you?'[960] See to it, brethren, for he who in his sickness has recourse to the Church will merit, obtaining recovery of his health and pardon for his sins."[961]

[958] Jas 5:15
[959] Cf. Gn 3:15
[960] Jas 5:14-15
[961] *P.L.*, xxxix, 2238, *inter Opera Sti. Augustini.*

QUESTION 473

For the Council of Trent, see above, q. 470.

QUESTION 479

Second Council of Lyons, A.D. 1274, *Profession of Faith by Michael Palaeologus*:

> "The same holy Roman Church also holds and teaches that there are seven sacraments of the Church...; another is the sacrament of order."[962]

Council of Florence, Session 8 (November 22, 1439), "Bull of Union with the Armenians":

> "The sixth sacrament is that of order; its material part is that by the handing of which the order is conferred: thus the priesthood is conferred by handing the chalice containing wine and the paten with bread, the diaconate by the bestowal of the book of the gospels; the subdiaconate by handing the empty chalice with an empty paten laid on it: and in like fashion for the other orders by indicating the things pertaining to their offices. The form for the priesthood is: 'Receive power to offer sacrifice in the Church for the living and the dead, in the name of the Father and of the Son and of the Holy Ghost.' Similarly for the forms of the other orders, as fully given in the *Roman Pontifical*. The ordinary minister of this sacrament is a bishop. Its effect is the increase of grace so that the recipient may be a fit minister."[963]

Council of Trent, Session 23, Can. 3:

> "If any one shall say that order or sacred ordination is not really and truly a sacrament instituted by Christ the Lord, or that it is a human figment devised by people unlearned in ecclesiastical affairs, or that it

[962] Mansi, *Concilia*, xxiv, 70
[963] Mansi, *Concilia*, xxxi, 1058

is merely a rite for the election of ministers of the word of God and of the sacraments, let him be anathema."

Pius X, Decree *Lamentabili sane*, July 3, 1907, the forty-ninth and fiftieth condemned Propositions:

Prop. 49: "As the Christian supper took on by degrees the character of a liturgical action, those who presided at the supper acquired a priestly character."

Prop. 50: "The elders whose function it was to watch over the gatherings of the Christians were appointed by the apostles as priests or bishops, so as to provide for the regulations necessary in the growing communities, but not properly speaking for the perpetuation of the apostolic mission and authority."[964]

QUESTION 480

Council of Trent, Session 23, Can. 2, 6, 7:

Can. 2: "If anyone shall say that in the Catholic Church there are not, in addition to the priesthood, other orders both major and minor, whereby, as it were by steps, a man ascends to the priesthood, let him be anathema."

Can. 6: "If anyone shall say that in the Catholic Church there is no divinely instituted hierarchy composed of bishops, priests, and ministers, let him be anathema."

Can. 7: "If anyone shall say that bishops are not superior to priests, or that they have not got the power to confirm and ordain, or that their power to do so they only have in common with a priest, or that orders conferred by them without the consent or invitation of the populace, or of the secular authorities, are invalid, or that those who have neither been rightly ordained by ecclesiastical and canonical authority,

[964] *Acta Sanctae Sedis*, vol. 40, p. 476

nor commissioned by them, but came in from elsewhere, are lawful ministers of the word and of the sacraments, let him be anathema."

QUESTION 482

Pius XI, Epistle *Officiorum omnium*, Aug. 1, 1922:

"Of all the sacred duties comprised in the fullness of the apostolic office, none assuredly is of greater importance than care in securing that the Church should have a sufficient supply of good ministers for the fulfillment of her divine task. For this matter is one which affects the dignity, the efficiency, and the general life of the Church: it also affects in the most intimate manner possible the salvation of the human race; for the immense benefits wrought in the world by Jesus Christ our Redeemer can only be communicated to men by 'ministers of Christ and dispensers of the mysteries of God.'"[965]

QUESTION 487

Council of Florence, Session 8 (November 22, 1439), "Bull of Union with the Armenians":

"The seventh sacrament is that of matrimony, which, as the apostle says, is a sign of the union between Christ and his Church: 'This is a great sacrament, but I speak in Christ and in the church.'[966] The efficient cause of matrimony is, generally speaking, mutual consent expressed by words in the present tense. Three good things are pointed out in matrimony: the first is the bringing up of children, and their education for the worship of God; the second is the fidelity which each of the parties has to observe with regard to the other; the third is the indissolubility of matrimony arising from the fact that it signifies the indissoluble union between Christ and his Church. And though separation owing to fornication committed by one of the parties is

[965] 1 Cor 4:1; *Acta Apostolicae Sedis*, yr. 14, p. 449
[966] Eph 5:32

allowable, yet it is not lawful to contract another marriage, since the bond of marriage, when lawfully entered into, is perpetual."[967]

For the Council of Trent, Session 7, "On the Sacraments in General," Can. 1, see above, q. 325.

Council of Trent, Session 24, Can. 1:

"If anyone shall say that matrimony is not really and truly one of the seven sacraments of the gospel law and instituted by Christ, but merely a human figment in the Church, or that it does not confer grace, let him be anathema."

Leo XIII, Encyclical *Arcanum Divinae Sapientiae*, Feb. 10, 1880:

"'What our fathers, the councils, and the tradition of the universal Church have always taught'[968] must be referred to our teachers the apostles; namely, that Christ the Lord raised matrimony to the dignity of a sacrament and at the same time brought it about that married people—hedged about and defended by the grace of heaven which their merits have won for them—should be able to sanctify themselves in the married state, and in it—marvelously modeled as it is on the mystical espousals between Christ and his Church—has perfected that love which is in accordance with nature, and more effectively knit together by the bond of charity, the natural companionship of one man with one woman."[969]

St. Cyril of Alexandria, *On John*, Ch. 2, n. 1:

"When the marriage was to be celebrated, chastely and honestly, the Mother of the Savior was present, and he, too, being invited with his disciples, came, not so much to feast as to work a miracle, and, further

[967] Mansi, *Concilia*, xxxi, 1058
[968] Council of Trent, Session 24, Proem.
[969] *Acta* of Leo XIII, ii, 16

still, to sanctify the principle of human generation which is an affair of the flesh."[970]

QUESTION 488

Leo XIII, Encyclical *Arcanum Divinae Sapientiae*, Feb. 10, 1880:

"Nor ought we to be disturbed by the distinction so strongly urged by the Royalists between the marriage contract and the sacrament, clearly with the object of reserving to the Church all that concerns the sacrament while handing over the contract to the power and discretion of the state. But such a distinction, or rather such a violent disruption, cannot be upheld, for it is an established fact that in Christian marriage the contract cannot be dissociated from the sacrament, and that, consequently, it is impossible to have a real and legitimate contract without its being by that very fact a sacrament. For Christ our Lord raised matrimony to the dignity of a sacrament, and marriage is the actual contract provided it be rightly performed...It is evident, then, that every valid marriage between Christians is in itself and of itself a sacrament; nor is there anything further removed from the truth than the notion that the sacrament merely adds a certain decoration, or is some feature added from without and distinguishable and separable from the contract at men's whim."[971]

QUESTION 491

Leo XIII, Encyclical *Arcanum Divinae Sapientiae*, Feb. 10, 1880:

"The union of husband and wife has from the very beginning had stamped and impressed on it two peculiarly striking characteristics in order that it might more adequately correspond with the wise counsels of God; these are unity and perpetuity...This we see declared and patently confirmed in the gospel by the divine authority of Jesus Christ

[970] *P.G.*, lxxiii, 223
[971] *Acta* of Leo XIII, ii, 25-26

who testified to the Jews and to the apostles that matrimony, even from the time of its institution, ought to be only between two, a man and a woman, that of those two was made one flesh, and that the marriage bond was by God's will so intimately and closely knit that it can be neither dissolved nor broken by any man: 'A man...shall cleave to his wife and they two shall be in one flesh. Therefore, now they are not two but one flesh.'"[972]

St. Augustine, *De Conjugiis Adulterinis*, Bk. 1, Ch. 9:

"If, then, we were to say, 'Whosoever marries a woman put away by her husband for any other cause than fornication commits adultery,' we should certainly be saying what was true; yet it does not therefore follow that we can pronounce him innocent who marries a woman who has been put away because of her fornication; we have not the remotest doubt but that they are both of them adulterers. And in the same way we pronounce him an adulterer, who, for some other cause than fornication, puts away his wife and marries another; yet we do not on that ground pronounce innocent of adultery a man who puts away his wife because of her fornication, and then marries another. We regard both of them as adulterers, although the sin of one is graver than that of the other."[973]

St. Augustine, *On Marriage and Concupiscence*, Bk. 1, Ch. 11:

"Now, since not only fecundity, whose fruit is offspring, nor chastity, whose safeguard is fidelity, but also a certain nuptial sacrament is set before the married members of the faithful, for the apostle says, 'Husbands, love your wives, as Christ also loved the church,'[974] it follows that the *thing* of this sacrament consists in husband and wife remaining inseparable for the rest of their lives once they have been joined in wedlock, and in the unlawfulness of separation between part-

[972] Mt 19:5-6; *Acta* of Leo XIII, ii, 12-13
[973] *P.L.*, xl, 456
[974] Eph 5:25

ners except it be because of fornication.[975] But if a man has done so (taken another wife during the lifetime of his former partner), then by the gospel law he is guilty of adultery, as also is the wife if she marries another,[976] though not so by the law of this world whereby, owing to divorce, marriage can be added to marriage and no legal crime incurred; in fact, as the Lord himself testifies, even holy Moses conceded this to the people of Israel owing to the hardness of their hearts. Between married people, then, there remains, so long as they live, a certain conjugal bond which neither separation nor subsequent union with another can remove. But this bond then remains, not as a bond of fidelity, but as the penalty of a crime; just as the soul of an apostate who withdraws from Christ's espousals, even though his faith has gone, does not lose the sacrament of faith which he received in 'the laver of regeneration.'"[977]

QUESTION 492

For the Council of Trent, Session 7, "On the Sacraments in General," Can. 1, see above, q. 325.

Council of Trent, Session 24, Can. 2:

"If any one shall say that a Christian can lawfully have more than one wife at the same time, and that this is not forbidden by divine law, let him be anathema."

Innocent III, Epistle *Gaudemus in Domino*, A.D. 1201, to the bishop of Tiberias:

"Now, since pagans share their conjugal affections among several women at the same time, it is a reasonable question whether on their conversion they are to retain them all, or, failing that, which one of them. The former notion seems discordant with, nay opposed to, the Christian faith, since in the beginning, out of one rib was made one woman; and holy scripture tells

[975] Cf. Mt 5:32
[976] Cf. Mt 19:8-9
[977] Ti 3:5; *P.L.*, xliv, 420

us that 'for this cause shall a man leave father and mother and shall cleave to his wife, and they two shall be in one flesh';[978] it does not say 'three' or 'several,' but 'two'; not 'he shall cleave to his wives,' but 'to his wife.' Nor was it ever lawful for a man to have several wives at the same time unless this was conceded him by divine revelation; the practice is sometimes even regarded as right, so that just as Jacob was excused from a lie, the Israelite from theft, Samson from murder, so too are the patriarchs and other holy men who are said to have had several wives at once, excused from adultery. In fact, that this opinion is true is proved even by the testimony of the truth himself, who in the gospel testifies that: 'Whosoever shall put away his wife, except it be for fornication, and shall marry another, committeth adultery.'[979] If, then, a man is not permitted to marry another when he has put away his wife, still less is he allowed to do so when he has not put her away. Whence it is evident that plurality in marriage on the part of either sex is to be reprobated, since the same judgment applies to either. Whosoever, then, has, according to his rite, repudiated his lawful wife, can never—since the truth himself has in the gospel condemned such repudiation—not even when he has been converted to the faith, lawfully have another wife during the lifetime of the former unless after his conversion she refuses to cohabit with him, or, if she does agree to do so, yet will not refrain from offering insult to the Creator, or tries to lead him into mortal sin. For in that case, he has to refuse to render to her the debt (of marriage) when she asks for it, even though such privation should be proved unjust; for, according to the apostle: 'A brother or sister is not under servitude in such cases.'[980] If, however, on his conversion, she follows his example and is herself converted before he has, owing to the aforesaid reasons, married a lawful wife, he must be compelled to take her. And although according to gospel truth 'he that shall marry her that is put away committeth adultery,'[981] yet the husband who has put her away cannot urge fornication against her on the ground that she has married another husband after this putting away unless she has been guilty of some other fornication."[982]

[978] Gn 2:24; Mt 19:5; Eph 5:31
[979] Mt 19:9; Mk 10:11
[980] 1 Cor 7:15
[981] Mt 19:9
[982] *P.L.*, ccxvi, 1269ff

QUESTION 493

Council of Trent, Session 24, Can. 6-7:

> Can. 6: "If any one shall say that a marriage which has been ratified but not consummated cannot be annulled by the solemn religious profession of one of the partners, let him be anathema."
>
> Can. 7: "If any one shall say that the Church errs when she has taught, and now teaches, that, according to the doctrine of the gospels and of the apostles, the bond of matrimony cannot be dissolved owing to the adultery of one of the partners, and that neither party, not even the innocent party who has not by committing adultery given any ground (for separation), is free to contract another marriage during the lifetime of the other partner, and that he who after putting away his adulterous wife marries another commits adultery, or the wife who after putting away an adulterous husband marries another, let him be anathema."

Pius IX, *The Syllabus of Errors*, the sixty-seventh condemned Proposition:

> "The marriage bond is not indissoluble by the law of nature, and in various cases divorce strictly so-called can be sanctioned by the civil authorities."[983]

Leo XIII, Encyclical *Arcanum Divinae Sapientiae*, Feb. 10, 1880:

> "Christ restored marriage to its state of primitive excellence when he condemned the morals of the Hebrews who had many wives and who misused the permission to put away their wives; for he sternly forbade anyone to dare dissolve what God had bound by a perpetual bond of union. When he had solved the difficulties alleged from the decisions given by Moses, he, in the Person of the supreme lawgiver, laid down this law for married people: 'And I say to you, that whosoever shall put away his wife, except it be for fornication, and shall marry another, committeth adultery, and he that shall marry her that is put away, committeth adultery.'"[984]

983 *Acta* of Pius IX, I, iii, 703
984 Mt 19:9; *Acta* of Leo XIII, ii, 15

QUESTION 497

Council of Trent, Session 24, Can. 4:

> "If anyone shall say that the Church cannot institute impediments which make a marriage null, or that she has erred in so doing, let him be anathema."

QUESTION 504

Council of Trent, Session 24, Can. 12:

> "If anyone shall say that ecclesiastical judges have nothing to do with matrimonial cases, let him be anathema."

QUESTION 511

Council of Trent, Session 6, "Decree on Justification," Ch. 7:

> "Hence in justification itself a person, together with the remission of his sins, receives simultaneously infused into him through Jesus Christ—into whom he is engrafted—all the following: faith, hope, and charity. For faith, unless there be added to it hope and charity, does not perfectly unite a person with Christ, nor does it make him a living member of his body; whence it is most truly said that faith without works is dead and unprofitable."

Clement V, Constitution *De Summa Trinitate et fide Catholica*, at the Council of Vienne, A.D. 1311, against the errors of Peter John Oliva:

> "As regards the effect of baptism on children, since certain learned theologians are found to have held conflicting opinions, some of them saying that by the power of baptism children's sins are remitted but no grace conferred, while others on the contrary maintain that the sins of children are remitted in baptism and also the virtues and informative

grace infused—so far, that is, as the habit is concerned, not however the use of it then: We, considering the universal efficacy of Christ's death, which by baptism is applied to all the baptized alike, have, with the approbation of this holy council, decided that the latter opinion is to be preferred, that, namely, which holds that in baptism there is conferred on children as well as on adults informative grace and the virtues, as being the more probable and more in harmony and agreement with the sayings of the saints and the theological teaching of modern doctors."[985]

St. Polycarp, *Epistle to the Philippians*, Ch. 3:

"St. Paul, when absent from you, wrote to you letters which, if you study them closely, will enable you to be built up in that faith which has been given to you 'which is the mother of us all,'[986] in hope which follows, and in that love of God, of Christ, and of our neighbor, which leads the way. If any one is in these things, then he has fulfilled the law of justice; for he who has charity is far removed from all sin."[987]

St. John Chrysostom, *Homily 40 on Acts*, Ch. 2:

"By baptism we have the starting-point of good works; we have received the forgiveness of our sins, sanctification, a participation in the Holy Spirit, adoption, eternal life. What more do you want? Signs? But they have ceased. You have faith, hope, and charity which abide. Seek these, for they are better than signs. Nothing equals charity: 'The greatest of these is charity.'"[988]

[985] Clement, i, 1
[986] Cf. Gal 4:26
[987] *P.G.*, v, 1007
[988] 1 Cor 13:13; *P.G.*, lx, 285

QUESTION 513

For Benedict XII, see above, q. 62.

St. Clement of Rome, *Epistle to the Corinthians*, Ch. 49:

> "Who can fittingly set forth that bond which is the love of God? Who can sing the grandeur of his goodness in fitting fashion? The height to which charity can carry us can never be told, for charity glues us to God, 'charity covereth a multitude of sins':[989] charity beareth all things, patiently endureth all things; in charity there is nothing sordid, nothing proud; charity allows of no schism, stirs up no sedition, makes all things harmonious. In charity are all the elect of God perfected; without it, nothing is acceptable to God. In charity did Christ take us to himself; by reason of the charity which he had for us, Jesus Christ our Lord gave his blood for us by the will of God, his flesh for our flesh, his soul for our souls."[990]

QUESTION 514

Alexander VII, Decree of Sept. 24, 1665, the first of certain condemned Propositions:

> "At no moment of his life is a man bound by force of any divine precept concerning those virtues to elicit acts of faith, hope, or charity."[991]

Innocent XI, Decree of the Sacred Congregation of the Inquisition, March 2, 1679, the sixth, seventh, sixteenth, and seventeenth condemned Propositions:

> Prop. 6: "It is probable that not even once in five years is a man rigorously bound to make an act of the love of God."

[989] 1 Pt 4:8
[990] *P.G.*, i, 310ff
[991] Du Plessis, *Collectio Judiciorum*, III, ii, 321

Prop. 7: "Such a precept only binds when we are bound to be justified and have no other means whereby we can be justified."

Prop. 16: "Faith is not reckoned as of itself falling under any special precept."

Prop. 17: "It is enough to make an act of faith once in one's life."[992]

QUESTION 515

First Vatican Council, Constitution *Dei Filius*, Ch. 3:

"Since man wholly depends on God as his Creator and Lord, and since created reason is wholly subordinated to uncreated truth, we are bound to render by faith full allegiance of our intellect and will to God in his revelation. Now, this faith, which is the starting-point of man's salvation, the Catholic Church declares to be a supernatural power whereby, through the inspiration and assistance of God's grace, we believe those things to be true which he has revealed, not because their intrinsic truth is evident by the natural light of reason, but because of the authority of God who reveals them and who can neither deceive nor be deceived. For faith is, as the apostle testifies, 'the substance of things to be hoped for, the evidence of things that appear not.'"[993]

St. Leo the Great, *Sermon 27*, n. 1:

"When...we draw nigh to understand the mystery of Christ's birth, namely, that he was born of a Virgin Mother, we have to put aside all the obscurity attaching to human reasonings, nor should the fumes arising from worldly wisdom be allowed to obscure eyes illumined by faith. For it is on divine authority that we believe, the teaching we follow is divine."[994]

For St. John Chrysostom, see above, q. 373.

992 Du Plessis, *Collectio Judiciorum*, III, ii, 348
993 Heb 11:1
994 *P.L.*, liv, 216

QUESTION 516

Innocent XI, Decree of the Sacred Congregation of the Inquisition, March 2, 1679, the twenty-second and sixty-fourth condemned Propositions:

> Prop. 22: "Only faith in the one God seems to be necessary as a means (*necessitate medii*); not explicit faith in God the rewarder."
>
> Prop. 64: "A person is capable of receiving absolution even though ignorant of the mysteries of the faith; even if through culpable ignorance he does not know the mystery of the most Holy Trinity and of the incarnation of our Lord Jesus Christ."[995]

Decree of the Congregation of the Holy Office, Jan. 25, 1703:

> "2. The question is put: whether before admitting an adult to baptism the minister is bound to explain to him all the mysteries of our faith, more especially when he is on the point of death, when his mind may be disturbed. Would it not suffice if the sick person were to promise that if he recovered he would take care to get instruction and put in practice what had been told him?
>
> "Reply: The promise is not sufficient; the missionary is bound to explain to an adult, even though sick—provided he is not wholly incapable of understanding—those mysteries of the faith which are necessary as means (*necessitate medii*), more particularly the mysteries of the Trinity and of the incarnation."[996]

[995] Du Plessis, *Collectio Judiciorum*, III, ii

[996] *Codicis Juris Canonici, Fontes*, iv, 41, 42

QUESTION 517

First Vatican Council, Constitution *Dei Filius*, Ch. 4, "Of Faith and Reason":

"Although faith is above reason, yet there can never be any real disagreement between faith and reason. For it is the same God who reveals mysteries and infuses faith into us, and who bestows on man the light of reason. Neither can God contradict himself, nor truth truth. That there should seem to be some such contradiction is generally due to the fact that the dogmas of the faith are not explained in the sense in which the Church understands them, or that mere conjectural opinions are taken for the pronouncements of reason. We define that every assertion contrary to a truth of illumined faith is wholly false."

QUESTION 518

For the First Vatican Council, see above, q. 517.

Pius IX, Encyclical *Qui pluribus*, Nov. 9, 1846:

"You, venerable brethren, are aware that these implacable foes to the Christian name, miserably carried away by the blind fury of a senseless hatred of religion, have gone so far in their rash opinions that, 'opening their mouths in blasphemies against God,'[997] they are not ashamed to teach openly, publicly, and with an unheard-of audacity, that the holy mysteries of our religion are but lies and the fictions of men, and that the doctrines of the Catholic Church are opposed to the well-being and profit of human society; nor are they afraid to abjure even God and Christ. And that they may the more easily delude people, more especially in cautious and unlearned folk, and seduce them by their errors, they pretend that the road to prosperity is known to themselves alone, and even venture to arrogate to themselves the title of philosophers, as though philosophy—which is wholly concerned with investigating the

[997] Apoc 13:6

nature of truth—ought to repudiate those things which the supreme and most merciful author of all nature has, out of his singular kindness and mercy, deigned to reveal to men so that they may win true happiness and salvation.

"Hence, by a distorted and most fallacious way of arguing, they never cease from lauding the power and excellence of human reason, extolling it in opposition to our most solidly established faith in Christ, which faith they boldly declare will be wrecked by human reason. Nothing more crazy, more profane, more in contradiction with reason itself, could well be devised. For though faith is above reason, no real disagreement or conflict between them can ever occur, since both derive their origin from one and the same source of immutable and eternal truth, the great and supreme good. Indeed, they mutually support one another; in such fashion too, that sound reason can demonstrate, safeguard, and defend the truth of faith; while faith can free reason from all errors, marvelously illumining, confirming, and perfecting it by the knowledge it affords us of divine things.

"By a no less fallacious reasoning, venerable brethren, do these foes of divine revelation, extolling human progress in every way possible, endeavor boldly and sacrilegiously to set it in opposition to the Catholic religion; as though religion itself were not God's work but man's, or some philosophical discovery which needed to be perfected by human endeavors. The words wherewith Tertullian deservedly assailed the philosophers of his own day most aptly fit these unhappy ravers: 'They have devised a Christianity which is Stoic, Platonist, and dialectical.'[998] And assuredly, since our most holy religion is not the outcome of human reason but was most mercifully revealed to men by God, anyone easily can see that religion derives its whole strength from the authority of God who has spoken to us; it cannot be deduced from reason nor brought to perfection by it.

"Yet lest it should be deceived in a matter of such moment, human reason ought to make diligent enquiry about the fact of divine revelation,

998 Tertullian, *Prescription against Heretics*, Ch. 7

so as to learn for certain that God has so spoken, and may therefore be able to render him, as the apostle so wisely expresses it, 'reasonable service.'[999] For who does not know, who can be ignorant that full credence must be given to God when he speaks, and that nothing can be more in accordance with reason than to acquiesce in and firmly adhere to those things which it is clear have been revealed by God who can neither deceive nor be deceived?

"How many, how wonderful and luminous are the arguments at our disposal whereby human reason ought to be overwhelmingly convinced that the religion of Christ is divine, and that 'the entire foundation of our doctrines is based upon what has come down from the Lord of heaven.'[1000] Hence, nothing can be more certain, established, and secure, more based on solid principles, than our faith. For this faith is the teacher of life, the guide to salvation; it drives out all vices and is the fruitful parent and nurse of all virtues; it is confirmed by the birth of its divine author and consummator, Jesus Christ; by his life, death, and resurrection; by his wisdom, miracles, and prophecies. Everywhere it shines with the light of a teaching that is from on high; it is enriched with the treasures of the riches of heaven, rendered peculiarly glorious and conspicuous by so many predictions of the prophets, the splendor of so many miracles, the constancy of such a host of martyrs, and the glory of so many saints. It sets before men Christ's laws, and day by day it gains greater force even from the cruelest persecutions. It has invaded the whole world, both land and sea, from the rising to the setting of the sun, though carrying but the standard of the cross. It has destroyed lying idols, has rolled back the dark clouds of error, triumphed over enemies of every sort. It has brought the light of the knowledge of God even to the most barbarous peoples, tribes, and nations, though differing in characters, manners, laws, and institutions; it has made them subject to the most sweet yoke of Christ himself, 'declaring peace to all, bringing good tidings.'[1001] All these things are everywhere so clear, lit up as they are by the splendor of God's wisdom and power, that any thinking mind can readily understand that the Christian faith is the work of God.

[999] Rom 12:1

[1000] Chrysostom, *Homily 1 on Isaias*

[1001] Is 52:7

"Hence human reason, clearly and openly recognizing, from arguments as luminous as they are solid, that God, the author of the said faith, exists, can progress no further, but, putting aside and leaving behind it all difficulty and hesitation, must offer to God the complete allegiance of faith, since it knows for certain that whatsoever that faith sets before it to believe or do has been taught by God."[1002]

QUESTION 519

For the Fifth Lateran Council, see above, q. 60.

First Vatican Council, Constitution *Dei Filius*, Ch. 4, "Of Faith and Reason":

"Not only can faith and reason never be in conflict, but they mutually support one another, since sound reason can demonstrate the foundations of the faith, and, illuminated by its light, can cultivate a knowledge of divine things; while faith can free reason from errors, safeguard it and furnish it with varied knowledge. Consequently, so far is it from being the case that the Church is an obstacle to the cultivation of the arts and sciences, that, on the contrary, she helps and furthers them in many ways. She does not ignore or belittle the advantages thence accruing to men's lives; rather does she acknowledge that the arts and sciences, since they have their origin in the God of all knowledge, do, if rightly handled, lead men by God's grace to God. Nor does she in the least prohibit these sciences from making use, each in their own ambit, of their own principles and their own peculiar methods. But while according to them this just liberty, the Church is particularly careful lest those who cultivate these arts and sciences should, by assailing divine doctrine, fall into error, or, going outside their proper sphere, should invade the domain of faith and so cause confusion."

[1002] *Acta* of Pius IX, I, i, 6-9

QUESTION 524

For Benedict XII, see above, q. 62.

St. John Chrysostom, *Homily 14 on Romans*, Ch. 6:

"What, then, saved you? Only hope in God and the fact that you have faith in him with regard to the things he has promised you and given you; you have nothing else to offer him. If, then, this faith has saved you, then hold fast to it now. For since it has brought you so many good things, it will certainly not deceive you about the future. For that same faith which made you, dead, lost, captive, and an enemy, into a friend, a son, free, just, and fellow-heir, and which has bestowed upon you such things as no one could have expected—how can you imagine that after such generosity and kindliness he will refuse to admit you hereafter?...What, then, is hope? Confidence regarding the future."[1003]

QUESTION 530

St. Gregory the Great, *On the Gospels*, Bk. 2, Homily 30, n. 1-2:

"But consider: if any one of you were asked whether he loved God, he would with absolute confidence and security answer: 'I do love him.' But at the very outset of what has been read to you, you heard what the truth says: 'If any man love me he will keep my word.'[1004] The proof, then, of love consists in exhibiting good works. Hence, in his epistle, the same John says, 'He who saith "I love God" and keepeth not his commandments, is a liar.'[1005] For we truly love God if, at his command, we restrain ourselves from our pleasures. But a man who continues to give himself up to his illicit desires clearly does not love God, for in his own will he sets himself in opposition to him.

[1003] *P.G.*, lx, 532
[1004] Jn 14:23
[1005] Cf. 1 Jn 2:4

"...When, then, a person truly loves God and keeps his commandments, into his heart the Lord both comes and there abides, for the love of his Godhead so penetrates him that in the hour of temptation he does not withdraw from that love. Now, he truly loves whose mind is not overcome by consenting to illicit pleasures. For the more a person is separated from that supernal love, the more does he find pleasure in what is inferior. Hence Christ goes on to say: 'He that loveth me not keepeth not my words.'"[1006]

QUESTION 532

Council of Trent, Session 6, "Decree on Justification," Ch. 15:

"As opposed to certain people of ingenious minds who by deceptive and flattering words lead innocent people astray, we have to assert that not only by unbelief, whereby faith itself is lost, but also by any other kind of mortal sin which does not involve the loss of faith, men do lose the justifying grace they have received. This we assert in defense of the teaching of the law of God, which excludes from the kingdom of God not only unbelievers but also believers who are fornicators, adulterers, effeminate, liers with mankind, thieves, covetous, drunkards, railers, extortioners,[1007] and all others who commit mortal sins from which they could, by the help of divine grace, refrain, and by reason of which they are cut off from the grace of Christ."

Council of Trent, Session 6, Can. 27-28:

Can. 27: "If any one shall say that the only mortal sin is that of unbelief, or that grace once received can be forfeited by no other sin—however heinous and grave—save that of unbelief, let him be anathema."

Can. 28: "If any one shall say that when grace is forfeited through sin, faith is also lost, or that the faith which remains is not true faith—though it is true that it is not a lively faith—or that a person who has faith without charity is not a Christian, let him be anathema."

[1006] Jn 14:24; *P.L.*, lxxvi, 1220ff
[1007] Cf. 1 Cor 6:9-10

QUESTION 534

Innocent XI, Decree of the Sacred Congregation of the Inquisition, March 2, 1679, the tenth and eleventh condemned Propositions:

> Prop. 10: "We are not bound to love our neighbor by any formal exterior act."
>
> Prop. 11: "We can satisfy the command of loving our neighbor by purely interior acts."[1008]

QUESTION 540

St. Augustine, *Tractate 8 on First John*, to the Parthians:

> "Works of mercy, feelings of charity, scrupulous holiness, inviolate chastity, modest sobriety, to these we must always cling...All the above-named are interior virtues. Who can enumerate them all? They are like the hosts of the Emperor who dwells within, in your spirit. For just as an emperor does what he wills with his hosts, so does our Lord Jesus Christ, when he begins to dwell in our inner man—that is, in our spirit—by faith,[1009] use the aforesaid virtues as his servants."[1010]

QUESTION 544

St. Ambrose, *On the Mysteries*, Ch. 7, n. 42:

> "You have received the spiritual seal, the spirit of wisdom and understanding, the spirit of counsel and fortitude, the spirit of knowledge and piety, the spirit of holy fear; hold fast, then, to what you have received. God the Father has sealed you, Christ the Lord has confirmed you and has given the pledge of his Spirit in your hearts."[1011]

[1008] Du Plessis, *Collectio Judiciorum*, III, ii, 348
[1009] Cf. Eph 3:17
[1010] *P.L.*, xxxv, 2035ff
[1011] *P.L.*, xvi, 419

St. Ambrose, *On the Sacraments*, Bk. 3, Ch. 2, n. 8:

> "On baptism there follows the spiritual sealing...; for after (cleansing in) the font a certain completion remains to be added, when, that is, at the priest's invocation, the Holy Spirit is poured out (on you): the spirit of wisdom and understanding, the spirit of counsel and fortitude, the spirit of knowledge and piety, the spirit of holy fear, the seven powers of the Spirit."[1012]

QUESTION 545

Leo XIII, Encyclical *Divinum illud munus*, May 9, 1897:

> "Further still, a just man, that is, a man leading the life of divine grace and acting by virtue or faculties in harmony with it, assuredly needs those sevenfold gifts which are fittingly termed the 'gifts of the Holy Spirit.' For by the bestowal of these the mind is furnished and strengthened so as to obey more readily and promptly his voice and his impulses. Such is the efficacy of these gifts that they can lead a person to the heights of sanctity; indeed so excellent are they that even in the kingdom of heaven they remain, though in more perfect fashion."[1013]

QUESTION 549

Leo XIII, Encyclical *Divinum illud munus*, May 9, 1897:

> "...By the help of these gifts, the soul is stirred up and led on to desire and to obtain the beatitudes promised in the gospel. These, like the flowers which blossom in the spring, are as it were couriers declaring in advance the blessedness that is to abide forever."[1014]

[1012] *P.L.*, xiv, 453
[1013] *Acta* of Leo XIII, xvii, 141
[1014] *Acta* of Leo XIII, xvii, 14

QUESTION 563

St. Jerome, *Against Jovinianus*, Bk. 2, n. 30:

"There are light sins, there are grave ones. It is one thing to owe ten thousand talents, another to owe a farthing...You see that if by prayer we can win pardon for light ones, and if for graver ones it is difficult to win pardon, then there must be a difference between light sins and grave ones."[1015]

St. Caesarius of Arles, *Sermon 104*, n. 2, among sermons attributed to St. Augustine:

"Now, though the apostle has mentioned several capital sins, yet, lest we should make you despair, we will tell you briefly which they are: sacrilege, murder, adultery, false witness, theft, robbery, pride, envy, avarice, and—if it be cherished for a long space—anger; also drunkenness, if it be constant; these have to be reckoned among the capital sins. For if any person recognizes that some of these sins have got dominion over him, then unless he really amends his life and, if he has time, does protracted penance for them, gives abundant alms and refrains himself from such sins, then he will not be purified in that transitory fire of which the apostle speaks but will be tormented without alleviation in the fire of eternity.

"As for the lesser sins, everybody knows them; yet, since it would take a long time to enumerate them all, we must be content to mention a few of them here. So often as a person takes more food or drink than is needful, he should understand that this comes under the lesser sins, similarly when a man says more than he should, or is silent when he should not be...Now, while we are not to imagine that such sins kill the soul, yet they do—like pimples and an objectionable itch—disfigure the soul when it is full of them, and they hardly allow the soul access to the embraces of its spouse, not, at any rate, without a great sense of shame...

[1015] *P.L.*, xxiii, 327

> "Moreover, if we do not render thanks to God in time of tribulation, if we do not make amends for our sins by good works, then shall we abide in the fires of purgatory until the aforesaid lesser sins—like wood, hay, and stubble—are consumed. Someone may, perchance, say to this: 'I do not mind how long a time I spend there provided I do get to eternal life.' But do not any of you, brethren, speak like that, for the fire of purgatory is worse than anything that one can dream of or see or feel in this suffering world."[1016]

QUESTION 567

St. Pius V, Constitution *Ex omnibus afflictionibus*, against the errors of Baius, Oct. 1, 1567, the twentieth condemned Proposition:

> "No sin is of its nature venial, but every sin deserves eternal punishment."[1017]

QUESTION 580

St. Basil the Great, *Sermon on Psalm 33*:

> "When temptation to sin assails you, I would have you reflect on that awful, insupportable judgment seat of Christ when the judge will preside on his high and lofty throne, when the whole of creation will stand before him and tremble at the sight of his glory. For one by one we shall be brought before him to give an account of what we have done during our lives. Speedily will the terrible and misshapen demons stand beside those who have committed many crimes during their lives; they will show their fiery countenances and will breathe out fire, thus betraying their cruel mind and purpose; their faces will be like the night owing to their own gloom and their hatred of the human race.

[1016] *P.L.*, xxxix, 1946, *inter sermones Sti. Augustini*
[1017] Du Plessis, *Collectio Judiciorum*, III, ii, 110

"Then think of that deep pit, of the indescribable darkness, of that fire that affords no light, for, though it has the power to burn, it lacks light; think of the worms that discharge their poison, that devour the flesh, that eat and are never sated nor filled but inflict insupportable pain by their gnawings. Finally—and this is the worst punishment of all—think of the disgrace and the everlasting shame. Dread these things and, overwhelmed by your dread, keep your soul, as by a bit in your mouth, from the concupiscence of sin."[1018]

QUESTION 582

For the Council of Trent, see above, q. 74.

QUESTION 583

For Benedict XII, see above, q. 62.

St. Augustine, *On the Soul and Its Origin*, Bk. 2, Ch. 8:

"Do you mean to say that you were ignorant of what Vincentius Victor most rightly and most profitably believes, namely, that men's souls are judged when they quit the body, and before coming to that judgment whereat they will be judged, when their bodies are restored to them, and will be either tortured or glorified in that flesh in which they have passed their lives? Who can so obstinately shut his ears to the gospel story as not to realize, or refuse to believe when he does not realize, that all this is contained in the story of that poor man who after death was carried to Abraham's bosom, and of the rich man whose torments in hell are there set forth?"[1019]

[1018] *P.G.*, xxix, 370-371
[1019] *P.L.*, xliv, 498

QUESTION 585

Council of Florence, Session 6 (July 6, 1439), "Decree for the Greeks":

"Further, if they have departed this life repenting of their sins and with love of God, but before they have, by fruits worthy of penance, made satisfaction for things they have done or omitted, then after death their souls are purified by the punishments of purgatory; also that for their relief from such punishments, the suffrages of the faithful still living avail, namely, the Sacrifice of the Mass, prayers and almsdeeds, and other offices of piety which, according to the Church's appointment, are wont to be offered by the faithful for one another. Also, that the souls of those who, after receiving baptism have never incurred any stain of sin, or have been purified of such stain while as yet in the body, or—as has just been stated—after leaving the body, are straightway admitted into heaven and there enjoy the open vision of God himself, three in one, as he is, one person, however, more perfectly than another according to the diversity of their merits. But the souls of such as depart, whether in actual sin or only in original sin, straightway go down to hell, there to be punished with differing degrees of punishment."[1020]

St. John Damascene, *An Exposition of the Orthodox Faith*, Bk. 4, Ch. 27:

"We shall, then, rise again, that is, with our souls rejoined to our bodies which will have shed their corruption; and we shall all stand before the tribunal of Christ; then the devil and his angels, as also his man, Antichrist, as well as wicked and criminal men, will be cast into eternal fire; I call it 'fire,' not because it is a material thing like our fire; though what it is, God knows. But they who have done good things shall, with the angels, shine like the sun, in life eternal, with our Lord Jesus Christ, to see him and be seen by him, thence to derive unspeakable joy, praising him with the Father and the Holy Spirit throughout endless ages."[1021]

[1020] Mansi, *Concilia*, xxxi, 1031
[1021] *P.G.*, xciv, 1228

QUESTION 586

For the Fourth Lateran Council, see above, q. 179; for the Council of Florence, see above, q. 585; for Benedict XII, see above, q. 62; for Pius IX, see above, q. 162.

Vigilius, *Adversus Origenem*, Can. 9:

> "If anyone says or thinks that the punishment of the demons or of sinful men is but for a time, and that its end will come some day, or that there will be some restoration or renewal of the demons and wicked men, let him be anathema."[1022]

QUESTION 588

For the Council of Florence, see above, q. 585.

St. Gregory the Great, *Dialogues*, Bk. 4, Ch. 43:

> "Though there is but one fire of hell, it does not torment all sinners alike; for there each will experience as much pain as his sin demands."[1023]

St. Augustine, *Enchiridion*, Ch. 111:

> "After the resurrection, when the general judgment is over and completed, these two cities—the city of Christ and the city of the devil—will come to an end; both of them—the city of the good and the city of the wicked alike—will contain angels as well as men. Those in the former city will have no will to sin; those of the latter no power to do so; in neither will there be any dying; those who belong to the former living truly and happily in eternal life; the others lasting on in the misery of eternal death with no chance of dying, for the members

[1022] Mansi, *Concilia*, ix, 534
[1023] *P.L.*, lxxvii, 401

of either have no end. Yet in that happiness some will surpass others, just as in that misery some will suffer less than others."[1024]

QUESTION 589

Second Council of Lyons, A.D. 1274, *Profession of Faith by Michael Palaeologus*:

"And if they depart this life in charity before having, by fruits worthy of penance, made satisfaction for the sins committed or the good they have omitted, then, as Brother John has just explained, their souls are purified after death by expiatory punishments; for relieving these sufferings, the suffrages of the faithful who are living avail, namely, the Sacrifice of the Mass, prayers, almsdeeds, and other pious offices which, according to the Church's appointment, the faithful are in the habit of offering for one another."[1025]

For the Council of Florence, see above, q. 585.

Council of Trent, Session 25, "Decree concerning Purgatory":

"Since the Catholic Church, instructed by the Holy Spirit, has, from the scriptures and the ancient tradition of the fathers, always taught in her councils and has now repeated in the present holy synod, that there is a purgatory and that the souls of the faithful there detained are helped by the suffrages of the faithful, more especially by the acceptable Sacrifice of the Altar—this holy synod bids the bishops take great pains to see that sound doctrine on purgatory, as handed down to us by the holy fathers and the sacred councils, is believed, held, taught, and set forth by all Christian believers...The bishops should also see that the suffrages of the faithful, that is to say, Masses, prayers, alms, and other works of piety such as the faithful are wont to offer for the departed according to the Church's appointment, should be performed religiously and devoutly, also that such suffrages for the dead as are due owing to testamentary

[1024] *P.L.*, xl, 284
[1025] Mansi, *Concilia*, xxiv, 70

> foundations or from any other source, should not be performed in perfunctory fashion, but faithfully and accurately carried out by priests, ecclesiastical ministers, and others whose duty it is."

For Benedict XII, see above, q. 62.

Leo X, Bull *Exurge Domine*, against the errors of Luther, June 15, 1520, the thirty-seventh through the fortieth condemned Propositions:

> Prop. 37: "Purgatory cannot be proved from any portion of holy scripture found in the Canon."
>
> Prop. 38: "The souls in purgatory are not secure of their salvation, at least not all of them; nor can it be proved by any arguments or by any scripture that they are not in a state in which they can merit or grow in grace."
>
> Prop. 39: "The souls in purgatory sin without intermission so long as they crave for rest or shrink from pain."
>
> Prop. 40: "Souls delivered from purgatory by the suffrages of the living gain a less degree of beatitude than if they had made satisfaction themselves."

Pius IV, Constitution *Injunctum nobis*, Nov. 13, 1564, *Professio Fidei Tridentina*:

> "I firmly hold that there is a purgatory and that the souls there detained are assisted by the suffrages of the faithful; also that the saints reigning with Christ are to be venerated and prayed to, and that they offer prayers to God for us, also that their relics are to be venerated. I emphatically assert that images of Christ and of the Virgin Mother of God, as well as those of the other saints, should be kept and retained and that due honor and reverence should be paid them; also that the power of granting indulgences has been left to the Church by Christ, and that the use of them by the faithful in Christ is salutary."[1026]

[1026] Mansi, *Concilia*, xxxiii, 221ff

St. Gregory the Great, *Dialogues*, Bk. 4, Ch. 39:

"As each person is as he quits this life, so is he presented for judgment. Yet we must believe that for certain lighter faults there exists, previous to the judgment, a purgatorial fire. For the truth himself says that if any man blaspheme the Holy Spirit 'it shall be forgiven him neither in this world, nor in the next.'[1027] By this pronouncement we are given to understand that certain sins can be forgiven in this world, and certain others in the next. For when something is denied in one case only, the clear implication is that it is not denied in the other cases. Yet, as I have said, this is only to be believed in the case of small and trifling sins."[1028]

QUESTION 592

St. Augustine, *City of God*, Bk. 21, Ch. 13, n. 16:

"Some suffer their temporal punishment in this life only, some after death, some both now and then; yet this is always previous to the last and most stern judgment. Not all, however, are destined for that eternal punishment which is to follow on that last judgment, not those, for example, who suffer temporal punishment after death...

"It may well be thought that there are no purgatorial punishments save previous to that tremendous judgment. But we cannot question but that that eternal fire will be more terrible for some than for others in proportion to their differing merits—or rather demerits; whether that means that that fire's power to burn varies according to the degree of punishment due to each, or that, while its power to burn is constant, some feel it less than others."[1029]

[1027] Mt 12:32
[1028] *P.L.*, lxxvii, 396
[1029] *P.L.*, xli, 728, 731

QUESTION 593

For the Fourth Lateran Council, see above, q. 179; for the Council of Florence, see above, q. 585; for Benedict XII, see above, q. 62.

Council of Vienne, A.D. 1311-1312, against the errors of the Beguards and the Beguines, the fifth condemned Proposition:

> "That every intellectual nature is naturally and of itself blessed, and that the soul has no need of the 'light of glory' uplifting it that it may see God and enjoy him in blessedness."[1030]

QUESTION 594

For the Council of Florence, see above, q. 585; for the Council of Trent, see above, q. 282.

St. Gregory the Great, *Moralia in Job*, Bk. 4, Ch. 35, n. 70:

> "Just as in this life we perform differing tasks, so doubtless in the life to come there will be degrees in dignity, so that in proportion as here one has surpassed another in merit, so there one will surpass another in the reward he has earned. Hence in the gospel the truth says: 'In my Father's house there are many mansions.'[1031] Yet even in those 'many mansions' there will be in some way an amicable diversity in rewards; for such will be the bond there uniting us all in harmony that the reward which one sees that he himself has not received he will rejoice to see realized in the case of another. Thus, though in the vineyard all did not toil equally, yet all alike received the same 'penny.'[1032] So, too, with the Father there are 'many mansions,' yet the unequal toilers all receive the same 'penny'; for while all alike will enjoy beatitude, yet not all will have led the same sublime life."[1033]

[1030] Mansi, *Concilia*, xxv, 410
[1031] Jn 14:2
[1032] Cf. Mt 20:10
[1033] *P.L.*, lxxv, 677

Aphrahat, *Demonstration 22*, n. 19:

> "Now listen to the apostle saying: 'Every man shall receive his own reward, according to his own labor.'[1034] He who has toiled but little will receive in proportion to his fatigue. He whose course has been a long one will receive a reward in proportion to that course...Again, the apostle says: 'Star differeth from star in glory, so also is the resurrection of the dead.'[1035] Surely you realize, then, that even when men 'enter into life,'[1036] the reward of one will be greater than the reward of another, the glory of one more eminent than that of another, the prize more rich."[1037]

St. Ephraem, *Hymni et Sermones*, 11:

> "Those who have done good things shall pass to a place filled with good things; but the wicked shall abide in hell, food for the fire; the stream of fire will hurry them away so that each may 'go to his own place.'[1038] The demons will drown one in the mud, never to be drawn out of it; another they will hurl into the fire, to abide there forever; another will go into 'the exterior darkness,'[1039] never even to see the fire; yet another will go down into the abyss, never to climb out again; but another will pass into the holy place, there to abide forever. There some will sit in the second rank, some in the third, others will be raised to the fifth, to the tenth, the thirtieth, others again to the highest places of all...But each will be given by the supreme justice a reward 'according to his labor.'"[1040]

St. Jerome, *Against Jovinianus*, Bk. 2, n. 32-34:

> "Here we have to toil so as to win rewards proportionate to our varying degrees of virtue...If in heaven we are all to be equal, then vainly do

1034 1 Cor 3:8
1035 1 Cor 15:41-42
1036 Mt 18:9; 19:17; Mk 9:42, 44
1037 *Patrologia Syriaea*, I, i, 1030
1038 Acts 1:25
1039 Mt 8:12; 22:13; 25:30
1040 1 Cor 3:8; *Ed.* Lamy, *Sti. Ephremi Hymni et Sermones*, ii, 424

we humble ourselves here that we may be the greater there…Why do virgins persevere, widows toil, the married contain themselves? Let us all sin then, and after repentance be all equal to the apostles!"[1041]

St. Jerome, *Apology against Rufinus*, Bk. 1, n. 23:

"Just as one is not termed an 'archangel' unless he is chief of the angels; so, too, principalities, powers, and dominations are only so-called because they have their subordinates of inferior degree…In the same way as amongst men there is a hierarchy of dignity owing to the diverse character of their work—for bishops, priests, and all ranks in the Church have their proper place, though all are men; so too amongst the angels there are differing merits, though all possess the same angelic dignity."[1042]

St. Augustine, *Sermon* 87, n. 4, 6:

"In that reward we shall all be equal, the first last, the last first; for that 'penny' is eternal life, and in eternal life all will be equal. For while all will shine out by their different degrees of merit, some more, some less, yet so far as eternal life is concerned it will be equal in all."[1043]

St. Augustine, *Tractate 67 on John*, n. 2:

"That 'penny' is the same for all; the householder bids it be given to all who have labored in his vineyard; in it he makes no distinction between those who have labored less and those who have labored more,[1044] for by that 'penny' is signified eternal life where no one 'lives' more than another, since in eternity there is no room for differing degrees in 'living.' But the 'many mansions'[1045] signify the differing degrees of merit in the one eternal life."[1046]

[1041] *P.L.*, xxiii, 344ff
[1042] *P.L.*, xxiii, 435
[1043] *P.L.*, xxxviii, 533
[1044] Cf. Mt 20:9
[1045] Jn 14:2
[1046] *P.L.*, xxxv, 1812

Appendix VII

SOME DISPUTED QUESTIONS TOUCHED ON IN THE CATECHISM

ON QUESTION 112

Much discussion exists among theologians about the state of those who will be living at the last day.

Some maintain that those then alive will not die before the general judgment but will be judged while still alive. They argue from the words of the Creed: "Thence he shall come to judge the living and the dead," also from a well-supported reading of 1 Corinthians 15:51, where many Greek manuscripts have: "We shall not all sleep, but we shall all be changed."

Many theologians, however, hold that all then alive will die, rise again at once, and be judged with the rest at the general judgment. And certainly, scripture does say, "Death passed upon all men, in whom all have sinned,"[1047] and, "As in Adam all die, so in Christ shall all be made alive."[1048] This view is regarded by St. Thomas as the safer and the more probable one.[1049]

Consequently, if competent authorities regard this latter opinion as certain, it will be easy to reply to Question 112 by adding to the words "still living" some such words as "and straightway to die."

ON QUESTION 151

If the Church, by any solemn pronouncement, or in the exercise of its ordinary but universal teaching office, proposes for general acceptance some

[1047] Rom 5:12

[1048] 1 Cor 15:22

[1049] See *Summa Theologiae*, I-II, q. 81, a. 3, rep. 1. Cf. Billot, *De Novissimis*, thesis xii; Père Hugon, *De Novissimis*, q. 1, n. 4; Lepicier, *De Novissimis*, p. 19ff

truth on the ground that such truth is divinely revealed, then all agree a) (see under Question 148) that in putting forward such a truth in this way, the Church is infallible; b) that all are bound to assent to it with divine and Catholic[1050] faith; c) that those who obstinately refuse to assent to it or who call it in question are heretical.

But if the Church proposes some truth for general acceptance, not on the ground that such truth is in itself divinely revealed, but by reason of its connection with some truth that is divinely revealed, as, for example, dogmatic facts or the censures attached to propositions proscribed or prohibited by the Church (see under Questions 150-151), then all likewise agree a) that the Church in thus proposing some truth for general acceptance is infallible; b) that all are bound to assent to such a truth with an internal assent, so that anybody who obstinately repudiates it or calls it in question commits a grave sin; and c) that such a person, however, is not a heretic strictly speaking. We accept, then, such a truth by faith, though not by "Catholic faith"; but then with what kind of faith do we accept it?

Many therefore maintain that we assent to such truths with ecclesiastical faith, since the truths of which we are speaking are not declared by God but only by the Church with God's assistance.[1051] Yet others would urge that we really do believe these truths with divine faith since we assent to them owing to the Church's infallibility; and since the infallibility of the Church rests on the word of God promising his assistance, it seems to follow that, in the final analysis, our faith rests on the word of God; and what else is that but divine faith?[1052] Others state the nature of this faith in other terms.[1053]

In our catechism, we say nothing about this controversy among theologians. See the answer given to Question 151.

[1050] The word *Catholic* appears to have been added by the Vatican Council in order to show that such faith is necessary if a person is to be considered a member of the Catholic Church; for a person who obstinately denies or calls in question any of these truths is a heretic and consequently no longer belongs to the Catholic Church.

[1051] See Cardinal Billot, *De Ecclesia*, thesis xviii; *De Virtutibus infusis*, thesis xiii. See, too, Palmieri, Schultes, etc.

[1052] See P. Schiffini, S. J., *De Virtutibus infusis*, Disp. iii, 4; P. Marin Sola, O. P., *La evolucion homogenea*, Ch. 5.

[1053] See P. Marin Sola, O. P., *La evolucion homogenea*, Ch. 5.

ON QUESTIONS 158 AND THE FOLLOWING

It is disputed whether excommunication, which is the gravest of all spiritual penalties, implies separation from the body of the Church so that a person who is excommunicated is no longer a member of the Church.

There are three opinions:

The first affirms this both of excommunicated persons "who are to be shunned" (*vitandi*) as well as of tolerated excommunicates; the upholders of this opinion refer to the words: "If he will not hear the Church, let him be to thee as the heathen and the publican,"[1054] and they allege in their favor various expressions of the fathers and doctors of the Church, also the form of excommunication and absolution used in all excommunications alike.

The second opinion, while affirming it in the case of *vitandi*, denies it in the case of excommunicated persons who are to be tolerated; their view is the one generally accepted among recent theologians who explain the passages given above as referring only to *vitandi*.

The third opinion refuses to allow it even in the case of *vitandi* on the ground that in the *Codex Juris Canonici*, Canons 2257-2267, where the penalties following upon excommunication are enumerated, this gravest of all penalties—separation from the body of the Church—is not mentioned even in the case of *vitandi*.

We have followed the second opinion which, as we have said, is the one most generally held among recent theologians; but if any competent authority feels that the first or the third opinion has solid probability in its favor, it will be easy for him to correct the answers given to Questions 151ff.

ON QUESTIONS 175 AND 296

It is disputed whether we can pray to the souls detained in purgatory to obtain their intercession for us with God.

The affirmative opinion is not only the one more generally accepted among theologians, especially more recent writers, but, what is of graver moment, it would seem to be in conformity with a general practice of the

1054 Mt 18:17

faithful which the Church has never opposed. Yet there are theologians of great reputation, some of whom quote against this view the words of St. Thomas, where he teaches that "the souls in purgatory are not so much in a state to pray for us as for us to pray for them."[1055] Not all Thomists, however, agree with this interpretation of his words, for some think that St. Thomas only means that the souls in purgatory have not the power to practice meritorious prayer—such as we have in this present life, nor the power of effective intercessory prayer which belongs to the state of glory. But he does not, so they maintain, mean to deny to them the capacity for such prayer as is common to all who have charity, a capacity for prayer which is a necessary feature of the communion of saints.

We ourselves regard the opinion which maintains that the holy souls can pray for us as certainly the correct one, more particularly because, as we have said, it is in harmony with a practice of the faithful which the Church has never opposed; hence the answer we have given to Questions 175 and 296. Still, if any competent authority feels that this view is unsound or not quite accurate, it will be easy to correct the answers we have given.

ON QUESTION 359

As regards children who die with original sin only, the doctrine given in our catechism is the one generally held in the Church today, namely, that they do not enjoy the beatific vision of God—in other words, they suffer the penalty of original sin, namely, the pain of loss; but that they do not suffer any penalty for personal sin, namely, the pain of sense. But even then the question arises whether such children are aware that they have not the beatific vision of God, and whether in that case they are grieved by the knowledge of their loss. Opinions differ. For first of all, we have St. Thomas teaching that the souls of such children are aware that they are deprived of eternal life and that they know why they are so deprived, yet he adds that such knowledge does not cause them any grief.[1056] Later on,

[1055] *Summa Theologiae*, II-II, q. 83, a. 11, rep. 3

[1056] See Aquinas, *Sentences*, II, d. 33, q. 2, a. 2.

however, he changed his opinion and held that the souls of such children were punished simply by being deprived of this beatific vision but were unconscious of the fact and therefore suffered no grief from it: "The souls of children," he says, "are not without that natural knowledge which belongs to the separated soul owing to its very nature, but they have not that supernatural knowledge which is implanted in us here by faith; for they have never here on earth actually exercised faith, nor have they received the sacrament of faith (baptism). Now while natural knowledge means that the soul is aware that it is made for created happiness and that such happiness consists in the attainment of what is perfectly good, yet that that perfect good for which man is made should consist in that glory which the saints possess, it is beyond natural knowledge to discover. Hence the apostle says that 'eye hath not seen, neither hath it entered into the heart of man what things God hath prepared for them that love him,'[1057] and the same apostle immediately adds, 'But to us God hath revealed them by his Spirit,'[1058] a revelation which belongs to faith. Consequently, the souls of children are not aware that they are deprived of this great good thing and therefore do not grieve about it, but the good they possess owing to their nature they possess without any grief."[1059]

But some theologians will not admit this. Thus Cardinal Bellarmine regards it as probable that "children dying without baptism will be grieved at the realization that they are deprived of beatitude and cut off from the society of their parents and brethren, shut up in the prison of hell, and condemned to spend their lives in a perpetual gloom; at the same time, the grief they experience from this is of the most trifling kind."[1060] Similarly, the theologians of Wurzburg lay down the thesis that children who die without baptism are punished by being deprived of supernatural beatitude, also by being deprived of natural beatitude, while it is probable that they are not punished by the pain of sense

[1057] 1 Cor 2:9

[1058] 1 Cor 2:10

[1059] Aquinas, *Disputed Questions, De Malo*, q. 5, a. 3, c.

[1060] Bellarmine, *De amissione gratiae et statu peccati*, Bk. 6, Ch. 6

though they are saddened by the loss of beatitude.[1061] We omit the even harsher views of certain theologians.

In our catechism, we have given the answer generally endorsed by theologians, basing ourselves in the main on the authority of Popes Innocent III, Pius VI, and Pius IX.

ON QUESTION 510

All agree that the theological virtues, faith, hope, and charity, are divinely infused, as is expressly stated in our catechism, q. 510, and that they cannot be acquired by any natural means. But the question remains undecided for the moral virtues. To understand the problem, certain points have to be noted:

It is not a question of acts of moral virtue directed to the attainment of some purely natural end; for all agree that natural moral virtue enables us to make such acts and that for so doing no assistance of divine grace is required. Similarly, for acts of moral virtue directed toward the attainment of a supernatural end, as when a person chastises his body and brings his body into subjection by fasting. For all agree that if a person is in a state of mortal sin, such acts can be made by the natural moral powers under the influence of the theological virtues of faith and hope and with the assistance of actual grace; also that in order to make such acts there is no necessity for an infused moral virtue; though it remains true that such acts cannot merit for us eternal life, though they do prepare the way for our being justified. But what if a person is in a state of sanctifying grace? For in his case such acts do merit eternal life. Whence arises the question whether such acts can be made by the natural moral powers under the influence of the three theological virtues and with the assistance of actual grace, or whether it is necessary to have an infused moral virtue.

The Thomists hold that for such acts infused moral virtues are absolutely necessary and that these are infused at the same time as sanctifying

[1061] See *Theologia Dogmatica, De Peccatis*, n. 134ff.

grace and are, with sanctifying grace, lost by sin. These theologians rely on the authority of Pope Innocent III and of the *Catechism of the Council of Trent*,[1062] as well as on theological arguments. For, so they argue, the faculties of the soul when left to nature's forces are, even when acting under the influence of the theological virtues and with the help of divine grace, unable to elicit acts proportioned to that supernatural good which is eternal life. Consequently, it becomes necessary for God to infuse into the faculties of the soul habits capable of producing such acts, and such habits are the moral virtues.

This view held by the Thomists is generally accepted by theologians. But the Scotists maintain that it is not necessary to hold that the moral virtues are infused by God. They base themselves on the authority of the Council of Trent,[1063] where the Council, while laying down that in justification the theological virtues are infused, says nothing about the moral virtues. They add, too, a theological argument: there can be no question but that, after being justified, a righteous person can, under the influence of the theological virtues and with the help of actual grace, elicit acts of the moral virtues by his purely natural powers. For if, as all admit, he can do so previous to justification, then equally or even moreso must he be able to do so after justification. And that after justification such acts can merit eternal life can be argued from the Council of Trent,[1064] as also from the general teaching of theologians on sanctifying grace. For through sanctifying grace, a person is uplifted so that he becomes a living member

[1062] Pope Innocent III (*Majores, De Baptismo*, Ch. 3): "As for the argument alleged by opponents, namely, that faith and charity or the other virtues are not infused into children since they cannot consent to it. Many refuse to concede this absolutely since this very point is in dispute among learned theologians, some of them maintaining that, by the power of baptism, sin is forgiven in the case of children though grace is not conferred upon them, while others hold that their sins are forgiven them and the virtues are infused into them, though children have only the habit of the virtue, not its use, until they come to the age of reason; see the *Catechism of the Council of Trent*: 'Here (namely, at baptism) is added the glorious company of all the virtues which, together with divine grace, are infused into the soul.'" (See TCCI 7:218.)

[1063] See Council of Trent, Session 6, "Decree on Justification," Ch. 7.

[1064] See the words of the Council of Trent given under q. 282, above, also those of St. Augustine under q. 66, above.

of Jesus Christ, a temple of the Holy Spirit, a sharer in the divine nature, an adoptive son of God. "But if a son, then also an heir of God,"[1065] says St. Paul; in other words, through sanctifying grace, such acts are now the acts of sons of God; but, if the acts of a son, then also are they acts of one who is heir to the glory of heaven; and, if acts of an heir to the glory of heaven, then they are meritorious of eternal life.

On this point—as indeed on many other points affecting the infused or acquired virtues which are much discussed by theologians—all catechisms are silent.

ON QUESTIONS 180 AND THE FOLLOWING

It will hardly be amiss if we give here briefly some of the various opinions held about the last things and especially about hell and purgatory.

As regards hell, we must believe as of divine faith:

1. That there is a hell appointed for the demons and for those who die with even only one mortal sin.

2. That in hell the damned suffer a twofold punishment—the pain of loss and the pain of sense, especially that of fire.

3. That the pains they suffer in hell are eternal, without end or mitigation.

4. That these pains, however, are not the same for all but differ according to the number and gravity of the sins whereby they have deserved eternal damnation.

It is theologically certain, though not "of faith," that the fire of hell is a real or corporeal, not a metaphorical fire, see Hugon, O.P.: "The Church has nowhere defined the nature of the fire, but the teaching of theologians who speak of this fire as real and not a figure of speech has been so accepted by the Church that to hold the contrary would be intolerably rash."[1066] The same is held by Cardinal Lepicier,[1067] also by Cardinal Billot.[1068] There ex-

[1065] Gal 4:7. The apostle says the same, Rom 8:16ff.

[1066] *De Novissimis*, q. III, i, n. 7

[1067] See Lepicier, *De Novissimis*, q. IV, art. 2.

[1068] See Billot, *De Novissimis*, q. III, thesis 4.

ists also a reply given by the Sacred Penitentiary to the question "whether penitents can be absolved if they only allow of a metaphorical and not a real fire of hell"; the reply runs: "Such penitents are to be carefully instructed and, if obstinately holding to their views, cannot be absolved."[1069]

But theologians freely discuss how it is possible for real fire to affect pure spirits such as are the demons and the souls of the damned previous to the resurrection of the body; of what nature, too, this fire is; where hell is situated, above the earth or beneath it; whether it is a place or a state, etc.

As regards purgatory, it is of faith:

1. That there exists a purgatory where are detained the souls of such as have departed this life without mortal sin but who have yet to pay a certain debt of temporal punishment.

2. That in purgatory souls are punished by the pain of loss as well as by the pain of sense; they are, that is, deprived for a time of the beatific vision of God and they suffer other grave pains.

3. The pains they endure in purgatory vary in length and intensity in proportion to the debt of temporal punishment due to them.

4. Their sufferings can be mitigated or shortened by the suffrages offered for them.

It is not "of faith" that the souls in purgatory are tortured by a real or corporeal and not merely by a metaphorical fire. The Council of Florence was loth to define this, since the Greeks held that the souls in purgatory did not suffer pain of sense from a real or corporeal fire but rather from the gloom of that realm of woe...Even to this day in the Eastern Churches, the catechisms say nothing about the fire of purgatory, and the same is true in the Latin Church: see the *Catechism of Pope Pius X*[1070] as well as several others.

On the other hand, the general feeling of the faithful in the Latin Church, as well as the teaching of theologians,[1071] admits of suffering by a

[1069] April 30, 1890.

[1070] Editor's note: The *Catechism of Pope Pius X*, or *Compendium of Christian Doctrine*, is included in full in Volume VIII of this series.

[1071] See Hugon, O. P., *De Novissimis*, q. 9, art. 5, n. 3; Cardinal Lepicier, *De Novissimis*, q. 5, art. 3, n. 1; Cardinal Billot, *De Novissimis*, thesis 7; also Bellarmine, Suarez, etc.

real fire; these theologians base themselves on the authority of St. Gregory the Great and of St. Gregory of Nyssa.[1072] Consequently, in our own catechism (q. 590), we have said nothing of the fire of purgatory; but if any competent authority feels that the existence of such fire should be maintained, it can easily be added to the answer given to that Question.

Theologians freely discuss whether, granted that there is a fire of purgatory, it is of the same nature as the fire of hell though with less excruciating power; also how it can affect souls separated from the body; where precisely purgatory is situated; whether it is a place or a state; whether, too, the guilt of venial sin is remitted by the fire of purgatory, for the Angelic Doctor teaches that venial sins are remitted in purgatory not by the fire, but an act of love of God expressly detesting the venial sins committed during life.[1073]

In accordance with what we laid down in our Preface, we say nothing in this catechism about these questions still disputed by theologians. Rather than waste time in discussing such things, let us strive with might and main to live well as befits Christians and so escape the pains of hell, even—so far as human frailty will allow—by penance and the works of mercy, let us strive to escape the pains of purgatory or at least to render them shorter and milder.

[1072] St. Gregory the Great: "Yet we have to believe that there is, previous to the judgment, a purgatorial fire for certain light faults" (*Dialogues*, Bk. 4, Ch. 39). St. Gregory of Nyssa says: "The soul that has departed from the body cannot become a sharer in the Godhead unless the fire of purgatory entering into the soul removes its stains" (*Oratio pro mortuis*; P.G., xlvi, 530).

[1073] See Aquinas, *Disputed Questions, De Malo*, q. 7, a. 11.

ABOUT THIS SERIES

Tradivox was first conceived as an international research endeavor to recover lost and otherwise little-known Catholic catechetical texts. As the research progressed over several years, the vision began to grow, along with the number of project contributors and a general desire to share these works with a broader audience.

Legally incorporated in 2019, Tradivox has begun the work of carefully remastering and republishing dozens of these catechisms which were once in common and official use in the Church around the world. That effort is embodied in this *Tradivox Catholic Catechism Index*, a multi-volume series restoring artifacts of traditional faith and praxis for a contemporary readership. More about this series and the work of Tradivox can be learned at www.Tradivox.com.

SOPHIA INSTITUTE

Sophia Institute is a nonprofit institution that seeks to nurture the spiritual, moral, and cultural life of souls and to spread the Gospel of Christ in conformity with the authentic teachings of the Roman Catholic Church.

Sophia Institute Press fulfills this mission by offering translations, reprints, and new publications that afford readers a rich source of the enduring wisdom of mankind.

Sophia Institute also operates the popular online resource Catholic Exchange.com. *Catholic Exchange* provides world news from a Catholic perspective as well as daily devotionals and articles that will help readers to grow in holiness and live a life consistent with the teachings of the Church.

In 2013, Sophia Institute launched Sophia Institute for Teachers to renew and rebuild Catholic culture through service to Catholic education. With the goal of nurturing the spiritual, moral, and cultural life of souls, and an abiding respect for the role and work of teachers, we strive to provide materials and programs that are at once enlightening to the mind and ennobling to the heart; faithful and complete, as well as useful and practical.

Sophia Institute gratefully recognizes the Solidarity Association for preserving and encouraging the growth of our apostolate over the course of many years. Without their generous and timely support, this book would not be in your hands.

www.SophiaInstitute.com
www.CatholicExchange.com
www.SophiaInstituteforTeachers.org

Sophia Institute Press® is a registered trademark of Sophia Institute.
Sophia Institute is a tax-exempt institution as defined by the Internal Revenue Code, Section 501(c)(3). Tax ID 22-2548708.